THE ETERNAL BOOKS RETOLD

A RABBI SUMMARIZES THE 39 BOOKS OF THE BIBLE

ALEX J. GOLDMAN

JASON ARONSON INC.
NORTHVALE, NEW JERSEY
JERUSALEM

First Jason Aronson Inc. hardcover edition—1999

This book was printed and bound by Book-mart Press of North Bergen, NJ.

Copyright © 1999, 1982 by Alex J. Goldman

10 9 8 7 6 5 4 3 2 1

Library of Congress Cataloging-in-Publication Data

Goldman, Alex J.
   The eternal books retold : a rabbi summarizes the 39 books of the
  Bible / Alex J. Goldman.—1st J. Aronson hardcover ed.
     p. cm.
  Previously published: New York : Pilgrim Press, c1982.
  ISBN 0-7657-6049-5
  1. Bible. O.T.—Introductions. I. Title.
BS1140.2.G56   1999
221.6'1—DC21
                                                       98-40647

Printed in the United States of America on acid-free paper. For information and catalog write to Jason Aronson Inc., 230 Livingston Street, Northvale, NJ 07647-1726, or visit our website: www.aronson.com

To my wife
Edith
our children
Dr. Robert Goldman
Richard and Pamela Kesselman
our grandchildren
Steven and Sarah Kesselman

Contents

Contents

AUTHOR'S PREFACE

THE BIBLE IS THE MOST EXCITING AND REMARKABLE BOOK the world has ever known, containing the story of God and people. It is the basic book of human destiny. To the Jewish people, the Bible is more. It is the Book, the Book of Books, the raison d'etre of Judaism, the story of meeting with God. The Bible is, indeed, the "tree of life."

As one book, the Bible is actually a composite of many books spanning the vastness of time, compressing millenia of human events, struggles, failures, aspirations, successes. It portrays the endeavors of innumerable personalities . . . prophets, kings, priests and humble people. Tradition ascribes a unity to a group of twelve short prophetic books, counting them as one book, referred to as The Twelve. These are the Prophets Hosea, Joel, Amos, Obadiah, Jonah, Micah, Nahum, Habakkuk, Zephaniah, Haggai, Zechariah and Malachi. Some recognize I Samuel and II Samuel as one book, likewise I Kings, II Kings and I Chronicles and II Chronicles. Counting these as two books each, the total biblical books number thirty-nine.

The three major categories of the Bible are:

Torah or Pentateuch
Nevi'im or Prophets
Ketuvim or Sacred Writings (Hagiographa).

A convenient way to remember these divisions is by contracting the initial letter of the groups into one word TeNaKh, (Kh is the soft sound of the letter K), as the Bible is known in Jewish circles.

AUTHOR'S PREFACE

TORAH

The Torah known as the Pentateuch comprises the Five Books of Moses, sometimes referred to by other names: Torath Moshe, the Torah of Moses, because Jewish tradition asserts that Moses wrote the Pentateuch, with the exception of the last few sentences which record the death of Moses, included by Joshua. Since there are five parts or books, it is sometimes called Hamishah Humshay Torah or simply Humash, "The Five."

Over the period of time the term Torah has assumed ever-expanding connotations. It is the Scroll read in the synagogue as part of the central worship service. It may also signify the entire Bible, all three divisions: Torah, Nevi'im, Ketuvim. It is likewise the Written Law (Torah She-bi-khethav) as distinguished from the Oral Law (Torah She-be'alpeh). It is the Written Law because the events were recorded near or concurrent with the times of their occurrences, the Five Books being traditionally accepted as recorded by Moses at the behest of God. This differs from the Oral Law (Mishna and Gemara or Talmud)—an expansive compendium of law interpretation, and legend, based on the principles of the Bible, transmitted by word of mouth from generation to generation for many centuries until finally reduced to writing about 500 C.E. Although finalized into the written word, the name of the oral transmission method has been retained.

The connecting thread throughout religious literature, the Torah is the sum total of authoritative rabbinic studies, injunctions, regulative principles, and codes formulated and proclaimed after the Oral Law was recorded, and continuing to our own day. While each is apparently an individual effort, every layer is rooted in the Torah, that is, the Five Books of Moses. The Torah may be visualized in its structure as an inverted pyramid, the Five Books representing the foundation, and layers upon layers of larger bodies of law and tradition imposed thereon to keep pace with increasing experience. It can be compared to the Constitution of the United States, concise and brief, yet the source of the judicial and interpretive system in our country. Torah is, in addition, a concept, an ideology, a way of life. It becomes more conceptual as it embraces more and more of the totality of Jewish life and humanity in general. Torah is Judaism and Jewish religion encompasses every aspect of life.

While reference to Torah infers wide and not necessarily exclusive meanings, in its earliest and most limited sense Torah is the Scroll of Law which contains the Five Books of Moses and the first of the three letters of the contracted and symbolic word TeNaKh. Names of the Five Books derive either from the Greek translation of the Bible—known as

Septuagint—or from the Hebrew. In the English-speaking world, the Books are more familiarly known by their Greek names which in one word describe the contents. Genesis from the Greek "origin, source, creation" details the beginnings of the world, society and the Jewish people. Exodus from the Greek word "going out" narrates the departure of the Israelites from Egypt after centuries of bondage. Leviticus, devoted to the "Levites" includes the laws and regulations enjoined upon the Levites, the tribe of priests, as they served in the Sanctuary as well as commandments and rules of life given to the people. Numbers takes its name from the census or counting of the Israelites when they were in the wilderness preparing for their journey to the Promised Land. The fifth book Deuteronomy, "repetition," reviews the experiences described in Exodus, Leviticus and Numbers and also presents a summary of previously given laws.

On the other hand, the Hebrew names derive from the first, or first important Hebrew word of the opening sentence of the book. Thus, the Greek Genesis is Berayshith, in the beginning, from "In the beginning God created the heaven and the earth." The book Exodus, Shemoth in Hebrew, connotes names, the second word of the opening verse of this book being Ayleh Shemoth, "Now these are the names of the sons of Israel who came to Egypt with Jacob." Leviticus is Vayikra, "And He called," from the first sentence "And He (God) called to Moses" to instruct him about the laws of the Levites. Numbers is Bemidbar, meaning "In the wilderness" from the first sentence "And the Lord spoke to Moses in the wilderness of Sinai." Deuteronomy is Devarim, meaning words, from the opening words of the fifth book, "And these are the words which Moses spoke unto all Israel."

This practice of name referrals has been carried over into other areas of Jewish tradition. It is followed, for example, with each portion of the Torah read in the Synagogue on Sabbath morning. The Five Books, divided into fifty-four parts, are read over the period of the entire year, beginning on Simhath Torah (last of the days of Sukkoth, Feast of Tabernacles). A specific portion is assigned to each week, called Sidra, meaning order, and each section is named by its first word or first important word of the first sentence of that portion. Thus, the first portion of the Bible read in the Synagogue (in addition to being the name of the entire first book) is known as Berayshith from the opening word, "In the beginning." The second portion, beginning with Chapter VI is called Noah from the first important word of the first sentence, "These are the generations of Noah." Also, in traditional Hebrew correspondence, the salutation always refers to the portion to be read on the succeeding Sabbath. The name of the portion of the Torah is the name of the week.

In addition to these Hebrew names, ancient Hebrew names descriptive of the contents have also been appended to the individual books. Genesis, or Berayshith, is also known as Sayfer Mahsay Berayshith, Book of the Acts of Creation; Exodus or Shemoth is Sayfer Yetzi'ath Mitzrayim, Book of the Departure from Egypt. Leviticus or Vayikra is called Torath Kohanim, Laws of the Priests. Numbers or Bemidbar is Humash Ha-pekudim, Fifth (Book) of the Musterings (Numbers). And Deuteronomy or Devarim is called Mishneh Torah, meaning Repetition of the Torah.

FIRST DIVISION OF THE BIBLE
(Torah, Pentateuch)

| | TITLE | | NUMBERS OF | | |
Old Hebrew Name	Hebrew	Greek	Chapters	Verses	Portions, Sidroth
Sayfer Mah-say Berayshith	Berayshith	Genesis	50	1535	12
Sayfer Yetzi'ath Mitz-ra-yim	Shemoth	Exodus	40	1209	11
Torath Kohanim	Vayikra	Leviticus	27	859	10
Humash Hapekudim	Bemidbar	Numbers	36	1288	10
Mishneh Torah	Devarim	Deuteronomy	34	955	11

SECOND DIVISION OF THE BIBLE

The Prophets, Nevi'im, are symbolized by the consonant N of the contraction TeNaKh, appearing in two major divisions:
Earlier or Former Prophets (Nevi'im Rishonim)

Joshua
Judges
I Samuel
II Samuel
I Kings
II Kings

Latter Prophets (Nevi'im Aharonim)

Isaiah
Jeremiah
Ezekiel

The Twelve (T'ray Asar)

Hosea
Joel
Amos
Obadiah
Jonah
Micah
Nahum
Habakkuk
Zephaniah
Haggai
Zechariah
Malachi

In addition to the practice of reading fifty-four divisions of the Torah in the Synagogue on Sabbaths during the course of the year (each called Sidra), selections of the Prophets relating to the theme of the Torah readings are read. They are called Haftarot (singular, Haftorah) which means conclusion. On festival and holy days, when Torah readings are culled from parts of the Torah containing descriptions of the specific festival, selections of the prophetic books are also assigned for chanting. In this manner, considering all the Sabbaths, holy days and festivals, a substantial part of the books of the Prophets is included in the public worship service.

THIRD DIVISION OF THE BIBLE

The last consonant of the contraction TeNaKh stands for Ketuvim, the Sacred Writings, or Hagiographa:

Psalms (Tehillim)
Proverbs (Mishlay)
Job (Iyov)
Song of Songs (Shir Ha-shirim)
Ruth
Lamentations (Aykhah)
Ecclesiastes (Koheleth)
Esther (Estayr)
Daniel
Ezra

Nehemiah
I Chronicles (Divray Ha-yamim)
II Chronicles

The public religious service includes also readings from the Sacred Writings. Psalms, for example, form the basic pattern of the daily, especially the morning service. On Sabbath and holidays additional psalms are read. The thirty-first chapter of Proverbs which extols the virtues of the Jewish woman, is read Sabbath eve in the home at the dinner table. A number of passages from Proverbs are included at the early morning service primarily for the instruction of the children.

The Five Scrolls, known as Hamaysh Megilloth, are read publicly in the Synagogue. The Song of Songs is read on the Sabbath of the intermediate days of Passover (Shabbath Hol Hamoed). Ecclesiastes is read on the Sabbath of the intermediate days of Sukkoth, Feast of Booths or Tabernacles or on Shemini Atzereth, the eighth day of the festival, if it falls on the Sabbath. Ruth is read on Shavuoth, Feast of Weeks. Lamentations is read on Tish'ah Be-Ab (Ninth of Ab), the Jewish national fast day of mourning to commemorate the destruction of the two Holy Temples and other catastrophes. The Book of Esther is read on Purim, the Feast of Lots.

Thus, all three divisions form part of the regular synagogue ritual. The books of Job, Daniel, Ezra and Nehemiah, I Chronicles and II Chronicles, while they are not included in the regular synagogue service (with the exception of brief selections from I Chronicles and Nehemiah in the morning service), are interestingly drawn into a related ritual. In days of old, the high priest who ministered in the Holy Temple of Jerusalem was required to hear or to study these volumes on the evening of Yom Kippur, Day of Atonement, in preparation for his conduct of the service on the following day.

In presenting THE ETERNAL BOOKS RETOLD we have had reference to the generally used 1917 translation of the Holy Scriptures by the Jewish Publication Society of America which comprises 1,136 pages set in the customary biblical two columns of small face type text to a page. We have also had reference to the newly translated Torah from the traditional Hebrew text published by the Jewish Publication Society of America in 1962 which comprises 393 pages of average face type, reading from margin to margin, and the newly translated Nevi'im (Prophets) published in 1978 which comprises 898 pages. Ketubim, the third category of the Bible, comprising 624 pages, was published in May, 1982. These volumes deviate from previously presented translations in avoiding obsolete words and phrases. For the second person singular, the form "you" is used and in the second person plural, when referring to God, "You" appears in place of, respectively, "thou" and "Thou."

In this book, THE ETERNAL BOOKS RETOLD, we have adhered to the 1962 premise regarding the second person singular and plural of the personal pronoun, in keeping with the now accepted purpose of making the Holy Scriptures more comprehensible to all kinds of people, who look to the Bible for knowledge and inspiration, and are enabled to find rich treasures there otherwise inaccessible to them.

Understandably, numerous volumes were researched in preparing the narratives of each of the thirty-nine books of the Bible. I used Bibles with varied translations, history books and prayer books in which biblical selections are included. Acknowledgment is made of Rabbi Mortimer J. Cohen's *Pathways Through The Bible*, published in 1946 by the Jewish Publication Society. I have for many years studied this classic book, indeed, making it part of my being. Indeed, Dr. Cohen read the original manuscript and encouraged its publication. I have also referred to the comprehensive and profound *Soncino Books of the Bible*, published by the Soncino Press of London, edited by the Rev. Dr. A. Cohen and others.

Selections to elucidate the text of THE ETERNAL BOOKS RETOLD are often paraphrased to exact every nuance of meaning from the verses, and are therefore indicated as being taken "from" the scriptures rather than a word for word rendition of either the 1917 or 1962 translations of the Bible. The interpretations and explanations of the biblical text are intended to reveal spiritual truths of Judaism which may help the reader better to understand its tenets and better to cope with the complexity of life which will make the Bible even more meaningful and significant to him.

My purpose in presenting this book, THE ETERNAL BOOKS RETOLD, retelling and explaining the ancient books of The Holy Scriptures, is to place the whole body of this religious literature within the covers of a single volume, easily intelligible to readers of all ages, for their enlightenment, information, enjoyment and inspiration, and to perform the service of personal guidance through the labyrinth of the world's foremost book. Hopefully, the reader will be encouraged to read The Holy Scriptures both in the Hebrew and the translated English texts available to us.

I am indebted to many people in the creation of this book whose interest, assistance and kindness have been invaluable. I wish to thank the authors of the many books consulted, the librarians in the various libraries who assisted me in my researching information, and the Jewish Publication Society for permission to quote from *Pathways Through the Bible*, pages 235, 236, 272, 303, 323, 337, and 477.

Author's Preface

I acknowledge with profound gratitude the careful editing by Dr. Menahem G. Glenn, Mrs. Frances Diane Robotti; Dr. Gerald Shepherd; and the late Rabbi Abraham Burstein. Their erudition and diligence are part of this volume.

My deepest feelings of gratitude are for my wife, Edith, for her love, her constant, unstinting and unreserved motivation to write. Without her devotion and wise counsel, neither this book nor any other would have been brought to light.

Alex J. Goldman

Stamford, Connecticut

PART I

THE LAW

Pentateuch
Torah

GENESIS

Berayshith

THE FIRST BOOK OF THE BIBLE TELLS THE STORY OF ALL BEGIN-
nings, the creation of life, of people and of a good world in which to live.
Out of the void God fashions an ordered universe, creating in six days
the heavens, earth, light, firmament and seas, vegetation, fishes, birds
and animals; and when each day is completed God pronounces that what
has been performed is good. When the six days of creative effort are
over, God rests on the seventh, called the Sabbath. God sanctifies and
blesses the day, and we on earth are called upon to follow the same
practice, that is, work for six days and rest on the seventh.

The beginnings of life and of people on earth as told in the scriptures
are simple and dramatic. People are created by God. God is, therefore,
Creator and the Creator of all who follow. Adam is the first man. All
people derive from him. All people are alike and equal. Here we have
the basic religious teaching known as the Fatherhood of God and the
Brotherhood of Man. Created in the image and likeness of God, people
must always strive to live the good, divine, and godly life.

God fashions a helpmate for Adam out of one of Adam's ribs. Her
name is Eve. God places them together in the Garden of Eden; Adam is
told to till the garden and to tend it. He is given the liberty to eat of
every tree of the Garden but not of the tree of knowledge. Tempted by
the serpent, Eve encourages Adam to eat with her of the forbidden
fruit. God's will has been flouted. All three are punished, Adam, Eve,
and the serpent. Evil, wickedness, pain have been brought upon the
world early in the history of people.

3

THE LAW

The evil persists. Cain and Abel, sons born of Adam and Eve, are the first children of God's creation. Their lives end ignominiously in exile and untimely death. Cain brings an offering to God from the fruit of the soil, and Abel, for his part, brings the choicest of the firstlings of his flock. God pays heed to Abel and his offering but not to Cain's gifts. Thereupon Cain is much distressed, and, in a fit of envy and anger, sets upon his brother Abel and kills him. It is the first case of fratricide. Cain's denial of responsibility, vividly expressed by his retort to God's questioning as to the whereabouts of Abel is: "Am I my brother's keeper?" It has become the slogan of all who refuse to accept human roles of responsibility. Cain is driven out of the land and made to wander over the face of the earth.

The biblical plan is clear to see. God would establish a world for people to conquer and to dominate for universal good and for a blessing. And then, very early, evil enters and reduces the blessings. People must therefore be on a constant alert to recapture and restore the divine blessings which have evaded them. There arises the process of selectivity by which persons are named, generations recorded, until one individual is summoned to play the leading role of guiding people to seek restoration of their primeval blessings. The scriptures continue the account of the surviving son of Adam and Eve, in the report of Adam's descendants, generation by generation.

Ten generations are to elapse before the next striking individual is to emerge on the scene of history. Among them are: Enoch who "walked with God," and Methuselah, whose span of nine hundred and sixty-nine years has become the symbol of long life. He is the father of Lamech, who in turn is father of Noah.

Noah finds favor in the eyes of God. His life marks the end of a major period of history and the beginning of another. His arrival brings hope for people's return to the high estate that has been lost. Noah, the righteous man, is selected of God, destined to lead his generation out of corruption and wickedness which have spread throughout the world. The old world with its evil people is to be eradicated and a new world begun, with Noah and his family as a nucleus. Thus chosen, Noah and his sons build the famed ark as they prepare for the watery doom to be unleashed upon the world.

To assure life after the raging flood waters have subsided, paired creatures are led into the ark. Noah, with his sons, Shem, Ham, and Japheth, his wife and the wives of his sons, lead the procession into the ark. The deluge begins as the fountains of the great deep burst apart and the flood-gates of the sky break open. For forty days and forty nights, rain falls on the earth. The waters increase and raise the ark so that it rises above the earth and is launched. The swelling waters cover the

4

highest mountains, and all existence on earth is blotted out—people, cattle, birds—only Noah and his family survive, and all those with him in the ark.

After a hundred and fifty days the waters subside and recede. The ark comes to rest on the mountains of Ararat. At the end of forty days, Noah opens the window of the ark and sends out a raven. The raven finds no place to alight and returns. Seven days later, a dove is sent out and it, too, returns to the ark. Noah waits another seven days and again sends forth the dove. The dove returns to him toward evening, and in its bill is a plucked-off olive leaf. Then Noah knows that the waters have decreased on the earth. Pained by the heavy loss the world has sustained, God arches a magnificent rainbow across the skies. It is God's sign that a destructive deluge of such magnitude will never again revisit the earth.

Noah and his three sons, Shem, Ham, and Japheth, become progenitors of the generations of people. Families of the nations are enumerated. However, the infliction of the flood has not had the desired effect of eradicating evil. Once more evil dawns in the hearts of people. They plan conquest of the very heavens, as depicted in the account of the Tower of Babel in the land of Shinar. People imagine they can climb the heights and dethrone God, but God defeats them by confounding their speech and dividing them into groupings, nations, and peoples to avert concerted wickedness and to provide control over the actions and deeds of others.

Eleven chapters of the Book of Genesis are devoted to the background for the selection of Abram as the founder of the Jewish people. Activated from the early pages of Genesis, the selective process narrows to the group upon which the Bible will hereafter concentrate. The narrator has passed over many peoples and individuals to choose one to covenant with God and lead others in striving to restore blessings of God upon all people. The covenant will be agreed upon by both parties; and Israel will be its vehicle. With Abram (later Abraham), the history of the people of Israel begins.

Terah is the father of Abram, Nahor, and Haran. Haran (who was the father of Lot) dies within the lifetime of his father, Terah, in his native land, Ur of the Chaldees, in Mesopotamia. Abram's wife is called Sarai; Nahor's wife is Milcah.

God calls upon Abram to leave his native land and kindred and to devote his life to the glorious future planned for him and his people. He is assured of reward for fulfilling his part of the covenant. "I will make you a great nation and I will bless you. . . . And I will bless those who bless you and curse those who curse you, and through you all the families of the earth will be blessed."

Abram and his faithful wife, Sarai, willingly enter the covenant and set out southward (toward the Negeb) to the Promised Land of Canaan. There is a famine in the land, and Abram goes down into Egypt to sojourn there. As he is about to enter Egypt, he says to his wife, Sarai, "I am well aware that you are a beautiful woman. When the Egyptians see you, they will say, 'She is his wife,' and they will kill me, but let you live. Say then that you are my sister, that it may go well with me because of you." As he predicted, when they enter Egypt, the Egyptians see how beautiful Sarai is, and when the courtiers praise Sarai's beauty to Pharaoh, she is brought to the palace. Pharaoh extends himself because of Sarai and things go well indeed with Abram. He acquires sheep, oxen, cattle, and camels. When Pharaoh is afflicted by plagues, he discovers that Sarai is really the wife of Abram, and he sends them away. Now rich in cattle, silver, and gold, Abram goes into the Negeb as far as Bethel, where he erects an altar.

When strife arises between the herdsmen of Abram and the herdsmen of his nephew Lot, Abram and Lot decide to separate peacefully. Abram remains in the land of Canaan; Lot settles in the cities of the plain of Jordan. God gives to Abram all the land he sees, to him and to his offspring forever. Often gripped by anxiety, Abram is reinvigorated by the pledge of God of the grandeur which awaits him. He is unable to understand, however, the fulfillment of the promise without having an heir, for Sarai is childless. God promises him a son. Meanwhile Sarai advises Abram to consort with her Egyptian maidservant, Hagar, who bears him a son, Ishmael, who is not destined to be in direct line of succession.

The terms of the covenant are formulated. Abram's name becomes Abraham, meaning "father of multitudes," and Sarai's name becomes Sarah, conveying more descriptively the meaning of her name—princess. *God will be the God of Abraham and of his descendants, and they will be God's people.* There is to be an external sign of the covenant, the rite of circumcision, on the eighth day following a male child's birth.

God tells Abraham that his wife Sarah will bear him a son whom he is to name Isaac. God asserts that a covenant will be established with him and his offspring to come. And God blesses Ishmael and promises to make his issue exceedingly fertile, that he will be the father of twelve chieftains. At the age of ninety-nine, Abraham observes the rite of circumcision for himself, for all his retainers and home-born slaves.

Three messengers of God arrive to foretell the tidings of Isaac's birth and the forthcoming destruction of Sodom and Gomorrah, cities of evil and immorality from which Lot and his family are to be rescued. Abraham's kind heart, his benevolent and hospitable nature, as well as his deep feeling for the right and the just, are shown in his dramatic plea for mercy and justice. He asks God, "Will you sweep away the righteous with the wicked? Shall not the Judge of all the world act justly? What if there are fifty who are righteous? Will you destroy them too?" God agrees to stay the decree of destruction for the sake of the righteous. But fifty are not found. Abraham persists: "What if there are forty?" Again God agrees. There are not forty. Abraham asks again. Thirty? Twenty? Ten? But even ten good people are not to be found. Convinced that God is just and that no righteous people exist in Sodom and Gomorrah, Abraham bows to God's will.

Angels (messengers) arrive in Sodom to warn Lot of impending disaster and to urge him to leave at once with his family, lest they all be swept away because of the iniquity of the city. They instruct him to flee and not to look behind him, nor to stop anywhere in the plain, but to proceed to the hills. As the sun rises and Lot approaches the small town of Zoar, the Lord rains sulfurous fire upon Sodom and Gomorrah, annihilating those cities and all their inhabitants. Unable to restrain her curiosity, Lot's wife looks back and is turned into a pillar of salt.

When Isaac is born to Sarah, she urges that Abraham send Hagar and her son away lest their heathen practices contaminate Isaac. Abraham, receiving God's assurance that this is correct action, "for through Isaac will your seed be known," banishes Hagar and Ishmael. God promises Hagar that Ishmael will be progenitor of a great nation.

Abraham has been confronted with many difficulties and trials in his long life. After invoking the name of God at Beer-sheba, he lives for a long time in the land of the Philistines. To prove his complete, unreserved, unequivocal faith in God, he is put to the supreme test when God asks him to sacrifice Isaac, his only beloved son. Abraham's faith is unswerving. He prepares to set out for the appointed place, Moriah, which is several days' journey distant. He takes the wood for the burnt offering, placing it on the boy's back while he himself carries the firestone and the implement as the two walk off together. Isaac asks his father where the sheep is for the sacrifice, and Abraham replies that God will see to it that there is one. Abraham builds an altar on their arrival and lays out the wood, binds his son Isaac, and lays him on the altar. God, never intending to exact the sacrifice, sends an angel to stay Abraham's hand. In Isaac's stead, a ram, caught in the thickets nearby, is substituted. God now knows that Abraham's faith is wholehearted and reassures Abraham that he will be rewarded, "Because you have done this thing . . . I will multiply your seed as the stars of the heaven and as the sand on the seashore . . . and through your seed will all the nations of the earth be blessed."

Sarah dies at the age of one hundred and twenty-seven, and Abraham secures the cave of Machpelah in the land of Canaan (Palestine) for her interment. He pays four hundred shekels of silver to Ephron, son of Zohar. The cave of Machpelah, facing Mamre (Hebron), a basis for possession of Palestine, becomes the burial ground for all of the patriarchs of Israel and their wives (except Rachel).

With Abraham's advancing years, he realizes his work is not yet completed. He must make certain that Isaac fulfills his destined role, which can be accomplished only if he is not dominated by foreign influences. Abraham therefore plans for Isaac to contract marriage with a woman of the land of his birth and instructs his devoted servant, Eliezer, to carry out his intentions. Eliezer sets out with ten of his master's camels and makes his way to the city of Nahor. He asks for a divine sign, that the maiden to whom he shall say, "Please, lower your jar that I may drink," and who replies, "Drink, and I will also water your camels"—she shall be the one whom God has decreed as the bride for Isaac.

Scarcely has he finished speaking when Rebekah (who was born to Bethuel, son of Milcah, the wife of Abraham's brother Nahor) comes out with her water jar on her shoulders. She is very beautiful. She goes down to the spring, fills her jar, and returns. The servant, Eliezer, runs toward her asking for a drink. She lowers her jar for him to drink and offers a drink for his camels. He asks her name and if there is room in her father's house for them to spend the night. The man rejoices that he is on the road on which God has guided him, to the house of Abraham's kinsmen. Eliezer tells the household how God has greatly blessed his master Abraham, that Abraham has become wealthy, that Sarah has borne him a son in her old age, and that it is Abraham's wish that Isaac secure a wife from his kindred. There is much feasting and rejoicing. Rebekah leaves her family accompanied by her nurse, and the party returns to the home of Abraham.

As Isaac walks in the field toward evening, he looks up and sees camels approaching. Rebekah asks of Eliezer who he is; he tells her it is Isaac, the son of his master Abraham. They are married, and Abraham's noble life comes to an end at the age of one hundred and seventy-five years. Old and contented, he is gathered to his kin, and buried near his wife Sarah in the cave of Machpelah.

Isaac now appears as the second patriarch. His life story is not as detailed, however, as that of his father, Abraham. Isaac was forty years of age when he took as his wife Rebekah, daughter of Bethuel and sister of Laban. Rebekah conceives and bears twins, who struggle within her womb before they are born, for they are two nations, one of whom will be mightier than the other. Esau is born first, then Jacob. The boys grow to manhood. Jacob is the quiet, peaceful, home-loving man; Esau the skillful hunter and man of violence.

One day, when Esau returns famished from the fields, he finds his brother Jacob preparing a meal of lentil pottage. Jacob says he will give him the food if Esau will sell him his birthright, to which Esau readily consents. The episode signifies the transfer of leadership of the clan from Esau to Jacob.

As each patriarch must personally experience the awareness and presence of God, God appears to Isaac and reiterates the blessing destined for the descendants of Abraham, thus renewing the covenant with Isaac. Isaac has grown wealthy with large flocks and herds and a great household. Age draws upon him and his eyes are dimmed. He wishes to bless his elder son, a blessing which has the effect of conveying primacy and line of succession. Isaac's love for his son Esau is strong and deep. He summons him and bids him prepare venison and delicacies before the blessing. Rebekah, who possesses prophetic vision, overhears Isaac's request. She disguises Jacob in Esau's hunting habit, since Esau is hairy-skinned, and sends him in to Isaac with a tasty dish. Unable to see, Isaac reaches out for his son and is confused. He remarks pointedly, "The voice is the voice of Jacob, but the hands are the hands of Esau." Nonetheless, Isaac enjoys the food and then blesses Jacob, placing the mantle of leadership upon him.

Meanwhile Esau returns from the hunt and prepares delicacies for his father's enjoyment. He learns of the deception and vows retaliation upon his brother Jacob. After the blessing by Isaac, Rebekah urges Jacob to leave the house until Esau's anger subsides. Like his father before him, Isaac instructs his son Jacob to return to Rebekah's homeland, and there, from among the daughters of her brother Laban, to find a suitable wife, who will become the faithful matriarch of Israel. And so Jacob flees from the wrath of his brother Esau. He goes to Paddan-aram, to Laban.

Now Jacob's long, tumultuous life comes to the attention of the biblical narrator who is infinitely more expository, more biographical with Jacob, as he takes his place in the patriarchal triumvirate. Jacob, too, is to experience personally his selection by God. The occasion comes quickly. When Jacob leaves Beer-sheba as he sets out for Haran, he reaches a certain place where he stops for the night. Taking one of the stones, he places it under his head as his pillow. He dreams, and sees a ladder set on the ground with its top reaching into heaven. Angels of God ascend and descend. God appears to Jacob and reveals words which have been similarly expressed to his father, Isaac, and to his grandfather, Abraham. God will abide with Jacob and bless him and all of his descendants, and bring them into the Promised Land. Jacob awakens with awe, realizing and experiencing God's presence. Early in the morning, Jacob takes the stone and sets it up as a pillar. He names the site Bethel, meaning The House of God, but previously the name of the city had been Luz.

Jacob arrives in Haran, where he meets the daughters of Laban—Leah, the elder, and Rachel, the younger. Jacob sees Rachel, a pretty shepherdess, as she advances to the watering place with her father's flock. Some of the shepherds have refused to help her water the sheep, insisting they must wait for the others before they can remove the heavy stone covering the well. In a feat of super-human strength, Jacob rolls the stone from the mouth of the well. For Jacob it is love at the very first meeting with his cousin Rachel, the daughter of his mother's brother Laban. When Jacob tells Rachel he is her kinsman, he kisses her and breaks into tears of happiness. The radiant girl runs to tell her father, Laban, the glad news. He comes to greet and embrace Jacob, and as he takes him into the house, he says warmly, "You are truly my bone and flesh."

Jacob then tells Laban he is willing to serve him seven years for the hand of Rachel. He keeps his word, and the years seem to him but a few days because of his great love for Rachel. Laban prepares a wedding feast and gathers together all the people. At the time of the ceremony, however, Laban substitutes Rachel's sister Leah under the bridal canopy because she is the elder daughter. Disappointed, Jacob nevertheless now works an additional period for Rachel, whom he finally marries with Laban's consent. While Rachel remains childless, Leah bears Jacob his sons Reuben, Simeon, Levi, and Judah. When Rachel realizes she is not becoming a mother, she brings her handmaiden Bilhah to her husband Jacob, so that through this woman she may at last have a son. In due time Bilhah bears a son called Dan, and then a second son called Naphtali. When Leah, for her part, sees that she is not bearing more children, she likewise brings to Jacob her own maid-servant Zilpah, who bears a son named Gad and then a second son named Asher.

Then Leah, after bearing four sons, resumes motherhood and has a fifth son called Issachar and a sixth son Zebulun. Lastly, Leah bears Jacob his only daughter, named Dinah. And then God remembers and heeds Rachel's prayers for children and she bears a son and names him Joseph ("May the Lord add another son for me"). During the many years Jacob has spent with his uncle Laban, eleven of his twelve sons and one daughter are born. The youngest son, Benjamin, is born to Rachel near Bethlehem on the way to Ephrath. The twelve sons of Jacob become the founders of the twelve tribes of Israel.

Jacob has prospered in all of his undertakings. He wishes to return to the land of his fathers, and sends messengers on ahead to his brother Esau, who lives in the land of Edom, to seek a reconciliation. Jacob and his entourage proceed to the meeting place. The previous night, his mind troubled and his heart anguished, Jacob experiences a dynamic change. On this night, left alone, he wrestles with a man-angel. His thigh is strained as his hip is wrenched from its socket, but he prevails over his opponent. The divine being says, "Let me go, for dawn is breaking," but Jacob answers, "I will not let you go unless you bless me." The other asks, "What is your name?" Jacob replies simply, "Jacob." The being says, "Your name shall no longer be Jacob, but Israel, for you have striven with God and with men, and you have prevailed." The meaning of the name Jacob is "supplanter," implying inferior position. The meaning of Israel is "Champion of God" or "He who strives with God."

Jacob's meeting with Esau is friendly, brief, and uneventful, although vividly presented in the scriptures. Esau advances to meet his brother Jacob with a company of four hundred men. They embrace and exchange amenities. The reconciliation effected, the brothers part in good spirits; Jacob journeys on to Succoth with his wives, children, and flocks. Here he builds a house and stalls for his cattle. Then he proceeds safely to the city of Shechem, which is in the land of Canaan, pitches his tents on land purchased from the children of Hamor, Shechem's father, and sets up an altar which he calls El-elohe-Yisrael, meaning, "God, the God of Israel."

The patriarchate has been established with the theme of Abraham, Isaac, and Jacob firmly entrenched in Jewish consciousness. The balance of the Book of Genesis is devoted to detailed narratives of the lives of the children of Jacob. Jacob continues strong in his faith, urging his household to rid themselves of alien gods.

On the journey from Bethel, Rachel gives birth to Benjamin. She does not, however, survive his birth, and is buried on the road to Ephrath (now Bethlehem). Over her grave Jacob sets up a pillar before journeying onward and pitching his tents beyond Migdal-eder.

At length Jacob reaches his aged father Isaac at Mamre at Kiriath-arba (Hebron) where before him his father Abraham had lived. Shortly thereafter Isaac breathes his last (at one hundred and eighty years of age) and is buried by his two sons Esau and Jacob. Again, when the brothers part, they settle in different areas, Esau in the hill country of Seir, Jacob in the land of Canaan.

The stories about Joseph, son of Jacob's old age and his favorite, now begin to unfold in the scriptures in all their beauty and simplicity. Jacob loves Joseph more than any of his other sons. He showers him with gifts, including an ornamented tunic or coat of many colors, interpreted as the mark of chieftainship over the entire group. Joseph's brothers are

envious of him and their feelings intensify when he describes his dreams
to them. In one he envisions sheaves in the field bowing before him.
The sheaves represent the brothers. In the second dream, he pictures
the sun, moon, and stars prostrating themselves before him. They represent his mother, father, and brothers. Both dreams reflect a haughti-
ness which angers the brothers all the more.

Joseph, now seventeen, is tending his father's flocks. One day, at the
bidding of his father, Joseph follows his brothers and their flocks to Dothan. They see him from afar as he approaches. They conspire to kill
him and to throw his body into a pit, mockingly saying, "Here comes
that dreamer!" Reuben, the eldest, hears his brothers and intercedes,
pleading, "Let us not take his life. Shed no blood! Cast him into this pit
. . . but do not touch him yourselves. . . ." Reuben intends to save
Joseph from them and to restore him to his father. When Joseph comes
up, they strip him of his beautiful tunic and cast him alive into the pit.

They sit down to a meal and, looking up, see a caravan of Ishmaelites
coming from Gilead, their camels bearing gum, balm, and ladanum, to
be taken to Egypt. Judah says to his brothers, "What do we gain by
killing our brother? Let us sell him to the Ishmaelites—after all, he is
our brother, our own flesh." They pull Joseph up out of the pit and sell
him for twenty pieces of silver to the traders, who bring Joseph into
Egypt.

The brothers return home and tell Jacob that Joseph has been killed
by a wild animal and show his bloodied coat of many colors as evidence.
The father bitterly mourns the loss of his favorite son.

The most dominant individual of Genesis emerges when Joseph begins his life among the Egyptians. He is sold by the Ishmaelites to Potiphar, a courtier of the Pharaoh and his captain of the guard. He quickly
gains the confidence of his master. God is with Joseph and lends success
to everything he undertakes, so that Potiphar makes Joseph his personal
attendant, placing him in charge of his household and properties. All
was not to run smoothly, for, after a time, Potiphar's wife casts her eyes
upon Joseph, who is well built and handsome, coaxing him day after day
with her wiles. Joseph resists her, and with vindictive malice she tells
Potiphar that Joseph has approached her. Joseph is thrown into prison.
There his powers of interpreting dreams create interest and he insists
that the Lord is the source of these powers. Two former servitors of
Pharaoh have dreams. The chief butler envisions a three-branched vine
which, while budding, brings forth ripe grapes. He presses them into
Pharaoh's cup and hands it to him to drink. Joseph interprets the dream:
"The three branches are three days. In three days Pharaoh will pardon
you and restore you to your post; you will place Pharaoh's cup in his

hand as was your custom formerly when you were his cupbearer." He asks that the prisoner think of him when he is restored to his position and to mention him to Pharaoh so that Joseph may be freed from confinement. The chief baker dreams he is carrying three baskets of bread on his head and birds peck away at them. Joseph interprets the dream to mean that in three days he will be executed. The butler forgets Joseph, who remains in the dungeon.

Two years pass. Pharaoh dreams he is standing by the River Nile when seven cows, handsome and sturdy, come up and they graze in the reed grass. Soon seven other cows come up close behind them; they are ugly and gaunt, and these consume the sturdy cows. Pharaoh awakes. On the following night Pharaoh dreams of seven ears of corn growing on a single stalk, solid and full-kerneled, and of seven ears that are thin and scorched by the east wind; and the thin ears swallow up the seven full ears.

The next morning, his spirit agitated, Pharaoh sends for the magicians and wise men of Egypt. None can interpret the dreams to Pharaoh. Then his chief butler speaks up and tells of the Hebrew youth, a servant of the captain of the guard, who had correctly interpreted his dream. Joseph is rushed from the dungeon; his hair is cut, his clothes are changed, and he is brought before Pharaoh, who relates his two dreams. Asserting, "It is not in me; God will give Pharaoh an answer of peace," Joseph declares that both the dreams are the same, that God will see to Pharaoh's welfare and has told Pharaoh what is about to happen. The seven healthy cows are seven years and the seven healthy ears of corn are seven years. The seven lean cows and the seven thin ears are years. Immediately ahead, says Joseph, are seven years of great abundance in all the land of Egypt; after them will come seven years of famine, and all the abundance in the land of Egypt will be forgotten. These are divine warnings. The recurrence of the dream means that the matter has been determined by God and God will soon carry it out. Joseph tells Pharaoh to find a man of discernment and wisdom to make preparations during the years of abundance.

This plan pleases Pharaoh and his courtiers. He appoints Joseph his viceroy. Removing his signet ring from his hand, Pharaoh places it on Joseph's hand, and has him dressed in robes of fine linen with a gold chain about his neck. Joseph rides in the chariot of his second-in-command and the people cry before him, "Abrech!" ("Bow the knee"). Pharaoh gives Joseph the Egyptian name of Zaphenath-paneach ("Explainer of hidden things") and also gives him for a wife Asenath, the daughter of Poti-phera, priest of On. Thus Joseph emerges in charge of the land of Egypt. He is thirty years of age when he enters the service of Pharaoh.

He travels through all the land and has the grain of the seven abundant years stored in the cities, collecting produce in very large quantity until it can no longer be measured. Before the years of famine come, Joseph's wife bears him two sons. He names the first-born Manasseh (God has made me forget) and the second Ephraim (God has made me fruitful).

The years of famine come and afflict all of the lands, as Joseph has foretold, but in Egypt there is sustenance. The famine soon becomes severe, even in Egypt, so that Joseph has to ration out the grain, and all the world comes to him in Egypt to buy grain. The famine spreads to Canaan, and Jacob tells his sons to go down to Egypt to buy food. So ten of Joseph's brothers come to secure grain rations in Egypt. Jacob does not, however, permit his youngest son, Benjamin, to go with the others for fear a disaster may befall him, as with Joseph.

Joseph's brothers appear before him. He recognizes them, but they do not know him. At the sight of them, he does not think of revenge. He looks upon the experience as the providential working of God, who has prepared the way for him to help his family. Overtly he deals harshly with the men, ferreting out information about his father, Jacob. He accuses them of being spies, which they vehemently deny as they tearfully plead their case and review their family history, its composition, their father's age, and the disappearance of their brother, Joseph. Joseph persists, saying they can prove their innocence by returning home and bringing back their youngest brother Benjamin. Simeon, Jacob's second son, is to be retained as a hostage. The brothers feel certain their father will not permit Benjamin to join them, but they say they will try, and so they return home.

Jacob refuses to allow Benjamin to go to Egypt. Only when their food is gone does he bow to his sons' demands, for he now has no alternative but to relent and hope that the fate of Joseph will not be repeated with Benjamin. When the brothers present themselves before Joseph, the viceroy is moved at the sight of his youngest brother, but he retains his composure. The interview is brief; Simeon is released. Joseph continues to test his brothers when they prepare to return to Canaan. He orders their sacks filled with grain and the money paid for it put back in the bags. In Benjamin's sack he has placed his own personal silver goblet. The brothers depart, and are soon overtaken by Joseph's soldiers, who allege that the premier's goblet has been stolen. All sacks are emptied. The brothers are bewildered when the goblet is found in Benjamin's sack. They are escorted back to Joseph, who orders the guilty one, Benjamin, to be punished.

One of the most poignant portrayals in literature follows. The viceroy, unknown to them as their brother, stands before the accused brothers and one of them, Judah by name, steps forward to plead eloquently on behalf of Benjamin. In moving language and with deep feeling, Judah outlines the events up till the present moment.

He reminds Joseph that when they first came to Egypt, he had asked them if they had a father or brother, that they had responded affirmatively, and that he had insisted they bring the brother on their next journey. He describes for Joseph what had transpired in their home when they returned and reported to Jacob that Benjamin must come, that Jacob had firmly refused to allow Benjamin permission to go lest harm befall him, that only after compelling circumstances left no other recourse did Jacob submit, and then only after he, Judah, had solemnly guaranteed Benjamin's safe return. Judah's pleas soar majestically as he asks Joseph rhetorically, "How can I now return home, knowing that I have sinned against my father and not kept my promise! How can I possibly face him and confront what will surely happen when I come home without my brother!"

The dramatic plea apparently has its effect. Joseph can no longer contain his feelings. He dismisses all the attendants in the room, and in the presence of only his brothers, reveals himself to them. "I am Joseph. Is it really true that my father, so old, so sorely tried, is yet alive?" Astounded at the revelation, the brothers at first fear Joseph will retaliate, but he assures them they need have no fear and that all that occurred was predestined. He urges them to hurry home to Jacob in Canaan and bid him come with all of his household and possessions to Egypt where peace and plenty will be theirs.

Joseph bids his brothers tell their father that they will live in the region of Goshen where they can be near him. The news reaches Pharaoh's palace that Joseph's brothers have come. Pharaoh thereupon generously offers a home in Egypt to Jacob and his household. The brothers return to Canaan with the news that Joseph is still alive, yes, and that he is ruler over the whole land of Egypt. Doubt gnawing within him as to going to live in Egypt, Jacob hesitates, but God appears and tells him to go, promising to protect him and his descendants.

Once again, Jacob heads his family as they travel into Egypt where the region of Goshen is prepared for him and his families. Joseph orders his chariot and goes to Goshen to meet his father Jacob. When they meet, Jacob says to Joseph, "Now I can die, having seen for myself that you are still alive."

Jacob, now known as Israel, settles in the country of Egypt, acquires holdings, and his descendants increase greatly in number. He lives seventeen years in Egypt, so that the span of his life is one hundred and forty-seven years. When the time approaches for him to die, he calls his son Joseph and says to him, "Do not bury me in Egypt, but take me to Canaan." Joseph promises. Jacob summons his sons to his bedside and blesses them, foretelling to each his destiny. He dies peacefully and is gathered unto his forefathers after instructing his children to bury him in the cave in the field of Machpelah bought from Ephron the Hittite, in the land of Canaan, where Abraham and Sarah, Isaac and Rebekah and Leah are buried. Jacob is mourned in Egypt for seventy days, and Pharaoh instructs Joseph to go up to Canaan and attend to the burial.

When Israel is no more, Joseph's brothers again express fear lest Joseph take revenge upon them. But Joseph assures them repeatedly that all has been providential and for the best. Soon thereafter Joseph secures a promise from the children of Israel that his body will be taken with them when they leave Egypt.

Joseph remains in Egypt and lives to see the children of the third generation of Ephraim. The children of Machir, son of Manasseh, were born and brought to Joseph's knees. When Joseph reaches the age of one hundred and ten years, he says to his brothers: "I am about to die. God will surely take notice of you and bring you up from this land to the land which was promised to Abraham, to Isaac, and to Jacob."

EXODUS

Shemoth

THE BOOK OF EXODUS CONTINUES THE STORY OF THE CHIL-
dren of Israel in Egypt. The names of those who came down into Egypt
with Jacob, each with his household, are duly recorded, and almost immediately there is a change of emphasis; a shift which is to be maintained throughout the rest of the Bible. No longer does the theme
revolve around a patriarch, an Abraham, Isaac, Jacob, or Joseph. From
the second book on, the entire group, the children of Israel, becomes
the central figure on the pages of history. The people thus replaces the
individual in importance.

Eleven sons of Jacob have come to Egypt: Reuben, Simeon, Levi,
Judah, Issachar, Zebulun, Benjamin, Dan, Naphtali, Gad, and Asher.
Joseph, the twelfth son, is already in Egypt. The number of Jacob's
family totaled seventy.

Jacob's children live peacefully and happily for many years, until a
new king arises over Egypt who does not remember Joseph. Whether
he is actually a new king or new in the sense of a major change of policy
is not known. The monarch is fearful of the Israelites as they grow,
multiply, and prosper. Their numbers and strength arouse the jealous
apprehension of the Egyptian court. Pharaoh, who begins to regard the
Israelites as foreigners who will rise against him when opportunity is
afforded, decides that the only way to control them is to reduce them to
slavery. By forced labor, the Israelites, with harsh taskmasters cruelly
oppressing them, build for Pharaoh the garrison cities of Pithom and
Raamses. They are put to work with mortar and brick and in the fields.

17

The fears of Pharaoh, however, continue to plague him lest a leader arise from their number and direct the people in rebellion against him. He orders that all newborn males be cast to death in the River Nile. Now the scene is set for the coming of Israel's redeemer and great hero.

Jochebed, the Levite wife of Amram of the house of Levi, having given birth to a boy, refuses to heed the behest of Pharaoh that she destroy her child. She seeks a way to save her newborn baby from the Nile. Ingeniously, hopefully, she takes the three-month-old child, places him in an ark made of bulrushes, daubed with pitch and mortar, and with a prayer on her lips sets the little basket among the reeds near the river bank. Her daughter, Miriam, is left to watch the tiny ark to see what will befall the child.

Soon the daughter of Pharaoh and her handmaidens come down to bathe in the Nile. Seeing the drifting basket, the Egyptian princess sends one of her maidens to retrieve it. When the basket is uncovered, she feels pity for the crying infant and says: "This must be a Hebrew child." Miriam comes forward and asks Pharaoh's daughter whether she may call a Hebrew woman to nurse the child for her. Miriam brings her own mother, Jochebed, and the princess puts the boy in her arms, saying she will pay her wages to nurse him until he is old enough to be brought to Pharaoh's daughter. When this comes to pass, the princess adopts him, bestowing upon him the name Moses, which means "I drew him out of the water." Moses is reared as a prince in the palace of the king and tutored in the many arts of Egyptian culture and civilization.

Moses retains a sympathy and love for his own people which seem always to have been part of him. This is first seen in the incident in which Moses is deeply moved at the sight of an Egyptian striking an Israelite. Looking quickly about him to determine if there are any witnesses, he kills the Egyptian and buries him in the sand. By this deed Moses has cast his lot with his brethren. On the following day, he is swiftly confronted with the rebuke: "Do you mean to kill me as you did the Egyptian?" To his consternation, he learns that his action of the previous day has already become common knowledge. The news, in fact, has quickly traveled to Pharaoh, and Moses flees the ruler's wrath.

In his flight, Moses reaches Midian, where he marries Zipporah, one of the seven daughters of the Midianite priest, Jethro. She bears him two sons, Gershom and Eliezer.

In the meantime the King of Egypt dies, but the Israelites are still kept in slavery, enduring untold hardships at the hands of their taskmasters. Their cries reach to the heavens, and God remembers the covenant made with Abraham, Isaac, and Jacob to protect the children of Israel and bring them to the Promised Land. God decides that the time has come to put an end to their suffering.

EXODUS

Moses is now called into God's service as leader of the people. In the role of a shepherd tending the flocks of his father-in-law Jethro, he comes to what is later called the mountain of God, at Horeb. There, he sees a blazing fire emanating out of a bush which miraculously the fire does not consume. It is the angel of the Lord appearing to him, the Bible records. Moses is drawn to inquire why the bush does not burn and God then calls him, "Moses, Moses!" Moses responds, "Here I am." God tells him to remove his shoes for the spot on which he stands is holy ground. God repeats to Moses the covenant made with Abraham, Isaac, and Jacob, and instructs Moses to approach Pharaoh as spokesman of the Hebrew slaves to allow them to go free. Moses hesitates to assume this mission, pleading that he is unable to perform the task because he is "heavy of speech." In answer, God tells Moses that his brother Aaron will serve as the speaker for him. Moses therefore accepts God's command to ask Pharaoh to allow the children of Israel to leave Egypt temporarily on a three-days' journey to sacrifice to God. Aaron is sent by God to meet his brother Moses in the wilderness, where he finds him at the mountain of God. Moses tells Aaron all that God has committed to him and about the signs which he is instructed to employ to convince the people of the holiness of their experience.

Moses returns from Midian to Egypt and gathers together the elders of Israel and all the people. When they hear the words of Moses and Aaron promising God's redemption, they accept the leadership of Moses and his brother Aaron. The initial request made by Moses of Pharaoh is permission for a three-days' journey by the Israelites to the wilderness where they may celebrate a festival in God's honor. Permission is denied. Pharaoh's answer is an intensification of demands upon them. On that very day Pharaoh charges the taskmasters that the people no longer be provided with the straw needed to make bricks. They must therefore gather the straw in the fields, and even with this loss of time they must nevertheless produce their same quota of bricks.

God warns Moses that Pharaoh's heart will be hardened and Pharaoh will continue to resist the pleas of the Israelites so that God's wonders and strength over Pharaoh may be shown, thus convincing the children of Israel of the greater might of their God over the many deities of the Egyptians. Pharaoh resists the plagues invoked by Moses—of blood, frogs, gnats, flies, boils, hail, locusts, and darkness which descends on the land for three days. It is after the plague of darkness has harassed Egypt that Pharaoh again summons Moses and finally grants consent with these words: "Go! Worship the Lord! Only your flock and your herds shall be left behind; even your children may go with you." However, Moses asks that the Israelites be permitted to take their own livestock from which they will select those to be used for sacrifices in their worship. Thereupon God again hardens Pharaoh's heart: the monarch denies permission to the children of Israel for the journey they desire.

God tells Moses one more plague will be brought upon Pharaoh and upon Egypt, after which the people will not only be allowed to depart, they will indeed be driven out of the country. Thus the final plague is visited: Every first-born in the land of Egypt will die, from the first-born of its ruler Pharaoh to the first-born of the slave girl, as well as all the first-born of the cattle.

Pharaoh does not, however, believe Moses' warning.

The narrative pauses as the Israelites are given their first law—Passover, festival of freedom, and instructed how to celebrate it throughout time. The Israelites are to be delivered not only physically, but spiritually as well. They are told how to prepare the paschal offering as an everlasting sign of their redemption, and that they are to celebrate it annually.

The children of Israel are to be marked for delivery from the plague of death to the first-born through the paschal sacrifice, blood of the lamb, to be put on the doorposts and lintels of the houses. It is called a passover offering (Hebrew, Pesach) referring to God's passing over the homes so marked.

As threatened, the plague strikes. There is no house which has escaped. Pharaoh rises in the middle of the night and summons Moses and Aaron to his chambers. In the moment of Israel's greatest despair, the final plague frees the people. Moses leads the Israelites out of Egypt. The enslavement is over. There is much, however, to do before there can be a complete transformation from an enslaved to a free people. They must be given duties and responsibilities as a group; this will bring them together and bind them into unity. God must now renew and expound the covenant with the descendants of the patriarchs, the covenant implying obligations on both sides. Moses is instructed to lead the people to Sinai, where the covenant will be concluded between God and Israel.

Inspired, fortified, encouraged, the Israelites march courageously after their leader. Pharaoh realizes that he has sustained a severe loss. He orders pursuit, sending six hundred of his picked chariots and the rest of the chariots of Egypt, with officers in all of them. Frightened by the tumult, the people plead before Moses: "Why did you take us out? Was it for want of graves in Egypt you brought us to die in the wilderness?" But they are shown God's greatness and might. Moses is told to stretch his hand over the waters. The Red Sea is split in two, and the Israelites march through on dry land. Then the angry waters, held back by divine fiat, commingle, and the Egyptian pursuers are wiped out.

Exodus

In the presence of all the multitude Moses chants what has become known as the Song of Moses, parts of which are incorporated into the daily worship service. "Who is like unto Thee, O Lord, among the mighty? Who is like unto Thee, glorious in holiness, revered in praises, doing wonders?" Here is the first public expression by Moses of God's power and might, his Ode of Triumph. (He will sing a second song when his life draws to an end and when the Torah is concluded.)

I shall sing to the Lord, for He is highly exalted;
The horse and his rider has He thrown into the sea.
The Lord is my strength and my song,
And He has become my salvation;
This is my God and I will glorify Him;
My father's God, and I will exalt Him. . . .

(Chapter XV, Verses 1–2.)

From the Red Sea, the Israelites journey on, into the wilderness of Shur and then to Elim, where they encamp, and then set out to traverse the wilderness of Sin to Mount Sinai, scene of the God-ordained covenant. A slave people, their shackles still figuratively chained to them, cannot be expected to act as a free people in so brief a time. The moment they encounter difficulty, they long for a return to familiar surroundings. They recall not their physical enslavement, but the physical delights they enjoyed. The bread and the fleshpots of Egypt loom large in their minds beyond the promised glories of freedom. When they complain to Moses that there is no food to eat, no water to drink, Moses turns to God, who directs him to sweeten the bitter waters for the people to drink. God sends manna from heaven, like coriander seed with the taste of honeyed wafers. Manna is the food of the Israelites for forty years, until they come to a settled land, to the very border of the land of Canaan.

At long last, the children of Israel arrive at the foot of Sinai. A great unity is created as Israel encamps to await the event which will mark the beginning of its spiritual history as a select people of God. The covenant made between God and their ancestors is now to be made with an entire people. God will guide and help the people, and they will be true and faithful to God.

In awe and reverence and with understanding of the importance of the coming event, Moses ascends the holy mountain where he hears the voice of God setting forth the terms of the covenant. Israel is proclaimed

God's own treasure and is invested with the title, "a kingdom of priests and a holy nation." In turn, Moses brings the word of God to the elders of Israel, and then to the people of Israel. They hear him, and with one voice, Israel responds: "All that the Lord has spoken we will do."

Here follows the most momentous event in history, the Revelation. With supreme grandeur, overwhelming natural phenomena, thunder, lightning, dense clouds upon the mountain, the shofar sounding the clarion call, God speaks the words which have become the Ten Commandments. They reverberate throughout the world. There is presented for all time the most comprehensive yet succinct set of principles of behavior ever proclaimed. Israel listens and accepts the Tablets, significantly divided into two, the right dealing with laws affecting people's relationship with God, and the left with people's duties to fellow human beings.

I am the Lord your God, who brought you out of the land of Egypt, out of the house of bondage.

You shall have no other gods before Me. You shall not make a graven image for yourselves, nor any likeness of anything that is in the heavens above, on the earth beneath, or in the waters under the earth. You shall not bow down to them, nor serve them; for I the Lord your God am a jealous God, visiting the iniquity of the fathers on the children to the third and fourth generation of those who hate Me; and showing mercy to the thousandth generation of those who love Me and keep My commandments.

You shall not take the name of the Lord your God in vain; for the Lord will not hold him guiltless who takes His name in vain.

Remember the Sabbath day, to keep it holy. Six days you shall labor and do all your work; but the seventh day is a Sabbath to the Lord your God: on it you shall not do any kind of work, you, your son, your daughter, your male-servant, your female-servant, your cattle, nor the stranger who is within your gates; for in six days the Lord made heaven and earth, the sea, and all that is in them, and rested on the seventh day; therefore, the Lord blessed the Sabbath day and hallowed it.

Honor your father and mother, that your days may be lengthened upon the land which the Lord your God gives you.

You shall not murder.

You shall not commit adultery.

You shall not steal.

You shall not bear false witness against your neighbor.

You shall not covet your neighbor's house, you shall not covet your neighbor's wife, nor his male-servant, nor his female-servant, nor his ox, nor his ass, nor anything that is your neighbor's. (Chapter XX, Verses 1–14).

Israel is now prepared to accept not only the laws promulgated in the Decalogue itself, but also other laws and principles which carry out the spirit of the Commandments. Detailed guidance is given to help them live up to the covenant as a holy nation in the making. There are laws dealing with civil rights, personal injuries, rights of the slave, homicide; others concerning crimes against property, injury and damage caused by animals; laws touching on moral behavior, ethical conduct, seduction, oppression of the weak and strangers, loans and pledges, truth and impartiality in the application of justice, love of one's enemy. In addition, laws are set down describing the religious observance of the Three Pilgrimage Festivals: Passover, Pesach (Feast of Unleavened Bread), Shavuoth (Feast of Weeks and of the First Fruits) and Sukkoth (Feast of the Ingathering), on which holy days all adults are expected to journey to the Sanctuary.

Now that the Decalogue has been proclaimed within the hearing of the entire multitude and Moses reads before them the book of the covenant, the people assert: "All that the Lord has spoken we will do and hear." This is their ratification of the covenant. Moses then ascends the mountain to receive the stone tablets. He spends forty days and forty nights on the mountaintop with God.

Communion with God must continue even after the covenant is established and all obligations assumed. There must therefore be a visible emblem of God's indwelling. The balance of the Book of Exodus is devoted to the gifts of the people for the construction of the tabernacle and its furnishings. This is the Sanctuary, the Tabernacle, which God instructs Moses to build: "And let them build for Me a sanctuary that I may dwell therein." Specific architectural details are given. The furnishings which are designed to add depth and significance to the Sanctuary and its service are fully described as to materials, colors, measurements, placement, and use. Among other symbolisms there is to be an Ark to house the stone tablets.

From among the Israelites the tribe of Levi is selected for the ministry. Aaron, brother of Moses, and the sons of Aaron are to be priests to perform the actual service of the Sanctuary. Sacral vestments, indicative of their exalted positions, are carefully set forth "for dignity and adornment"—a breastplate, an ephod, a robe, a fringed tunic, a headdress, and a sash and turbans. When they are thus invested, anointed, and ordained they are consecrated as priests to the service of God.

The narrative of the Sanctuary is interrupted to record the grievous sin committed through the Golden Calf, which episode has become engraved on the consciousness of Israel. The people expect that Moses will return from his retreat to the top of the Holy Mountain on the fortieth day, inclusive of the day on which he ascended. When he fails to return, they become impatient to the point of complete helplessness. The people now gather, come to Aaron and demand a visible God. Divesting themselves of their gold and silver ornaments, they fashion a Golden Calf.

The people worship the graven image of the Golden Calf with festival, eating and drinking, and they are assuaged. When Moses and Joshua return—Joshua had gone up with Moses but remained on the lower slope of the mountain—Joshua hears the sound of the people in their boisterousness, and says to Moses: "There is a cry of war in the camp." But Moses answers: "It is not the sound of triumph or defeat; it is the sound of song that I hear!" When Moses draws near, he sees the Golden Calf. He is horrified, and hurls the stone tablets from his hands, shattering them at the foot of the mountain. He rebukes Aaron when he sees the people out of control and reprimands the people for their impatience and their lack of faith. But the impassioned people do not hear and are a menace to any who might oppose them. At this juncture, Moses asks the assistance of his devoted followers, and all the Levites rally at his side. Moses instructs them to put down the mutiny.

In his profound understanding, coupled with the people's contrition and regret, Moses is moved to plead with God for forgiveness of the heathen worship of which they are guilty. He beseeches God also for divine assistance in his task. In time, God bids Moses hew out two tables of stone and ascend the mountain with them. Again, Moses remains there for forty days and forty nights. God proclaims the divine characteristic qualities, known as Shlosh Esray Midot, Thirteen Attributes or Qualities of God, which are recited in the festival service of Pesach, Shavuoth and Sukkoth: "The Lord, the Lord God, merciful and gracious, long suffering, and abundant in goodness and truth, keeping mercy unto the thousandth generation, forgiving iniquity and transgression and sin. . . ." The complete proclamation continues: ". . . and that will by no means clear the guilty; visiting the iniquity of the fathers upon the children and upon the children's children, unto the third and unto the fourth generations." (Chapter XXXIV, Verses 6–7.)

The sin of the Golden Calf has destroyed the covenant and it is therefore necessary to re-establish it. The conditions set for renewal deal only with the relationship of God to people, since the sin of the Golden Calf affected half of the Decalogue. With the second set of tablets, the covenant is renewed and when Moses descends the second time, his countenance reflects great happiness: "The skin of his face sent forth beams." Divine radiance shines on his countenance as he feels his mission accomplished.

The description of the Sanctuary is resumed. The master builder, Bezalel, son of Uri of the tribe of Judah, and Oholiab son of Ahisamech of the tribe of Dan, are appointed, divinely infused with wisdom, knowledge, and understanding for construction of the House of God. The Israelites are to share in the offerings by being given the opportunity to contribute. Their giving is so intense that Moses asks them to desist from further flow of gifts.

The Sanctuary is built, faithfully, lovingly, gently; every single divine instruction is fulfilled. It is now ready for the service of the priests, with the presence of the Lord filling the Tabernacle.

The Israelites have traversed a great distance both physically and spiritually from the time they left Egypt. They have come to Mount Sinai where they have accepted the divine covenant. They have built the House of God and are becoming welded into a holy people, a people of God. They have reached the end of an important period in their national development. The Book of Exodus draws to a close as the glory of God fills the Tabernacle witnessed by all of the people of Israel.

LEVITICUS

∽∾∽∾∽∾∽∾∽∾∽∾∽∾∽∾∽∾∽∾∽∾∽∾∽∾∽∾∽∾∽∾∽∾∽

Vayikrah

THE THIRD BOOK OF THE PENTATEUCH IS THE LEAST IN length. With the Sanctuary completed and ready for worship, Leviticus sets forth the use to be made of it and who is to bear the responsibility for its proper operation. Leviticus may be called a manual of ritual instruction. It describes the kinds of services to be conducted; the elaborate system of sacrificial worship; the rituals to be established; the duties and responsibilities of the priests as individuals, as ministers in the ceremonials, and teachers of the people; and the role the Israelites as a "kingdom of priests" are to play in the Sanctuary service. This primary source book from which we derive and develop what has been referred to as "the Jewish way of life" is in its contents almost wholly legislative rather than historical.

The beginning chapters are devoted to a detailing of the laws of sacrifice. In days of old, the system of sacrifice was the normal way of worship. Every people followed some form of sacrifice. Leviticus describes them as natural and deeply felt expressions of religious feeling and of homage and fealty to God, similar to our prayer of today. It is significant that the Hebrew word for sacrifice is korban, from the word karov, meaning coming or drawing near.

There are many kinds of sacrifices, and their names reflect their purpose and spirit. Peace offerings were presented as gratitude for deliverance from illness or danger, for fulfillment of a promise made in times of distress and disturbance, or in appreciation of God's bounty. These were free-will offerings when one was moved to make them. The sin offering was an admission by the wrongdoer, implying a solemn promise on his part to correct the wrong committed. The daily offering symbolized the people's pledge of continued devotion and loyalty to God. The communal sacrifice taught the concept of interdependence of individuals upon each other, and of the people, as a sacred congregation upon its individual members. This sacrifice nurtured the consciousness of the sacred covenant with God and the mission of the chosen people on earth.

The principal sacrifices having been enumerated, Leviticus describes the inauguration of the sanctuary service and the consecration of the priesthood. In the Book of Exodus, Aaron and his sons had been appointed ministers of God, their princely garb and the symbols of their high sacerdotal position delineated. Reserved for the Book of Leviticus is the description of the dramatic ceremony of consecration and investiture (Chapters VIII–X) in the presence of the entire congregation. The offerings for Aaron and for the congregation are followed by the priestly blessing, after which Moses and Aaron enter the sanctuary and bless the assembled people. The impressive ceremony terminates with the appearance of the glory of God and the sacred fire which consumes the sacrifices placed on the altar. The continuous ceremony of seven days is followed by public worship on the eighth day, when Aaron and his sons officiate for the first time as priests. The service is now officially inaugurated.

The emphasis on holiness and purity, both personal and communal, underscored in the sacrificial system, permeates every area of life and contact. Holiness applies to all, priests and members of the congregation. Living a holy—that is to say a pure—life is the supreme motive which forms the basis of the laws of purity and impurity covered in the next five chapters (Chapters XI–XV). The mind is not only to maintain pure thinking, pure thoughts are to be expressed in the pure deed, and the body must also be pure. Thus dietary laws are enumerated in what foods are permissible and forbidden; laws dealing with the relations of men and women, marriages of specific blood relationships allowed and disallowed, physical diseases and their treatment, and other laws of purification are elaborated upon. There are rules for observance of an annual fast day, having for its object the purification of the people and the sanctuary. Thus the climax of holiness is reached in the ceremony of purification performed in the Sanctuary on the Day of Atonement. The Torah portion in the traditional synagogue on Yom Kippur is taken from this chapter (XVI), the service performed in the Sanctuary by the high priest becoming part of the Musaf (additional) service.

THE LAW

The second half of Leviticus, beginning with Chapter XIX, in the portion significantly called Kedoshim (holy), contains what has become known as the Code of Holiness. The chapter occupies a primary position in the Book of Leviticus and therefore a similarly high and central position in the entire Bible. The dominating theme is the injunction: "Be you holy, for I the Lord your God am holy." The principle is that the concept of holiness applies to personal conduct and behavior.

In this formative period of the nation's history, basic moral and ethical laws are formulated and recorded in maxim and principle bearing on reverence for one's parents; consideration of the poor; immediate payment of wages for labor performed; honorable dealing among people; control of tale-bearing, malice, taking advantage of the unfortunate such as the blind and deaf; love of one's neighbor, friendliness toward the stranger; equal treatment of and justice for both rich and poor; the maintenance of honest weights and measures. Contrariwise, there are set forth prohibitions against that which is immoral, improper, unclean, unethical, and impure. The precepts which form the major portion of this chapter are recognized as belonging to the left column of the two mosaic tablets reflecting man's relationship to his fellow man.

The famed Verse 18 (Chapter XIX) "Love your neighbor as yourself" is found here. Less often quoted is the beginning of the same verse "You shall not take vengeance nor bear any grudge against your kinsfolk," which is preceded by "You shall not hate your brother in your heart."

The Lord spoke to Moses, saying:

Speak to the entire congregation of the children of Israel, and say to them:

You shall be holy, for I the Lord your God am holy.

You shall fear every man his mother, and his father, and you shall keep My Sabbaths: I am the Lord your God. . . .

When you reap the harvest of your land, you shall not wholly reap the corner of your field, nor shall you gather the gleaning of your harvest. You shall not glean your vineyard, nor shall you gather the fallen fruit of your vineyard; you shall leave them for the poor and for the stranger.

You shall not steal; nor shall you deal falsely, nor lie one to another. . . .

You shall not oppress your neighbor, nor rob him; the wages of a hired servant shall not remain with you all night until the morning.

You shall not curse the deaf, nor put a stumbling block before the blind, but you shall fear your God. . . .

You shall do no unrighteousness in judgment; you shall not respect the person of the poor, nor favor the person of the mighty; but in righteousness shall you judge your neighbor.

You shall not go up and down as a talebearer among your people; nor shall you stand idly by the blood of your neighbor. . . .

You shall not hate your brother in your heart; you shall surely rebuke your neighbor, and not bear sin because of him.

You shall not take vengeance, nor bear any grudge against the children of your people, but you shall love your neighbor as yourself. . . .

You shall rise up before the hoary head, and honor the face of the old man. . . .

If a stranger lives with you in your land, you shall not do him wrong.

The stranger who lives with you shall be to you as the home-born and you shall love him as yourself; for you were strangers in the land of Egypt. . . .

You shall do no unrighteousness in judgment, in mete-yard, in weight, or in measure. . . . (Chapter XIX: Verses 2–3, 9–11, 13–18, 32–35.)

The theme of holiness proceeds to include the priestly class itself, elucidating their conduct in the Sanctuary, their function and concern for the ritual and its performance. The high point is reached in the memorable verse: "You shall not profane My holy name, but I will be hallowed among the children of Israel." (Chapter XXII, Verse 32) The virtue of reverence for the holy name is known as Kiddush HaShem, sanctification of the name of God. Its most extreme expression is that of martyrdom, that is, surrender of life itself rather than public apostasy or desecration of the Name.

Holiness is further described in the sacred seasons of the year and their celebrations. Each is to be hallowed and sanctified. Each religious holiday is called a "holy convocation" or "assembly" for worship in the Sanctuary. First is the Sabbath and its holiness as people's day of rest for all time. In order, the calendar of sacred seasons are set forth, beginning with Pesach (Passover), Feast of Unleavened Bread, which comes in early spring, on the fifteenth day of Nisan, considered the first month.

Forty-nine days of the Omer (an agricultural measure) are counted, and on the fiftieth day Shavuoth, Feast of Weeks, arrives. Exactly six months after Pesach, on the fifteenth day of Tishri, the seventh month, Sukkoth, Feast of Tabernacles or Booths, is celebrated. These are the three pilgrimage festivals when adults are expected to visit the Temple in Jerusalem. The cycle of holy days is completed by the enumeration of: Rosh Hashanah, the Day of Memorial or New Year, on the first day of Tishri, the seventh month, and Yom Kippur, Day of Atonement, on the tenth day of Tishri.

The law of holiness as applied to people's rest on the Sabbath relates as well to the land, for the earth is not a possession of people. It belongs to God who has entrusted the land to people's ministrations and use, and like people and beasts, is entitled to rest after the sixth year.

The cycle of sacred seasons continues with a description of Sabbaths of years. "Six years you may sow your field and six years . . . prune your vineyard and gather in the yield. But in the seventh year the land shall have a Sabbath of complete rest." When this is repeated seven times, the seventh or sabbatical year brings the fiftieth or Jubilee year, from the Hebrew word "yobel," ram's horn or blast of the Shofar, which ushers in the Jubilee Year. In this year, emancipation is decreed for all Hebrew slaves and all lands which had been alienated during the whole period now revert to their former owners.

In this section of Leviticus occurs the proclamation of the Jubilee: "And you shall hallow the fiftieth year and proclaim liberty throughout all the land unto all the inhabitants thereof: it shall be a Jubilee unto you; and you shall return every person unto that person's possession and you shall return every person unto that person's family." From this passage, the Founding Fathers of the United States took the remarkable words which are engraved on the Liberty Bell in Philadelphia, Pennsylvania: "And proclaim liberty throughout the land unto all the inhabitants thereof." (Chap. XXV, Verse 10.)

The Book of Leviticus has projected laws of every conceivable kind: priestly and ceremonial sections, ethical and moral chapters. The concluding chapters contain admonitions, exhortations, and rewards for obedience as well as penalties for disobedience. This is a common practice in a number of places in the Bible. The final chapter concerns itself with the subject of vows and tithes, and closes with the simple yet authoritative verse: "These are the commandments, which the Lord commanded Moses for the children of Israel on Mount Sinai."

As one is aware, with the passage of long periods of time many of the laws of Leviticus may no longer have practical application to our present-day life. For instance, the sacrificial system has long since been replaced by prayer. Abolishment came in the year 70 C.E. when the Temple in Jerusalem which was the site of the offerings of the sacrifices, was destroyed. However, it is interesting to note that in Jewish tradition, children begin the study of the Bible with the third Book, for the reason that "children are pure and sacrifices are pure; let those who are pure come and occupy themselves with that which is pure."

NUMBERS

Bemidbar

THE FOURTH BOOK OF THE TORAH, NUMBERS, DEALS ALMOST exclusively with the wanderings and experiences of the Israelites in the wilderness. Covering more than thirty-eight years of the four decades they were destined to spend from the time they left Sinai, it traces their forward movement until their final arrival at the banks of the River Jordan, within sight of the Promised Land.

Numbers is the continuation of the accounts and legislation set forth in the previous Books: Genesis was historical in background and composition. Exodus depicted the birth of a nation, its rise from slavery to a God-accepted and God-accepting people, and recording the laws and ordinances by which they were to live as a "kingdom of priests and a holy nation." Leviticus dealt with civil, social, ethical, and ritualistic legislation and expanded upon the themes of the Ten Commandments, detailing the laws and standards of living. The laws expounded in Leviticus were also those imparted at Mount Sinai and are part of the total experience.

Thus far very little has appeared in regard to the emotions and attitudes of the people in the great change which has transpired—the transition from centuries of slavery to new-found freedom, entailing new regulations, demands upon them, and the establishment of living standards. There is likewise the novel experience of a great number of people being constantly on the move as they travel to the Promised Land. The Book of Numbers richly portrays many of the human elements and characteristics noted in the thirty-eight years of wandering. The trials, problems, fears, and frustrations lead first to murmurings of discontent, rebellions and mutinous uprisings against Moses and the leaders of Israel. The noble character of Moses is reflected in his great patience as he strives constantly to assuage the feelings of anger, hatred, and strife which pervade the vast camp.

Included in this Book are a number of supplementary laws relating to the Sanctuary and offerings, to the purification of life and to other civil and political injunctions designed to enable the children of Israel to fulfill the great work assigned to them by God.

The Book of Numbers opens with the roll call of the people to determine the fighting strength of the Israelites and the enumeration of the ministering Levites. The census revealing 603,550 adult males (Chapter I, Verse 46) is conducted one month after the erection of the Sanctuary. Described in detail is the arrangement of the camp with the Tabernacle kept ever in the center of the march. Each tribe proceeds under its own banner, maintaining the position initially assigned to it, with the entire camp set up in the form of a quadrilateral. In the center is the Tent of Meeting, and surrounding it on four sides are the Levites. Farther beyond them—and enclosing the whole of the camp—are the twelve tribes of Israel. In the lead is the sacred Ark containing the engraved Tablets. When the Ark is raised on high, indicating the march forward, Moses recites a prayer. When the Ark is lowered, indicating the halt, Moses reads another prayer. These same prayers inaugurate and conclude the Torah reading service in the synagogue.

The mustering of the tribes of Israel is duly recorded, followed by the tribe of Levi, who are to play a specific role in the service. A smaller group of the Levites is to comprise the Kohanim, the priests. They as ministers of God, perform the actual service. The Levites are to be their assistants, setting up and dismantling the Ark. Not only are the duties of the priests recounted but also their prayers. The instructions and Levitical prayers are climaxed by the simple and beautiful Hebrew fifteen-word benediction the priests are to invoke upon the children of Israel in God's name.

"The Lord bless you and keep you. The Lord make His face to shine upon you and be gracious unto you. The Lord lift up His countenance upon you and give you peace." (Chapter VI, Verses 24–26.)

The forward movement of the people begins as a period of great privation and tribulation. Ill-feeling and resentment are generated with the accumulation of difficulties. The people complain, recalling foods and especially delicacies they sometimes enjoyed in Egypt, and forgetting their physical sufferings while in bondage. They come to Moses and plead for food, for meat. Moses turns to God, seeking help in providing their necessities. He asks also for help in guiding and leading the people as he can no longer rule the vast multitudes alone. Seventy elders are summoned to his aid, infused with the spirit of God, and appointed to assist Moses in his leadership.

Then God sends quail in from the sea to satisfy the craving of the people for flesh. It was meat in overabundance covering the ground "a day's journey on both sides of the camp." The people set to gathering quail day and night and all of the next day to satisfy their hunger. Then God's anger blazes against them for their passionate cravings for food, and the people are stricken with a severe plague. Many perish and are buried there, the place being named Kibroth HaTaavah, Graves of Lust.

The trials of Moses entail disagreement with the people, and his unbearable loneliness is magnified as he bears the brunt of murmurings from members of his own family. Aaron, his brother, and his sister, Miriam, speak against Moses because of the Cushite woman he has married. With humility, resignation, and courage, Moses with the help of God overcomes these confrontations which continually test his patience and his strength. His burden is very great.

When information is needed about the land of Canaan, which is the Promised Land, Moses, by God's command, sends twelve scouts, each man a leader of his ancestral tribe, including Hoshea, whose name Moses changes to Joshua (God saves). They are directed to go up into the Negeb and into the hill country, to find out and report on the land, its vulnerability, accessibility, its wealth and fortifications, and the kind of people who dwell there. They go up and scout the country thoroughly from the wilderness of Zin to Rehob, the Negeb, to Hebron and the Valley of Eshcol (cluster) from which they return with grapes, pomegranates, and figs.

They present two reports. The first is a majority and pessimistic view, climaxed by the familiar passage of fear and defeat—"And we saw there the Nephilim (giants) and we were in their eyes as grasshoppers and so we were in our own sight." The other, a minority and optimistic report, presented by Joshua of the tribe of Ephraim and Caleb of the tribe of Judah, asserts that fearlessness coupled with the help of God will assure the success of an invasion, that indeed it was a land flowing with milk and honey, abundant with fruits; however, the people inhabiting it are powerful and their cities fortified and very large.

The people give more credence to the majority report. They panic and wail. The whole community, breaking into loud cries and weeping that night, rebel against Moses and Aaron and say to each other, "Let us return to Egypt." It is apparent that a free people has not emerged. They are still spiritually chained to the past, and God decrees that the generation which came out of Egypt cannot enter the Promised Land. Because of the many times they have tried God and disobeyed, they shall not see the land promised to their fathers. The entire generation will die out in the wilderness, and only their children (a new generation) will enter the land. Caleb, son of Jephunneh, is exempt from the decree because he is imbued with a different spirit and is loyal to God. Joshua, son of Nun, is also exempt.

The wandering must, therefore, continue until the new and free-born generation is prepared to cross the River Jordan and fulfill the promise of God.

Rebellions continue to plague Moses. A great mutiny (Chapter XVI) is instigated by its principal spokesman, Korah, who heads a group of malcontents, including Dathan, Abiram, and On, to rise up against Moses and question his leadership. Taking with him two hundred and fifty recognized chieftains of the community, Korah complains that Moses has usurped all of the high and important offices for himself and for his own family. Dathan and Abiram directly accuse Moses of misguiding and misleading the people as they inveigh against his leadership. God vindicates Moses and Aaron by bringing death upon Korah and his followers, "and the earth opened its mouth and swallowed them up with their households, all Korah's people and all their possessions . . . the earth closed over them and they vanished from the midst of the congregation."

Over and over again, the Bible evokes the brilliant qualities of leadership possessed by Moses, his profound humility, his modest nature, his extreme fidelity to God and to the people, and most of all his unending patience. These character traits are easily recognized when Moses is confronted by an angry, unhappy, and complaining people.

When Miriam, the sister of Moses and Aaron, dies, she is buried as the Israelites arrive at the wilderness of Zin, where they stay at Kadesh. The community is without water, and in despair the people quarrel with Moses and call for water to quench their thirst and that of their flocks and herds. God instructs Moses and his brother Aaron to assemble the community and to speak to the rock to yield water, to provide drink for the congregation and their beasts. Moses smites the rock with his rod once and then a second time, and as he is carried away by anger, he temporarily loses control of his patience. On the second blow, the rock yields a copious flow of water and the people and their livestock drink of it. "Because you believed not in Me to sanctify Me in the eyes of the children of Israel" is the reason for God's decree that Moses, like the elder generations of the people whom he leads, forfeit his right to enter the Promised Land. Moses is destined to die in the wilderness and to remain on this side of the Jordan.

From Kadesh, Moses sends messengers on to the King of Edom as he continues, with determination, to lead his people onward following the incident at the waters of Meribah (Waters of strife). He asks leave for the children of Israel to cross the King's territory. Permission is denied, and the people set out from Kedesh, arriving at Mount Hor on the boundary of the land of Edom. At God's command, Aaron is gathered to his fathers on the summit of the mountain and his son Eleazar is vested in his priestly garments. The house of Israel mourns Aaron for thirty days.

Finally, the Israelites arrive at the steppes of Moab, at the peak of Pisgah, overlooking the land. When Sihon, King of the Amorites, denies Moses the right to lead the people through his territory, he takes the offensive against the Israelites at Jahaz. The Israelites conquer the Amorite kings, occupy their land, and encamp at the border of Moab.

Moses asks Balak, King of Moab, to allow the Israelites passage through his land, promising no harm or damage to people or property. Balak refuses and instead sends for Balaam, famed throughout the East for his magical powers, to come and cast a curse upon the people who have come out of Egypt. But God will not have it. God appears to Balaam in a dream, at first forbids him to go, and then allows him to proceed, with instructions, however, that he speak only those words which are put into his mouth. On the way from his home in Pethor, near the Euphrates River, Balaam experiences the episode of the talking donkey. This lowliest of animals, by his actions and miraculous speech, teaches Balaam a great lesson: that he must speak against the blindness and obstinacy of man. Balaam arrives at length in Moab, but instead of cursing the Israelites, the purpose for which Balak summoned him, Balaam speaks words of blessing foretelling Israel's victory and greatness. One of the blessings he offers begins with a phrase that has become part of the synagogue ritual: "How goodly are your tents, O Jacob, your dwelling places, O Israel!"

Almost forty years have passed since the first numbering, and a second census is now necessary. The census is of the new generation which has grown to adulthood. God instructs Moses and Eleazar, son of Aaron, to take a census of the whole Israelite community from the age of twenty years up, by their ancestral houses, all Israelites able to bear arms. The numbering takes place on the plains of Moab, at the Jordan near Jericho, with the enrollment of the Israelites: 601,730 (Chapter XXVI, Verse 51), 1,820 less than the total of the initial census.

God instructs Moses to appoint Joshua his successor and to invest him ceremoniously with leadership: "And you shall put of your honor upon him that all the congregation of Israel may listen."

The entire generation which left Egypt has passed away and the free-born generation has taken its place. The people at last arrive at the

Jordan and make preparations for crossing the river into the Land of Promise. All the tribes are united in their goals with the exception of the tribes of Reuben, Gad, and part of the tribe of Manasseh. They secure permission from Moses to settle permanently on this side of the river, subject to the provision that they strive together with their brethren until the conquest of the territory has been achieved. Moses assigns specific areas to them.

In addition to the numberings, there is recorded the marches of the Israelites who started out from the land of Egypt, troop by troop, in the charge of Moses and Aaron. Moses has recorded the starting points of their marches and the directions they traversed, as well as the time of the year.

The land of Canaan is to be dispossessed of its inhabitants and the symbols of their cults destroyed. The boundaries of the land of Canaan are recorded, as are the names of the people to whom the land is to be apportioned by lot. Allowance is made for the Levitical cities (since Levites are not permitted to own land or property because of their responsibilities in the Sanctuary); also cities to be places of refuge to which anyone who commits involuntary murder may escape pending trial and judgment.

The Israelites, a great multitude, are at the banks of the Jordan as the Book of Numbers concludes with the stirring passage: "These are the commandments and ordinances which the Lord commanded by the hand of Moses to the children of Israel in the plains of Moab by the Jordan at Jericho."

The Israelites prepare for the crossing.

DEUTERONOMY

Devarim

THE BOOK OF NUMBERS ENDS WITH THE ARRIVAL OF THE Israelites at the banks of the Jordan. Moses, their leader for forty turbulent years, brings them to the very entrance of the land promised by God. He prepares to deliver what may be termed his last will and testament, his final Book containing three major addresses to the new generation which has grown to adulthood during the era in the wilderness.

In Greek, this Book is known as Deuteronomy, from deuteros, (second) and nomos, (law) . . . the second law, or second giving of the law by Moses. In Hebrew, this Book is called Mishneh Torah, meaning copy or repetition of the Law, a term based upon Verse 18, Chapter XVII, which appears again in Joshua, Chapter VIII, Verse 32. It reviews some of the experiences of the Israelites, many of the laws, precepts, and regulative principles enunciated in the previous books.

More than any other in the Bible, the Book of Deuteronomy is a work of literary genius. In style, content, and concept it is a masterpiece. The structure of the final book of the Torah falls into well-marked divisions:

Five verses provide the introduction, and then Moses launches into his major discourses. The first is devoted to reviewing the great journey and to an exhortation to observe the laws of God. (Chapter I, Verse 6, to Chapter IV, Verse 40.)

The second address deals with the religious foundations of the covenant, together with a Code of Law, the manner in which it is to be kept and the motivations which lead to proper obedience. Israel's affirmation of faith as well as the Decalogue are recorded in this section. (Chapter IV, Verse 44, to Chapter XXVI inclusive.)

The third address of Moses contains the re-establishment of the covenant, how the Law is to be enforced, and instructions for the solemn ratification of the Law after the conquest of Canaan, the Promised Land. (Chapters XXVII–XXX inclusive.)

Before his death at the age of one hundred and twenty years, the great leader offers concluding exhortations of farewell to his people, and sings his final Ode to God.

As Deuteronomy opens, Moses, lawgiver and epic hero of Israel, continues to plead with the people ever to strive for closer communion with God, the righteous, merciful and living Lord. He stands before his people and explains in moving, elevating and inspiring words that it is not granted to him to cross the river with them. He explains that his faithful follower, Joshua, strong and determined, will lead them forward, and calls upon them to understand the covenant between themselves and God, to accept it wholeheartedly, to abide by its terms, and to receive as reward the blessings to accrue.

In his first address, Moses has laid the foundation for popular acceptance of the covenant. Recognizing the difficulties the people have endured, he reviews the events which have come to pass in their wanderings in the wilderness, the adventure of the twelve scouts into the land of Canaan, the pessimistic, fear-inciting report with which some of them returned, and the favorable report of a land flowing with milk and honey; the decree of the Lord that the generation which came out of Egyptian bondage shall not enter the Promised Land, but that it die and be replaced by a completely new generation to live and cultivate the land. Those who listen to the words of Moses are the new generation, and they are to enter into the covenant with God like their ancestors before them. As Moses reveals his own fate and approaching death, he does not conceal his emotions. He pleads with reason and passion that the children of Israel not forget the marvelous truths revealed at Sinai when God spoke out of the burning bush, promising to bring the people to the new homeland of fertility and contentment. He asks them to remember God's concern for Israel, the Chosen People, God's declaration of the covenant, and the Ten Commandments engraved on tablets of stone. Moses again exhorts the people to abstain from socializing with the idol-worshipers, from giving credence to pagan ideas and influences, and finally he assures them that God is always near and will always hear a contrite and repentant heart which seeks forgiveness.

The second address of Moses, the longest of the three, continues the theme of the first. He addresses the generation born and bred in the wilderness, the men, women, and children who are unacquainted with the momentous events at Mount Sinai. To them in particular he explains the covenant once again, impressing upon them its eternity, that it was not arrived at only for their parents and grandparents, but for them as well, "for the Lord made not this covenant with our ancestors alone but with us who are all of us here alive this day."

With the foundation established in these preliminary addresses, Moses now explains the terms of the covenant and the spirit in which it is to be maintained for all generations for all time. He enumerates the principal laws to be observed in the new land, the religious foundations of the covenant, and specifies that, included in this code, are: worship, rituals of the Sanctuary, the government, domestic life and laws, and criminal law.

He speaks of the close relationship between God and Israel and of the spiritual demands which the bond imposes. Then he repeats the Ten Commandments given at Sinai to their ancestors. The address has reached a climax of drama. Moses clearly declares that the greatest proclamation of the Torah is the Oneness of God and Israel's loyalty to God. He evokes the keynote of all Judaism as he enunciates what has since become known as the Shema, the watchword or confession of faith of Israel:

Hear, O Israel: the Lord our God, the Lord is One. And you shall love the Lord your God with all your heart, with all your soul, and with all your might. And these words which I command you this day shall be upon your heart. And you shall teach them diligently to your children, and shall talk of them when you sit in your house, when you walk by the way, when you lie down, and when you rise up. And you shall bind them for a sign upon your hand, and they shall be for frontlets between your eyes. And you shall write them upon the door-posts of your house, and upon your gates. (Chapter VI, Verses 4–9.)

In repeating the code of laws, encompassing many areas of life, there are included regulations of religious institutions, the Sanctuary, and the sacrificial system. The code stresses the marked difference between the divine mode of worship and that of the heathen neighbors. Moses speaks of the concept of holiness; of dietary laws—what is pure and what is not; the tithe system; redemption and release of slaves; and the discourse concludes with an additional description of the Three Pilgrimage

Festivals: Pesach, Shavuoth, and Sukkoth, their relationship to the Sanctuary, and the expectation that every Israelite then assemble at the Sanctuary in order to present an offering.

A detailed description follows of the government which is to be set up to rule over the people and to guide their destiny. Defined in the scripture are: the status of judges, how they are to be appointed, the principle by which they are to serve, the judicial system ("Justice, justice, shall you pursue"); the qualifications and selection of the king; the roles of the prophets, priests and Levites—all of whom are to be officials of the envisioned commonwealth when the Israelites inhabit and develop the land of Canaan.

The code is further elucidated with respect to laws concerning criminals, regulations as to cities of refuge for those who have committed involuntary murder.

Chapter XX reveals details of the code in regard to warfare, with emphasis on the essential dependence of Israel upon the help of God. "When you take the field against your enemies, and see horses and chariots—forces larger than yours—have no fear of them, for the Lord your God, who brought you from the land of Egypt, is with you. Before you engage in battle, the priest shall come forward and address the troops . . . saying to them: 'It is your God who marches with you to do battle for you against your enemy, to bring you victory.'"

Even the waging of war is to bear the stamp of human kindness. Many are to be exempted from military service: those who have built houses but have not dedicated or begun to live in them; those who have planted but have not yet seen the fruits of the soil; those who are just betrothed; or those fearful and fainthearted.

Offers of peace are to be made to every city attacked. During a long siege, fruit trees are not to be destroyed, since they are not human and cannot retreat. Only trees known not to bear food may be cut down for construction siege work against the city engaged in war.

Moses prescribes principles of domestic life, family laws, laws of equity, relationship of employer and worker, exercise of justice for the stranger, the orphan, the widow; kindness to animals and justice to their owners in regard to livestock; honesty and integrity in weights and measures.

Near the conclusion of the second address, Moses portrays the beautiful ceremonies to accompany the presentation of first fruits and the tithes to God in the Sanctuary, as tokens of thanksgiving for God's merciful bounty and beneficent favor. Each supplicant is to recite before

God how he came out of bondage in Egypt and was delivered of oppression by God's outstretched arm and awesome power, by signs and portents into a land flowing with milk and honey, "Wherefore I now bring the first fruits of the soil which You, O Lord, have given me."

The second discourse of Moses ends as he once more focuses attention on the original theme of the covenant between God and Israel.

The third and final address of Moses directs the priests and the Levites to prepare appropriate and expressive ceremonies for public acceptance of the covenant when the people enter the Promised Land. As soon as the Jordan is crossed, the people are to set up twelve large stones on Mount Ebal and inscribe upon them all the words of the Torah, building an altar to God of unhewn stones.

The covenant is to be ratified on Mount Ebal and on Mount Gerizim. On Mount Ebal are to stand: Reuben, Gad, Asher, Zebulun, Dan, Naphthali as the solemn dooms are proclaimed by the Levites for negators. On Mount Gerizim are to stand for the people: Simeon, Levi, Judah, Issachar, Joseph, and Benjamin as the blessings for those who abide by the covenant. The cursed and the blessed deeds, invoking the covenant to be inscribed on the twelve great stones, renews the covenant of the children of Israel with their God.

Moments of sublime exaltation are the due of Moses as he arrives to view the order of the multitude gathered before him. Forcefully he addresses his people: "You are standing this day, all of you, before your God . . . to enter the covenant of God." He asserts that the covenant, to the end that God may establish the Israelites this day as God's people and be their God as promised to Abraham, Isaac, and Jacob, is, with its sanctions, not alone with those standing before him but, "with him that is not here with us this day."

Moses, eloquent with fervor and the warmth of sincerity, urges that the nature of God's laws and commandments are not too difficult to follow nor are they too distant and unrelated, ". . . for this commandment, it is not too hard for you . . . neither is it far off. It is not in heaven . . . neither is it beyond the sea . . . but it is here, in your mouth, in your heart, that you may do it. See, I set before you this day life and good, death and adversity. For I command you this day to love the Lord, your God, to walk in God's ways, and to keep the Lord's commandments, the Lord's laws, and the Lord's norms, that you may thrive and increase, and that God may bless you in the land which you are about to enter and occupy."

Having thus spoken in regard to the Torah, Moses concludes this third address, touched with poignant drama of the forthcoming entry into Canaan.

I call heaven and earth to witness against you this day, that I have set before you life and death, the blessing and the curse. Therefore, choose life that you may live, you and your seed—to love the Lord your God, to listen to His voice and to cleave to Him; for that is your life and the length of your days; that you may dwell in the land which the Lord swore to your fathers, to Abraham, to Isaac, and to Jacob, to give them. (Chapter XXX, Verses 19, 20.)

With the address of Moses completed, there remain four chapters in the Book of Deuteronomy which relate his last days on earth. Cognizant of his mortality, Moses appoints Joshua as his successor in leadership with the simple admonition: "Be strong and of good courage." Moses commits the words of the Torah to writing and delivers the papyri into the hands of the priests and the elders of Israel, charging them with the duty of their periodic public reading. The elders take the written instructions of Moses as recorded in his Pentateuch and deposit them in the Ark of the Covenant alongside the stone tablets engraved with the Ten Commandments.

Then Moses recites the words of his song, in the presence of the whole congregation of Israel. Beginning his ministry at the Red Sea, with his triumphant Song of Moses, he is prepared to end his life of service with another epic hymn of joy in which he summons heaven and earth to witness and to listen to him. In eloquent language he surveys once more the history of Israel and again draws lessons of wisdom from the people's past. His song of praise vindicates the way God has treated Israel. He contrasts God's lovingkindness and faithfulness with Israel's faithlessness and ingratitude. He extols God, always and ever present, willing to give ear whenever called upon by the sincere supplicant.

The last portion of the Torah is significantly called VeZoth HaBerakhah ("This is the blessing.") This is the blessing which Moses, man of God, confers upon the children of Israel before his death. It envisions for them a luminous and joyful destiny. In symbolic closeness of the father who places his hands on the heads of his children, the departing leader blesses each of the twelve tribes of Israel. With the name of God on his lips, he speaks of the revelation of Mount Sinai, of the Torah, and then of the unity of Israel with God. With words which Jewish children recite during their morning prayers, he blesses the people. "Moses commanded us the Torah, an inheritance of the congregation of Jacob." In doing so, Moses follows in the path of Jacob, third of the patriarchs, who at the close of Genesis blesses each of his twelve sons before his death. Now Moses blesses the descendants who sprang from Jacob's twelve sons. The name of the last portion of the book of Genesis is Vayechi—"And he lived." This theme may well apply to Moses.

The last moments of his stay on earth are poignantly dramatized. The concluding chapter of Deuteronomy rises to a high point in living literature as it details how Moses went up from the steppes of Moab to Mount Nebo, to the summit of Pisgah, opposite Jericho, and he looks out upon the whole land: Gilead as far as Dan; all Naphtali, the land of Ephraim and Manasseh; the whole land of Judah as far as the Western Sea; the Negeb; and the Plain—the valley of Jericho, the city of palm trees—as far as Zoar. And God tells Moses that this is the land which was promised to the offspring of Abraham, Isaac, and Jacob.

Moses gazes longingly and long over this vast expanse of the Promised Land lying before him, and then the fact of his demise is simply recorded. "So Moses, the servant of God, died there in the land of Moab, according to the word of God . . . and no one knows his sepulchre to this day." The scripture says it was near Beth-peor. Moses was a hundred and twenty years of age, yet his eyes were undimmed and his vigor unabated. For thirty days the Israelites mourned Moses in the plains of Moab.

The Torah pays its highest tribute to Moses in the words: ". . . and there has not risen a prophet since in Israel like Moses, whom the Lord knew face to face."

PART II

THE PROPHETS

Nevi'im

JOSHUA

J OSHUA, THE FIRST BOOK OF THE PROPHETS, WHICH CONSTITUTES
the second general division of the Bible, continues the narrative of the
Five Books of Moses. Joshua is also the first of the four historical books
recording the story of the Israelites from the time they were posed at
the banks of the River Jordan until the fateful destruction of the First
Temple in Jerusalem in 586 B.C.E. The books are: Joshua, Judges, Samuel I and II, and Kings I and II. The book of Joshua fulfills the promise
God made to Abraham, Isaac and Jacob, the events contained therein
bringing to a close the striving and yearning for the Promised Land so
vividly portrayed in the Five Books of Moses.

The book differs from the Pentateuch in the absence of legal matter
and in its intimate connection with the contents of the books devoted to
the earlier prophets immediately following. It is, however, the proper
sequel to the origins of the people as related in the Book of Genesis,
their exodus from Egypt, and their journeyings in the wilderness. Some
scholars therefore attach Joshua to the Pentateuch and call the entire
group the Hexateuch, or Six Books.

The book takes its name from Joshua, son of Nun, an Ephraimite,
who became the successor of Moses, for Moses, at God's behest, had
invested him with the mantle of leadership. Tradition ascribes to Joshua
the writing of the last eight verses of Deuteronomy concerning the
death of Moses.

The book falls naturally into two main parts, of which the first is the
long-anticipated crossing of the Jordan and the subsequent military victories over the inhabitants of Canaan.

It opens dramatically with preparations for the crossing of the people and the capture of the powerful city of Jericho. God appears to Joshua and charges him with the duty of leadership with stirring words of assurance and courage:

As I was with Moses so shall I be with you. I will not fail you nor forsake you. Be strong and of good courage, for you shall cause this people to inherit the land which I swore to their fathers to give them. Only be strong and very courageous and be sure to observe the law, which Moses, my servant, commanded you. Turn not from it to the right hand or to the left, that you may succeed wherever you go. This book of the law (Torah) shall not depart out of your mouth. You shall meditate on it day and night that you may observe all that is written in it; then you shall make your ways be prosperous and you shall have good success. (Chapter I, Verses 5–9.)

Joshua responds to the charge with a ready acceptance. Summoning the leaders of the people, he instructs them to make all necessary preparations for the crossing; stating that the great event will take place within three days. He urges them to remember well the words Moses spoke to them. The people solemnly pledge obedience and support to Joshua as they had to Moses.

All that you command us we will do and wherever you send us we will go. As we obeyed Moses so shall we obey you; only the Lord your God be with you as He was with Moses. (Chapter I, Verses 16, 17.)

Joshua carefully maps the plans for the river crossing. The first city to be conquered is the fort of Jericho. He dispatches two spies to determine the strength of the city, its fortifications, and the attitudes of the inhabitants toward the approaching Israelites. The men come to the house of Rahab, a harlot. The king of Jericho, hearing that spies have entered the city, and are in fact in the house of Rahab, sends soldiers to capture them, but Rahab frustrates their mission by concealing the spies of Israel. She admits that two men have come but says that they are already gone. Rahab misdirects the soldiers and reveals to the spies that all the inhabitants of Jericho, from the king to the average citizen, are aware that God has given over Jordan to the Israelites and that Jericho is a doomed city.

She exacts a promise from the spies that, because of her cooperation, she and her family be spared. The promise is made, and the sign of assurance to Rahab and her family is a scarlet cord to be hung from her window. The Israelites will know the sign and will not molest this home. Rahab then lets the spies down by the window and tells them to hide for three days before returning to their leader Joshua. They follow her instructions; the king's soldiers despair in their search for the spies who return safely to the camp at Shittim. When Joshua hears their favorable reports, he declares that "God has delivered the land into our hands" and proceeds to take immediate action.

The priests are summoned to carry forward the Ark of the Covenant. When the carriers step into the River Jordan, the waters separate and they walk across on dry land. The children of Israel follow and the crossing is achieved. When the priests resume their places on the other side of the Jordan, the waters reunite in a flowing stream. God has re-enacted for the Israelites the miracle of the crossing of the Red Sea when they left the land of bondage in Egypt.

Joshua has twelve stones, representing the tribes of Israel, taken from the river and brought into Gilgal where the people encamp. They are set up for future generations as a memorial that the children of Israel traversed the Jordan over dry land. In Gilgal, the Israelites observe the Passover. At this time, in an experience reminiscent of Moses and the burning bush, a "captain of the hosts of the Lord" appears to Joshua to inspire and encourage him in the great work assigned to him by God.

The manner in which the fortified city of Jericho is to be captured is carefully detailed: The people are to march around the city once for each of six days, led by the Ark carried by their priests. They are not to raise a shout until told to do so. On the seventh day, they are to march around the city seven times. Seven priests, each bearing a shofar, are to sound the rams' horns strongly and loudly, and it is then the people are to raise a great shout. The Israelites follow the instructions of their leaders and at the given signal, Joshua exclaims: "Shout, for the Lord has given you the city." The people utter a tremendous outcry in unison; the cry from thousands of human throats rising in a deafening roar is answered by the roaring thunder of tumbling bricks as the huge wall collapses. With the wall down, the city is easily conquered; only Rahab and her family are spared.

Joshua forges ahead. En route, he selects thirty thousand soldiers and moves on to the city of Ai near Bethel. The strategy is to ambush the city from the rear while Joshua approaches the city with his armed soldiers, and, pretending flight, withdraw the enemy. While thus inciting pursuit, the army at the rear of the city will enter and subdue Ai, and no soldiers to defend it will be left within the city itself. The soldiers of Ai, caught in a military vise, quickly capitulate. Joshua has an altar erected upon Mount Ebal, north of Shechem.

The book of Joshua continues with the account of the subterfuge perpetrated by the Gibeonites to make peace with Israel. Living in the very path of the marching, conquering Israelites, the Gibeonites learn of their victories and send a delegation to Joshua, disguised as weary travelers. They are to say they come from a distant land to propose a treaty with Joshua. They avoid direct response to questions put to them as to their homeland, and they show Joshua their moldy dry bread and their torn and tattered clothes. Joshua agrees to a peace treaty. Learning shortly thereafter that the Gibeonites are in fact neighbors, he is unable to rescind the treaty. Instead he imposes servitude on this people making them hewers of wood and drawers of water for the House of God.

The five kings of Canaan learn of the Gibeonite trick and join forces to punish Gibeon. The Gibeonites in turn call upon Joshua to fulfill his obligations under the treaty, and he comes to their aid. He leads his army against the Amorite kings. God assures him a victory, and Joshua at the head of his troops, marches through the night from Gilgal to confront them. On this day Joshua issues his memorable command to the heavenly bodies:

Sun, stand still upon Gibeon, and Moon, in the valley of Ajalon. And the sun stood still and the moon stayed . . . And the sun stood still in the midst of the heavens and did not set for about a whole day. And there was never a day like it, before or since, that the Lord listened to the voice of a man: for the Lord fought for Israel. (Chapter X, Verses 12–14.)

Joshua continues his campaign of military conquest until he has prevailed over the five kings and their countries and Canaan has been won, with the exception of outlying land remaining to be possessed.

The second part of the book is devoted to the division of the conquered districts among the tribes of Israel. With the completion of the division, the mission of Joshua has been accomplished. That is, for all the tribes with the exception of two and one-half (Reuben, Gad, and half of Manasseh) who wanted their inheritance to materialize on the other side of the Jordan. They have fought side by side with the other tribes, and return to the land Moses had agreed to give them. Now advanced in years, Joshua, at God's command, proceeds to apportion the territory.

He summons all Israel to assemble at Shilo. Three people of each tribe are selected to investigate the terrain. Upon their return, Joshua draws lots for the land and divides it. He gives Hebron to Caleb, his co-scout in the searching out of the land as recorded in the Book of Numbers. Joshua also assigns cities and lands for pasture to the Levites who (because they are to perform the service in the Sanctuary and Temple) are not permitted to own land. Cities of refuge (mentioned in Numbers and Deuteronomy) are established.

Joshua grows older as the role to which God has assigned him draws to a close. Like Moses, his predecessor, he assembles all of the people in the city of Shechem and delivers to them his farewell address. He reviews the historical record and renews the covenant between them and God. He reminds the people that it was God who fought for them and fulfilled the promise made to their forebears. He enjoins upon them the worship of God and God alone, faithfully and loyally. They are not to worship other gods, and God is their one God. The people respond to his exhortation: "We will serve God." Joshua emphasizes that they have reached a decision and that the decision is theirs. Again they respond, "We are witnesses." Thus Joshua renews the solemn covenant between Israel and God.

To dramatize the covenant, Joshua takes a huge stone, sets it under a large oak tree near the Sanctuary, and says to the people:

This stone will be a witness against us, for it has heard all the words of the Lord which He spoke to us; it will therefore be a witness against you, lest you deny your God. (Chapter XXIV, Verse 27.)

His mission fulfilled on earth, Joshua, military and religious leader, servant of the Lord, dies at the age of one hundred and ten years. The record of his life and conquests constitutes a conviction of the destiny of Israel and of the greatness of the God of Israel and God's works for the people.

JUDGES

Second of the historical books in the division of the Earlier Prophets, the Book of Judges constitutes a sequel to the Book of Joshua. It covers the period of history between the death of Joshua and the birth of the Prophet Samuel.

In the Promised Land, the Israelites renew the covenant with God with a solemn promise to their leader Joshua to keep the commandments. The vows are kept during the lifetime of Joshua and his elders. Upon the death of Joshua and his generation, the new generation is unaware of the covenant, its terms and obligations. They find it difficult to grasp the hereditary spiritual concept of God while living among the surviving Canaanites, who worship visible idols headed by Baal and the Ashtereth (plural Ashtaroth).

God is angry with them for their heathen practices and punishes the Israelites by subjecting them to the Canaanites. When they are tortured and oppressed, they cry out to God for help. God sends a leader to save them. While the leader lives, peace prevails. Upon his death, the Israelites revert to pagan practices.

The Book of Judges comprises cycles of repetitive episodes tantamount to a set formula: The perpetration of evil, submission to a foreign power as punishment, pleading to God for help, the arrival of a leader, the leader's success in achieving peace during his lifetime—this is the history-repeating-itself theme of the Book of Judges.

The term "judge" is used in the sense of champion of the people rather than in the normal meaning of examining and deciding a case in dispute. Before the Israelites had established a monarchy, their govern-ment was in the hands of certain leaders who appeared to have formed a continuous succession although the office was not hereditary.

The opening chapters (I and II) deal with the occupation of Palestine by the Israelites, reviewing parts of the previous Book of Joshua, and covering the initial efforts of the Israelites to gain a firm footing in the land at Hebron, Ebir and Bethel, the cities Joshua subdued.

Judges then treats with the first of the cycles. Othniel, younger brother of Caleb, is first of the judges. He is followed by Ehud ben Gera, who, although lamed in his right hand, delivers the Israelites from the oppression of Eglon, king of Moab. Ehud, employing a subter-fuge, humbly presents himself to Eglon, bringing with him substantial tribute. With a plan for assassination in his mind, he requests a private audience which is granted him. Ehud thereupon slays Eglon, flees the palace, and escapes to the nearby mountains where his men await his return. He sounds the trumpet—the prearranged signal—and with a surging call, "Follow me, for God has delivered your enemies into your hands," the people of Israel subdue Moab. Saved thus by God's leader, the people are returned to God's good graces and enjoy relative peace for fourscore years, until their leader Ehud dies. Shamgar, the second leader, who proves victorious over the Philistines, "also saved Israel."

After Shamgar, the Children of Israel "did that which is evil in the sight of the Lord," and are oppressed under Jabin, king of Canaan, who had nine hundred chariots of iron. Sisera is Jabin's general of the armies and overlord of the king's chariots, constituting the nucleus of a large armored division. There is now related the famous episode of the prophetess Deborah, wife of Lappidoth, who became a judge of Israel, holding court and dispensing justice under a palm tree, between Ramah and Bethel in the hill country of Ephraim. To relieve her people's pain-ful servitude, Deborah summons Barak, the son of Abinoam, to lead an offensive for freedom. Barak accepts the charge but demands that Debo-rah join him in the actual battle, otherwise he will not proceed. Fearless and dynamic, Deborah agrees to his terms, declaring, "I will go with you. But the glory of this campaign will not be yours. God will deliver Sisera into the hands of a woman." Ten thousand soldiers are assembled to meet General Sisera and his iron chariots. They go forward from Mount Tabor with Deborah's courageous leadership inspiring Barak on-ward. "Let us go. This is the day God has given Sisera into your power."

Suddenly confronted by Barak's large number of troops, Sisera and all his host ("the Lord discomfited Sisera and all his chariots") are con-founded and flee; Sisera alights from his chariot and escapes on foot to the tent of the woman Jael, whose husband Heber the Kenite is on good terms with Sisera's king Jabin. Jael bids Sisera come into her tent. She gives him milk to drink and provides a covering for him to sleep. While he sleeps, Jael slays him so that as Barak, pursuing Sisera, reaches the tent of Jael she shows him that their enemy is dead. Thus God subdues Jabin, king of Canaan, before the Children of Israel. Once again, God has sent a savior to the Israelites. Peace reigns once more.

There follows one of the beautiful expressions of religious feeling in literature, as Deborah offers her ode to God. In her song of triumph and faith, Deborah recounts the oppression of the Israelites by the enemy, the battle lines drawn and fought, the destruction of Sisera, and an imaginative passage portraying the mother of the young general awaiting in vain her son's return from war. The Song of Deborah reaches its climax with the prayer that the enemies of Israel will vanish. "So perish all your enemies, O Lord; But they that love Him be as the sun when it goes forth in his might." (Chapter V, Verse 31.)

Again there is rest in the land for forty years, but the period without conflict is temporary. When the Israelites depart from God's ways, history finds them in the power of Midian for seven years. The Israelites are oppressed by the Midianites and the Amalekites from the east, who take possession of their crops and livestock. The enemy, numerous as locusts, come with their cattle, their tents and camels to destroy the land. The Israelites are forced to take to the mountains where they establish their strongholds and dwell in caves.

The children of Israel cry out for surcease to God who once more sends them a prophet of peace and humility to champion Israel. God's selection is vividly portrayed. An angel of God sits down beside Gideon, a son of Joash, who is beating out wheat in the winepress in order to hide it from the Midianites. The angel says, "The Lord is with you, you mighty man of valor." Gideon responds, "If the Lord is with us, why have all these things befallen us? And where are all the wondrous works of which our ancestors spoke?" The angel replies, telling Gideon he has been chosen by God to lead the cause of Israel. Gideon demurs, pleading his lowly station in life. God, through the angel, reassures him, but Gideon, still unconvinced, asks for visible signs to indicate he is divinely appointed for this mission. The signs are given and Gideon assumes his role.

Gideon builds an altar to God there in Ophrah. He destroys the altar of Baal and cuts down the Ashtereth by it. The people of the city complain to Joash, the father of Gideon, that he surrender his son to be killed for his blasphemy to the country's idols. Joash, heroic for his own part, defends Gideon by answering the people against Gideon: "Will you contend for Baal?" Inspired by the God of Israel, Joash faces the people successfully and the scriptures tell that Gideon's name is changed to Jerubbaal, meaning "let Baal contend against him," because he broke down Baal's altar.

Clothed with the protection of God, Gideon sends messengers throughout all Manasseh, to Asher, to Zebulun, to Naphtali, and assembles thirty-two thousand soldiers. Gideon asks God to demonstrate that he will be victorious. He places a fleece of wool on the threshing floor and says that in the morning, if there is dew on the fleece alone, and the ground around it is dry, it will be a sign that Israel is to be saved through him. So it was. Still in doubt, Gideon asks for final proof in that the reverse occur, that there be dew on the ground and the fleece be dry. So it happens.

God tells Gideon that the number gathered is too large; the people will boast that they and not God have saved themselves against the Midianites. Gideon is to send home the fearful and faint-hearted. Twenty-two thousand return to their families and ten thousand remain. God tells Israel that the number is still too great and instructs Gideon to bring the entire contingent to the water for another test of elimination. Those who lap up the water with their tongues, using a hand as a cup, are to be separated to one side; those who kneel down to drink with their mouths directly in the water are set to another side. The former, who numbered three hundred, will contend against the enemy. The latter who knelt, in the habitual stance before Baal, are rejected.

God bids Gideon to take his servant Purah and go down secretly to the camp of the Midianites. There he overhears two soldiers speaking, one telling the other of a dream. "I dreamed," the soldier says, "that a cake of barley bread tumbled into the camp of Midian with such force that it struck the tent and knocked it down." The other soldier comments, "This is nothing else save the sword of Gideon, son of Joash, a man of Israel into whose hand God has delivered Midian." When Gideon hears this conversation and the interpretation of the dream, he realizes it is a sign from God. Quickly he returns to camp, divides his three hundred soldiers into three companies, gives to each a trumpet and an empty pitcher, and places a torch in the pitcher. He commands his soldiers to watch him and to make no move until instructed.

When Gideon reaches the outskirts of the camp, he blows his trumpet, and all those who are with him, numbering the first contingent of one hundred soldiers, break the pitchers at the same time, and the other two companies comprising the balance of two hundred soldiers, blow their horns, break their pitchers while holding their torches in their left hands in order to do so. With swords in their right hands they cry out: "For the Lord and for Gideon." The enemy, shocked out of sleep by the blowing of three hundred horns, awakens and is routed.

Thus is Midian defeated, and peace again reigns over Israel.

The people ask Gideon to rule over them . . . "both you and your son and your son's son, for you have saved us." Gideon responds: "I will not rule over you, neither shall my son rule over you; the Lord shall rule over you." (Chapter VIII, Verses 22, 23.) The land is at peace for forty years during the balance of Gideon's lifetime.

After his death, the Israelites revert to the worship of Baal, defecting from the ways of God. The cycle again is in effect.

Gideon is buried in the sepulchre of his father Joash, in Ophrah. He had many wives and seventy sons; and his handmaiden in Shechem also bore him a son, calling him Abimelech. When the Israelites are again in straits, Abimelech goes to Shechem, to his mother's people, prevailing upon his family to speak to the leaders of Shechem that he be appointed to rule. When they are persuaded, the first act of Abimelech is one of treachery. He enters the home of his father and slays all seventy of his brethren, the sons of Gideon, with the exception of Jotham, the youngest, who escapes with his life.

The men of Shechem assemble and crown Abimelech king. When Jotham learns of this event, he returns to the city, remaining on the outskirts. He climbs to the top of Mount Gerizim and tells the people a fable, a tale of trees:

"Once upon a time the trees wanted to anoint a king over them. They said to the olive tree, 'You reign over us.' The olive tree declined the honor, saying, 'Should I give up the richness of my fruit by which God and people are honored and become king over the trees? No!' They asked the fig tree, but it too declined, saying, 'Should I give up my sweetness and productiveness to be king? No!' Then the trees went to the vine, and it, too, responded, 'Should I leave my wine through which God and people rejoice?' Then all the trees said to the bramble, 'You be our king.' The bramble said, 'If you really want me as your king, then come and take refuge in my shadow. If not, let a fire come out of the brambles and devour the cedars of Lebanon.'" (From Chapter IX.)

Jotham applies the moral of his fable to the anointing of his brother Abimelech as king. He indicates that his father, Gideon, would not accept the offer to become king and here is Abimelech, the son of Gideon's maidservant, murderer of his children, now being crowned king. Is this just? Is this proper action toward Gideon and his family? When Jotham concludes speaking against his brother's ascension to kingship, he flees the jurisdiction of his brother and goes to live in Beer.

Abimelech is prince over Israel for three years, in a brief but evil reign because of the hatred between him and the people he rules. There are skirmishes of violence, and finally Abimelech and his followers encamp against Thebez. They take this city except for a strong tower which became the refuge of many people of Thebez. Abimelech storms the very door of the tower to burn it when a woman hurls a millstone from the height of the tower which strikes him and wounds him fatally. He calls his armor-bearer to draw his sword against him lest it be said he is slain by a woman. When the people of Israel see their leader is dead, they depart for their homes. Thus is vindicated the wickedness of Abimelech against his father, Gideon, in the slaying of his seventy brothers and the wickedness of the people of Shechem.

A number of other judges rule over Israel during this period of unrest after the settlement of the Israelites in Palestine, the locale being the central area. The Israelites are torn by external oppressions, Moab, Ammon, Philistines, and others, and by internal rivalries which are apparent in this Book. An important feature is the alternative apostasy or abandonment of God, the penitent return to the Lord, and their deliverance by judges, the temporary leaders whose years of rule are indicated as well as their waging of successful warfare, all forming a preface to the institution of the Israelite monarchy, and thus constituting an important segment of biblical history.

After Abimelech there arises to save Israel a man by name of Tola, the son of Puah of the tribe of Issachar. Tola lives in Shamir, in the hill country of Ephraim, and he judged Israel for twenty-three years. His successor is Jair, the wealthy Gileadite who judged Israel for twenty-two years.

Jephthah, the Gileadite, is the next mighty man of valor to rule the people. As the Ammonites wage war against the Israelites, they come to him and say: "Come and be our chief, that we may fight against the children of Ammon." (Chapter XI, Verse 6.) Under his leadership, the Israelites wage war against the people of Ammon and conquer twenty cities. Jephthah likewise subdues the people of Ephraim who rise against him. Jephthah judges Israel for six years.

After him, Ibzan of Bethlehem judges Israel for seven years. He is followed by Elon the Zebulunite, who judges Israel for ten years. Abdon succeeds Elon as judge and serves for eight years.

Following these fairly brief judgeships, the Children of Israel revert to idolatry and are delivered into the hands of the Philistines for forty years until salvation comes when God raises up a mighty champion, Samson, whose strength and courage have become legendary. His birth is described in detail. Chapter XIII relates how one Manoah, of the family of the Danites, and his wife have no children. An angel of God appears to her, reveals that she will conceive and bear a son, and instructs her that no razor is to touch his head, for the child shall be a

Nazirite, dedicated to God, and is to be the deliverer of Israel from the Philistines. He tells her to be careful not to drink wine or other strong drink, to eat no unclean thing. When her son is born, the woman calls him Samson. God blesses him and infuses him with the divine spirit.

When Samson is grown to manhood, he is attracted to a woman in Timnah, of the daughters of the Philistines who at this time rule over the land of Israel. His disapproving parents plead with Samson not to marry a woman of the Philistines, but he is adamant. Accompanied by his parents, they all go down to Timnah to make the nuptial arrangements. As his father and mother precede Samson and they pass through the vineyards, a young lion roars toward him. The spirit of God comes over Samson, although he is bare-handed, he rends the lion asunder, but says nothing of his experience to his parents. They arrive in Timnah and wedding plans are made. After a time, when he returns for his betrothed, he sees the body of the lion he has killed. There is a swarm of bees on him and a cache of honey, which Samson scrapes into his hands and gives to his parents, not revealing the source of his find.

At the wedding festivities, Samson presents a riddle to the thirty young men in attendance, saying that if they can solve it within the seven days of the feast, he will give them thirty linen garments and thirty changes of raiment; but if they fail, they are to give him the same: "Out of the eater came forth food. And out of the strong came forth sweetness." The thirty companions cannot fathom the riddle, and finally come to Samson's wife, asking her to persuade her husband to explain it. Since their failure would involve a costly forfeit, they threaten to destroy her and her father's house. Angered, they declare: "Have you called us here to impoverish us?" (Chapter XIV, Verse 15.)

Samson's wife weeps and tells her bridegroom he loves her not, for he has set forth a riddle to young men of her people which he will not reveal to his own wife. Samson answers that since he has not told his own mother and father, should he tell her? The bride weeps for the remaining seven days of the wedding feast. Finally, the new husband relents as his wife presses him persistently. She promptly gives the answer to her people, who appear before Samson with the solution: "What is sweeter than honey? And what is stronger than a lion?" Samson retorts angrily: "If you had not plowed with my heifer, you would never have solved my riddle." Feeling great strength rising within him, he goes to Ashkelon and smites thirty men, taking their raiment and giving it to the men who have solved his riddle. Samson then returns to his father's house without his wife. His father-in-law, thinking Samson will never return, gives his wife to another man—in fact, to his companion who has been his friend.

Somewhat later, in the time of the wheat harvest, Samson returns to visit his wife, bringing gifts, but her father refuses to allow him to enter, saying that in the belief that Samson had no love for her, he gave his daughter to another. He offers her younger sister in her stead. Samson, in his anger at the rebuff, vows great mischief to the Philistines. Using three hundred foxes and torches tied to their tails, he sets them loose in the fields so that all the standing corn and the olive groves are burned out. The Philistines retaliate. Learning that it is the son-in-law of the Timnite who has perpetrated this damage, they wipe out Samson's wife and her family.

Not satisfied with this, the Philistines take a stand against all Judah. They declare that they have come to bind Samson and to punish him. At this juncture three thousand men of Judah come to Samson at Etam. "Do you not know," their spokesman says, "that the Philistines are rulers over us? What then is this that you have done to us?" Promising not to kill Samson themselves, the hero allows himself to be bound with ropes for delivery to the enemy. When he is turned over to the Philistines, they are overjoyed with their good fortune: they have captured Samson! Again he is infused with divine strength. Under his powerful muscles, the ropes which bind him captive melt like flax burnt with fire. Finding the jawbone of a donkey, he smites a thousand people. The place where Samson casts away the jawbone that served as his mighty weapon is called Ramath-lehi. In answer to his cry for God to quench his thirst, God cleaves the hollow place in Lehi and water springs forth. Samson drinks and his spirits are revived.

Philistine oppression of the Israelites continues in the narrative of the Book of Judges. The Philistines constitute a confederation of five cities— Ashdod, Ascalon (Ashkelon), Ekron, Gath, and Gaza. Philistia itself refers to the ancient district embracing the rich lowlands on the Mediterranean coast from the area of Jaffa (Joppa) to the Egyptian desert south of Gaza.

Chapter XVI tells of the exploit of strength by Samson at Gaza where the people hoped to ensnare and kill him. Before he can be trapped, Samson grasps the doors of the gate of the city, picks up the two posts, places them on his great shoulder, and carries them to the top of the mountain near Hebron. Eventually Samson, the unconquerable, will be conquered by feminine wiles. The heroine of Samson's last love story is a Philistine woman named Delilah from the valley of Sorek (modern Suruk). She is approached by lords of the Philistines with the promise of eleven hundred pieces of silver from each of them if she can fathom the secret of her lover's great strength, so that they may incapacitate and destroy him.

Samson replies to Delilah's questioning that if he be bound with seven fresh bowstrings that were never dried, he will become like any other man. He is bound, but breaks the strings easily. On the second attempt he also breaks new ropes as if they are threads. As Delilah persists, Samson tells her that if she will weave the seven locks of his head with the web, he cannot escape. She does so, fastening it with a pin. At her warning cry, "The Philistines are here after you, Samson!" he awakes from his sleep, removes the pin and the web, to the woman's frustration. She now cajoles, entreats, and presses him intensely, saying, "How can you say you love me when your heart is not with me? You have mocked me three times and have not told me wherein your great strength lies."

Delilah pressures him daily with her words and urges him to tell his secret so that "his soul was vexed unto death." Now Samson tells her all that is in his heart, that a razor has never touched his head, for he has been a Nazirite, dedicated to God from birth. "If I am shaven, my strength will leave me." Delilah knows that this time Samson is telling her the truth. Delilah tells the lords of the Philistines to come up. They arrive with the promised silver as Delilah's reward. Delilah induces Samson to sleep with his head in her lap. Then she calls for a man to shave off the seven locks of his head. For the last time she calls out, "Samson, the Philistines are here after you!" Samson awakens, but he is now powerless. His strength is gone. The Philistines capture him and blind him in both eyes. Bringing him down to Gaza and binding him with fetters, Samson becomes their prisoner. Samson's hair begins to grow again, and in his hair lies his strength.

Meanwhile, as an expression of their gratitude for the capture of Samson, the Philistines arrange a sacrifice to their god Dagon in their great temple. As thousands of people make merry, they call out for Samson to be brought forth from prison so that they may make sport of him. Samson is brought forward. He asks the guard to place him between the two supporting pillars of the temple, so that he may lean upon them. The temple is full of men and women; the lords of the Philistines are present, and there are about three thousand people on the roof to watch the spectacle of Samson brought to his humiliation. In his suffering, Samson calls out: "O God, remember me! Give me strength only this once so that I can avenge myself for the loss of my eyes." And with this prayer Samson takes hold of the pillars upon which the building rests, leans against them, one with his right hand and the other with his left. So doing, he cries out: "Let me die with the Philistines." He bends and presses with all his might so that the pillars crumble and the house collapses in a heap of ruins. All are crushed to death, Samson with them. His family comes down to bear his body away for burial with his father, Manoah. Samson has ruled over Israel for twenty years.

The recorded judges in this book in résumé are: Othniel, Ehud, Shamgar, Deborah, Barak, Gideon, Abimelech, Tola, Jair, Jephtha, Ibzan, Elon, Abdon, and Samson.

I SAMUEL

THE TWO BOOKS OF SAMUEL CONTAIN ONE CONTINUOUS NARrative, divided for convenience into I and II. They complete the history of the judges of Israel of the eleventh century B.C.E. and relate the events which led to the institution of the monarchy under Saul. The role of Samuel is especially prominent.

The experiences, problems, intrigues during the lives of Samuel, of Saul, and of his successor David comprise the content of the books of Samuel. Their language is clear and succinct, and the characters and their relationships show them to be human and real.

The books of Samuel open with the story of Elkanah, who lives in the city of Ramah. Elkanah has two wives, Hannah and Peninah. Since Hannah is childless, it is her husband Elkanah's custom to go with his family to the temple at Shiloh to offer prayers and sacrifice to God. Following the sacrifice, he would give Peninah a portion to eat, but to Hannah, whom he loved more dearly, he would give a double portion. This husbandly concern, however, does not ease her unhappiness, which is so acute that she cannot eat or drink. One day Elkanah, seeing Hannah's distress, asks her, "Why are you crying? Why do you not eat? Why are you so unhappy? Am I not better to you than ten children?" Hannah remains silent.

Some time later, when they are at Shiloh, Hannah goes into the temple to pray. Nearby sits Eli, the priest. He sees Hannah enter the temple and pray devoutly. She vows that if she were to be blessed with a child, she would give her child to God for all the days of its life. Eli sees

62

her lips move soundlessly and mistakenly believes that Hannah has partaken too much of the cup. When he realizes his error he says to Hannah: "Go in peace. May God grant you your prayer."

In due time, Hannah's pleas are answered. She gives birth to a son whom she calls Samuel, the name meaning either "God has heard (my prayer)" or "I asked him of the Lord." When Elkanah goes the following year to offer his annual prayers at Shiloh, his wife Hannah does not accompany him, explaining that when she weans the infant Samuel, she will then take him to the temple to fulfill her promise. Shortly thereafter Hannah brings her son Samuel to Eli and says: "I am the woman who was praying for a child. God has granted my prayer and now I lend my son to God for as long as he lives." Samuel is thus dedicated to the service of God. In her happiness and gratification, Hannah offers a magnificent psalm in praise of the providence of God which is reminiscent of the hymns of thanksgiving throughout the Book of Psalms.

Samuel, as a child, ministers to God, and grows to manhood in God's service in the temple. When he is still small his mother begins to make him a little linen robe, and continues to bring him a new garment each year. Eli blesses Hannah and Elkanah, praying that God might remember Hannah for her loan of Samuel to God. God remembers Hannah, who bears three sons and two daughters.

Eli rears Samuel as his own son, drawing him close to him, and placing his hopes of succession in Samuel, for his own sons are wicked, immoral men, not given to the divine service. The narrative proceeds to Samuel's call by God. One night, when Eli is about to retire, Samuel lies down to sleep near the Ark of the Covenant to protect it as he was accustomed to do. The Lord calls him, "Samuel! Samuel!" He awakens and responds, "Here I am!" He hastens to Eli, who is growing old and whose eyes are dim, but Eli says, "I did not call you, Samuel. Go back and lie down." This occurs again and then a third time. Eli now understands that it is God calling to Samuel. He tells him that if he hears his name called again, he should reply, "Speak, O Lord, Your servant is listening." God calls again, and tells Samuel that the house of Eli is doomed because of the wickedness of Eli's sons and because Eli has not been able to keep them from evildoing. Samuel fears to reveal God's words, but Eli persists and finally Samuel tells his experience. The priest simply affirms: "It is the Lord. Let Him do what seems right in His eyes to do."

Israel's problems with her neighbors continue as the Philistines renew their wars against them. In a fierce battle with the enemy, Israel loses four thousand soldiers. The elders of Israel decide to bring the Ark of the Covenant out of Shiloh in order that God may be among the people and lead them to victory. When the Ark arrives, there is rejoicing in the

Israelite camp. Hearing the shouts of joy, the Philistines know that the Ark of God has come. They redouble their efforts, defeat the Israelites, and capture the Ark of the Covenant. Among the slain are two sons of the priest Eli—Hophni and Phinehas. A soldier of Benjamin's army arrives in Shiloh with news of the bitter defeat and the people cry out in their despair. Hearing the tumult, Eli, now blind and ninety-eight years of age, trembles for the safety of the precious Ark of the Covenant. The messenger comes to Eli and Eli inquires how things are. When the messenger tells of the defeat of the Israelites by the Philistines, the death of his sons, and the capture of the Ark of God, Eli collapses and expires. He has judged Israel for forty years.

The Philistines bring the Ark of God from Ebenezer to Ashdod, setting it up near their god Dagon. During the night the statue of the pagan god falls forward and is broken. The people are smitten so that they remove the Ark to Gath, then to Ekron. In each place, God's hand is heavy against the Philistines. After seven months, they decide to return the Ark to the Israelites, and it is brought by cart to Beth-shemesh. The Ark is preserved here for twenty years.

Meanwhile the Israelites turn to their new leader, Samuel, for help in relieving the pressure of Philistine oppression. Samuel speaks to the people, insisting they remove the foreign gods and the heathen symbols from among them, and that they direct their hearts to God and serve God only. Only then will they be delivered from their enemies. Samuel assembles all of the people at Mizpah, where he prays; the people fast, confessing their sin against God. When the Philistines attack, God sends great thunderclaps, reverses the battle from defense by the Israelites to the offensive, so that the Philistines are subdued. The cities which the Philistines have taken are restored to the Israelites, from Ekron to Gath, and the border delivered.

Samuel has made his sons, Joel and Abijah, judges in Beersheba. However, they do not walk in his ways but pervert justice, accepting bribes, so that they are not worthy to be Samuel's successors. Concerned for the future, the elders of the people come to Samuel and ask that he appoint a king to rule over them. Samuel is distressed, for he fears the effect a king would have over the people. He turns to God for counsel and God tells him to comply. Samuel delivers an eloquent discourse on tyrannical kingship and the terrors of dictatorship, warning the people of the change in their lives, how a king would rule with an iron hand, how all would be subject to work for the monarch, that he would take their sons to be his horsemen, their daughters to be cooks and bakers, their vineyards subject to his use—in short, that everyone governed would be answerable to the regal governor. The people are adamant in their desire for a king. They want to be like other nations, have a king to judge them and to lead them in battle. When Samuel again turns to God, the Lord tells him, "Listen to them and give them a king." (I Samuel VIII, Verse 22.)

The events leading to the coronation of Saul as first king of Israel are recorded in great detail. Saul is identified as the son of the Benjaminite Kish, "a mighty man of valor." He is a strong and handsome young man who stands head and shoulders above all of the people. One day, when his father's donkeys are late in returning home, Saul and a servant are dispatched to look for them. They go to a number of places where the donkeys may have wandered, but to no avail. When Saul suggests they return home, the servant tells Saul that he knows of a man of God who lives in a nearby place and they could seek his help. The servant refers to this man as a "seer." The early seers were consulted about lost articles, animals that went astray, the success of journeys, and the outcome of wars. Samuel, however, is a prophet, a leader who desires for his people a better life and future, with the help and protection of the God of Israel. Saul agrees; when they arrive, they learn Samuel has just that day returned and is preparing for a religious service. They go to meet him as Samuel advances toward them.

The day before, God had said to Samuel, "About this time tomorrow, I will send a man from the land of Benjamin. You shall anoint him king over Israel." As Saul and his servant approach the prophet, God says to Samuel: "This is the man about whom I spoke. He shall rule over My people." Samuel greets Saul and brings him to his home, where there are thirty guests. Saul is given a place of honor and choice meat. Samuel tells Saul to be no longer concerned for the donkeys because they have been found.

Saul is surprised as Samuel says: "The glory to lead Israel belongs to you and to your house." . . . "Do I not come from the smallest of the tribes?" Saul asks. Samuel does not pursue the matter for the moment. On the day following, Saul accompanies Samuel on a walk through the city. Samuel sends the servant ahead, takes a vial of oil and pours it upon the head of Saul, anointing him and saying: "The Lord has anointed you to be prince over the Lord's inheritance." Samuel gives Saul two signs to prove the anointment is of God. The first will be when Saul reaches the tomb of Rachel, where he will be told that his father's donkeys are safe. The second sign will occur when he meets three men at Tabor on their way to Bethel who will greet Saul and give him two loaves of bread and as he will come to the hill of God, he is to meet a band of prophets. The spirit of God will come upon Saul and he will be moved to prophesy with them. Both signs are fulfilled. Saul does not reveal his experiences with Samuel to his uncle except to say that the prophet told them the donkeys were found. Concerning the matter of the kingdom and also the anointment, Saul remains silent.

Samuel lays his plans for the announcement of the selection of Saul as king. He calls the people together, chastises them for demanding a king (which to him means they are dissatisfied with God as their ruler) and speaks to them of the laws, regulations and duties of the monarchy. Samuel records this in writing. The people return to their homes.

Saul's first test comes when the Ammonites besiege the town of Jabesh-gilead. Frightened, the people seek Saul as their leader. Saul takes a census of the children of Israel. They number three hundred thousand and the people of Judah thirty thousand. Saul divides them into three companies who march against the Ammonites and defeat them mightily. Then Samuel says to the people "Come and let us go to Gilgal and renew the kingdom there." And all of the people go to Gilgal and there they make Saul king with peace-offerings to God and there Saul and all the people of Israel rejoice greatly. (From Chapter XI, Verses 14 and 15.)

Samuel now proceeds to have the people elect Saul their king. With deep feeling he reviews his career as Moses and Joshua reviewed the historic events heretofore. He pleads with them to revere God and to keep their part of the covenant as it is kept by God.

Samuel said to Israel: "I have listened to you and have made a king over you. Now, the king walks before you; I am old and gray-headed; and my sons are with you; and I have walked before you from my youth to this day. Here I am; testify against me before the Lord, and before God's anointed: whose ox have I taken? Or whom have I defrauded? Or whom have I oppressed . . ." And they said: "You have not defrauded us, nor oppressed us." (Chapter XII.)

The people extol Samuel as a great judge. "You have not mistreated or defrauded us," they proclaim. Samuel reviews the history of their fathers from the days of Moses and Aaron in Egypt to the present, and then calls forth Saul as their king. He warns that if they do wickedly they shall be swept away, they and their king.

Chapter XIII opens with the statement of ascension. "Saul was — years old when he began to reign; and two years he reigned over Israel." (The age is wanting in the Hebrew text.) Israel is now a monarchy. To defend the land and his people, Saul selects three thousand soldiers. He himself will lead two thousand, and his son Jonathan the other thousand. When the Philistines mass against Israel, they meet defeat by King Saul and his army. Now the Philistines ready a tremendous army which includes thirty thousand chariots and six thousand cavalry as they prepare for a major war.

Samuel sets a seven-day waiting period, during which time he does not appear before the people. They become frightened and hide in caves, in thickets, and in pits. Some cross the Jordan into the land of Gad and Gilead, with the enemy encamping at Michmas, east of Beth-aven. Saul is still at Gilgal. Many desert his leadership because of their great fears of the outcome with so powerful an enemy.

Still Samuel does not appear at Gilgal after the seven-day waiting period. As the people scatter before him, Saul decides to offer the sacrifice to God before he leads his soldiers into battle. He has no religious right to do so, since this service is Samuel's responsibility. No sooner has he finished the offering than the prophet arrives, and as Saul goes forward to greet him, Samuel says: "What have you done?" Saul replies that he saw the people scattered from him, that Samuel had not come, and that the Philistines had gathered at Michmas. He thought the Philistines would come down upon the Israelites at Gilgal and he had not sought the favor of God, and therefore he forced himself to perform the service.

Samuel reprimands Saul, saying that he has acted improperly, therefore indicating his lack of faith in God; that if he had obeyed the command of God, then God would have established Saul's kingdom over Israel forever. This initial unwise act is the beginning of Saul's downfall and the eventual disappearance of his household. Samuel tells Saul that his monarchy will not endure, and that God has selected another to be his successor. He then leaves Gilgal. Saul now numbers six hundred soldiers who remain with him; and his son Jonathan who is with him at Gibeath-Benjamin, and the Philistines are encamped at Michmas.

One day, Jonathan without telling his father, takes his young armor-bearer with him to the Philistine outpost with the intent to penetrate the enemy camp. As the young men crawl up the rocky terrain they are detected by the Philistines, who surmise that there are many Israelites now emerging from the caves and valleys. They are disturbed when Jonathan and his aide succeed in killing twenty men. Meanwhile, King Saul's guards, viewing the scene from another mountain top, note the confusion and report it to Saul, who has the camp searched. Jonathan and his armor-bearer are found to be missing. Saul quickly moves his soldiers into battle and scatters the Philistines, who are panic-stricken over Jonathan's feat. Then, when the people of Israel who were hiding in the hill country of Ephraim hear of the flight of the Philistines, they, too, pursue the enemy, and thus God saves Israel that day.

Saul enjoins his people from eating of food until he has avenged himself on the enemy. The people obey. They see honeycombs on the ground and, although they are hungry, they do not disobey the order. On the other hand, Jonathan has not heard of the instruction, and when he finds a honeycomb, he eats of it as he returns home. Later, learning of his father's edict, he stands ready to be treated as any other violator. For his part, the king feels he, too, must fulfill the oath he has made, but the people plead for Jonathan's life: "Shall Jonathan die, he who brought us this great victory? This shall not be. Not one hair of his head shall be touched, for he is responsible for our victory with God's help." Saul is moved by their pleas and Jonathan is released.

Samuel tells Saul that God has instructed him to rise up against the Amalekites, who have acted so treacherously toward the Israelites when they left Egypt. He is to destroy Amalek and their king, Agag. Saul assembles his troops and leads them in the assault. Contrary to instruction, however, Saul and the people take pity on Agag. They also spare the best of the cattle. Once more Saul has disobeyed, and God regrets having selected Saul as king. Samuel is so distressed at the turn of events that he weeps throughout the night. The next morning, Samuel goes out to meet Saul, and when Saul hears of the prophet's approach, he goes to welcome him with the news that he has performed God's will in defeating the Amalekites. Samuel responds by asking Saul about the sound of bleating sheep. Saul admits that the sheep have been spared and admits he has again been disobedient. However, he counters that he went into battle, captured Agag, and destroyed the Amalekites, and that not he, but the people, took the sheep to offer them as sacrifices to God. In a stirring retort which teaches that prayer is far superior and infinitely more desirable than sacrifices, Samuel declares:

Does the Lord delight in burnt offerings and sacrifices as much as He does in obeying Him? To obey is better than sacrifice, and to listen is better than the fat of rams. You have denied the word of God and God, in turn, has rejected you. (Chapter XV, Verses 22, 23.)

Saul admits his sin, saying he acceded to the demands of the people, but Samuel refuses to listen to his plea. As the prophet turns to leave, the desperate king grasps the holy man's cloak, and a piece is torn from it. Looking at his torn mantle, Samuel says symbolically: "The Lord has torn the kingdom of Israel from you and has given it over to someone who is a better man than you." Samuel goes on to Ramah, and Saul returns to his house in Gibeath-Shaul. The relationship is severed. Samuel never sees Saul again until the day of his death. This juncture marks the beginning of a series of events which lead to Saul's eventual removal as monarch of Israel.

The story of the secret crowning of David unfolds. God tells Samuel to fill his horn with oil and proceed to Bethlehem to the house of Jesse. Jesse has eight sons, of whom David is his youngest. When Samuel arrives at Bethlehem, the elders of the town come forward hesitantly to welcome him and inquire anxiously, "Does your visit mean peace?" Samuel replies that he has come peaceably to offer sacrifice and bids the people join him. Jesse and his sons are invited. When Samuel sees Eliab, who is strong and handsome, he thinks he is the man to be anointed.

But the Lord said to Samuel: "Look not on his countenance, or on the height of his stature; because I have rejected him; for it is not as man sees: for man looks at the outward appearance, but the Lord looks at the heart." (Chapter XVI, Verse 7.)

Then Abinadab and Shammah pass before Samuel, in fact all the seven sons who are present. Samuel says to Jesse, "Are all of your children here?" Jesse answers that there remains only the youngest, but that he is a shepherd boy tending the sheep. Samuel requests that he be sent for. Jesse sends for his son David and Samuel sees a handsome young man with beautifully expressive eyes and a ruddy complexion. The Lord said: "Arise, anoint him; he is the man." Samuel takes the horn of oil and anoints David in the presence of his father and brothers. From that day on, the spirit of God strongly inspires David. Samuel leaves for Ramah.

The succession begins to take effect as the spirit of God departs from Saul. He becomes disturbed and troubled with "an evil spirit." Seeing the king's distress, Saul's servants suggest that a harpist be summoned to play soft music to soothe him. One of his courtiers tells the king about David, skillful in playing the harp, and a valiant, intelligent young man of good demeanor. Much impressed, King Saul bids them bring the shepherd to him. He immediately appoints David his armor-bearer. In David's playing of his instrument and singing, Saul finds welcome relief, and David soon becomes an integral part of the king's household.

There follows the account of the challenging Philistines who have gathered their armies for battle at Socoh in Judah. The soldiers of Israel under Saul's leadership pitch in the vale of Elah. The opposing forces are arrayed on the tops of two mountains with a valley between them. A champion named Goliath, a giant of Gath, whose height is ten feet, is the mighty man of the Philistines. He advances to ask for an opponent to fight with him. Arrayed in heavy armor with a brass helmet, a coat of mail weighing five thousand shekels of brass, with brass greaves on his legs, a javelin, a spear, and a shield-bearer walking before him, he calls out:

"Select one of your army and let him come down to me. If he will fight with me and kill me, then we will be your servants; but if I defeat him, then you will be our servants. . . . Give me a man that we may fight together." (Chapter XVII, Verses 8, 9.)

The Israelites and their king are fearful as to how they might meet the challenge. For forty days Goliath strides forth every morning and issues his taunt, and no man volunteers to fight him. One day, when David brings food to his three brothers who are encamped with Saul's forces, he hears of the challenge and learns of the great reward of riches awaiting the man who is successful in combat with Goliath, as well as the hand in marriage of the daughter of the king. David's interest is kindled, but his brothers reprimand him for leaving their father Jesse's sheep unattended. Disregarding their warnings, David goes to King Saul and volunteers to fight the Philistine giant. Saul at first demurs. "You are only a youth, and he is a man of war." David describes how he has been able to protect his father's flocks from wild animals by engaging them in single-handed combat, tearing apart a ferocious lion and a bear that had attacked the flocks. "The Lord," avers David, "saved me from the power of the lion and the bear and will also save me from this Philistine." When Saul hears David's confident words, he is convinced and gives his consent.

David is clad in Saul's own armor and a bronze helmet. He buckles on his sword and tries to walk, but finds his defensive gear heavy and burdensome. Complaining, "I cannot walk with these things. I have never worn them before," he removes them, takes his shepherd's staff in his hand and, carefully choosing five smooth stones from the brook, places them in his shepherd's pouch. He then takes his sling and draws near to the Philistine. The gigantic Goliath comes heavily forward, clad in his armor and carrying his iron shield. When he sees the man chosen by the Israelites as their champion, he scorns him. He is only a youth! "Am I a dog," he thunders at David, "that you come against me with sticks? I will give your flesh to the birds that fly and to the beasts of the field." David replies fearlessly:

You come against me with a sword and a spear and a javelin, but I come to fight you in the name of the Lord of hosts, the God of the armies of Israel whom you have insulted. The Lord will deliver you into my hands today. I will defeat you. Everyone will know that there is a God in Israel. Everyone will know that the Lord does not save by the sword and spear alone. (Chapter XVII, Verses 45, 46.)

The massive Philistine lumbers toward David, who hurries lithely to meet him. So doing, David takes a stone from his shepherd's bag, puts it into his sling, aims unerringly, and releases the sling. The stone strikes Goliath on the forehead and he falls forward. David dashes over, takes Goliath's sword and slays him. The Philistines, seeing their hero fallen, retreat. The Israelites, thrilled by the turn of events, raise a joyous battle shout of victory and pursue the fleeing Philistines.

David and the Israelites, returning victorious over the enemy, are warmly welcomed by young women who come forward dancing and singing paeans of praise, with a recurring chant, "Saul has killed his thousands and David his ten thousands." Hearing these words, envy enters the heart of King Saul. David's fame spreads throughout the land and Saul's jealousy, nurtured from the first experience of David's success over Goliath, is destined to become the basis of their ensuing unhappy relationship. Saul develops an obsessive and deadly hatred of David as well as a secret fear of his popularity and strength as a possible rival of the people's commendation. There is the incident of Saul attempting to kill David by hurling a spear at him, which misses David and is buried in the wall; David's deft movement has saved his life.

Saul sees the esteem in which David is held by the people and determines that the young man must be removed from court. He reduces his status by appointing him commander of a thousand men, which is a lesser office than he has heretofore enjoyed. Saul keeps his bargain and offers David his daughter Michal in marriage, believing that she may prove to be an effective means of controlling David. In all that he does, David has great success, and all Israel and Judah love him. The Princess

Michal loves him, too, and is proud to have David as her husband. David is thoughtful, it being, he says, no light matter for a poor man, a man of no position, to become the son-in-law of the king.

One of the world's most beautiful stories of friendship is that of Jonathan, the son of Saul, and David, now his brother-in-law. "And Jonathan loved David, as his own soul." He warns David against the danger of the king's enmity and also speaks favorably to Saul, his father, pleading that David has always acted most faithfully. Saul listens to Jonathan and solemnly promises he will not harm David. So the breach is healed for a time and David attends the king as before. The tension is temporarily eased, but the evil spirit comes over Saul again, as a fog creeps through the crevices of his mind. He forgets David's loyalty and seeks once more to kill him. This time David flees from the palace and returns to his home in Bethlehem. Saul sends messengers to David's house to kill him in the morning, but Michal warns her husband of his danger and David escapes. He makes his way to the Prophet Samuel at Ramah and tells him all that has occurred. Then David and Samuel go and dwell in Naioth.

Later when David and Jonathan meet, David pleads, "What have I done? What crime did I commit that your father wants to kill me?" Jonathan reassures him by saying his father does nothing, great or small, without letting his son know and that he would not hide his intent against David. David answers doubtfully, "Your father knows that you are fond of me, so he says to himself, Jonathan must know nothing of this, lest it grieve him."

A test is agreed upon. The following day is the festival of the new moon, the first of the month. The palace will be celebrating and David is expected to be in attendance. Jonathan and David set a series of signals which will reveal Saul's true intention and which will tell David what to do—to return or to flee. David is to hide in the fields and if, during the feast, Saul asks David's whereabouts, Jonathan is to say that David has had to go on a mission to Bethlehem. Saul's reaction will indicate his feelings. "If your father says, 'It is well,' then I will know that he has no evil thoughts against me. If, on the other hand, he does not react favorably, then I will know that he is still intent on killing me."

And how will Jonathan reveal this information to David? They go to the field and point out the landmarks. After David's three days' absence from the palace, Jonathan will come to the field and shoot three arrows toward a certain large stone. David will be hiding nearby. Jonathan will send his boy after the arrows. If he calls out to the boy, "Go and get the arrows; they are on *this* side," it means that all is well and David may return to the palace. But if he says to the boy, "Go and get the arrows; they are beyond you," this is the signal to David that he must leave and not return. Three days later, Jonathan's call to the boy tells David he is unwelcome in the palace of King Saul. David flees and must thereafter be constantly on the move.

A number of incidents are related which describe Saul's increasing passion to destroy David. On various occasions David pleads with Saul to make peace between them as he, David, has no ill will toward his father-in-law and his king. Saul, when the evil spirit is not stirring always agrees that David's plea is proper, that justice is on David's side, and yet his bitter hatred has now become a corroding disease which he cannot control. David becomes a refugee from Saul for many years. The king pursues him whenever there is a respite from war. Meanwhile the fear of David replacing him still disturbs Saul. A number of men adhere to David and become the core of his faithful army.

The episode of David and Ahimelech and the priests of Nob is recounted. At the core of this incident, too, is the enmity of Saul. Without revealing his true identity or plight, David comes to Ahimelech, receives and partakes of hallowed food, part of the sacrifice, and also takes the prized sword of Goliath. When Saul hears of this, he summons Ahimelech, accuses him of collusion with David, and orders all the priests of Nob killed. Only Abiathar, son of Ahimelech, escapes. He flees to David who promises him sanctuary.

When Saul returns from his wars with the Philistines, he is told that David is in the wilderness of En-gedi. Hot in pursuit, Saul, with three thousand selected men, sets out to ensnare David and his followers. They reach a large cave, and Saul enters it, unaware that David and his men are there. David's followers suggest the opportunity to destroy the king, but David replies: "The Lord forbid that I should do this to Saul, to the Lord's anointed!" David arises in the night, secretly approaches the sleeping Saul, cuts off a piece of his robe and retreats. When Saul leaves the cave, David, who has followed him, calls out: "My lord, the king!" Saul looks back, David bows and says: "Why do you listen to men who tell you that David seeks to injure you?" He lifts up the piece of the king's robe he has cut off so that he may convince Saul that he could have taken the opportunity to kill him, but that he has no evil intent toward him. Moved by David's words, Saul asks: "Is this your voice, David, my son?" He tells David that he, too, has no evil designs.

". . . Saul raised his voice and wept. He said to David: "You are more righteous than I; for you have rendered . . . good, whereas I have rendered evil to you . . . for when the Lord delivered me into your hand, you did not kill me . . . wherefore the Lord reward you with goodness . . . and now I know you will surely be king, and that the kingdom of Israel will be established in your hand." (Chapter XXIV, Verses 18–21.)

King Saul asks David not to destroy his name from his father's house. They enter into a pact in which David promises never to cut off Saul's family, and they part in good spirits, Saul returning to his palace and David to his stronghold.

At this period, the great prophet Samuel dies at Ramah and all Israel mourns him. He had risen to prominence in the dark days of Philistine oppression and has given the Israelites their first reigning monarch.

David now travels to the wilderness of Maon, where Nabal, a prosperous man, lives. David and his men have given protection to Nabal. A churlish, rough-mannered man, he is married to a beautiful and intelligent woman whose name is Abigail. David sends messengers to Nabal, who is shearing his sheep at Carmel, to advise that he and his men have come in peace to ask for their well-earned reward. Nabal answers David's young men gruffly. Rebuffed, David decides to retaliate and heads four hundred armed men, leaving two hundred with the baggage. Meanwhile one of the young shepherds has reported the occurrence to Abigail, who, cognizant of the dangerous situation to her husband and their possessions, does everything within her power to ward off the impending violence. Her servants prepare a great store of food, and placing the supplies on donkeys, she proceeds to bear the food to David, pleading with him to disregard the insulting actions of her husband, Nabal. David, acknowledging her wisdom, accepts the food, commends her for her devotion to her husband and her wish to avoid bloodshed. Abigail says nothing of all this to Nabal, who is sitting at table with guests when she returns home. Nabal eats, drinks, and becomes very merry with his friends. Then he retires, and Abigail lets him sleep the deep sleep of wine. In the morning, she tells him what she has done. His heart "dies within him and he becomes like stone." About ten days afterward, Nabal is stricken and expires.

David learns of Nabal's death, thanks God who has stayed his hand from doing wrong, and sends messengers to Abigail to ask her to become his wife. Abigail accepts. She and five of her maids hasten to David's side. David also takes Ahinoam of Jezreel as his wife. As to the

Princess Michal, David's first wife, King Saul has given her in marriage to Palti, the son of Laish of Gallim.

Meanwhile the anger of Saul against David does not abate. When the evil spirit comes over him, he continues the pursuit. He learns that David and his men are in the hills of Hachilah. David observes Saul's army from a distance and once again steals into the royal camp during the night. Together with Abishai, the brother of Joab, head of David's forces, they enter the king's tent and find Saul sleeping, surrounded by his general, Abner, and other high officers. Abishai whispers to David that he be allowed to strike down the king with his own spear with one stroke. But David replies that he must not destroy the king for he is God's anointed, that his day will come at the hand of God. He bids him instead to take the cruse of water near the king, and also the spear. They steal out of the camp undetected. A safe distance from the camp, David calls out to Abner, taunting him for not guarding well the person of the king. He holds up Saul's spear and the cruse of water. Recognizing David's voice, Saul says: "Is that your voice, my son David?" David replies: "It is my voice, my lord, O king."

Saul admits his error saying, "I have done wrong; return, David my son, I will never harm you again, since you held my life precious this day." David asks that one of the king's young men come to him and retrieve the spear. Saul says: "Blessed are you, my son David! You shall do great things and you shall surely prevail." They part, each to go his own way.

Knowing that someday he will be destroyed by Saul, David decides to escape with his six hundred men to territory within which the king will not think to seek him. He goes to Achish, the son of Maoch, who is king of Gath among the Philistines. Achish gives David Ziklag for a dwelling place for him and his family, for his men and their families. David remains in Gath for a year and four months.

Not long after the death of Samuel, the Philistines resume their harassment of the Israelites. No longer sure of himself, Saul is frightened when he sees the large encampment of the enemy confronting him. He seeks God's counsel and guidance, but God does not answer him either by dream or by the prophets. In disguise, Saul goes to the woman of En-dor and asks her to bring up Samuel's spirit. The woman reminds Saul that the king has outlawed the mediums and those who divine by the spirits of the dead, but Saul promises that no harm will come to her. The woman then brings up Samuel, and Saul pleads:

I am greatly distressed. The Philistines are making war against me and God has departed from me. God does not respond to my call. (Chapter XXVIII, Verse 15.)

Samuel tells Saul with brutal truthfulness that no help can be granted him and that the kingdom of Israel is to be given over to David. Saul, overcome with fright and fatigue, falls in a faint "full length upon the earth" in the woman's hut.

As the Philistines fight against the forces of Saul, many Israelites flee and many fall in the battle of Mount Gilboa. The enemy closely pursues Saul and his sons. They slay Jonathan, Abinadab, and Malchi-shua. Saul is critically wounded and asks his armor-bearer to draw his sword and thrust it through him so that the heathen Philistines may not make mockery of him as their prize captive so long sought for. Overcome with horror, the armor-bearer is unable to do his royal master's bidding. Saul therefore takes his sword, rises painfully, and falls upon it. Thus Saul the mighty warrior, first king of Israel, his three sons, and his armor-bearer die on the same fateful day. They are buried in Jabesh.

And thus comes to a close the exciting, and melancholy life of King Saul, a warrior of mighty abilities, strapping and handsome in appearance, a man of munificence who has loved the prophet Samuel and David but whose family relationships have been marred by his evil spirit, or mental affliction. He has not been successful in conquering the Philistines. He has, however, shown the Israelites how to oppose them. On this foundation, King David is able to break their power over the Israelites. Saul will always be memorialized in Jewish history as a king who first united Israel and won its loyalty, which he lost while striving for his throne and for his people.

II SAMUEL

DAVID, IN THE MEANTIME, HAS BEEN WARRING ON THE
Amalekites and defeats them. On the third day after the victory, a refu-
gee from the war of Saul and the Philistines, torn and tattered, arrives at
David's camp, to disclose that Saul and Jonathan have been killed.

David and his men tear their clothes in symbolic mourning to lament
the great loss Israel and they personally have sustained. David then
chants his majestic and unforgettable lamentation:

Your beauty, O Israel, upon your high places, is slain!
How have the mighty fallen!
Tell it not in Gath,
Publish it not in the streets of Ashkelon,
Lest the daughters of the Philistines rejoice,
Lest the daughters of the uncircumcised triumph.
O mountains of Gilboa,
Let no dew nor rain fall upon you;
Nor fields of choice fruits;
For there the shield of the mighty was cast away;
The shield of Saul, as though he had not been anointed
   with oil. . . .

. . . . .

Saul and Jonathan were beloved and dear in their lives;
Even in their death they were not divided.
They were swifter than eagles,
They were stronger than lions.
O daughters of Israel, weep for Saul
Who clothed you in scarlet and
Who put ornaments of gold upon your apparel.
How are the mighty fallen in the midst of the battle!
Jonathan upon your high places is slain!
I am distressed for you, my brother Jonathan.
Very dear have you been to me.
Wonderful has been your love to me,
Exceeding even the love of women.
How are the mighty fallen
And the instruments of war perished.

(Chapter I, Verses 19–27.)

After mourning for Saul and Jonathan, David asks God if he should go to any of the cities of Judah. God bids him go to Hebron where the men of Judah anoint him king.

Informed by the men of Jabesh-gilead that they have buried Saul and his sons, David sends messengers to their leaders, advising that God will show them kindness for the kindness they have proffered to the dead ruler, announcing that David has been anointed king over them as Saul's successor. There is, however, a struggle for regal power. Saul's general, Abner, the son of Ner, still faithful to the house of Saul, has at Mahanaim made Saul's son, Ish-bosheth, king over Israel, but mostly the people of Judah follow David.

Abner and the followers of Ish-bosheth march from Mahanaim to Gibeon. Meanwhile the commander of David's forces, Joab, leads his men forward. Both groups meet at the pool of Gibeon where they encamp, each on one side of the pool. The battle is bitter as David's men defeat Abner's soldiers. The conflict between the house of Saul and the house of David lasts a long time, with David becoming gradually stronger and Saul's house growing weaker. When Ish-bosheth accuses his general of infidelity, Abner in anger sends messengers to David asking for a treaty with him and offering to help bring all Israel over to his side. David accedes to this treaty with the provision that his wife, Michal, the daughter of Saul, be restored to him.

Abner communicates with the elders of Israel, reminding them that in times past they sought David for their king, that David has delivered them from the hands of their enemies, and that David had been appointed by God as their king. Abner comes to Hebron, accompanied by twenty men; an agreement is reached, and David gives a feast in Abner's honor. The former general of King Saul departs with his men. Just then Joab and soldiers of David return from a raid, bringing rich spoils with them. Joab is astounded at what has occurred. He remembers that his own brother, Ashael, years ago, was slain by Abner at Gibeon, and he tells David that Abner came to deceive him. Without the knowledge of David, Joab orders that Abner be overtaken and returned with his men. Abner is brought back and slain by Joab. David learns of the foul deed, is shocked, and declares himself guiltless. He orders Joab to mourn Abner's death, and he himself follows the bier of Saul's commander in chief in the funeral procession. They bury Abner in Hebron, and the people weep for him, for Abner, a great man and a leader, has fallen. Joab himself is too powerful and useful to the king to be severely punished.

When the son of Saul, Ish-bosheth, hears of Abner's end, he loses courage, and the Israelites who are his followers become frightened. Without Abner's help, things go from bad to worse, and his own men turn against him. Two captains of his troops, Baanah and Rechab, assassinate Ish-bosheth. They hasten to report their deed to David, expecting commendation. David, however, is angered for their having killed a king and repays them in kind. Ish-bosheth, son of King Saul, reigned two years.

The tribes of Israel come to David at Hebron. Their elders make a covenant with David before God and anoint him king over Israel. David is thirty years of age when he begins to reign, and his reign lasts forty years. In Hebron, he ruled over Judah seven years and six months; and in Jerusalem, thirty-three years over all Israel and all Judah.

Before Joshua, the successor of Moses, invaded Palestine (c. 1400 B.C.E.), the town of Jerusalem, then known as Urusalim, was a vassal of Egypt. When the Jebusites captured it from the Amurren and Mitanni, they transformed it into a fortress regarded as impregnable by its inhabitants. Nevertheless, David is successful in capturing Jerusalem from the Jebusites. An advance guard climbs through the city's water-supply shaft, gains entry to the city, and opens the gates. David takes up residence with his family and courtiers within the captured fortress, which he renames the City of David. On the steep eastern hill on the site of the citadel of Jebusite Zion, he constructs his palace and the royal city.

To the north, King David chooses the place for the temple his son Solomon is to build. Hiram, king of Tyre, sends messengers of friendship to David, and shipments of cedar logs, carpenters and masons, who remain and build David's palace which is of vast dimensions and truly regal grandeur. David constructs a wall around the city from Millo and inward. "And David became greater and greater; for the God of hosts was with him." (II Samuel, Chapter V, Verse 10.)

After transferring his rule from Hebron to Jerusalem, David enlarges his household. In the women's quarters of the palace there are: his first wife, the Princess Michal, daughter of King Saul; Achinoam, who gives David his first son, Amnon; Abigail, the widow of Nabal, who is the mother of a son, Cheleab; Princess Maacha, daughter of King Talmai of Geshur (whose marriage to the king is by way of political alliance), who becomes the mother of Absalom. David loves Absalom dearly. There are, also, Haggith, Abital, and Egla, and within five years in Jerusalem six sons and four daughters are born to David. The scriptures enumerate his children: Shammua, Shobab, Nathan, Solomon, Ibhar, Elishua, Nepheg, Japhia, Elishama, Eliada, Eliphelet. David's parents, his sisters, and his brothers remain in Moab. Only one of his relations comes to Hebron while he is monarch—his nephew Assael.

Living expansively in his royal palace, David becomes uneasy that God, who has been his shield and protection, has not a fitting dwelling place. He consults with the chief people of Israel, and it is decided that the proper place for the sacred Ark of God is in the City of David. It is therefore brought from Perez-uzzah and remains in the house of Obed-edom, the Gittite, for three months pending proper arrangements and preparations for its entry into Jerusalem. The priests, the king, his attendants, and courtiers, as well as all of the inhabitants, participate in the great event. Special songs are composed and set to the music of several instruments. There are choruses and chantings honoring the Ark as it is escorted on its specially built cart, to the accompanying expressions of joyous welcome of the populace in an upsurge of religious fervor. The sounding of the shofar (the ram's horn) thrills through the streets of Jerusalem. David's heart is uplifted as "he dances with all of his might, girded with his linen ephod." The Ark is thus escorted to its place of safety in the new tabernacle tent provided for it. David offers sacrifices to God and blesses the people in God's name. In celebration of the historic event, special cakes are distributed from the royal storehouse to all of the people of the city.

With gratification and a sense of achievement, King David returns to his own household to greet and bless his family. Flushed with excitement of the day's activities and supremely happy, he is met first by his wife Michal. Instead of the warm reception he anticipates, she rebukes him scornfully because from her window she had looked down and seen the monarch as he danced in his linen ephod with the other participants. David hotly defends his joyous behavior in honor of the triumphant return of the Ark to the care of Jerusalem, and asserts that before God he will always "make merry." The episode marks the permanent separation of David and Princess Michal.

King David reveals to the Prophet Nathan, once the pupil of the great Prophet Samuel, that he would like to provide a house of God for the Ark. "See now, I dwell in a house of cedar but the Ark of God dwells within curtains of the tent which is its tabernacle." Nathan tells him to do all that is in his heart, for God is with him. During that night, however, God appears to Nathan and tells him David is not to erect the Temple because hands that have spilled blood cannot build a house of God. His son, after him, will be the builder. "When your days are fulfilled and you shall sleep with your fathers, I will set up your seed after you, that shall proceed out of your body and I will establish his kingdom. He shall build a house for My name and I will establish the throne of his kingdom forever. I will be to him as a father and he shall be to Me as a son . . ." (From II Samuel, Chapter 7, Verses 12–14.) At the same time David is assured that his monarchy will endure and that God will be with his son as God has been with him. In a magnificent ode, David accepts the divine proclamation:

You are great, O God; for there is none like You, neither is there any God beside You. . . . And who is like Your people, Israel, a nation one in the earth, whom God went to redeem to Himself for a people. . . . May Your name be magnified forever that it may be said: The Lord of hosts is God over Israel; and the house of Your servant David shall be established before you. . . . You alone are God and Your words are truth. . . . (Chapter VII, Verses 22–28.)

David and his general, Joab, achieve a number of military successes which fill the royal coffers with much gold and brass taken from the nations subdued by Israel's military might: Aram, Moab, Ammon, Philistines, Amalek, Zobah, and the Arameans in the battle in the Valley of Salt. Throughout Edom David places armed garrisons. In consolidation of his realm, the royal court is organized under King David who executes justice and righteousness to all of his people. Joab, son of Zeruiah, is commander in chief of the army. Jehoshaphat, son of Ahilud, is court recorder. Zadok, son of Ahitub and Ahimelich, son of Abiathar, are the chief priests. Seraiah is court scribe. The sons of David represent him as chief ministers.

King David remembers the past and inquires if any of Saul's house survives. A son of Jonathan is sought out, Mephibosheth. When he was five years old and the dreadful news came of Saul and Jonathan out of Jezreel, his nurse took him and fled. In the confusion, the boy fell and became lame thereafter in both of his feet. Now many years later, Mephibosheth is invited to David's court with his family; the king commands that for the balance of his life he is to have a place at the royal tables. Thus he becomes a pensioner in token of the old affection the king bears to his father Jonathan, once his dearest friend.

A friendly embassy from King David to Hanun, the newly crowned king of Ammon, son of Nahash, is met with insult to David's messengers who are basely treated as spies, their garments cut, and half of their beards shaved off to shame them. When David receives news of this event, he sends men to meet the mistreated delegation and advises that the men stay at Jericho until their beards are grown and then return to him in Jerusalem.

After this, war naturally ensues with the Ammonites, and even though they initially gained considerable support from the Arameans, they are completely defeated by David's forces. A long siege ensues and their chief city, the strongly fortified Rabbah, is captured by the Israelites. The Syrian allies of Ammon are reduced to submission and Edom is subjugated by Joab. During the course of this campaign with the Ammonites, the lovely Bathsheba of Jerusalem comes into the life of King David.

One evening while David walks on the roof of his palace, he observes on a nearby housetop a very beautiful young woman bathing, unaware that she can be seen. The king inquires about her and finds that she is Bathsheba, the daughter of Eliam, commander of thousands, brother of Achitophel and the wife of Uriah, the Hittite, commander of hundreds who is at the front under General Joab. The king sends for her. Soon after this visit, when Bathsheba advises the king that she is to have a child, he hastily sends for her husband Uriah, granting him leave of absence from battle to be at home with his wife. To the chagrin of the king, the soldier refuses for three days to leave the other guards attending the gate, saying his first duty is to his lord, the king. In desperation, David writes to Joab instructing that Uriah be placed in the very heat of the Ammonite assault, in which he is subsequently killed. When Bathsheba learns that her husband is dead, she duly observes a period of mourning for him, then David takes her to his household and makes her his wife.

David's misdeed displeases God and God sends the Prophet Nathan, who recites a parable to the king:

There were once two men who lived in a city. One was wealthy and the other poor. The rich man had many flocks and herds and the poor man had nothing except a little lamb. He had bought the lamb, cared for it, tended it, nourished it, and it grew up together with his family. One day a traveler came to the city to visit the rich man. The rich man wanted to have a festive meal in honor of his guest, but did not care to use his own flocks. So he took the lamb from the poor man and prepared it for his guest to enjoy. (From II Samuel, Chapter XII. Verses 1–4.)

Aroused by the story, David tells Nathan that such a man should be put to death for having shown no compassion or pity. Nathan looks intently at David:

"You are the man," he says. "Thus says the Lord, The God of Israel: 'I anointed you king over Israel. I saved you from Saul's hands. . . . Why have you despised Me and My word and done this wicked thing?'" (Chapter XII, Verses 7–9.)

Stunned by the prophet's direct accusation, David admits his guilt. Nathan says that God has pardoned him, but that the child born of this union, will not live. So it happens. In due time, Bathsheba bears another son whom she names Solomon, and whom Nathan calls Jedidiah, meaning Beloved of the Lord.

David's reign is undisturbed from foreign attack. Internal conflicts, however, develop within the king's household and among the members of his immediate family. David's sons quarrel bitterly with each other. The eldest, Amnon, defiles Tamar, the sister of his half brother Absalom. Angered by Amnon's base deed, Absalom, the king's third son, takes revenge on Amnon, killing him. Absalom flees from the country for refuge with his maternal grandfather Talmai in Geshur, where he lives in exile for three years.

In spite of his son's crime, David's heart longs for Absalom. His faithful general, Joab, tries to arrange a reconciliation. He has a woman from Tekoa come to David, and through a cleverly presented hypothetical case, similar to David's, prevails upon the king to invite Absalom back to Jerusalem. Perceiving that Joab is behind this maneuver, David agrees to allow his son Absalom to return to Jerusalem. However, two years are to pass before the son is restored to royal favor and a full reconciliation effected.

Dissatisfied with his position, Absalom (married to a princess of Geshur and the father of children), rebel that he is, secretly plots against the king, attracting a large number of followers. He has a fine chariot and horses and fifty men to run before him. Furthermore, his party is able to raise the standard of revolt against David in Hebron. Absalom's spies are sent among the tribes of Israel with the word that upon the signal of the horn, Absalom is to be declared king in Hebron. Two hundred men depart with Absalom from Jerusalem unaware of the perfidy of the prince. Absalom sends for Ahithophel, the Gilonite, David's counselor, and the conspiracy gains in strength as many people adhere to Absalom's leadership.

Absalom enters the city in full regalia. David is compelled to abandon his palace and flee to Gilead with his household. The rebellion gains in momentum toward full civil war as father and son are arrayed against each other with their respective forces. David divides his men into three main camps. A third he places under the command of Joab, a third under Ittai the Gittite, and the king reserves a third for his own personal command. Loyally and devotedly, David's followers protest:

You shall not go forth; for if we have to flee, no one will care for us; if half of us die no one will care, but you are worth ten thousand of us; therefore it is better that you be ready to help us from the city. (Chapter XVIII, Verse 3.)

Touched by the concern and loyalty of his followers, David agrees. He calls Joab to his side and commands his generals, Abishai and Ittai: "Deal gently, for my sake, with young Absalom."

The battle takes place in the forest of Ephraim. Absalom meets with a freak accident. As he rides his mule and passes under the thick boughs of a great terebinth tree, he is caught by his hair as the startled animal escapes. Joab himself arrives and dispatches the king's son, leader of the rebellion, in spite of the peading of David to deal gently with Absalom. Anxiously awaiting word of the battle, it is not long in reaching David. "Is the young man Absalom safe?" he asks when two messengers come. The king is greatly moved when informed of Absalom's death. He weeps with words of grief which have become unforgettable for their depth of pathos and poignancy:

O my son, Absalom, my son, my son Absalom! Would I
had died in your stead, O Absalom, my son, my son! (Chapter XIX, Verse 1.)

The people are touched by the king's grief and return to the city
quietly, even though they have won a great victory which secures the
throne for David. Joab finally prevails upon David to go out from his
chamber and address the people, who are confused by the king's continuing to mourn for Absalom, who is their enemy, responsible for the
loss of many lives by his rebellion, and yet David seems to be more
impressed by the death of his son than by the people's victory. David
appears before his people, who welcome him and restore him to the
throne, but envy continues to plague his reign.

There are revolts, famines, and further wars with the Philistines, but
David maintains his faith in God, and conducts affairs of state to the best
of his ability. A number of psalms of praise, reminiscent of those which
appear in the Book of Psalms, are attributed to David's eloquent authorship. These are songs of triumph, words of praise of God, and recognition of God's help and guidance.

The Lord is my rock, my fortress, and my deliverer,
The God who is my Rock, in Him I take refuge. . . .
He stretched out from above His hand, took me, and
   drew me out of the mighty waters. He delivered me
   from my enemy. . . .
The Lord rewarded me according to the purity of my
   hands for I have kept the ways of the Lord and did
   not depart from my God. . . .
For You are my lamp, O Lord.
And the Lord illumines the darkness.
            (Chapter XXII, Verses 2, 3, 17, 18, 21, 29.)

David takes a census of Israel and Judah from Dan to Beersheba,
finding that there are eight hundred thousand fighting men in Israel and
five hundred thousand in Judah. This is followed by a pestilence which
is stayed when David offers burnt offerings to God.

The Book of II Samuel comes to a close as David approaches old age.
The powerful Prophet Samuel; Saul, the first king; and David, king of

Judah and Israel, have dominated the two books of Samuel, filling major roles in Israel's development from tribal groups into a unified kingdom. In spite of conflicts, revolts, external and internal, the third and fourth of the historical books of the Earlier Prophets end with a sense of unity which has been achieved under David's kingship. David is real. His very inconsistencies and frailties, in contrast to his valor and kingly might, prove him all the more human and lovable. His life and his lengthy reign have been tumultuous. He now prepares to turn over his crown to his successor, his son by Bathsheba, the wise and regal Solomon.

I KINGS

I KINGS AND II KINGS, WHICH CONTINUE THE ACCOUNTS OF
the history of Israel, were originally a single work like the two books of
Samuel. They are the last two historical books of the Earlier Prophets.
Tradition ascribes authorship to the Prophet Jeremiah who lived toward
the end of the narrative in II Kings.

Kings begins with a united kingdom of Israel under King David, recounts the building of the Temple by Solomon, the central event of his
long life and reign, continues through the division of the kingdom into
Israel and Judah after Solomon, sees the destruction of Israel and the
disappearance of the Ten Tribes, eventually the disintegration of Judah,
the fall of Jerusalem, the destruction of the Temple of Solomon by the
Babylonian conquerors, and the removal of a greater part of the population to Babylon for the period known as the "exile." Kings and prophets
dominate the scene throughout this historic era which spans the period
from before the death of David and the ascension of his son Solomon as
king, in 965 B.C.E., to the fall of Jerusalem in 586 B.C.E.

The opening pages of Kings portray King David, now advanced in
years, making provision for his successor. A lovely young girl called
Abishag, a Shunammite, has been brought to minister to the enfeebled
monarch. Adonijah, the son of Haggith, has taken steps to forward his
claim to the throne, and has provided himself with chariots and horsemen and fifty men to run before him. He is described as a goodly man,
born after Absolom. There are two parties in the politics of the palace.
Adonijah confers with the general, Joab, and with the priest Abiathar,

who are sympathetic to his claim. But Zadok, the priest, and Benaiah, the son of Jehoiada, and the Prophet Nathan, as well as Shimei and Rei and the "mighty men" of David's special guard, are not with Adonijah's party.

At a great banquet tendered at Zoheleth, near En-rogel, Adonijah is host to his brothers, the king's sons, and the king's servants of Judah, but excludes Nathan, Benaiah, the "mighty men," and his brother Solomon from the festivities, designed to proclaim himself king. Nathan bids Bathsheba, the mother of Solomon, hasten to the king, and counsels her to remind him of his promise that Solomon shall reign after him, and why is it that at this very moment Adonijah reigns? Nathan says that he will assist her cause. Bathsheba enters the king's presence and is shortly followed by Nathan, Zadok, Benaiah, the captain of the guard, all summoned to the royal bed chamber. David confirms the oath made before Bathsheba and Nathan, "Assuredly, Solomon will reign after me."

David instructs Solomon's supporters to have him mount the royal horse and proceed to Gihon where he is to be anointed king over Israel by Nathan and Zadok; the ram's horn is to be sounded and they are to proclaim, "Long live King Solomon." Benaiah responds "Amen; so says the Lord, the God of my lord the king. As the Lord has been with my lord the king, so may the Lord be with Solomon, and make his throne greater than the throne of my lord King David." (I Kings, Chapter I, Verses 36, 37.)

The king's instructions are followed; Solomon is anointed king, and the people exclaim "Long live King Solomon." They follow him as he returns to the palace, rejoicing, piping with pipes "so that the earth rent with the sound of them." Solomon's brother Adonijah meanwhile hears the tumult while feasting and celebrating his own elevation to the kingship. A messenger brings him the news of the event of Solomon's anointment and repeats to Adonijah the words of David, "Blessed be the God of Israel, who has given one to sit on my throne this day, my eyes even seeing it."

The disappointed banquet guests depart. Adonijah, terror-stricken, flees to the tabernacle, taking sanctuary by grasping the horns of the altar. Seeking pardon from Solomon, he is granted his life, conditioned upon his proper conduct.

As the days of David draw to a close—after forty years as king—he calls Solomon and charges him: "Be strong and be a man." The dying father instructs his son to keep God's statutes, commandments, and ordinances that he may prosper in all that he undertakes. "And David slept with his fathers, and was buried in the City of David. . . . Solomon sat upon the throne of David his father; and his kingdom was established firmly." (Chapter II, Verses 10–12.) David had reigned seven years in Hebron and thirty-three years in Jerusalem. Musician, poet, singer, protector of the Ark of the Covenant, David was a devout worshiper of God, loved and revered by the people.

Soon after, while Solomon is offering sacrifices at Gibeon, God appears to him in a dream, saying, "Ask what I shall give you." To this Solomon replies:

You have shown great kindness to my father, David. He walked before You in truth and righteousness and with upright heart. Now You have made me, his son, ruler after him. I am but a young man. I know not how to rule. Give me, therefore, an understanding heart to judge Your people and to discern between good and evil. How else can one judge Your people?

And the speech pleased the Lord, that Solomon had asked this thing.

Because you have asked for this and have not asked for long life nor for wealth nor for the death of your enemies, I will give you a wise and understanding heart. In addition, I will give you what you did not ask for, wealth and honor. There will never be another king like you. Also, I will give you long life. (Chapter III, Verses 6–9, 11–13.)

Solomon's wisdom is soon evident as he decides the now legendary case of the two women who claim to be the mother of the same child. One says, "This woman and I live in one house. We each had a child the same night. Her son died during the night, and while I was asleep, she took my child and replaced him with hers. When I awoke in the morning to feed my child, he was dead. But when I looked more carefully, I realized he was not my son." The second woman exclaims, "It is not so! My son is the living one and her son is the dead one." The first mother retorts with equal vehemence.

King Solomon considers the problem thoughtfully, and with an astuteness revealing his deep knowledge of human character says, "Bring me a sword." It is presented to him. Thereupon Solomon orders, "Divide the living child into two and give each woman one half."

The mother of the surviving son, hearing the king's decision, cries out, "Pardon, my lord! Give her the living child! Do not kill him!" The second woman calls loudly "No! Divide him! He shall belong neither to you nor to me!"

Solomon passes judgment. "Give the first woman the living child. She is its real mother."

All Israel hears of the wise decision of the king with great admiration for Solomon's judgment. They understand that the wisdom of God is Solomon's. Soon his wisdom becomes known throughout the world and his name as a wise man and ruler becomes a byword among people everywhere. He speaks three thousand proverbs and composes over a thousand songs. At home in many areas of knowledge, he can speak of trees, animals, birds, reptiles, and fish. From all countries of the world, people come to listen to the king's brilliant dispensation of justice. Solomon rules over all the land from the Jordan to Philistia and to the very border of Egypt. His possessions, grandeur, and splendor are graphically portrayed. By many alliances, beginning with his marriage to the daughter of the Pharaoh of Egypt, Solomon brings untold wealth to his reign according to the pattern set forth in his dream at Gibeon.

His kingdom securely established, Solomon turns his attention to his chief work, the building of the great Temple in Jerusalem. Hiram, the Phoenician King of Tyre, who learns of the death of his friend David and the succession of his son Solomon, offers his friendly assistance, proffering congratulations to the new ruler in reply to Solomon's message: "You know that my father, David, was not permitted to build a temple in honor of the Lord because of his constant wars with surrounding peoples. God has blessed me with peace and I propose now to build a temple to the Lord. I ask you to cut cedar and cypress timber from Lebanon. My servants will work together with your servants."

King Hiram responds, "Blessed be the Lord for giving David a wise son to rule over the great people of Israel." He arranges to deliver the timber, floating it down the coast on rafts. His men, who are experts in the field, are to do the felling, but Solomon is to provide the unskilled labor. He contracts to pay Hiram in wheat and oil. The stones for the Temple's foundation are quarried in the hill country of Ephraim with hired Phoenician stone masons performing the actual cutting. The vastness of the labor force allocated is indicated as Solomon gathers together thirty thousand workers whom he sends to Lebanon in shifts of ten thousand each month. In addition the king summons eighty thousand carriers, eighty thousand stone masons, and three thousand, three hundred supervisors of the work.

The site of the Temple had been determined by King David. It is the northern extension of Zion, the area corresponding nearly to what is known today as the Haram, the present remains of the western enclosure belonging to the times of King Herod, but the foundation is that of Solomon.

Seven intensive years of building are required. In Solomon's eleventh year as king, the magnificent and majestic House of God is completed. Built entirely of stone prepared at the quarry, no hammer, ax, iron tool or implement has been employed. Exclusive of surrounding galleries and parapets, the Temple is sixty cubits long, twenty cubits wide, and thirty cubits high. Chapters VI and VII are devoted to a minute description of the awe-inspiring structure and its furnishings.

Solomon's reign has begun in 965 B.C.E., the year marking David's death; the completion of the Temple of Jerusalem is in the year 954 B.C.E. The Temple structure, with its large squared stones and cedar beams, lies east and west, with the entrance on the eastern side as in Egyptian temples. Its two main apartments are separated by a wall in which there is a door constructed of precious olive wood. The outer and larger apartment, the Hekal or Nave, accommodates the Table of Showbread for the exposure of twelve cakes, six in a row, baked fresh for the Sabbath; the Altar of Incense; ten golden candlesticks, five on each side, at the entrance of the smaller apartment. The candelabra furnish light since the windows, high above the ground, with wooden lattices, narrow without, although widening within, are not calculated to relieve the darkness. Behind and lower is the inner room, the Debir or Sanctuary, formed as a perfect cube. This is the most holy part of the sacred edifice, the Holy of Holies, the depository of the Ark of the Covenant, the paneling of cedar, richly adorned with carvings, and the floor of cypress wood.

Three stories of chambers attached to the thick walls on three sides (the front has a porch with two bronze columns at the entrance) are used for the Temple utensils and votive offerings and thus constitute the treasury of the Temple. Within the Court where there is a Bronze Altar for public and private sacrifices, the worshipers assemble, and it is here where the prophets address the people, since the Temple proper can be entered only by the priests and the Holy of Holies only by the High Priest once a year.

Thirteen years are consumed in the building of Solomon's magnificent palace and state building, which occupy the area south of the Temple on the lower terraces of the hill. The palace compound contains more than one building. Solomon's Egyptian wife dwells in a mansion built expressly for her. From the Palace court, there is an entrance to another compound in which stand the Hall of Justice and the House of the Forest of Lebanon, a two-story structure, the lower story of which has forty-five cedar columns, giving the appearance of a forest, the large hall serving as an assembly room for the elders of Israel and the upper story being used as an arsenal.

It is an imposing spectacle which the entire complex of buildings present. Phoenician craftsmen, supplied by Hiram, King of Tyre, have executed the larger part of the work upon well-established architectural models with the Israelite artificers proving good pupils.

Under Solomon's guidance, prosperity prevails throughout the land, commerce flourishes, nations pay tribute to him, and his navy of ships brings in gold and costly gems. The magnificence of Solomon's court is dazzling. His great throne of ivory inlay is overlaid with finest gold. His drinking cups are of gold, as are all the vessels in the house. Once every three years the royal navy which sails with Hiram's navy returns laden with gold, silver, ivory, apes, and peacocks.

Upon completion of the Temple, Solomon assembles the elders of Israel, all the heads of the tribes and other leaders for the ceremony of bringing the sacred Ark of the Covenant of God from the City of David in Zion to the Temple in Jerusalem. The priests and the Levites bring the Ark containing the two stone Tablets of the Law received by Moses into the inner shrine, the Holy of Holies. They also bring in all the sacred vessels of old from the Tent of the Tabernacle.

Deeply grateful, Solomon blesses the congregation of Israel as they rise before him. He tells them that it was in the heart of David, his father, to build a house for God, but it is his own destiny to achieve this Temple he now dedicates. Standing before the altar of the Lord, he spreads his hands toward heaven, and says:

O Lord, God of Israel! There is no God like You in heaven above or on earth beneath. . . . Let Your word, I pray which you have promised to Your servant, David be kept. . . . All the heavens cannot contain You. How, then, can this house which I built contain You? Yet listen, to the prayer of Your servant. (Chapter VIII, Verses 23, 26–29.)

Solomon offers thanks to God for keeping the covenant made with David and raised up an heir to rule. He prays that the Temple will always be the place to which Israel may turn for forgiveness; for God's intercession in the dealings of people; for the stranger, the non-Jew, who comes to the Temple to pray, "so that all the nations of the earth may know Your name and revere You, so that they may understand that this house which I have built is called by Your name." He blesses the people and prays that God's promise of old be fulfilled in them. To this end, he pleads that God incline their hearts that they keep God's ways with faith and zeal. Thus he prays:

Blessed be the Lord, who has given rest to His people Israel as He promised to Moses. The Lord our God be with us as He was with our fathers. May He never leave us nor forsake us. May He incline our hearts to Him to walk in His ways and keep His commandments. May He maintain always the cause of His people Israel, so that nations may know that He is God; there is none else. May your hearts, therefore, be completely at one with God. (From Chapter VIII, Verses 56–61.)

The Temple is dedicated by Solomon by the inauguration of the regular daily sacrifice and by celebrating with feasts for a period of seven days. After the feast he again blesses the people and they return to their homes, joyful and glad of heart because of all the good that God has done for David, for Solomon, and for Israel.

Soon after completion of the Temple, God again appears before Solomon, assuring him that his prayer has been heard and that it will be answered. "I have heard your prayer and I have hallowed this House which you built for Me." It is conditional upon proper observance of the laws and statutes God has ordained. "If you will continue to walk before Me as David your father did, with uprightness of heart and in rectitude, and keep the commandments, I will establish forever your throne in Israel. If, on the other hand, you or your children turn away from Me and My commandments, I will cast Israel off from the land which I gave them, and also this House will I remove."

Whereas David rose to his pinnacle of fame by virtue of his indomitable energy and vision, his son Solomon was born to it inheriting great wealth. As king, his fame spreads far and wide. The countrymen of his realm are taxed heavily to provide the luxuries of the royal table. Barley and straw have to be provided for the royal horse—Solomon has one thousand four hundred chariots and twelve thousand horsemen, stationed in chariot cities and in Jerusalem. Materials and labor are needed for his vast building enterprises, and the services of foreign (chiefly Phoenician) craftsmen are paid for in products of the soil, which is a very great burden to the people.

King Solomon is alert to the conditions of his times and to the advantage of the geographical location of Palestine. The commerce of the world, from Egypt, from Arabia, from lands beyond, pass through Palestine and pay tribute. In addition his wealth is increased by mercantile enterprises, importing and exporting horses. As he enters into association with the large world beyond his realm, distinguished guests frequent his palace, admiring his brilliance.

Like so many others, the Queen of Sheba has heard of King Solomon's greatness. Considered a wise woman herself, she wishes to confirm his magnificence and to enjoy a visit to his splendid palace. She brings with her a large entourage of servants, her camels bearing rare spices, gold, and precious stones. In an audience with Solomon, she tells him all that is in her heart, poses complex questions and riddles, to which Solomon gives correct answers, and none is too difficult for him to solve. The Queen of Sheba has listened to the king, seen the palace and other buildings, dined at his luxuriously appointed table, inspected the housing of his officers, observed the manner in which his servants attended him, and is deeply impressed. She says to Solomon:

It was a true report that I heard in my own land of your acts and of your wisdom. However, I did not believe the words until I came and saw with my own eyes; and indeed, the half was not told to me; you have wisdom and prosperity exceeding the fame which I heard. Happy are they who are privileged to stand before you continually and are privileged to hear your wisdom. Blessed be the Lord who has placed you on the throne of Israel. (Chapter X, Verses 6–9.)

Sheba presents Solomon with a hundred and twenty bars of gold, abundance of spices and jewels. No supply of spices ever again came to Solomon as great as the Queen of Sheba's gift. Solomon reciprocates the queen's generosity by giving her appropriate gifts out of his royal bounty before she returns to her own land.

The story of Solomon's splendor, grandeur, and wisdom has been told. Now I Kings reveals a completely different aspect of his reign. Over the years, while accumulating wealth and bringing prosperity to the land, the king has married many foreign women besides the daughter of the Pharaoh—Moabites, Canaanites, Edomites, Hittites, and Ammonites. Since it is customary for the ruler of a country to marry the daughter of a king with whom a treaty of alliance has been culminated, many women came from nations to whom marriage is forbidden to the men of Israel. They bring with them their religious altars, priests and idols. Solomon has seven hundred wives, princesses and three hundred handmaidens, and his wives "turn away his heart, for Solomon cleaves to them in love. And his heart is not whole with the Lord his God as was the heart of David his father." King Solomon who honors his wives, builds shrines and altars for them.

Solomon's action greatly displeases God. God appears to him and says:

You have not followed My covenant and My commandments. Therefore, I will take the kingdom away from you and give it to your servant. Nevertheless, I will not do this during your lifetime because of My love for David, your father. I will rend the kingdom from your son after you. However, I will not destroy it completely. I will give your son one of the tribes to rule over. (Chapter XI, Verses 11–13.)

The pendulum of peace and prosperity has begun to swing the other way. Solomon's happy reign nears an end. Strife enters the pages of the Book of Kings. There is a prologue to the revolt destined to rob the Davidic dynasty of its large territory and its monarchy. Rumblings of rebellion are heard. In the king's palace, a young, brilliant officer named Jeroboam, the son of Nebat, beloved by Solomon, is industrious, capable. He is appointed over the house of Joseph.

One day, soon after his appointment, Jeroboam leaves Jerusalem on an assignment. He is met on the road by Ahijah, the prophet, who takes hold of the new cloak Jeroboam is wearing and tears it into twelve pieces, saying, "Take ten pieces for yourself, because this is the word of God who has ordained that the kingdom of Solomon will be divided and that you will be the ruler over the ten tribes. Solomon will have only one tribe."

Thus encouraged, Jeroboam rebels against Solomon, and the king seeks to capture his officer now turned traitor. Jeroboam flees to Egypt, where he remains until the death of Solomon. After forty years of ruling Israel, Solomon dies in the year 926 B.C.E and is buried in Jerusalem, the City of David, and Rehoboam, his son, succeeds him to the throne.

Jeroboam, still in Egypt, learns of Solomon's death and returns to his native town, Zeredah, in the highlands of Ephraim. The people send for him, assembling, to speak to Rehoboam in Shechem where he has come to be crowned king. Groaning under their heavy taxes paid in produce or forced labor, they demand that the new king relieve them of some of their burdens. The king tells them to return in three days and in the meantime he consults the elders of Israel. They advise him to listen to the pleas of the people, lighten their burdens, and they will serve him well as they did King Solomon. Rehoboam then turns to the younger men with whom he grew up, and asks their counsel. They advise him not to submit to the pressure of the people. "Tell them that your little finger is thicker than your father's thigh. Tell them that you will show them what burdens really are, that if your father taxed them heavily, you will increase their burdens."

When the three days are over and the people return to hear the king's decision, Rehoboam arrogantly refuses to listen to their pleas, thus following the counsel of the younger men.

. . . my father burdened you with a heavy yoke. I will add to your yoke; my father chastised you with whips, but I will chastise you with scorpions [painful scourge, the scorpion being a club studded with nails]. (Chapter XII, Verse 11.)

The defiant reply of the king, promising the use of force, is answered by open revolt. The Israelites give this answer "We have no portion in David any more. We are at an end with the son of Jesse. To your tents, O Israel! Look after your own house, David!" They depart. But as for those who live in the cities of Judah, Rehoboam continues to reign over them. He sends Adorom, the hated master of the levy, to the north where he is stoned to death and Rehoboam flees in his chariot to Jerusalem.

The north immediately secedes and establishes the Kingdom of Israel. Jeroboam returns from exile and is proclaimed king in Shechem. He rules over ten tribes of Israel which become the Northern Kingdom and Rehoboam is king over Judah and Benjamin, which becomes the Southern Kingdom. Thus, Ahijah's prophecy is fulfilled, as God had warned Solomon.

King Rehoboam enlists all the people of Judah and Benjamin to proceed against King Jeroboam and to reunite the divided kingdom. When God sends word through Shemiah, a prophet, not to pursue the matter of waging war against Israel, Rehoboam sends his people home.

The kingdom is divided, never to be reunited.

Jeroboam knows that in order to maintain the secession, he must establish a religious center to preclude any movement for a reuniting with Judah. If the people return to Jerusalem and to the Temple to offer their sacrifices, they may clamor for unity with Judah. He therefore erects two golden calves, one at Beth-el and the other at Dan, telling the people that these are their gods and there is no longer any reason to offer sacrifices in Jerusalem. He sets up temples and appoints men who are not priests to perform the service, consecrating them himself. This sinful deviation from the ways of God marks the beginning of the decline of Jeroboam's dynasty. A prophet appears at Beth-el while the king is sacrificing, and predicts the destruction of both altar and priests. The fall of his monarchy is also foretold by Ahijah, the prophet who originally brought the news of his selection as king over the ten tribes. After ruling for twenty-two years, Jeroboam dies, and is succeeded by his son Nadab.

Rehoboam and Jeroboam had warred continually against each other during their reigns. Rehoboam also had set up shrines for idol worship. After having ruled for seventeen years, he was succeeded by his son Abijam who reigned for three years in Jerusalem following the sinful ways of his father. There had been war between Abijam and Jeroboam. When Abijam died he was buried in the City of David and his son Asa ruled in his stead. Both kings who succeeded King Solomon strayed from the path of God. From that point, there were two separate lines of kings. Every king has been recorded in proper historical order in each kingdom, from ascension to the throne until death.

The kings who rule Judah and Israel have great power, but the prophets, as messengers of God, assume major roles in the development of the Jewish people. They are a courageous, fearless group who combat all manner and form of idolatry, exposing and condemning evil and wrongdoing, whether by king or individual. They wage relentless attacks against oppression and injustice, teaching that love of God and fidelity to the Lord will bring about peace and righteousness. They prophesy the future history of both kingdoms, Judah and Israel.

An able and energetic ruler, Omri (884–873 b.c.e.), king of Israel, chooses for his capital a new site, a hill six miles northwest of Shechem, rising over three hundred feet high from the valley leading to the coast. As later events prove, the choice is a propitious one. In honor of Shemer, the former owner of the land, Omri calls his new capital Samaria. It is almost impregnable, and its reduction by attacking armies is a lengthy undertaking. Omri for all time disposes of the Philistine threat; the Moabites are reduced to vassalage, paying enormous amounts of tribute to Israel in the form of wool from the herds in which that country abounds. Omri allies himself with the Phoenicians (interrupted since the days of Solomon). To check inroads, commercial and political, by the rulers of Damascus, Omri arranges for the marriage of his son Ahab, heir to the throne, and Jezebel, the daughter of Ethbaal, king of Tyre.

Toward the end of Omri's reign and in the first years of Ahab's accession, an Assyrian army marches into northern Syria. The Assyrian King Ashurnazirpal receives the tribute of Tyre, Sidon, Byblus, and other Phoenician towns, and it is only a question of time before the Assyrian colossus penetrates deeper into the south. For the present time, King Ahab is more concerned with the peril indicated by the Arameans, and he holds fast to the policies of his father. Like Solomon, Ahab beautifies his capital and enlarges his father's palace building, which becomes known as Ivory House from the profusion of ivory used. Again like his ancestor Solomon, Ahab builds a temple to the deity of Tyre for his Tyrian wife Queen Jezebel. An imperious person, she seeks to make her religion of Baal the religion of the royal court and of the people.

During the reign of Ahab, the prophet Elijah appears on the scene of history. He seeks to keep the nation from accepting Jezebel's religion with its cruel practices. Numerous legends have come down about the life of Elijah, the Tishbite, and no one in Jewish history is so admired, revered, and immortalized.

Elijah comes from Gilead to see King Ahab to advise him that God is sending a drought as punishment for divergence from the worship of the true God. The message delivered, Elijah is directed by God to leave Ahab and to hide near the brook Cherith. The water there will quench his thirst and the ravens will be commanded to sustain him. Elijah follows God's word. After a while, he is sent to Zarephath, where he is told he will be fed by a poor widow who lives there. Elijah meets the widow and asks her for a drink of water. While she is securing it, Elijah asks for a slice of bread. The widow explains that she has only a handful of meal and a little oil, hardly enough to feed her own son and herself. Elijah tells her that she need have no fear. "The jar of meal shall not fail, nor shall the cruse of oil diminish until God sends rain upon the land." The widow agrees, and is thus able to provide for the three of them. Soon after, her son becomes seriously ill and his breathing ceases. The widow in her grief confronts the prophet angrily and holds him responsible for bringing tragedy to her door. Elijah takes up the boy in his arms, carries him to the upper floor, and places him on his own bed. He prays to God that the child be restored to life and stretches himself out gently on the child three times, praying fervently, "O God, cause this child's life to return to him." God listens to Elijah's prayer and life is restored to the widow's son. She then says, "Now do I know that you are a man of God and that the message of the Lord which you bring is truth."

Almost three years pass with the drought unbroken and famine is now stalking in the land. Ahab calls Obadiah, the overseer of the palace, a loyal servant to God. Indeed, when Queen Jezebel ordered the prophets of God to be slain, he hid a hundred of them in caves and kept them supplied with bread and water. Ahab now calls on Obadiah to search the land for springs of water and brooks, and for grass and fodder for the cattle. They divide the land between them, one to go one way and the other to take the alternate road. Elijah meets Obadiah and orders him to return to Ahab and tell the king of the prophet's coming. At first Obadiah hesitates for he fears Elijah will vanish, but is reassured that the prophet will meet with Ahab. The king goes to meet Elijah and asks him pointedly, "Are you the troublemaker of Israel?" Elijah responds, "It is not I who have troubled Israel, but you and your father's house, because you have forsaken the command of God and followed Baal."

Elijah orders Ahab to assemble all of the people on Mount Carmel and also the four hundred and fifty prophets of Baal supported by Queen Jezebel. Elijah determines to stage a dramatic contest to prove to the Israelites that the idolatry of Baal is the cause of all the evil in the land and that the future of the religion of Israel is in jeopardy. He will show the people that the Lord, not Baal, is God. On Mount Carmel the momentous contest is held. The prophets of Baal lay out an offering upon the altar of their god. But all their prayers, artifices, and wild contortions avail nothing to bring down heavenly fire. When the time is right to offer the evening sacrifice, fire descends from heaven and consumes Elijah's offering upon the altar of God which he has prepared, using twelve stones to represent the tribes of Israel. This is the answer to Elijah's confrontation to the people: "How long will you halt between two beliefs? If the Lord be God, follow the Lord; if Baal, follow him." The people, seeing this response of God to Elijah's call, fall upon their faces and exclaim: "The Lord is God! The Lord is God!"

Elijah commands the Israelites to destroy the false prophets of Baal. He then turns to King Ahab to tell of signs of the long-awaited rain. Before long the heavens darken thickly and a great rainfall descends. The interminable drought is ended. Ahab returns to the palace to tell the queen of Elijah's victory over the priests of Baal. Jezebel threatens Elijah, and the prophet escapes by way of Beer-sheba into the southern wilderness. Disheartened and weary, he sits down under a broom-bush and prays that he may die, crying, "I have had enough. O Lord, take away my life now, for I am not better than my fathers." He lies down to sleep, but suddenly feels the touch of an angel who commands him to rise and eat. Elijah looks about and sees cakes and water. He eats and drinks. He lies down again. Once more the angel awakens him and commands him to eat, because a long journey is in store for him. Elijah follows instructions and has now enough strength for the forty-day trip to Horeb (Sinai), the seat of the revelation of God to Moses, where he finds shelter in a cave. God appears to him and tells him not to fear but to anoint Jehu king of Israel, and reveals also that Elisha is to be Elijah's successor. On his way to meet Elisha, who at the moment is plowing with twelve yoke of oxen, Elijah approaches him and casts his mantle over Elisha's shoulders, in this way placing the cloak of responsibility on him. Elisha takes leave of his mother and father, and departs with Elijah.

A story of Queen Jezebel typifies her wickedness. The palace of the rulers is located near a very beautiful vineyard belonging to Naboth, the Jezreelite, in Samaria. The king asks Naboth to relinquish his vineyard that there may be a royal herb garden planted in its place. He promises the vintner a more desirable vineyard in another location, but Naboth refuses to part with his inheritance. Ahab can do nothing about it legally, but when Jezebel learns of the matter, she assures Ahab: "Are you not the ruler of Israel? Rise up and eat, and let your heart be merry. I myself will give you Naboth's vineyard."

The queen writes letters in the king's name, sealing them with his signet ring, and sends the letters to the leaders and nobles who live in the city along with Naboth. "Proclaim a feast and arrange Naboth to be seated at the front. Also, seat two evil men near him and have them testify, 'You have cursed God and the king.' Then take him outside the city and kill him." The nobles carry out her instructions. When it is done, Jezebel tells Ahab to take possession of the vineyard which he covets.

In the meantime, God appears to Elijah and sends him to warn Ahab that his evil deeds will not go unpunished and that both he and Jezebel will pay for their crimes. Elijah is also to inform Ahab that his dynasty is doomed. Ahab meets with Elijah and learns of his fate. He repents and fasts. God then tells Elijah that inasmuch as Ahab humbles himself, the punishment will not be executed in his lifetime but in the days of his son. Ahab meets his end in battle with the Arameans, and his death brings to a close the first turbulent Book of Kings. With the death of the king, the cry goes through the camp: "Back to your towns, back to your country, every man of you, for the king is dead! His followers leave the battlefield and return to Samaria, where they give Ahab burial. And Ahab sleeps with his fathers, and his son Ahaziah reigns after him.

II KINGS

AS INDICATED IN I KINGS, DURING THE GREATER PART OF Ahab's reign, the country of Israel under Ahab has enjoyed peace. By virtue of a victory over the Arameans, Ahab repossesses the Galilean cities previously wrested from him. The merchants of Israel set up their bazaars in the city of Damascus, which Ahab wishes to take, and with this King Jehoshaphat of Judah is in agreement. The royal houses are connected by marriage: The son of Jehoshaphat, Jehoram, is the husband of Athaliah, daughter of King Ahab and Queen Jezebel. The prophet Micaiah warns against personal participation, but the two kings nevertheless go into battle. Ahab, disguised as a soldier, is stricken by an enemy archer and killed. King Ahab reigned in Samaria over Israel more than twenty years (875–853 B.C.E.). II Kings opens as Moab rebels against Israel after the deaths of Ahab and Jezebel.

The story of Elijah continues. His work has been completed and the time approaches when he will ascend in a whirlwind to heaven. His faithful disciple Elisha accompanies Elijah as far as Gilgal, and three times, at Gilgal, Beth-el, and Jericho, the young prophet asks Elijah to linger. At each place, a group of prophets question Elisha as to his knowledge of Elijah's impending departure from earth. Elisha replies that he is aware of the matter and remains close to his master. They cross the narrow Jordan River as the waters miraculously divide for them. As they walk, Elijah says thoughtfully to Elisha, "Before I am taken from you, ask what I can do for you." Elisha earnestly responds,

101

"Let me have a double portion of your spirit." Elijah says, "You have asked a difficult thing. If you see me when I am taken from you, your request will be fulfilled. But if not, it will not be granted."

As they continue to walk, a fiery chariot drawn by horses of fire suddenly races between them and separates master and disciple. Elijah vanishes in the whirlwind sweeping him to heaven, as Elisha calls out, "My father, my father, the chariot of Israel and their horsemen!" He sees his beloved prophet no more and rents his clothes in grief. Picking up the mantle that has fallen from the shoulders of Elijah, Elisha returns to the banks of the Jordan where fifty disciples of the prophets stand some distance away. With simple recognition of the divine event they say, "The spirit of Elijah now rests upon Elisha," thus acknowledging him as successor. They ask Elisha for permission to search the countryside. Perhaps the spirit of God has left the beloved prophet on one of the mountains or in one of the valleys. They return in three days to admit that Elijah cannot be found. The disciple follows in the footsteps of Elijah, performs miracles of healing and many acts of kindness and understanding.

Chapter IV tells of the poor widow of a disciple of the prophets, threatened by a creditor who wants to take her two children as bondmen to settle her husband's indebtedness. When she comes to Elisha for help, he bids her borrow all the containers possible from her neighbors, fill them with the oil she still has in her home, which is only one cruse. Miraculously, the one cruse yields enough oil for all of the borrowed vessels. Selling the oil, she derives sufficient money to pay the debt and her sons are saved.

Elisha revives the little son of the wealthy Shunammite woman who has befriended him and his steward. In her home he had always found a warm welcome whenever he passed by the city in which she lived. She had suggested to her husband that since Elisha vists their area so often that they furnish a small upper room for him with a bed, table, stool, and candlestick. One day, Elisha sends his servant, Gehazi, to inquire what he may do to express his gratitude. The woman makes no request. Gehazi notes, however, that she has no children. The prophet sends for the woman and tells her she will be blessed with a son and in due time, Elisha's words come to pass as the Shunammite woman becomes a mother. Her son grows and is soon strong enough to help his father in the fields. One day as they are with the reapers, he complains of severe head pains. The father rushes home with his son in his arms. The anxious mother administers to him and cradles the child on her lap, but he expires at noon.

The distraught mother takes the lifeless body of her son to Elisha's chamber and lays him on the prophet's bed, then hurries to Elisha, who is now at Mount Carmel. Seeing her approach, the prophet sends Gehazi to greet her and to inquire if she, her husband, and her child are well. She replies laconically that all is well, but when she meets Elisha, he immediately notes her distress. "Did I ask for a son?" she cries out. "Did I not say, do not lead me astray?" Elisha tells Gehazi to accompany her home and to lay his staff on the child's face. The woman refuses to move unless the prophet himself comes with her. Sending Gehazi on ahead, Elisha prepares to leave. Gehazi follows his master's directions, with no results. When Elisha reaches his room, seeing the child in the stillness of death, he locks the door and begins to pray. He stretches himself out gently on the small body, completely covering it; the child begins to breathe. The prophet has Gehazi summon the woman, whom the prophet welcomes with words of joy, "Here is your son. Take him!"

Elisha's fame as a man of God spreads throughout the land and into surrounding countries. His miraculous powers are recognized by Naaman, captain of the army of the king of Aram, a mighty warrior, highly honored by his king and famous for bringing victory to the Arameans. Naaman has received every honor in his country; good fortune has blessed him. He is, however, a leper. In one of the battles against Israel, a young girl is captured and she becomes a servant of Naaman's wife. She tells her mistress that the prophet Elisha is able to cure Naaman's distressing affliction. Naaman requests his king to write a letter to the king of Israel in his behalf. The king of Israel is greatly concerned, fearful that the Syrian king, Naaman's chief, may seek to incite him to conflict. "Am I God to kill and to make alive, that this king sends me a man to be cured of his leprosy?" Learning of the letter, Elisha sends word: "Why do you rend your clothes? Let this man come to me and he will know that there is a prophet in Israel."

Naaman and his entourage come to the house of Elisha. The prophet sends a messenger ahead to the commander, instructing him to "Go bathe in the Jordan seven times, and you will be cured." The king's general is angered at the impudence of the prophet transmitting a message through one of his followers instead of in person. "I thought he would come out to me and call on the name of his God, hold his hand over me, and heal the leprosy. Are not the rivers of Damascus better than all the waters of Israel? Can I not bathe in them and become clean?" He turns in disappointment to leave. One of his servants approaches and says, "If the prophet had asked you to do a great thing, would you not do it? How much better, then, when he tells you simply to bathe in the Jordan and become cured?" Impressed by the wisdom of his servant, Naaman follows the orders of Elisha and is completely healed. He returns joyously to the prophet, grateful for the miracle, and offers him costly gifts which Elisha does not accept. In an outburst of religious fervor, Naaman acknowledges the Lord as God over the entire universe, and leaves for his home directly.

Gehazi, however, feels that he may profit a little for himself from Naaman's proffered generosity. Without revealing his intent to his master, he overtakes Naaman and declares that Elisha has changed his mind and will after all accept some of the gifts he has offered the two sons of the prophet. Naaman gladly gives Gehazi double the amount requested. He is rebuked by Elisha: "Is this a time to take money and garments and other costly things?" Gehazi, unable to resist so great a temptation which opportunity presented, is punished and leaves the presence of the prophet "a leper as white as snow." (Chapter V, Verse 27.)

Elisha, following his master Elijah in his loyalty to the God of Israel, wins the love of people everywhere through his patience, kindness, and his eagerness to assist the poor, the afflicted, and the ill. His kind deeds abound. The disciples of the prophets receive permission from Elisha to build larger quarters and go to the Jordan to fell trees on its bank. One of the men loses his axhead in the water and is distressed because it is a borrowed implement. He seeks Elisha's help. The prophet cuts down a stick, throws it into the water and retrieves the axhead.

Elisha's qualities of leadership are evident in the account of the king of Syria who, during one of the battle skirmishes, takes counsel with his officers and decides upon a specific place to encamp. Aware of this, Elisha sends word of it to the king of Israel, urging extreme caution. The king avoids passing the camp. Believing there is a spy in his midst, the Syrian king is disconcerted that the location of his encampment has been revealed. However, his officers assure him that the prophet of Israel, Elisha, has by his miraculous powers knowledge of all secrets, even the king's innermost thoughts, and that it is he who advises the king of Israel. The Syrian ruler learns that Elisha is in Dothan and sends a large contingent to take him captive. They surround the city; Elisha awakens in the night, his servant frightened by the encircling soldiers. Elisha calms him: "Do not be afraid. We have many more than they have."

Elisha prays, "O God, open his eyes, I pray Thee, that he may see." The young man's eyes are opened and he sees that all around Elisha there is a mountain surrounded by horses and chariots. The troops of Syria descend on the house, and Elisha prays again, this time that God blind the opposing host. So God does. Elisha then tells the troops that they are going in the wrong direction. "Follow me," he says. "I will lead you to the man you are seeking." He takes them to Samaria. On their arrival, Elisha again prays to God asking that the troops be permitted to see again. When they open their eyes, they realize their location. The king of Israel asks Elisha for permission to destroy the army then and there. Elisha responds, "You shall not smite them. Would you smite those whom you have not captured with your own sword?" On the contrary, he counsels the king, set bread and water before them that they may eat, and then send them back to their master. The king of Israel thereupon prepares a great feast and afterward returns the men safely to the Syrian king.

Convinced that the royal house of Omri is, because of its persistent worship of false gods and idols, the source of all the evil which came upon Israel, Elisha decides to put an end to the dynasty. He sends one of his disciples to anoint Jehu king of Israel. The disciple reaches Jehu, finds him in the company of other army officers, calls him outside, pours oil over his head, saying, "Thus says the Lord, God of Israel. I anoint you king over the people of the God of Israel." The officers inquire of Jehu what happened outside. At first he refuses to tell them, but upon their persistence, discloses the act. Promptly they acknowledge him king. He is to rule from 841 to 814 B.C.E.

Jehu, the son of Jehoshaphat, the son of Nimshi, conspires against King Joram, King of Israel. To avoid the possibility that news of his anointment as king may precede him, Jehu sets out across the land to Jezreel where, in short order, his purpose is effected. King Joram has had his chariot made ready and, accompanied by Ahaziah, king of Judah, they ride forth each in his chariot to meet Jehu face to face, finding him in the portion of Naboth, the Jezreelite. When Joram is near enough he calls out to Jehu, "Is it peace, Jehu?" To which Jehu responds: "What peace, so long as the harlotries of your mother Jezebel and her witchcrafts are so many?" Joram turns and flees, saying to Ahaziah, King of Judah and Joram's cousin, who has been visiting, "There is treachery, O Ahaziah." Jehu kills Joram, and Ahaziah is pursued and killed as he holds the reins of his chariot in his flight.

When Queen Jezebel hears the dreadful news, she knows her own fate is sealed. She takes pains to prepare herself to greet Jehu, painting her eyes and arranging her hair. When Jehu victoriously enters the gate, Jezebel looks out of her window and calls out, "Your master's murderer!" The officers of the new king seize the queen and hurl her from the window; thus she meets the violent end Elijah had prophesied for her.

Samaria is still in the hands of the followers of King Omri. Within the well-fortified city is the principal royal palace with chariots, horses, and arsenal. Jehu fears that one of the surviving brothers (who are seventy in number) of Jehoram might be proclaimed king. He therefore dispatches a letter to the authorities in the capital, to the minister of the household, to the governor, and to the elders of the city as well as to the tutors of the royal princes, with a death warrant for the seventy males.

All remaining members of the house of Ahab in Samaria, including all sympathizers, perish at the hands of the revolutionaries led by Jehu.

Now the conqueror is free to enter Samaria in triumph. On the way he even slays forty-two Judean princes who have come in peace to inquire after the welfare of the royal family of Israel. After Jehu enters the capital in the company of Jehonadab, a Rechabite zealot, he instructs that all Baal worshipers be assembled in their temple, where they are attacked, killed, and the temple and its furnishings destroyed. Thus with appalling bloodshed, decisively and cruelly is the hated cult of the Tyrean god Baal uprooted.

Elisha becomes ill during the reign of Jehoash, the young successor of King Jehu. Jehoash visits the prophet and grieves over his final suffering. A poignant scene now unfolds: "My father! My father! the chariots of Israel and its horsemen!" the young monarch cries. The dying Elisha counsels: "Take bows and arrows." Then he says: "Draw the bow." Elisha lays his hands on the hands of the king, opening the window toward the east. "Shoot!" Elisha says. The king releases his arrow and the prophet cries: "God's arrow of victory! Victory over Aram! You shall smite the Arameans at Aphek and defeat them." The fervent, patriotic words are Elisha's last as his voice is stilled in death.

The Scriptures now turn to Athaliah, second of the evil women whose foul deeds are recorded in the Book of Kings. Daughter of King Ahab and Queen Jezebel and mother of King Ahaziah, Athaliah (like her Phoenician mother) is a worshiper of the Baal religion, and she hopes to establish the god of Tyre in the very heart of Jerusalem. Her opportunity comes when Jehu kills her son, King Ahaziah, during his visit to his cousin King Joram of Israel. Athaliah seizes the throne of Judah and declares herself queen. Without compunction Athaliah removes by massacre all the sons of King Ahaziah in the royal line of Judah. Only one grandson is saved, Jehoash, the youngest, whose mother is Zibiah of Beersheba. Ahaziah's sister Jehosheba, who is the daughter of Queen Athaliah (and aunt of the infant boy) secrets him by placing the prince in the care of his nurse within the precincts of the Temple.

Queen Athaliah and her priests take possession of the Temple treasures and further violate the House of God by introducing their pagan god Baal, whose worship continues during her rule. In the seventh year of her reign, 835 B.C.E., Jehoiada, the high priest, assembles the officers and guards in the Temple, swears them to loyalty to the king, and in a plot brought to a head on the Sabbath, while the Temple guard is being changed, crowns and anoints the seven-year-old boy king of Judah, and the witnesses cry: "Long live the King!" The queen hears the tumultuous celebration which accompanies the coronation, comes into the Temple and sees her grandson Jehoash, king of Judah, standing on the platform in kingly regalia receiving the respect and homage due a king. Athaliah exclaims: "It is treason!" But it is too late. Jehoiada, the high priest, commands that she be followed so that there be no violence committed in the Temple. As the deposed queen returns to the palace by way of the horses' entry, she is overtaken and slain.

The covenant is renewed with the God of Abraham, Isaac, and Jacob and the people. The temple of Baal, his altars and images are demolished. Builders and masons are hired to repair the House of God with new timber and mortar. Guided by the high priest since his infancy, Jehoash is devoted to the Temple where his early childhood was spent, and he walks in the ways pleasing to God. He provides a chest beside the altar for donations, and by virtue of this fund keeps the Temple in constant repair. Jehoash, whose reign began in the seventh year of King Jehu of Israel, rules in Jerusalem as king of Judah for forty years.

When the Assyrian campaign against Damascus fails, Hazael, King of Aram, takes Gath of the Philistines, the whole of the country east of the Jordan as far as the River Arnon falling into the hands of the Arameans. The invaders burn the fortified towns of Israel and then turn toward Jerusalem, the capital city of Judah. In this crisis, King Jehoash buys the departure of the enemy from his gates by a substantial tribute of the hallowed treasures of the Temple and the palace. Ultimately, as times change, a conspiracy builds up against the ruler of Judah and Jehoash is assassinated. Amaziah, his son, reigns in his stead from 796 to 767 B.C.E. He gains a signal victory over the Edomites in the Valley of Salt, southwest of the Dead Sea, and their rock-bound fortress is renamed Joktheel and incorporated into Judah. The roads to the south are now opened up for commerce.

In his pride, Amaziah now challenges the king of Israel to a test of power. Jehoash, with the same name as Amaziah's late father, replies with the fable of the thistle that asked for the hand of the daughter of the great cedar and is trodden underfoot by a passing beast. Nevertheless the battle is fought; Amaziah is defeated and taken captive; Jehoash, king of Israel, enters Jerusalem in triumph, breaking down a portion of its walls and despoiling the Temple of its treasures. The defeated Amaziah must deliver hostages as a guarantee of his keeping the peace. He falls into disfavor with his own people and is assassinated.

Amaziah is succeeded by his son Azariah (or Uzziah) (791–740 B.C.E.). Meanwhile in Israel, Jehoash is followed by his son Jeroboam II (786–746 B.C.E.). These two monarchs are able for nearly half a century, by virtue of the favorable political situation, to restore the territories of Israel and Judah to their geographical extent in the times of King David and King Solomon.

*　　*　　*

When Jeroboam II, great-grandson of Jehu and king of Israel dies, there is turmoil with kings rising and falling. Ultimately the greatness of Israel declines. Hoshea, son of Elah, ascends the throne as the last king of Israel (733–722 B.C.E.). He does evil in the eyes of God and Assyria is dominant. King Shalmaneser marches against Hoshea who conspires with the king of Egypt and refuses to pay tribute. In retaliation, Shalmaneser attacks the capital of Israel, Samaria, for three years, captures the city, and eradicates the kingdom of Israel. Large numbers of Israelites are carried away to Assyria. The king of Assyria brings some of his own people from Babylonia and other places and settles them in Samaria, which has been depopulated of Israelites. Thus is ended the kingdom of Israel, and its ten tribes disappear to become the Ten Lost Tribes of Jewish history. The year is 722 B.C.E.

Only the kingdom of Judah remains. King Hezekiah and the people of the Southern Kingdom are greatly disconcerted by the destruction of the Northern Kingdom of Israel. There is a new power rising in the far east beyond Assyria—Babylonia—and its ruler seeks allies, urging the country of Judah to join Babylonia against Assyria. Hezekiah, son of Ahaz, begins to reign in Judah in the third year of Hoshea, the last king of Israel. He walks in the ways of his ancestor King David and rules justly. He is a model of faith and piety, obeying God's commands as given to Moses, and he prospers in all his undertakings.

The king of Assyria, Sennacherib, exacts heavy tribute from Hezekiah, who is obliged to pay with gold and silver from the Temple furnishings. Sennacherib, however, is not satisfied. By a series of intimidations and a parade of force he tries to impress Hezekiah with the weakness of his position. He sends messengers to the king of Judah to boast that no one, not even the God of Israel, will be able to withstand the Assyrian attack. Hezekiah loses courage, but is strengthened by the encouragement of the prophet Isaiah who assures him the Assyrian king will not capture Jerusalem. A great army takes up its position outside the wall of the city. Miraculously the siege is raised and the capital of Judah is saved.

When Hezekiah becomes mortally ill, Isaiah comes to him and tells him to set his house in order. The king in tears turns his face to the wall and prays for an extension of life, since he has been faithful and loyal to God: "Remember now, O Lord, I beseech You, how I have walked before You in truth and with a whole heart, and have done that which is good in Your sight." The prophet Isaiah leaves, but the word of God comes to him, bidding him return to the king with word that God has heard his prayer and seen his tears and has granted him another fifteen years of life. Hezekiah is also assured that he and his capital Jerusalem will be delivered from the threat of the Assyrian king.

Soon after his recovery, Hezekiah receives a delegation from Berodach-baladan, king of Babylon. Believing they have come as friends in peace, the king proudly shows them the wealth and resources of his kingdom. When Isaiah learns of Hezekiah's hospitable reception of the Babylonians, he is distressed and rebukes the king for his lack of wisdom. He predicts that Babylon will come and secure the treasures; he prophesies the Babylonian exile; but Hezekiah, appalled at the prophet's dire forebodings, takes comfort in the thought that the catastrophe will not occur during his lifetime.

The last years of his reign as king are peaceful. Upon his death, his son Manasseh, twelve years of age, ascends the throne, reigns for fifty-five years, and deviates from the ways of God. He reintroduces foreign cults and idols, soothsaying, and necromancy which his father abolished, and commits the ultimate desecration in setting a graven image of Ashtoreth in the Temple.

God speaks through the prophets, saying: "Because Manasseh king of Judah has committed these abominations, and has done wickedly . . . I will bring evil upon Jerusalem." They foretell the doom of the entire house of Judah, the destruction of Jerusalem and the Temple. Upon his death, his son Amon succeeds him at the age of twenty-two years. He walks in the wicked ways of his father until assassination removes him from the throne. He is succeeded by his son Josiah, who is eight years of age when he commences to reign. He rules for thirty-one years.

Babylonia comes to its full power after conquering Assyria. Meanwhile the prophets Zephaniah (who condemns the people for their idolatry and the leaders for their corruption), Nahum, and Habakkuk are active among the people and the prophet Jeremiah emerges as a great force and towering figure of antiquity.

In the eighteenth year of Josiah's reign (622 B.C.E.) he institutes a massive effort to restore the Temple to its original beauty and utility. When the work of renovation begins, a literary treasure is discovered, which marks an important event in Josiah's reign. Hilkiah, the high priest, tells Shaphan, the Temple scribe: "I have found the Book of the Law in the house of the Lord!" He brings the significant scroll to Shaphan, who reads it before the king. Josiah, profoundly moved, rends his clothes in symbolic mourning for the deviation of the people from the words of God and for the impending disaster because of the people's disobedience and idolatry.

Hilkiah, Ahikam, Achbor, and Shaphan, as well as Asaiah, go to see Huldah, the prophetess, who affirms that God will bring evil to Jerusalem and upon the inhabitants because they have forsaken the Lord for other gods, assuring them, however, that because of the king's fidelity, the destruction will not occur during his lifetime. Josiah summons all the leaders of Judah and Jerusalem to the courts of the Temple where the monarch himself mounts a platform and reads from the scroll of the covenant which was found in the Temple. Josiah makes a solemn promise before God to obey all the Lord's commands and to carry out all that is written in this holy work. The people also agree to abide by this.

Josiah then orders a complete cleansing of the Temple, destroying the vessels fashioned for Baal. He removes and burns the horses of the sun at the entrance of the Temple, given by the kings of Judah. Josiah breaks down the altar and the temple at Beth-el erected by Jeroboam, and, following this, observes the Passover which had not been properly celebrated since the distant days of the Judges. (Chapter XXIII, Verse 21.)

The wrath of God nevertheless does not turn away because of earlier deviations. King Solomon himself had built high places for Ashtoreth and other deities before Jerusalem. (Chapter XXIII, Verse 13.) At this time when Assyria is conquered by Babylonia, its hated capital Nineveh is destroyed. The king of Egypt Pharaoh-necoh rebels against the king of Assyria and marches against him as far as the Euphrates River. King Josiah meets the king of Egypt and is mortally wounded in the Valley of Megiddo. The people of Judah and Jerusalem mourn for Josiah, the good king.

The son of Josiah, Jehoahaz, twenty-three years of age, is anointed king. He is made a captive by Pharaoh-necoh after three months and deposed in favor of his brother Jehoiakim. The new king is twenty-five years old when he begins the reign and rules for eleven years.

The king of Babylonia, the most powerful country in this part of the world, captures Egypt and in this way releases Jehoiakim from Egyptian control. Jehoiakim serves Nebuchadnezzar for three years, then turns and rebels against him. Now Jerusalem is besieged by Babylonians, Arameans, Moabites, Ammonites. Jeohiakim dies and is succeeded by his son Jeroiachin, eighteen years of age.

Nebuchadnezzar, king of Babylon, himself comes to Jerusalem during the siege of 597 B.C.E. and takes the young king Jehoiachin and his family captive. He plunders Jerusalem and carries away all the mighty men of valor, ten thousand captives, all the craftsmen and the smiths numbering one thousand—indeed, any who could instigate a revolt or fashion arms of resistance. Only the poorest, the most humble of the people are allowed to remain in a desolated Jerusalem.

Zedekiah, Jehoiachin's uncle, is appointed king and rules for eleven years in Jerusalem. In the fourth year of his reign, the Prophet Jeremiah says to Zedekiah: "Submit to the yoke of the emperor of Babylonia and serve him and his people in order that you may live! Why should you and your people die by sword, famine, and pestilence? Do not listen to the words of the prophets who say to you 'You shall not serve the emperor of Babylonia! . . .'"

For eight years the king of Judah is submissive, and then he attempts a revolt. In doing this he signs the death warrant of his kingship and of the capital city of Jerusalem. Nebuchadnezzar retaliates. In the ninth year of Zedekiah's reign, on the tenth day of the tenth month, the king of Babylon arrives in person against Jerusalem with his entire army. They build forts around the city, and it is under siege until the eleventh year of Zedekiah's reign.

Finally there is no bread, and the famine is sore. When a breach is made in the wall, Jerusalem's men of war as well as their king flee by night. King Zedekiah is pursued, overtaken, and brought to Nebuchadnezzar, who kills his sons, blinds him, and sends him off to Babylon. The beautiful Temple of Solomon, the magnificent palace of the king and all of the great houses in Jerusalem are set to fire. The army breaks down the walls of Jerusalem, and the rest of the multitude are dispersed, leaving only the poorest to be vinedressers and workers of the land.

In order to preclude a political party forming to revive any revolt against Babylon, the chief priests, officers, and leaders are killed. So Judah is brought a captive, crying piteously to Babylonia and the great adventure begun in the days of Samuel and Saul, of David and Solomon becomes a nadir as the Kingdom of Judah ends in the year 586 B.C.E.— in the Jewish calendar, the ninth day of the month of Ab.

Gedaliah, grandson of Shaphan, is appointed by Nebuchadnezzar to govern the pitiful remnant of folk left in the demolished city. He urges the people not to fear, nor rebel, but to serve the king of Babylon that all may be well with them. He, too, meets with assassination at Mizpah, and as many people as are able escape to Egypt.

The Books of Kings, recording the history of two kingdoms, Judah and Israel, draw to a close with a sequel to follow in the two Books of Chronicles. Its last few verses impart a comforting note, telling how in the thirty-seventh year of the captivity of Jehoiachin, king of Judah, the king of Babylon Evil-merodach, releases him from prison, refreshes him with new garments, and he is welcomed to the king's table.

The Babylonian king "spoke kindly" to the unfortunate former king of ravished Judah. Here there is indication of a new beginning that is to follow after the people of Judah have endured an exile of seventy years. In God's own good time, the people will be restored to their homeland and to their Holy City of Jerusalem, the City of David.

ISAIAH

T HE LENGTHY BOOK OF ISAIAH COMPRISES THE LIFE AND WORK OF
the first of the three later prophets—Isaiah, Jeremiah, and Ezekiel—
Nevi'im Ahronim. The second division of the prophets will comprise
"The Twelve"—Hosea, Joel, Amos, Obadiah, Jonah, Micah, Nahum,
Habakkuk, Zephaniah, Haggai, Zechariah, Malachi—referred to as "mi-
nor." The distinction between them and the major works of Isaiah,
Jeremiah, and Ezekiel is based not on the content of their books but on
their length as contributions to literature.

Isaiah is not only a superb collection of the prophet's prophecies and
teachings but a reservoir of information on the historical events of his
times. According to tradition, Isaiah is recognized as the author of the
sixty-six chapters comprising the book bearing his name. However,
many scholars of biblical studies believe chapters forty to sixty-six were
written by another prophet whose name remains unknown, who probably lived in Babylonia shortly before that country was conquered by
Cyrus the Persian, about 545 B.C.E.

This view is based on two premises: First, because the first part of the
book refers to the kingdom of Judah and its inhabitants, whereas the
latter part deals with the Babylonian exiles. A time span of about one
hundred and fifty years is involved, from the fall of Israel in 722 B.C.E.
to the Babylonian exile which began with the destruction of Jerusalem
and the Temple in 586 B.C.E. Second, the first part of the book contains
the stirring warnings by Isaiah of the future, whereas the second portion, from Chapter XL to the close of the book, treats with messages of

comfort and hope to a depressed people. Known as the Book of Consolations, it is from the Book of Isaiah, beginning with Chapter XL, that the *haftarah*—prophetic portion of the week—is read for seven successive Sabbaths in the synagogue after Tisha B'av, the Ninth Day of Ab, national day of Jewish mourning.

Isaiah, the son of Amoz, is a native of Jerusalem, born into an aristocratic family whose connections with royalty allow for Isaiah's freedom of movement within the king's palace and ready access to the monarch himself. His prophetic work and ministry covers the period extending from 740 to 701 B.C.E. during the reigns of Kings Uzziah, Jothan, Ahaz, and Hezekiah of Judah, the southern kingdom. He is a child when the prophet Amos speaks at Beth-el, and he is a young man when the prophet Hosea pleads with Israel to return to the ways of the God of Abraham, Isaac and Jacob. His teachings reveal that he garnered much wisdom from both of his antecedents.

Isaiah calls his wife "the prophetess," and the two sons of whom we know have names symbolic of the ideas in which he so fervently believed. One son is called Maher-shalal-hash-baz—Speed-booty-hasten-prey—incorporating the direly frightening warning of impending disaster. Isaiah realizes incisively that Assyria of the North presses to swoop on little Judah. He called his second son Shear-Yashub—a remnant shall return—to express his conviction that while destruction may overtake Judah, a small yet significant remnant will survive into the future of the nation.

The prophet lives through a succession of political crises in connection with the intervention of Assyria in western Asia epitomized by history: the Syro-Ephraimitish War of 734 B.C.E., the fall of Samaria in 722 B.C., the seige of Ashdod by Sargon in 711 B.C., the death of Sargon in 705 B.C.E., and the invasion of Sennacherib in 701 B.C.E.

The prophet witnesses the destruction and disappearance of Israel. He looks now beyond the event he has seen, southward to Judah, still existing. He fears that Judah too might suffer a similar fate. He feels impelled to warn little Judah and pleads fervently with Judah not to become entangled in politics and intrigue with neighboring nations. In addition, he urges that Judah keep its internal world and structure untainted from evil and idolatry.

With the fall of Israel, founded by Jeroboam ben Nebat after Solomon's death, Judah remains alone in Palestine. The ten tribes composing the Northern Kingdom have lost their identity. Only Judah, the southern kingdom founded by Rehoboam, son of King Solomon, remains. Judah is now the only source through which the Torah and its teachings will continue, the only avenue by which the heritage of Abraham, Isaac, and Jacob can be transmitted to posterity.

THE PROPHETS

The prophet of faith, Isaiah towers as a sublime figure in Jewish history, believing with all his heart and mind and soul in the supremacy of the spiritual over worldly powers, the potency of high ideas and ideals over brute force and military might. To combine such a lofty faith with practical statesmanship—since the prophet is essentially a person of action—is an achievement worthy of the greatest persons of any era.

With the clarity of his prophetic vision, Isaiah sees the abuse of power, the evil, greed, injustice, and hatred of people. He regards the abuse of established sacrificial system as having degenerated into desecration and not a pure worship of God. His innate sense of justice and moral righteousness move him to speak out against all injustice, wrongdoing, and unethical conduct in the day-to-day activities of the people. In brilliant, flowing style and with vivid imagery, Isaiah inveighs bitterly against the current perversion of religion in idolatrous worship. With a passion born of deep spiritual fervor, he soars to heights of oratorical splendor as he bears down on the distortion of religious principles which have deviated so far from the laws of Moses.

Isaiah speaks to the mind and addresses himself to the heart in utterances which are both dramatic, expressive, incisive, and yet healing and comforting, knowing that the human spirit is frail. Thus he establishes rapport with his listeners, a master of the spoken word, the fiery orator, the passionate exponent and seeker after truth.

Isaiah views the relationship of people to the Holy One of Israel as direct and personal. God is omnipotent, majestic, universal—Lord of all the world. Israel is the Chosen People, which imposes special duties and demands absolute faith and the living of a moral life. Israel's destiny is to teach the message of religion to all the people of the world. To deviate from the holiness of God is a defilement. Worship alone is not sufficient. It must be coupled with proper living. Thus God's sovereignty is basic. God is Lord over all the earth and concerned with all that happens within it. True, evil exists and sometimes prevails, but punishment will follow as surely as night follows day. Retribution, however, will not be so intense as to destroy the world. "The saving remnant" will survive and will be firmly rooted in Zion, the Holy City, from which will flow inspiration to all people so that they will recognize and accept God as their monarch. This acceptance will precede the messianic era when peace will reign throughout the world.

The Book of Isaiah begins with a strong denunciation of the people, who are condemned because they have forsaken the Lord and the Lord's commandments, have misunderstood the Lord's principles and abused them. Their punishment will be removal from the homeland. God speaks:

Children have I reared and brought up,
And they have rebelled against Me.
The ox knows his owner
And the donkey his master's crib;
But Israel does not know,
My people does not consider.
Ah! Sinful nation. . . .

(Chapter I, Verses 2-4.)

Isaiah chastises the people for having misconstrued the purpose of prayer and religion, relying on ritual alone which cannot compensate for evildoing and unrighteousness. The observance of the ritual of offering sacrifices does not in itself signify that the worshiper is living righteously.

What is the value of your many sacrifices? I have had enough of them. I do not want nor desire them. Do not bring them to me anymore. They are worthless. They are a burden to me. Instead of bringing them, look to yourselves, wash yourselves and purify yourselves. Make yourselves clean. Put away evil which you may be doing. Learn to do well. Seek justice, relieve the oppressed, judge the fatherless, and plead for the orphan and widow. Come, let us reason together. We can change all this. We can change the evil which exists, and the sins you are committing, if you are but willing and obedient. (Chapter I.)

Isaiah prophesies destruction for transgressors, glory for those who heed the words of God. Justice will be the redemption of Zion.

Through a shimmering, golden haze, Isaiah envisions the euphoric, gloriously magnificent messianic days of the future, in the long-familiar portrayal of the Prophet's Golden Age:

It shall come to pass in the end of days,
That the mountain of the Lord's house shall be established as the top of the mountains,
And shall be exalted above the hills;
All the nations shall flow to it

And many peoples shall go and say
"Come, and let us go up to the mountain of the Lord,
To the house of the God of Jacob;
He will teach us His ways,
And we will walk in His paths."
For out of Zion will go forth the Law (Torah),
And the word of the Lord from Jerusalem.
He shall judge between the nations,
And shall decide for many peoples;
They shall beat their swords into plowshares,
And their spears into pruning-hooks;
Nations shall not lift up sword against nation,
Nor shall they know war any more.

(Chapter II, Verses 2-5.)

In Isaiah's philosophy, the love of God transcends the chosen people of Israel; it embraces all of mankind. Since Israel has been given special care and protection, this divine concern should have elicited a more loving and obedient response. Israel should have produced better fruit, more noble people with greater adherence to God's commandments, more righteousness and justice. Conversely, Israel has instead produced "wild grapes," negative responses to God's call. Isaiah graphically depicts this theme in his parable of the vineyard, capturing the attention of his listeners with a familiar subject.

My friend had a vineyard.
It was on a very fruitful hill.
He dug it, cleared it, and planted it with the choicest vines.
Then he built a watchtower in the middle of it and had a winepress installed there.
He then hoped that it would yield grapes—good, sweet, delicious grapes.
But he was disappointed . . .
The earth yielded wild, sour grapes. . . .
What should be done with the vineyard?
What more could any friend have done for it?
He has done all he could. Why should it have brought wild grapes? What went wrong? What was wrong?
What should he do now?

(Chapter V, Verses 1-5.)

The prophet answers his own questions. He will remove the fence of protection. The vineyard will be trampled upon and destroyed. The moral of the parable is brought into sharp focus. The vineyard symbolizes the house of Israel. God sought justice but found violence. God looked for righteousness. God heard only the cries of those oppressed by unrighteousness inflicted upon them by other people. God's anger is aroused, especially against those who wilfully distort and do evil.

Woe to those who call evil good and good evil;
Who change darkness into light
And light into darkness;
Who present bitter into sweet
And sweet into bitter.
Woe to those who are wise in their own eyes
And prudent in their own sight. . . .
(Chapter V, Verses 20-21.)

The God of Israel is patient and will always be ready to listen to the pleas of God's children, according to the hopefulness of the prophet.

The sixth chapter describes Isaiah's selection to prophecy and to his service of the ministry. He speaks in the first person, dramatically, from the courts of the Temple, portraying the Almighty sitting on a high and exalted throne. Above God hover the seraphim (angelic beings), each with six wings. They call to each other in a chant which has become part of the daily and festival synagogue service, underscoring Isaiah's basic concept of God:

Holy, holy, holy is the Lord of hosts;
The whole earth is full of His glory.
(Chapter VI, Verse 3.)

This supremely majestic passage has been called the quintessence of all prophetic teachings and true religion. It clearly differentiates between God and people, evaluating God's perfection and purity and embracing all the world as God's own domain.

The contrast of God's holiness is overwhelming. Isaiah experiences a deep sense of humility, feels that he is unclean in the presence of such divine purity. One of the seraphim grasps a glowing stone, flies with it to Isaiah, touches his mouth with it, and tells him his sins have been removed; he is forgiven and purged of impurity. Then Isaiah, finding his voice, describes the call:

Then I heard the voice of the Lord saying,
"Whom shall I send,
And who will go for us?"
And then I said, "Here I am. Send me!"
(Chapter VI, Verse 8.)

God bids Isaiah go forth to tell the people of Judah that punishment for wrongdoing is forthcoming. This warning is softened by the comforting reassurance that a remnant, even as small as a tenth, will remain, which will be the seed of the eventual salvation of Israel.

In chapter after chapter of this literary masterpiece, Isaiah combines his political astuteness with a passionate championship of God's cause. He sees Assyria gaining in power, yet he envisions Assyria as the implement of God, sent to impose punishment for evildoing. Assyria, he says, will not endure, so there is little reason for Israel to ally itself politically with her.

Almost immediately after his ministry begins, Isaiah's challenge comes. (Chapter VII.) The kings of Israel and Aram have formed an alliance against Assyria. They plan to impose a king on Judah, to join the alliance and, to prove their determination, lay siege to Jerusalem. Threatened, Ahaz and his people consider turning to Assyria for help.

Isaiah attacks the decision because it is sacrilegious and reveals lack of faith in God. God says to him, "Go forth now to meet Ahaz, you and Shear-Yashub, your son." Isaiah comes to Ahaz and encourages him, in God's name, "Keep calm. Do not be afraid of 'these two tails of smoking firebrands.' They will not succeed." But Ahaz is not convinced.

Isaiah makes another attempt in the name of God. "Ask God to give you a sign to verify my message." Ahaz refuses. "I will not test the Lord," he says. Angered, Isaiah insists that God will indeed give him a sign: "A young woman will conceive, bear a son, and will call him Immanuel, (meaning, 'with us is God'). He will eat curds and honey but before he can distinguish good from bad, the land whose kings you fear will be forsaken." Isaiah thus tells Ahaz that the two kings who are striving with human forces are no match because *immanu-el*, with us is God. Ahaz does not listen to the prophet's exhortation.

A number of statements in Isaiah posit names reflective of concepts and divine goals. Isaiah's sons are called *She'ar-Yashub*, (Chapter VII, 3) meaning *a remnant will return* and *Maher-Shalal-bash-baz* (Chapter VIII, 1, 3) meaning *pillage hastens-looting speeds,* or *the spoil speeds, the prey hastens.* Ahaz's son is called *Pele-joez-el gibbor* (Chapter IX, 5) meaning *wonderful in counsel is God the mighty, the everlasting Father, the Ruler of Peace,* or *the mighty God is planning grace; the Eternal Father, a peaceable ruler.* (See also, Chapter XXV, 1, "O Lord, You are my God, I shall extol You, I will praise Your name. For You have done marvelous things, counseled us in faithfulness and truth.")

So also *immanuel,* which is further recorded in Chapter VIII, 8, and 10. Verse 10 reads: "Take counsel together and it shall be foiled; speak words and it shall not succeed, for *immanuel,* God is with us."

This verse forms the lyrics of a folk-song sung especially on Purim, Feast of Lots. (See, Story of Esther.)

Isaiah's exhortations and condemnations of wrong thunder through the pages with sublime cadence:

Woe to them who decree unrighteous decrees,
And to the writers who write iniquity;
To turn aside the needy from judgment,
And to take away the right of the poor of My people,
That their widows may be their spoil
And that they make the fatherless their prey.

(Chapter X, Verses 1, 2.)

As Isaiah's attacks against unrighteousness gain in intensity, so do his assurances and hopes for redemption. He promises that a great future will spring from the remnant of Israel; that indestructible spirit will be its nucleus.

A remnant will return, even the remnant of Jacob, to God the Mighty.

(Chapter X, Verse 21.)

Surging through the words of Isaiah is the magic ingredient of hope.

A shoot shall come forth from the stock of Jesse,
A twig out of his roots.
The spirit of the Lord shall rest upon him,

The spirit of wisdom and understanding,
The spirit of counsel and might,
The spirit of knowledge and the fear of the Lord.
His delight shall be in the fear of the Lord;
He shall not judge after the sight of his eyes,
Nor decide after the hearing of his ears;
But with righteousness shall he judge the poor,
And decide with equity for the meek of the land;
He shall smite the land with the rod of his mouth,
With the breath of his lips will he slay the wicked.
Righteousness shall be the girdle of his loins,
Faithfulness the girdle of his reins.
The wolf shall dwell with the lamb,
The leopard shall lie down with the kid;
The calf and the young lion and the fatling together;
And a little child shall lead them.
The cow and the bear shall feed;
Their young ones shall lie down together;
The lion shall eat straw like the ox.
And the babe shall play on the hole of the asp,
And the child shall put his hand on the basilisk's den.
They shall not hurt nor destroy
In all My holy mountain;
For the earth shall be full of the knowledge of the Lord,
As the waters cover the sea.
It shall come to pass on that day,
That the Lord will set His hand again a second time
To recover the remnant of His people . . .
He shall assemble the dispersed of Israel,
And gather together the scattered of Judah
From the four corners of the earth.
And there shall be a highway for the remnant of His people.
(Chapter XI, Verse 1-9, 11, 12, 16.)

In the messianic days, men will express their gratitude to God, the Lord of all men, recognizing God as the Holy One of Israel.

Give thanks unto the Lord, proclaim His name . . .
For great is the Holy One in your midst.
(Chapter XII, Verses 4, 6.)

Many nations will be doomed, Isaiah prophesies, the great and mighty ones will fall—Babylonia, Moab, Syria, Egypt, Arabia, and Phoenicia. He commingles denunciation of evil kingdoms with promises of salvation, many of his prophecies beginning with the words, "In that day." With terrifying drama, he reveals the wasteland to which the earth will be reduced, while he remains staunch in his faith in God's justice and righteousness.

Isaiah's vision foretells the tragic destruction of the holy city of Jerusalem, the proud City of David. The contents of Chapter XXXVIII and XXXIX are similar to the material in the II Kings. Hezekiah, recovered from his grave illness, receives the envoys of Babylon gladly, showing them his treasure-house. He is rebuked by Isaiah, who foretells the days when all the wealth of Temple, palace and city stored up from antiquity will be carried away to Babylon. Isaiah's unrolled scroll of prophecy becomes historical fact.

A new theme enters the pages of the Book of Isaiah with Chapter XL. Attributed by many biblical scholars to another whom they call Isaiah, the Isaiah of the Exile or the Second Isaiah, the writings henceforth are similar in grandeur of ideas, ideals, and in literary beauty, and therefore become a natural portion of the book. All that Isaiah has prophesied is now a reality. The kingdom of Judah has been destroyed, its people carried away to bondage in what has come to be known as the Babylonian Exile, Jerusalem razed, the Temple treasures appropriated. Now great Babylon, the conqueror, is itself about to be destroyed as Cyrus, King of Persia, rides the crest of power.

This monarch is Cyrus II, who became king in 558 B.C.E. His first successful rebellion was against the Medians. He plundered Ecbatana and took its king prisoner, after which he called himself king of the Persians. Soon after the conquest of the Median empire, Cyrus is attacked by a coalition of Babylonia, Egypt, and Sparta, greatest military power of Greece. (In fourteen years, Persia is so strong that Babylon is compelled to surrender to the great Persian general Gobyras in 539. With the fall of the Babylonian capital, the Babylonian provinces in Syria fall to Persia.) From the year 538 B.C.E. Cyrus calls himself also the King of Babylonia and of the countries (of the world).

In Cyrus, the Jewish people see a shining light of salvation, a burning hope, the hand of God sent to redeem them. Cyrus is the instrument of God to fulfill the promises God has made. For his part, Cyrus believes it his divine mission to free the Jews for their return to Palestine and for the rebuilding of Jerusalem and its sacred Temple. The cylinder bearing his historic proclamation, which is included in the work of Ezra and

Nehemiah, is, in fact, among the scanty original sources about this great king.

In its supreme hour, Isaiah speaks comfortingly to a people discouraged and disheartened by a long exile:

Be comforted, be comforted, My people, says your God.
Bid Jerusalem take heart and proclaim to her,
That her time of service is over,
That her guilt is paid off;
That she has received at the Lord's hand
Double for all her sins.
Hark! one calls;
Clear in the wilderness the way of the Lord
Make clear in the desert
A highway for our God.

(Chapter XL, Verses 1-3.)

Isaiah calls on his people to acknowledge God's greatness and providential care:

Do you not know? Do you not hear?
Has it not been told you from the beginning?
Have you not understood the foundations of the earth?
It is He who sits above the circle of the earth,
And its inhabitants are as grasshoppers,
Who stretches out the heavens as a curtain,
And spreads them out as a tent to live in. . . .
Look up and see. Who created these?
He who brings out their host by number,
He who calls them all by name,
By the greatness of His might and for that He is strong
in power
Not one fails.

(Chapter XL, Verses 21, 22, 26.)

Chapter XL is the first of seven *haftaroth*, prophetic portions, recited in the synagogue from the fast day known as Tisha B'Av, considered the national day of mourning, until the Sabbath of Repentance between

Rosh Hashanah and Yom Kippur. The name of the Sabbath on which this chapter is read is taken from its first word, Na-cha-mu—"be you comforted." The Sabbath is called the Sabbath of Comfort.

Isaiah has been called the Prophet of the Restoration. Israel will be restored and will be a light unto the nations of the world:

But you, Israel, my servant,
Jacob, whom I have chosen,
The seed of Abraham My friend;
You whom I have taken hold of from the ends of the earth,
And called you from the most distant parts;
And said to you, "You are My servant,"
I have chosen you and have not cast you away,
Do not fear, for I am with you. . . .
(Chapter XLI, Verses 8-10.)

Behold My servant, whom I uphold;
My elect, in whom I delight;
I have put My spirit upon him,
He will make the right to go forth to the nations . . .
I, the Lord, have called you in righteousness,
And have taken hold of your hand.
And kept you, and set you for a covenant of the people,
For a light of the nations . . .
(Chapter XLII, Verses 1, 6.)

For I am the Lord your God,
The Holy One of Israel, your savior.
(Chapter XLIII, Verse 3.)

The position of Israel is that of a witness for God, to the end that every generation shall know, understand and believe in God as the Creator of heaven and earth and the Savior of mankind.

You are my witnesses, says the Lord,
And My servant whom I have chosen;
That you may know and believe Me, and understand
that I am He.

The Prophets

Before Me no God was formed,
Nor will any be after Me.

(Chapter XLIII, Verse 10.)

In God, Israel has inexhaustible, unlimited strength. God will not fail to carry through His great purposes for mankind through Israel, God's servant. Their faith in God will engender strength and courage in themselves. And should they feel that their small number militates against fulfilling their destiny, God who has created a design for their lives as the light unto the nations, reminds them that their forefather Abraham was a lone person when God allied him in service. They are reassured not to fear, not to be concerned, for "I am with you."

Isaiah continues his mission to encourage the people. He speaks of the fate of the nations who oppose the will of God. He tells them over and over again that their sufferings will not be in vain. They will become stronger in loyalty because of it. There was plan and purpose for their tears. What was that high purpose? That the Israelites become messengers of God to mankind. As God's messengers, Israel is to teach righteousness, morality, justice. In passages of rare beauty and spiritual depth, Isaiah speaks of the "servant of the Lord." Israel is God's collective servant, the dedicated minority willing to bear suffering and even to die for their faith. This small group is cognizant of the fact that it performs a sacred duty for God and humanity.

Dramatically, with sustained suspense, Isaiah develops Israel's historic, destined role as God's collective servant. Israel is God's suffering servant. In chapter after chapter God speaks words of encouragement to Israel which suffered despairingly, as in the Babylonian exile, where Israel was attacked, despised by other people. God had never rejected Israel. A small group called *the remnant*—an eternal divine spark imbedded within them—always waited patiently for the redemption, for assurance that Israel would be the light unto the nations. "I will make you a light of the nations." (Chapter XLIX, 6) They will yet see the great astounding transformation of Israel from humiliation to exaltation, from a suffering tantamount to martyrdom, to an ultimately exhilarating triumph and restoration. They will marvel at the incredible change which will come to a people forsaken, pained, diseased, crushed—almost destroyed. But not completely. God, the Redeemer of Israel, would not permit it; God would fulfill the promise. "Behold, My servant will prosper. He will be exalted and raised to great heights." (Chapter LII, 15)

The climax of Isaiah's portrayal of Israel's extraordinary powers of en-

durance and survival is expressed in the words of those who would see
the remarkable transformation.

"Who would have believed our report,
  (Who can believe what we have heard?)
To whom has the strength of the Lord been revealed?
He shot up like a sapling
Like a root out of dry ground."
                                        (Chapter LIII, Verse 1.)

God would now, says the prophet, create a new heaven and a new
earth. God who created the heavens and the earth in the very beginning, will now, through the righteous remnant, establish:

I have put My words in your mouth,
And I have covered you in the shadow of My hand,
That I may plant the heavens,
And lay the foundations of the earth,
And say to Zion, "You are My people."
                                        (Chapter LI, Verse 16.)

Israel is to be the instrument through which the new conception of
heaven and earth will be established. Heaven is to be construed in human terms of righteousness, mercy and justice, truth and peace, the
ideals taught by Israel, the collective servant of God. Then Zion (Israel)
will arise, redeemed, restored, ready to assume its rightful place among
the nations.

Awake, awake
Put on your strength, O Zion;
Put on your beautiful robes,
O Jerusalem, the holy city . . .
How beautiful upon the mountains
Are the feet of the messenger of good tidings,
Who announces peace, the harbinger of good tidings,
Who announces salvation;
Who says to Zion;

'Your God reigns!'
Hark, your watchmen lift up their voices,
Together do they sing;
For they will see, eye to eye,
The Lord returning to Zion.

(Chapter LII, Verses 1, 7-8.)

The call goes out to all people everywhere to put aside evil and wrongdoing:

Seek the Lord while He may be found,
Call upon Him while He is near. . . .

(Chapter LV, Verse 6.)

Keep justice and do righteousness. . . .

(Chapter LVI, Verse 1.)

A redeemer will come to Zion,
And to those who turn from transgression in Jacob;
Says the Lord: This is My covenant with them, says the
   Lord; My spirit which is upon you,
And My words which I have put into your mouth,
Will not depart from your mouth, nor from the mouth of
   your children,
Nor from the mouth of your children's children
Says the Lord, from now and forever.

(Chapter LIX, Verses 20, 21.)

Isaiah's message moves to its climax. Zion will be restored, transformed, a light and glory for all humankind. He proclaims the glories of Jerusalem in the end of days. The long era of suffering is to draw to a close. Rising to the greatest of oratorical heights, Isaiah's words roll forth in a stream of eloquence:

Arise, shine, for your light has come,
And the glory of the Lord has risen upon you.
For, indeed, darkness will cover the earth,
And great darkness upon peoples;
But upon you the Lord will arise,

And His glory will be seen upon you.
Nations will walk by your light,
And kings at the brightness of your rising. . . .
(Chapter LX, Verses 1-3.)

For, behold, I create a new heaven
And a new earth;
The past will not be remembered,
Nor come to mind.
Be glad and rejoice forever
In that which I create;
For I create Jerusalem as a rejoicing,
And her people as a joy,
And I will rejoice in Jerusalem,
And rejoice in My people,
The voice of weeping shall be no more heard there,
Nor the voice of crying. . . .
For they are the children blessed of the Lord,
And their offspring with them.
Before they call, I will answer,
And while they are yet speaking, I will hear.
The wolf and the lamb shall feed together,
And the lion shall eat straw like the ox;
And earth shall be the serpent's food.
They shall not hurt nor destroy
In all My holy mountain,
Says the Lord.
(From Chapter LXV.)

Isaiah, the Prophet of Hope, concludes his message by speaking of the new heaven and the new earth, symbolizing the new order which will be ushered in:

And it will come to pass
That from one new moon to another
And from one Sabbath to another,
Will all come to worship Me,
Says the Lord.
(Chapter LXVI, Verse 23.)

JEREMIAH

SECOND OF THE THREE MAJOR BOOKS OF THE PROPHETS, Jeremiah comprises fifty-two chapters, in contrast to the sixty-six chapters of Isaiah. Nevertheless, Jeremiah in content is the longest of the prophetic books. It contains poetry in the form of actual oracles delivered by the prophet, prose in the first person by Jeremiah, and prose in the third person, giving the account mainly of events in the life of the prophet, and usually this part is attributed to the scribe Baruch.

The son of Hilkiah, Jeremiah is born about 650 B.C.E. in Anathoth (now the Arab village of Anata), a few miles to the northwest of Jerusalem, into an honored, illustrious, and priestly family. He is the last of the great prophets of Judah before the fall of Jerusalem and the exile to Babylon. It is his destiny to perform his ministry and to prophesy during a long period of turbulent, rapidly moving events when world powers rose and declined. Judah is falling—and actually falls, and in a soaring climax of national agony the capital city of Jerusalem is destroyed. The forty years of Jeremiah's divine work end as the long exile of the people of Judah in Babylon begins, to endure until their liberation by Cyrus of Persia.

The historic background which forms the canvas for Jeremiah's ministry is also recorded in the second Book of Kings. Jeremiah's life falls within one of the most striking and critical periods not only of Palestine but in the history of the ancient world. Historically and politically, Assyria, the great power of the times, is beginning to wane in her might. Asshurbanipal, last of the great kings of Assyria, dies in 626 B.C.E. at a

128

time when all western Asia is being laid desolate by the inroads of the hordes of northern barbarians known to the Greeks as Scythians or Cimmerians and to the Babylonians as Umman-manda. Fortunately, they by-pass the interior of Palestine. Babylonia under King Nebuchadnezzar rises to secure domination. Egypt, south of Palestine, always manages to maneuver the kings of Judah, and Judah is caught in the web of intrigue. Judah's kings are confused, do not know which way to turn. Some advisors counsel open battle with Babylon, the ill-advised influence leading to the eventual collapse of the kingdom of Judah.

Jeremiah's work begins in 626 B.C.E. He is an actual witness to the historic event of the complete overthrow of Assyria which culminates in the destruction of the proud capital of Nineveh in the month of Ab of 612. Under the combined attack of Babylonians, Medes, and Scythians, Nineveh becomes a mound of ruins. This is followed by the decisive defeat of Egypt's final attempt at world empire in the battle of Carchemish in 605.

Startling events occur in his own country. In his youth, King Amon, son of King Manasseh, is assassinated in the second year of his reign. The people suppress the revolution; place Amon's son, Josiah, eight years old, on the throne. The prophets Nahum and Zephaniah foresee the oncoming downfall of Nineveh. To the strict followers of Moses, it means a world judgment from which Judah will emerge purified. The uprooting of idolatry, imitation of foreigners, and social injustice is needed. In 621 when King Josiah is twenty-six, he is ready to listen to the anti-Assyrian reform party. It is when the Temple is repaired and restoration in progress that the high priest Hilkiah chances upon a copy of the Torah of Moses, sequestered by Manasseh or immured during the repairs of King Jehoash, if not the very volume deposited at the time of the building of the Temple by Solomon. In 621 occurs the great reform of King Josiah, who meets a tragic end in the battle against the Egyptians at Megiddo in 609. He is succeeded by his son Jehoahaz, who reigns three months, then is removed to Egypt where he dies. Judah becomes a vassal in turn of Egypt and of Babylon, and it is in rebelling against Babylon in 597 that she suffers consequent invasion, siege, and deportation of her young king Jehoiachin and the finest of her people. Jehoiachin's uncle and successor, Zedekiah, after years of vacillation, yields to the machinations of his corrupt nobility and to the intrigues of Egypt, with the ultimate result that the kingdom of Judah perishes in 586 with the climactic capture of Jerusalem and the destruction of Solomon's Temple.

When Judah suffers from Scythian raids on its coast, and even Jerusalem is threatened, Jeremiah's call comes in the thirteenth year of Josiah's reign. While Jeremiah approves the sweeping reforms of Josiah, deprecating the exaggerated value placed on the sacrificial cult, it is easy to understand the hostility of his own family (Jeremiah XI, Verses 18-20, and XII, Verse 6) if he were concerned in a movement that will deprive the priests of Anathoth of their ancestral rights. The prophet has a deep respect for King Josiah. The reaction under his son Jehoiakim, who is friendly to Egypt, calls for the condemnation of Jeremiah when his boldness endangers his life.

With all of his heart, in emotional outbursts, in tragic, heartful pleading, Jeremiah urges the kings to make peace with Babylon. But his words are regarded as treasonable and he is shunned, disdained, humiliated, and degraded. Add to the historical, political and external circumstances affecting Judah, another—and perhaps more difficult—disturbance exists in the land. In terms of religion, corruption and wrongdoing are common. Idol-worship is rampant. Sacrifices are offered without inner feeling. Jeremiah inveighs fearlessly against these evils. He foresees that the evil practices of the day will only bring punishment in their wake.

He calls on the people to repent their wrongdoing and to return to the paths of God and of their ancestors. He is not opposed to ritual and ceremony. They need, he avers, emotional strength and significance to be of value. Like Ezekiel, he berates the assumption among the people that the Temple in itself serves as a protection for them. No, indeed, thunders the prophet, the Temple cannot make them more secure. It is a physical structure and its existence does not create religiousness. This must come from within, from their inner beings, their feelings, attitudes, and deeds.

Both kingdom and people of Judah are caught in the vortex of conflict. Jeremiah as a person finds himself embroiled in his own nature. He is a gentle, sensitive, reticent, peace-loving, introspective person, opposed to violence. Yet, when the call to be a prophet of God comes to him, he takes his role earnestly. Tender, shy, of a nervous temperament, with a deep-rooted love of nature and of man, his temperament demands a life of quiet domestic obscurity. His calling and his devotion to God demands that he live a life of lonely publicity, always on the unpopular side, always confronted with the disaster which finally overwhelms his country, always conscious of sharing in responsibility for evils which he is so powerless to avert or to postpone. His is a double passion, a love of his people and a love of God: the longing of his heart is to see his people validly wedded to the God of their forebears; and the tragedy of his life lies in the steady drift of the children of Israel away from the God of Abraham, Isaac, and Jacob.

Few characters in history have stronger claims on our affection and sympathy than Jeremiah. A man of fluctuating moods, he is variously called the weeping prophet, the prophet of sorrows, or a man of great problems. His audiences are angry, disrespectful, so that he often despairs; his disappointments and frustrations are many. Grief overcomes him often, pain and hurt are his lot. He emerges out of his periods of despondency, soaring on wings of poetry and prose to heights of exaltation. His love of God and of his people inspire him to persist and to carry onward, no matter what the response, as he looks beyond the present, holding out a message of hope and faith. He does not hesitate to condemn those about him who deserve to be denounced. At the same time, his message is hopeful, portraying a glorious era, a new covenant with God, a yet closer, more personal relationship, and restoration of the kingdom of the children of Israel.

The faith of Jeremiah is contagious. There is a complete honesty and sincerity in him, creating admiration, almost love for the prophet. There grows a sense of close affiliation with his ideals through understanding. The strength of the prophet transfers itself to his listeners and to his readers so that he becomes real across the shoals of time. We look deeply into the lives of a people through the narrative of the prophet as the chapters of the Book of Jeremiah unfold.

The first chapter vividly describes Jeremiah's call to service as God's prophet. Simple, dramatic, succinct, yet encompassing, it is presented in dialogue form. God speaks. Jeremiah answers. Jeremiah learns that his role has been predestined. He does not readily accept. He pleads shyness, timidity, incapability, immaturity. God is insistent that he must accept the divine call to the ministry. God in turn promises Jeremiah that the Lord will be with him always, and encourages him to be fearless in word and deed.

Jeremiah experiences two visions. They are portents of the message to be proclaimed to the people. The first is an almond tree, signifying that God is awake and will fulfill the word. The second is a seething pot or caldron, facing the north. This symbolizes the direction from which Israel, the ten tribes of Israel, met destruction years before. From the north the Assyrian invasions originated. Judah, also, will be destroyed from the north.

When the visions are completed, the introductory chapter bringing Jeremiah on to the scene of history, ends with an added word of inspiration. Jeremiah is told that he has a strong position to maintain. It will, however, be placed in jeopardy because the people will prove unwilling to listen. They will fight against him, seek to destroy him, but he will prevail, for God will be at his side throughout his ministry.

*   *   *

Jeremiah begins immediately to speak to the people. He recalls their
history, their past. In earlier days the people were loyal to God, holy to
God.

I remember for you the affection of your youth,
The love of your espousals,
How you followed Me in the wilderness,
In a land that was not sown,
Israel is the Lord's hallowed portion. . . .
(Jeremiah II, Verses 2, 3.)

When Israel entered Palestine, a strange change transpired. Safely
arrived in the Promised Land, they began to desert God and to worship
false, strange gods familiar to the people of their new surroundings.
Israel strayed from the path of God and began to do evil, to pursue
wealth.

Jeremiah portrays the relationship of Israel and God as that of a loyal,
devoted bride to her bridegroom. It must have been true love which
drew her and impelled her to follow God. Israel's love of God must have
been the reason for the willingness to endure the hardships of the their
wanderings in the wilderness. Then Israel began to regress from God's
path, not wanting to remember the close relationship, their covenant
with God. For this reason, the people must be considered guilty. Yet,
God, they must know, is always ready to pardon people and to restore
them to favor if they but put aside their evil and turn back.

Return, you backsliding Israel,
Says the Lord,
I will not frown upon you;
For I am merciful, says the Lord. . . .
(Chapter III, Verse 12.)
If you will return, O Israel,
Says the Lord,
Yes, return to Me;
And if you will put away your detestable things out of
   My sight,
And will not waver;
And will swear: "As the Lord lives"

In truth, in justice, and in righteousness;
Then shall the nations bless themselves by Him
And in Him will they glory.

(Chapter IV, Verses 1, 2.)

Jeremiah's thinking conveys a thought and then sees reality. A hope is projected, and then he returns to things as they are. He summons his people to halt their faithlessness, picturing the enemy out of the north who poses ready to heap destruction upon them. However, the people can deter catastrophe even though the moment is so close at hand. Jeremiah notes dejectedly that they are too far entrenched in their evil practices for salvation. There is no hope of return. False prophets prophesy and the people listen, are influenced by them, and revel exuberantly in their wicked practices.

This people has a revolting and rebellious heart;
They have revolted and gone away. . . .
For among My people there are wicked men;
They pry, as fowlers lie in wait;
They set a trap to catch men.
As a cage is full of birds,
So are their homes full of deceit;
Therefore they have become great and wealthy;
They have become fat, they have become sleek;
Yes, they surpass the bounds of wickedness;
They do not plead the cause, the cause of the fatherless,
    yet they prosper;
The right of the needy they do not judge.
Shall I not punish for all these things?
Says the Lord;
Shall not My soul be avenged
On such a nation as this?

(Chapter V, Verses 23, 26-29.)

In these denouncing, condemnatory words, one senses the element of pleading, of hopefulness. God does not want to send deserved punishment because God loves Israel and because of Israel's earlier loyalty and devotion. It is as if God expresses anguish and pain because of the forthcoming destruction. The door is left open for the children of Israel to come back to the Lord.

God sends Jeremiah to preach to the people at the gates of the Holy Temple. A huge multitude assembles. His subject is social evils. He delivers blasting denunciations of wrongdoing. They must mend their ways before they can be forgiven. They cannot assume they can hide behind the structure of the Holy Temple as their protective mantle. It will not help them, unless they themselves correct their ways of life. The Temple, and the offering of sacrifices, do not guarantee salvation from the impending dangers. They cannot expect to practice evil and cry out, "We are delivered. We are saved."

Correct your ways and your doings and I will cause you to dwell in this place. Trust not in lying words, saying, "The Temple of the Lord, the Temple of the Lord, the Temple of the Lord, are these." If you indeed correct your ways and doing, if you perform justice between man and his neighbor, if you do not oppress the stranger, the fatherless, and the widow, and do not shed innocent blood in this place, nor walk after other gods to your own detriment, then will I cause you to dwell in this place, in the land which I gave to your fathers, for ever and ever. You rely on lying words that cannot profit. Will you steal, murder, commit adultery, swear falsely, offer to Baal, walk after other gods whom you have not known, and then come and stand before Me in this house which bears My name and say, "We are delivered," to do all these abominations? Has this house by which My name is called become a den of robbers in your eyes? I have seen it, says the Lord. (Chapter VII, Verses 3-11.)

God prepares Jeremiah for the reality of his situation. He will warn but his warnings will go unheeded. The people will have to endure the penalty for their blindness in refusing to depart from the ways to which they are long accustomed which are evil in the eyes of God. Deeply grieved, Jeremiah mourns: "My heart is faint within me . . . woe is me for my hurt, my wound is grievous." He so clearly sees the impending eruption of a volcano, the hot lava streaming down the mountain sides, voraciously engulfing all in its wake while the people in its furious path refuse to depart and save themselves. Suppressing his personal feelings of disappointment in the obtuseness of his people, the prophet still realizes God's greatness, omnipotence and omnipresence. Proclaiming the

JEREMIAH

very omniscience of God, he rises to glorify the Lord:

There is none like You, O Lord;
You are great, and Your name is great in might. . . .
The Lord God is the true God,
He is the living God and the everlasting King. . . .
(Chapter X, Verses 6, 10.)

In this enduring faith, Jeremiah finds his consolation. In his clarity of vision, he knows that salvation awaits all who have this faith and trust.

Once again, Jeremiah is sent to the people of Judah. This time he is to declare the terms of the covenant. God persists in the desire to bring Judah back. Jeremiah goes forth and speaks:

Listen to My voice. Observe the terms as I command you, so that you will be My people and I will be your God; that I may establish the promise which I swore to your ancestors, to give them a land flowing with milk and honey. (Chapter XI, Verses 4, 5.)

Jeremiah's prophetic words fall on deaf ears. He learns that a conspiracy has developed against him. For the first time in prophetic literature, Jeremiah raises the eternal question, "Why do the wicked prosper?" God responds that Jeremiah must learn patience, that this will not be the only time he will be plotted against. There will be further conspiracies, more intensive attacks and trials launched against him; he will have to withstand them and remain strong as God's minister.

Continuing undeterred, Jeremiah foretells the coming destruction to be rained upon Judah, his message becoming more graphic and more sharply delineated. He employs symbols so that the people may more readily grasp his meaning. There is still time in which they may yet take steps to ward off the coming darkness. Within his heart, however, Jeremiah realizes the hour is too late for any staying hand. Change is not possible. Salvation is not possible.

Can the Ethiopian change his skin? or the leopard his spots? Then can you also do good, you who are accustomed to do evil? (Chapter XIII, Verse 23.)

Jeremiah introspectively considers his personal position. He is obligated to deliver God's messages, although they are unpopular. People are content with life as it is, its comforts, its associations of security, whereas he, as a person, has become identified with his unpopular platform. He is despised and shunned.

Woe is me, my mother, that you bore me.
A man of strife and a man of contention to the whole earth!
I have not lent, nor have men lent to me;
Yet everyone of them curses me.

(Chapter XV, Verse 10.)

Jeremiah speaks his heart. Now that calamity approaches which people can readily understand. A severe drought afflicts Judah so that vegetation, both garden and grain crops, as well as the herds of cattle and other livestock, are parched for want of rain. The people thereupon confess their sins and cry out to God for help as of old. And Jeremiah pleads with God in behalf of the suffering people. The response is negative. Jeremiah loves his people. It grieves him to see their distress.

Added to the grief of unpopularity, Jeremiah now finds his loneliness unbearable as God draws him away from his fellowmen.

You, O Lord, know,
Remember me, and think of me, and avenge me of my
    persecutors;
Take me not away because of Your long-suffering;
Know that for Your sake I have suffered taunts.
Your words were found, and I did eat them;
And your words were a joy to me and the rejoicing
    of my heart;
Because Your name was called on me,
O Lord God of hosts.
I did not sit in the assembly of those who make merry,
    and rejoice;
I sat alone because of Your hand;
For You have filled me with indignation.
Why is my pain unceasing,

And my wound incurable, so that it refuses to be healed?
Will You indeed be a deceitful brook to me
Like the waters that fail?

(Chapter XV, Verses 15-18.)

Jeremiah does not hesitate to express his bitterness. He knows, however, that only faith and trust in God will help. This applies not only to the people but also to him. God assures him of strength to meet the challenges of his enemies.

At the outset of his career, he received a promise of support in the face of dissenting men. He never was fearful before priest or king or people. Yet in facing his God, he stands alone, often rebelling, sometimes even doubting. The beauty of the character of Jeremiah is projected in all of its poignancy as we understand that his experiences brought him an agony parallel in holy writ only to that of Job, the man of sorrows. Accepting the doctrines and attitude of his towering predecessors, especially the Prophet Hosea, he sees that the union between God and humanity must be spiritual, not material, and he expresses this eternal truth in his proclamation of a "new covenant with the house of Israel." It is to be a covenant of individual faith and direct relationship to God, to be written on the heart.

Faith in God will be the victor. The day will come when everyone will recognize God, when God will bring them all back to their homeland as promised to their fathers. In a passage which contrasts the fate of those who trust in people and those who place their trust in God, similar to the first chapter of the Psalms, Jeremiah confidently declares:

Blessed is the man who trusts in God,
and whose trust God is.
For he will be as a tree planted by the waters,
That spreads out its roots along the river.
And will not see when heat comes,
But its foliage shall be luxuriant;
And will not be anxious in the year of drought,
Nor cease from yielding fruit.

(Chapter XVII, Verses 7-8.)

For the first time in prophetic literature, Jeremiah calls upon the people of Judah to observe the Sabbath day. He stresses its importance. He urges them not to carry burdens, which is forbidden by the Torah. He elicits a promise of Sabbath observance and assures them that this will help to usher in the return of the glorious day: "Then shall there enter in by the gates of this city, kings and princes sitting upon the throne of David, riding in chariots and on horses, they and their princes." They will bring equipment for ritual and sacrifices. Here one notes that the prophet has recognized the value and importance of the beauty of the ritual, and emphasizes that external physical offering of sacrifices is valueless without a spiritual propriety of inner attitude and feeling.

Again, the prophet foretells impending doom through symbols of the potter and the vessel. What does the potter do with a damaged piece of pottery? He repairs it, making it as nearly perfect as possible. Cannot the people of Israel learn a lesson from this? Cannot the people act similarly, mend their ways, and return to their original relationship with God? His message is so well chosen and yet so simple, it succeeds in hitting the mark with much impact. The people are moved, disturbed, and now conspire to do him harm:

Come, let us devise devices against Jeremiah.
For instruction will not perish from the priest,
Nor counsel from the wise, nor the word from the prophet.
Come, let us smite him with the tongue,
Let us not listen to any of his words.

(Chapter XVIII, Verse 18.)

Jeremiah is dispirited. He now cries out to God against his tormentors, against this open antagonism and hostility of the very people he seeks to save. Is it not to help them, for their good, that he preaches? Jeremiah does not become easily disconcerted. He continues the parable of the potter, but adds a note of finality. He portrays the vessel broken, shattered. It cannot be mended, for the damage is beyond repair. Again, Judah is the object of the lesson. Grieve for the people. Grieve for Judah. Grieve for Jerusalem. It is too late, too late for Judah. The people's consciousness finally grasps the significance of the symbol. With this import, they plot against him, imprison him. Once again, Jeremiah, from an anguished heart, cries out in bitter prayer.

I have become a laughing-stock all the day,
Everyone mocks me. . . .

(Chapter XX, Verse 7.)

Yet Jeremiah does not hold his peace. He cannot contain his feelings and thoughts. There is an inner compulsion to express what is in his heart:

And if I say, "I will not make mention of Him,
Nor speak any more in His name,"
Then there is in my heart, as it were, a burning fire
Shut up in my bones,
And I weary myself to contain it,
But cannot.

(Chapter XX, Verse 9.)

Again, Jeremiah personalizes his feelings as he laments his difficult life:

Cursed be the day
In which I was born;
The day which my mother bore me,
Let it not be blessed.

(Chapter XX, Verse 14.)

Jeremiah directs his condemnation to the number of kings of Judah and the false prophets, criticising them severely for their foreign alliances, for misleading the people of Judah and for promises made to the people which cannot be fulfilled. He has special words for the prophets whose assurances of security create lethargy among the people when it is clear to them that the final hour is drawing near, yet they urge the people not to be concerned.

While Jeremiah denounces, he does not preach complete and perpetual darkness. Beyond the destruction certain to come, there is always a better day. He sees the return of a king from the true line of David. He envisages Israel's new glory and prestige among the nations of the world.

Behold, the days come, says the Lord,
That I will raise to David a righteous shoot,
He will rule as king and prosper,
And will execute justice and righteousness in the land.
In his days, Judah will be saved,

Israel will dwell safely;
And this is his name by which he will be called
The Lord is our righteousness.
(Chapter XXIII, Verses 5, 6.)

Employing a symbol to illustrate his message, the prophet describes good and bad figs in comparison to the people of Israel:

One basket had very good figs, like the figs that are first ripe, And the other basket had very bad figs, which could not be eaten, they were so bad. . . .
Thus says the Lord, the God of Israel:
"Like these good figs, so will I regard the captives of Judah. . . . I will set My eyes upon them for good, I will bring them back to this land, and I will build them, and I will plant them. . . .
And I will give them a heart to know Me, that I am the Lord, and they will be My people, and I will be their God; for they will return to Me wholeheartedly." (Chapter XXIV, 2, 5-7.)

As to the bad figs, this foretells the coming of Babylon and Judah's eventual seventy-year exile. Jeremiah's senses are paralyzed as he so vividly foresees impending disaster approaching relentlessly, to which the populace is blind and unprepared to face. He rises to dramatic heights of oratory as he pleads with his people to mend their ways before it is to late. His words are not interpreted as warnings of imminent danger but arouse antagonism, especially among the priests and false prophets, whose positions are threatened.

Jeremiah is arrested. His accusers seek to have him put to death. Their indictment is that he has spoken against the city and deserves to die. Jeremiah does not cower. He maintains that his words were spoken in the name of God and that he is God's messenger, and as such cannot be adjudged guilty.

The Lord sent me to prophesy against this house and against this city all the words which you have heard. Therefore, now mend your ways and your doings. (Chapter XXVI, Verses 12, 13.)

The accusers, impressed with his claim that he speaks the words of God, withdraw their indictment. "This man is not worthy of death, for he has spoken in the name of the Lord our God." (Chapter XXVI, Verse 16.)

The First Captivity has ended. The year is 597 B.C.E. Eight years earlier (605 B.C.E.) the Babylonians rebelled against Assyria, sacked its capital of Nineveh and at the historic battle of Carchemish annihilated the Assyrians. The former Assyrian empire fell into the hands of Babylonia and with it, Judah. After a rule of three years, Judah rebelled. King Nebuchadnezzar came at the head of his combined forces to besiege Jerusalem. Only after three years does Jerusalem capitulate through starvation. Zedekiah, the last king of the house of David, is elevated to the throne of Judah, which aligns itself with Egypt to strike for independence. Again the Babylonian king marches on his enemies. The Egyptians succumb within a few weeks, but the people of Judah hold out for a year and a half. Finally, in the fateful year of 586 B.C.E., the Babylonians breach the walls of Jerusalem. King Zedekiah is captured and the royal family slain. The Temple is destroyed, the city looted and reduced to ruins. Everyone is deported to Babylonia except the poor, the caretakers of the land, the old and ill. This remnant, however, is strong enough to slay Gedaliah, the governor appointed over them by Nebuchadnezzar. Finally, after three wars and three defeats, the kingdom of Judah is at an end—one hundred and thirty-six years after the fall of Israel.

Jeremiah tries to prevent the devastation of Jerusalem by urging King Zedekiah not to ally Judah against Babylon but to retain allegiance with Babylon. The false prophets assure the king that the Babylonian exile is of temporary duration and succeed in influencing him. Jeremiah is rewarded by the king of Babylon for his loyalty by a pension. Concerned for the welfare of the deportees, Jeremiah addresses letters to the exiles in which he counsels them not to expect an early return to Judah, suggesting rather that they plan to live normal lives in Babylonia, prepare for a permanent settlement there, become full citizens and work for the good of their new country. His message has become a classic pronouncement of loyalty to the land of one's residence:

Build houses and live in them. Plant gardens and eat of their fruit. Take wives and have children and take wives for your sons and give your daughters to husbands that they may have sons and daughters and multiply there. Seek the peace of the city where I have caused you to be taken captive, and pray to God for it, for in its peace will you have peace. (Chapter XXIX, Verses 5-7.)

In this message Jeremiah has not only counseled his people to establish permanent residence, but has also taught his brethren that they may worship God in their new land. Prayer to God is not limited nor confined to Judah, Palestine, or Jerusalem. He is telling them, in effect, that their practice of religion is not dependent upon residence in Palestine.

You will call upon Me and go and pray to Me and I will listen to you. You will seek Me and find Me, when you search for Me with all your heart. . . . (Chapter XXIX, Verses 12, 13.)

In the Babylonian captivity, as the religion of Judah is restudied, the people create two new ideas, inspired by Jeremiah: the building of synagogues for religious assembly, and prayers offered to God in lieu of temple sacrifices. Through the synagogue and prayer, the people are no longer tied to temple or country. Thus, survival of the people of Judah in captivity and in dispersion is assured.

In the sixth century before the common era, Babylonia is ruled by a series of enlightened kings who treat their captives with tolerance. While the faithful weep by the rivers of Babylon, in the words of the psalmist, the balance, in keeping with Jeremiah's counsel, settle down and prosper. Babylonian trade routes take them to every corner of the then known world, evolving many into men of commerce, international trade and culture. Many, however, long for their familiar homeland.

In the midst of the confusion of the exile, Jeremiah does not, however, lose sight of the future. His prophecy of the fall of Jerusalem and the destruction of the Temple has been fulfilled. He has taken a step, as far as is known unprecedented in prophecy. He has secured the services of a professional writer, the scribe Baruch, who becomes his secretary and close friend. To him he dictates his earlier prophecies read at public gatherings. Now he puts on permanent record the events which have taken place.

In a change of tone, Jeremiah now speaks and writes of the restoration of Jerusalem to its pristine beauty. There will be renewed joy for the people. A ruler from the house of David will reign. Tragedy will end in joy. One of Jeremiah's greatest contributions is his complete confidence that in the coming days God will again make a covenant with the people of Israel. It will not be the same as the covenant of days gone by, the one entered into at Sinai. That one was broken by Israel. The new covenant will be one written and inscribed in the heart, in each one's heart. There will be a new motivation to fulfill God's laws. And through this new covenant the Jewish people will be re-established and reunited with their God.

Behold, the days come, says the Lord, that I will make a new covenant with the House of Israel, and the House of Judah, not like the covenant which I made with their fathers on the day I took them out of the land of Egypt, since they have broken My covenant although I was a lord over them, says the Lord. But this is the covenant which I will make with the House of Israel after those days. I will put My law into their inmost being. On their hearts will I inscribe it. I will be their God and they will be My people: They will no more teach every man his neighbor and every man his brother, saying, "Know the Lord." For they will all know Me, from the least of them to the greatest of them, says the Lord. For I will forgive their iniquity, and their sin will I remember no more. (Chapter XXXI, Verses 31-34.)

When Jerusalem was under siege, Jeremiah felt a divinely ordained necessity to demonstrate his faith in the coming restoration. He wanted to show that the land, the very earth, had a future, that it could not be completely destroyed. This faith in the future he expressed by purchasing a plot of land in his home town of Anathoth and summoning witnesses to the sale to take note how he preserved life and deed to the land.

Take these deeds, this deed of the purchase, both that which is sealed and that which is open, and put them in an earthen vessel; so that they may continue many days. For thus says the Lord of hosts, the God of Israel: Houses and fields and vineyards shall yet again be bought in this land. (Chapter XXXII, Verses 14, 15.)

Nothing dismayed Jeremiah in his appointed tasks. When the king Jehoiakim wants to verify the truth of Jeremiah's words, he calls for the documents of parchment on which Baruch, Jeremiah's faithful secretary, had written. He commands them to be read. He listens but a few moments and then in a passionate fury draws out his knife and rips the parchment, throwing the documents into the fire. God instructs Jeremiah to rewrite the messages. He does so, adding other thoughts. Jeremiah and Baruch are arrested and cast into a dungeon. The then King Zedekiah secretly sends for them and asks advice. Again, Jeremiah advises surrender to the Babylonians since it is inevitable that Judah must fall. Zedekiah does not listen nor heed, and Jerusalem is destroyed and the exile he so long predicted becomes a reality. After lending support to the governor Gedaliah, whose brief reign ends with his assassination, Jeremiah is taken much against his will to Egypt, which he abhors, by a group determined to settle in that country in the delta where there are some Jewish communities. Jeremiah's teachings there are likewise met with resistance.

In a brief, touching chapter, the prophet, sensitive and wounded by events and rebuffs, consoles his secretary Baruch, who is tired and depressed. He assures his friend that God will watch over and protect him.

The final chapters of the Book of Jeremiah contain a series of prophecies dealing with various kings and nations. As they parade before the prophet's vision, one by one and in turn, Jeremiah tells each what to expect in stinging, fiery words, sometimes in poetic verse. Each will be conquered and their end is near.

Nevertheless the love of Jeremiah for God and his people are insinuated into the last section, which is not harsh nor denunciatory. His kindly words assuage the heat and bring balm to the contrite spirit:

Do not fear, Jacob, My servant,
Nor be dismayed, Israel;
For I will save you from afar,
And your children from the land of their captivity,
Jacob will again be quiet and at ease,
And none shall make him afraid.
(Chapter XLVI, Verse 27.)

Thus Jeremiah's comforting words, from the beginning of what may be called his great song, are offered. Though smitten, denounced by his own, his sensitivity and gentle spirit, have remained at the core of his heart and demeanor. He has been destined to foretell a fearful experience for his people, but the tragedy has not stultified his faith in God. He remains soft and kind, his love for his people constant and true.

Reminiscent of the last chapters of II Kings, the Book of Jeremiah draws to its close. There is a brief summation of the reign of Zedekiah, the incredibly tragic burning of the great Temple buildings and courts, the exile of the people to a foreign land. As in the Book of Kings, the final incident suggests the days of the restoration of the holy City of David and House of the Lord. There is a light of human kindness in the darkness of evil when the king of Babylon releases the king of Judah, Jehoiachin, from prison, speaks kindly to him, refreshes his garments, and welcomes him to the royal table in a gesture which beseeches rather than extends forgiveness. The turbulent Book of Jeremiah ends on a hopeful note.

EZEKIEL

PROBABLY THE MOST UNUSUAL OF THE BIBLICAL BOOKS BE-
cause of its almost complete dependence on rich symbolism, ecstatic
visions, fantasy and imagery, Ezekiel, third and last of the major books
of the Prophets, Nevi'im Aharonim, is made up of forty-eight chapters.

Ezekiel (Ye'hezke'el—God will strengthen), the son of Buzi, is born in
Judah of a priestly family, a member of the Jerusalem priesthood, sons
of Zadok. Greatly influenced by the teachings of Jeremiah, Ezekiel as a
young man is among those carried off into Babylonian exile during the
First Captivity, 597 B.C.E. In a foreign land, Ezekiel continues his ministry for a period of twenty-two years. There is some overlapping with
Jeremiah, who in the beginning preaches at the same time in Judah.
Ezekiel is first called to prophesy in 592 B.C.E. After this year he lives in
a house of his own among other Jewish exiles in the village of Tel-abib
(Tel-Aviv), south of the city of Babylon, by an irrigation canal known as
the River Chebar. The elders come and sit before him. His ministry,
which continues until 571 B.C.E., has covered two periods. Before
Jerusalem meets its doom, he preaches against the worship of idols, the
injustices of the wealthy, the weakness and treachery of the kings of
Judah. Like Jeremiah, he believes that Nebuchadnezzar is the agent of
God to punish a faithless people. After the fall of Jerusalem, the prophet
changes his message from despair and pain to comfort and hope.

Ezekiel's role as both prophet and priest makes it easier to bear the
period of crisis and transition from a people living on its own land to an
exiled people living in a foreign land. His ministry makes their adjust-

146

ment possible. His understanding of his people's anxieties, denouncing them when necessary, comforting them when indicated, is in large measure responsible for Jewish survival then, and consequently for the future of the Jews as a nation.

He is credited with preserving the Jewish way of life in the pattern he sets for conduct and living. His service to his people is based on the recognition of the imperative need of the moment. He brooks no compromise with wrong, but holds out hope to the sinning. He teaches the doctrine of individual responsibility, that a person has within himself the power of decision to be righteous or wicked, irrespective of hereditary influences. Ezekiel repudiates the idea that if the parents eat sour grapes, their children's teeth are set on edge. To Ezekiel, it is a hopeful philosophy that the individual is the master of the individual's own destiny and responsible for the individual's own acts. This conception directs the present generation to look hopefully toward the future. Let it be said, however, that his primary concern is not with the individual alone but with the body of the Jewish people, with their salvation and preservation.

Ezekiel is therefore the prophet of the heart, the prophet of undying hope, the first prophet in Jewish history to serve God beyond Palestine. He teaches that God can be worshiped outside of Palestine. God is universal and omnipotent. He believes the Jewish people can surmount their catastrophe by a unified love for and faith in God and by nursing its mutual hope of returning to Palestine. He interprets his immediate work to prepare his people for the future. He knows God will return all of his people to Palestine, so he draws up definite architectural plans for the rebuilding of the Temple on Zion.

Ezekiel plays the role of both priest and prophet, retaining prophetic hopes and ideals and preserving the rituals and ceremonies of the Torah. Ezekiel emphasizes the importance of ritual and ceremony, viewing ritual as having a hallowing and sanctifying influence upon the people in its faithful observance. He combines the spirit of prophecy with priestly ministrations as required by divine law. Thus he becomes the leader of the religious community in exile in Babylon where the hopes remain alive for the return to Jerusalem and Zion.

He is opposed to building a temple of God in Babylonia because to him it means the renunciation of the future restoration of the Temple in Jerusalem. Ezekiel conceives of Zion as remaining God's Holy Mountain and there alone God's Temple shall be rebuilt, infused with "a new heart and a new spirit." (Chapter XI, Verse 19.)

Like Jeremiah, Ezekiel foresees the doom of Judah and the Temple and the insurmountable problems arising to plague his people. The exiles will need help and guidance. They will ask questions requiring satisfying answers. What will happen to us? May we worship in Babylon, a foreign land, when we no longer have our Temple? Does God dwell only in Jerusalem? If Jerusalem is destroyed, does it mean that our God is weaker than the gods of the heathens? If not, why did God lose? (The common belief is that not only nations fight, but their deities join the people in battle and the victorious god wins the worship and loyalty of those whose god is conquered.) And most of all, they ask, how long will we have to bear such woeful suffering? What about the welfare of our children? Shall they, too, be punished for the sins of their ancestors? Is this justice?

The design of Nebuchadnezzar, the conquering king, is to retain the people of Judah as a unified group rather than to disperse them. Ezekiel's leadership is therefore made more cogent and durable in that he can better minister to his people as both priest and prophet. They gather in his home and he guides and teaches the law to them on the Sabbath and holy days and is, indeed, the founder of what becomes the synagogue.

He replies to the queries of the people in allegories, symbolisms, and parables, making it possible for the people to hold steadfastly to their faith in God and their future as God's chosen people.

The defeat of Jerusalem is interpreted as God's way of bringing punishment upon the people for breaking God's covenant. When the news reaches Babylon of the devastation of Jerusalem in 586 B.C.E., Jeremiah's prophecies of punishment are fulfilled. Ezekiel immediately changes the tone of his discourses and turns his eyes and the minds of the people toward the restoration upon which the future of the exiles depends. He now preaches courage and strength, praying to God, asking forgiveness, and stoutly maintaining that God can be worshiped anywhere—not only in Palestine, because the whole world is God's dwelling place. Thus Ezekiel inspires the people with a desire to return to the ways of God, to repent their evildoing and to be forgiven. He moves them to great heights of hope for their eventual return to their homeland. Dramatically, symbolically, allegorically, he performs acts which teach the humbled people that he is certain of the final restoration and the return of God's glory to Jerusalem. Judah and Israel will be reunited in the Holy Land.

The book is divided into two general moods: the first foretells the approaching decline of Judah and Jerusalem; the second expresses Ezekiel's hope of the return to the homeland and the restoration of the Holy Temple in all of its splendor. The book opens with Ezekiel's call to prophetic office, and his great visual power is immediately evident in a majestic and mystic scene as he sees a vision with storm clouds, flashes of lightning, pealing thunder, strange and fearsome creatures composed of man and beast. In the midst of this fantastic scene, a divine chariot appears to summon him. The call is accompanied by the phrase characteristic of the book of Ezekiel—"Son of man." This is God's greeting to the new prophet. Ezekiel is charged with the duty of proclaiming Judah's destruction. The people will not listen, and Ezekiel hears God say that he must nevertheless persist. God shows Ezekiel a written scroll which contains words of lamentation and woe, and commands Ezekiel to consume the scroll, which Ezekiel does, symbolizing his complete assimilation of the words of God. The scroll tastes like honey, symbolizing the sweetness of God's words. Thus fortified with inspiration, Ezekiel begins his role as prophet and guardian over the house of Israel.

The prophecy now unfolds as messages come through visible symbols. The prophet sees visions through which God seems to address him and he teaches by relating these mystic experiences. Ezekiel is given to using cerain phrases such as "a rebellious house" in referring to Judah's people, and "son of man," implying mortal people.

Ezekiel's first concrete symbolic act simulates the coming destruction. He is called upon to plot out a miniature city, a replica of Jerusalem, on clay tile. Details are to be clearly visible, with enemy armies in position, besieging Jerusalem, and mounds set up for scaling the walls. Battering rams appear, and the enemy penetrates the fortifications. This is how Jerusalem will be possessed. Food is severely rationed. The people can no longer hold out and the end is in view. Every untoward event results from the violation of God's laws, so that people are urged to mend their ways.

Ezekiel's visions include visitations to the Temple where he witnesses evil practices. He constantly emphasizes that the misfortunes and sufferings of the people result from their sins. Many of his parables reveal Jerusalem in the throes of ruination. The holy city is allegorically described as an unfaithful wife, a worthless vine, useless, to be castigated. Yet he is aroused to great compassion: "Will you make a full end of the remnant of Israel?" The response allays Ezekiel's fears:

I will gather you from the peoples and assemble you from the countries where you were scattered, and I will give you the land of Israel. They will come here and remove all detestable things and abominations. I will give them one heart, and I will infuse a new spirit in you; and I will remove the

stony heart from their flesh and will give them a heart of
flesh so that they may walk in My statutes and keep My or-
dinanaces and do them; and they will be My people, and I
will be their God. (From Ezekiel, Chapter XI, Verses 17-20.)

Within his preaching of destined doom for wrongdoing, Ezekiel in-
serts his central religious doctrine that the individual bears responsibility for sin and that the sins of the parents are not visited upon the
children. With precise, stinging words, Ezekiel supplies the answer in a
doctrine which has become a cornerstone of Jewish thinking and living:

The soul that sins, it shall die. The son will not bear the
iniquity of the father with him, nor will the father bear the
iniquity of the son with him; the righteousness of the righteous will be upon him and the wickedness of the wicked will
be upon him. (Chapter XVIII, Verses 19-20.)

He calls upon the people to assume their responsibility, to cast aside
past patterns of conduct and behavior, counseling that they can now
help themselves and begin anew.

Therefore I will judge you, O house of Israel, everyone
according to his ways, says the Lord God. Return and turn
yourselves away from all your transgressions, so they will not
be stumbling blocks of iniquity to you. Cast away all your
transgressions and make for yourselves a new heart and a
new spirit; for . . . why will you die, O house of Israel?
(Chapter XVIII, Verses 30, 31.)

A number of chapters similar to those included in Isaiah and Jeremiah
direct attention to foreign nations. The interpretation of the political
situation of the world powers is religious. There is presented the view
that if Jerusalem, primarily the city of God and secondarily a coveted
military fortress, should fall, it would imply the weakness of God in
defending the Lord's dwelling place. Other gods, those of the heathen
peoples, would be deemed more powerful. This is the belief that one's
gods fight with a nation, that they win or fail with the people. This view
is disturbing to the prophet. In his opinion, the fall of Jerusalem means

God's judgment is being fulfilled, bringing punishment upon Jerusalem in a powerful manifestation of God's supremacy. Not only will destruction come to God's city but to all the nations who have violated the Lord's principles of justice and righteousness. Like Judah, they must bear the responsibility for their deviations.

The perspective thus far has been upon Jerusalem and Judah. The sudden shift of emphasis shocks the reader as the actual catastrophe shocks Ezekiel and the exiles in Babylon who learn of the disaster in Jerusalem. Anticipation is one thing. The reality of misfortune is another. Ezekiel rises from being the great denouncer to the great comforter. It is now his mission to uplift the spirit of a defeated people. Almost overnight Ezekiel changes. He begins to enlarge the horizons of hope. He calls upon his people to repent, mend their ways, and to begin preparations for their return to Jerusalem, to rebuild the city and the Temple, and to restore the devastated homeland.

While there is need to raise their dejected spirits, the need is just as great to justify his previous pronouncements and teachings. Ezekiel reiterates his view of individual responsibility. He reviews the grandeur of Jewish history from the times of Abraham, Isaac, and Jacob to Moses and the exodus from the bondage of Egypt, the wanderings in the wilderness, and the covenant with God at Mount Sinai. The people have sinned and the punishment is not unwarranted. While the promise is fulfilled, it does not signify complete destruction of the children of Israel. God will restore the chosen people to their Promised Land. God will infuse within them a new heart and a new spirit. The country of their forebears will once more flourish and bring forth its abundance. The people must merit this forgiveness and do their share in the future restoration, correct their ways, seek and obtain divine pardon. When they do, God, the shepherd of Israel, will lead them triumphantly back to their land.

Ezekiel's faith in the power of God to evoke new life for the seemingly lifeless Jewish people is dramatically expressed in one of the most unforgettable symbols of the restoration, in the strange but fascinating vision he sees of the dry bones strewn in the valley. The bones spring into life, are clothed in flesh and sinew, and are infused with God's spirit.

The hand of the Lord was upon me, and the Lord carried me out in a spirit, and set me down in the midst of the valley, and it was full of bones. He caused me to pass around them, and, behold, there were very many in the open valley;

and lo, they were very dry. He said to me: "Son of man, can these bones live?" And I answered: "O Lord God, You know." Then He said to me: "Prophesy over these bones, and say to them: O you dry bones, hear the word of the Lord; Thus says the Lord God to these bones: Behold, I will cause breath to enter into you, and you will live. I will lay sinews upon you, and will bring flesh upon you, and cover you with skin, and put breath in you, and you will live; and you will know that I am the Lord." I prophesied as I was commanded; and as I prophesized, there was a noise and a commotion, and the bones joined together, bone to its bone. And when I beheld, and, lo, there were sinews on them, and flesh came up, and the skin covered them above; but there was no breath in them.

Then He said to me: "Prophesy to the breath, prophesy, son of man, and say to the breath: Thus says the Lord God: Come from the four winds, O breath, and breathe upon these slain, that they may live." So I prophesied as He instructed me, and the breath came to them, and they lived, and stood upon their feet, an exceedingly great multitude.

Then He said to me: "Son of man, these bones are the whole house of Israel: Behold, they say: Our bones are dried up, and our hope is lost; we are completely cut off. Therefore prophesy and say to them: Thus says the Lord God: Behold, I will open your graves, and cause you to come up out of your graves, O my people; and I will bring you into the land of Israel. You will know that I am the Lord, when I have opened your graves, and caused you to come up out of your graves, O my people. And I will put My spirit in you, and you will live, and I will place you in your own land; and you will know that I, the Lord, have spoken it, and performed it," says the Lord. (Chapter XXXVII, Verses 1-14.)

Ezekiel portrays the principle of unity through the medium of comparison to two sticks, one to symbolize Judah and the other Joseph (Israel). These two will unify as will the two kingdoms of Judah and Israel:

The word of the Lord came to me, saying, "And you, son of man, take one stick, and write upon it: For Judah, and for the children of Israel, his companions; then take another stick and write upon it: For Joseph, the stick of Ephraim, and for all the house of Israel his companions: and join them one to another into one stick, that they may become one in your hand. When the children of your people will speak to you, saying, Will you not tell us what you mean by these, say to them: Thus says God: Behold, I will take the stick of Joseph which is in the hand of Ephraim, and the tribes of Israel his companions; and I will put them with him, together with the stick of Judah, and make them one stick, and they will be one in My hand. The sticks on which you write will be in your hand before their eyes. Say to them: Thus says God: Behold, I will take the children of Israel from among the nations, where they have gone, and will gather them on every side, and bring them into their own land; and I will make them one nation in the land. . . . so that they will be My people, and I will be their God. . . . They will dwell in the land which I have given to Jacob, My servant, where your fathers lived; and they will dwell in it, they and their children and their children's children, forever. David, My servant, will be their prince forever. I will make a covenant of peace with them which will be an everlasting covenant. I will establish them and multiply them, and will set My sanctuary in their midst forever, My dwelling place will also be with them; and I will be their God, and they will be My people. The nations will know that I the Lord do sanctify Israel. . . ." (Chapter XXXVII, Verses 15-28.)

In the last section of Ezekiel the theme of restoration, generalized in the earlier part of the book, now becomes more specific, and the vision centers around the Temple, its rituals and ceremonials. Ezekiel draws imaginatively upon the New Jerusalem. He envisions himself transported to the Temple mount, where, by a heavenly guide, he is escorted through the entire Temple area. Like an architect he reconstructs the buildings, places every item requisite for the rituals in its proper place and views the whole Temple rising in its extent like a city. This new, magnificent shrine will embody in ideal form the ideal of Israel. Israel will serve God in the Temple. The descendents of Zadok, the loyal house of priests of which Ezekiel is a part, will be the ministers in the Temple, directing the service with purity and reverence.

In this manner, the rituals and ceremonials will assume added significance. Not only will they require inner emotions of the heart and devotion, they will, as punctiliously followed, acquire greater religious spirit. The worshipers will be divinely inspired and will feel elevated. The

heightened spirit of true religion will affect the entire populace, sanctifying them, and in this way help Israel to live according to the terms of
the covenant with God.

The message of Ezekiel, the ritualist prophet of the heart, reaches its
glorious climax as his theme of the restoration ends, as does the book,
with the inspiring and hopeful words:

The name of the city from that day shall be "The Lord is
there." (Adonai Shamah.) (Chapter XLVIII, Verse 35.)

The prophecy and teachings of Ezekiel, occurring at the most crucial
period in the history of Judaism, preserved the people from disintegration for its destined future, precluding a permanent separation from the
past and cementing irrevocably the past, present and future. Ezekiel has
fulfilled his mission.

Section III THE TWELVE
(Tray Asar)

HOSEA

T HE BOOK OF HOSEA IS FIRST OF THE TWELVE (PROPHETS), TRAY Asar in Hebrew, all of which are shorter than Isaiah, Jeremiah, and Ezekiel. To make certain that these books were preserved intact, they were grouped into one literary collection and are counted as one. Chronologically, the Book of Hosea should follow the Book of Amos, but it appears first because of its greater length.

The opening verse of Chapter I declares: "The word of God that came to Hosea, the son of Beeri, in the days of Uzziah, Jotham, Ahaz and Hezekiah, kings of Judah, and in the days of Jeroboam, the son of Joash, king of Israel." This takes us back to the middle of the eighth century B.C.E., to the reign of Jeroboam II, king of Israel, the Northern Kingdom of Palestine, about three decades before the downfall of Israel. The period is one of grave national danger. Both Hosea and the prophet Amos, who live to see Israel destroyed, are called the Prophets of the Decline and Fall of the Northern Kingdom.

Outward appearances indicate prosperity and luxurious living prevalent, but Hosea and Amos detect the superficiality of economic conditions which conceal the crumbling foundations of the kingdom. What they perceive is disturbing and frightening. Moral and social decay eat away at the strength of the country. Injustice is rife and moral wrongs are commonplace. Israel is beset by a collapsing internal social structure and by powerful enemies from without. Assyria emerges as a terrifying impending threat over the land. In their weakness and terror the kings of Israel fence politics with Assyrian and Egyptian rulers and pay them

155

heavy tribute. A rapid succession of kings has risen to power by way of murder and assasination. Since the death of Jeroboam II, six kings, in some twenty-three years, rule the throne with four of them having been the slayers of the previous kings. This violence affects the people, who revert to idolatry and they crowd the sacred shrines of Beth-el and Gilgal where they worship visible images.

Where sacrifices are offered according to the religion of Israel, the performances are perfunctory and without significance. Alliances with neighboring powers bring foreign cultures and morality to the kingdom for the people to imitate. The priests are equally guilty of non performance of their duties. The people fall into further evil ways and their spirituality deteriorates. Assyria unabatedly continues to exert its forceful aggression so that the country drifts steadily toward disintegration.

Hosea appears in these hectic times to preach the word of God. "Set the trumpet to your lips like a watchman over the house of the Lord!" (Hosea, Chapter VIII, Verse 1.)

The general character of the book reflects the closing decades of the Northern Kingdom, the fall of Israel occurring in 722 B.C.E.

He warns the people of impending doom, urging them with tearful pleas to take heed to renounce their wicked ways and to return to the Lord's ways, restoring the covenant originally made at Sinai. Hosea's heart and soul go out completely to the people so that his sympathy for them is contagious. His affection is stirring and warming as with pathos and force he enters his ministry.

Hosea is tender, sensitive, affectionate for yet another reason. His entire approach to his people, to God, and to the interrelation between them parallels his own tragic and bitter personal experience which becomes the source of his insight and intuitive perception. Hosea is the first to draw the analogy between God's relationship to man and the institution of marriage.

Hosea has known marital love. He has known happiness and frustration. He can therefore speak more understandingly of the covenant and of the love God bears the people, of God's grief that they are unfaithful to the Lord. He knows instinctively that God's love is enduring. He conceives of this divine truth by virtue of his own life with Gomer, his wife; his love for her, his disappointment in her, and her redemption. He cannot banish his overwhelming love for her from his heart. Nor, by the same token, can God cast Israel away because God's love is abiding. Hosea cannot forget his unfaithful wife. He takes her back into his home and into his heart after she has experienced a period of repentance and discipline. In like manner is the marriage between God and Israel sacred and binding in a permanent relationship. Israel broke the covenant of Mount Sinai when the people worshiped idols, but God will not banish the beloved people. First Israel will be cleansed by punishment and then the enduring love of God will restore a purified Israel to glory.

According to the first biographical part of the book, Hosea is called to prophesy the imminent destruction of Israel by the power of Assyria. God summons him to marry Gomer. Three children are born of the union to whom he gives symbolic names: Jezreel meaning "God sows," a sign of the scattering of the kingdom; Lo-ruchama, "the unpitied one," or "the one who has not obtained compassion," signifying that since Israel has forgotten God, God can no longer have compassion on Israel; and Lo-Ami, meaning "not my people," a clear indication that the covenant has been broken and Israel is no longer God's people.

Even while he foretells the tragic future, Hosea's inner feelings urge him to speak words of hope and cheerfulness so that he foretells the ultimate redemption of Israel. He uses the same names for impending doom to spell hopefulness. "God sows" therefore becomes productivity; "one who has no compassion" becomes compassion, and "not my people" becomes my people, because God will show His mercy.

On that day I will make a covenant for them
With the beasts of the field and the birds of heaven,
And with the creeping things of the ground;
I will break the bow and the sword and the battle
out of the land,
And will make them to lie down safely.
(Chapter II, Verse 20.)

In tender, loving words, Hosea reaffirms the union of God with the people Israel:

I will betroth you to Me forever;
I will betroth you to Me in righteousness, and in justice,
And in lovingkindness, and in compassion.
And I will betroth you to Me in faithfulness;
And you will know the Lord.
(Chapter II, Verses 21, 22.)

Hosea reformulates the significance of the names of his children:

It will come to pass on that day,
I will respond, says the Lord,
I will respond to the heavens.
And they will respond to the earth;
And the earth will respond to the corn, and the wine,
    and the oil,
And they shall respond to Jezreel.
And I will sow her to Me in the land.
And I will have compassion upon her who has not obtained
    compassion;
And I will say to those who were not My people: You are
    My people;
And they will say, You are My God.

(Chapter II, Verses 23-25.)

The next part of the book contains Hosea's pronouncements against the ruling classes who in their power and wealth neglect the people. He describes the moral sins of vice and corruption, lashing out against the leaders who seek alliances with foreign powers declaring the kingdom will be benefited, when in reality the opposite effect results. Israel's practices and religion are defiled, assimilated, deprecated so that political alliances do not strengthen the nation. Strength lies, holds the prophet Hosea, only in moral fortitude, which is inner strength.

Hear the word of the Lord, you children of Israel!
For the Lord has a controversy with the inhabitants of
    the land,
Because there is no truth nor mercy,
Nor knowledge of God in the land.
Swearing and lying, and killing and stealing, and
    committing adultery!"

(Chapter IV, Verse 1, 2.)

Hosea rebukes the priests, alleging they bear a heavy responsibility in the moral degradation of the people whose confidence in them has been betrayed. On the other hand, he reprimands the people, as well, for the deviation from their religion. It is axiomatic that in times of despair the people naturally seek the help of God, but with little sincerity:

Come and let us return to the Lord,
For He has torn and He will heal us,
He has wounded, and He will bind us up.
(Chapter VI, Verse 1.)

Hosea re-emphasizes a theme which threads through the preachings and writings of the other prophets: moral living is primary. Sacrificial ceremony, without the heart, is meaningless and unacceptable to God. Righteousness and mercy are the essential elements of true worship.

For your goodness is as a morning cloud,
And as the dew that leaves early,
Therefore have I hewed them by the prophets;
I have slain them by the words of My mouth;
And your judgment came with the dawn;
For I desire mercy, and not sacrifice,
And the knowledge of God rather than burnt-offerings.
(Chapter VI, Verses 4-6.)

The prophet persists in inveighing against foreign political entanglements. While destruction approaches as God's punishment for evildoing, God looks longingly upon his first-born, as it were, in the simile of a human father and his child.

When Israel was a child, I loved him,
And from Egypt I called My son.
The more they called them, the more they went from them;
They sacrificed to the Baalim,
And offered to graven images.
And I, I taught Ephraim to walk,
Taking them by their arms.
But they did not know that I healed them.
I drew them with cords of a man,
With bands of love;

I was to them as those who impose a yoke on their jaws
And I fed them gently.

(Chapter XI, Verses 1-4.)

The prophet exhorts, cajoles, pleads with his people to turn from evil deeds:

Therefore, turn to your God;
Keep mercy and justice,
And wait for your God continually.

(Chapter XII, Verse 7.)

History's die is cast. Israel does not heed the pleadings of its prophets. The nation walks inexorably to destruction and its destruction as a people. Conquered by Assyria, the people of Israel are deported from Palestine and disappear, becoming known thereafter as the "Ten Lost Tribes of Israel," in 722 B.C.E.

In the last chapter, the call to return to God is resounded. It has re-echoed down the corridors of time in its incorporation into the service of the synagogue on the Sabbath of Repentance, the Sabbath occurring between Rosh Hashanah and Yom Kippur.

Return, O Israel, to the Lord your God;
For you have stumbled because of your iniquity,
Take with you words,
And return to the Lord:
Say to Him, Forgive all iniquity,
And accept that which is good;

(Chapter XIV, Verses 2, 3.)

And God replies:

I will heal their backsliding,
I will love them freely;
For My anger is turned away from them.
I will be as the dew to Israel,
He will blossom as the lily,

And cast forth his roots as Lebanon.
His branches will spread out,
And his beauty will be as the olive tree,
And his fragrance will be as Lebanon.
Those who dwell under his shade shall again
Make corn grow,
And will blossom as the vine;
Its scent will be as the wine of Lebanon. . . .
Whoever is wise, let him understand these things,
Whoever is prudent, let him know them.
For the ways of the Lord are right,
The just walk in them;
But transgressors stumble in them.

(Chapter XIV, Verses 5-8, 10.)

Many of the doctrines Hosea preached are continued in the prophetic books. The principle of the eternal covenant and the concept of the Chosen People are basic to his philosophy. Departure from the covenant merits punishment, but the punishment is not a harsh one for it is destined not to inflict suffering but to purify, encourage repentance and bring to the individual a realization of God's goodness and lovingkindness. God will heed repentance from the heart. Sacrifice and ritual are significant, but only as manifestations of inner feelings and convictions. Mercy and lovingkindness are the seeds from which true piety grows so that people will return to God.

JOEL

THE PREACHING OF JOEL, SON OF PETHUEL, CONSTITUTES THE
second of the books of the Twelve Prophets. There are conflicting views
as to the period in which Joel lived. The absence of any reference which
may serve to indicate the precise occasion of the prophecy has caused
the Book of Joel to be assigned to dates ranging from 835 to 360 B.C.E.
While it is true that many allusions are furnished by the general background of the book, these are, however, such that they lend themselves
to logical explanation in the circumstances of different periods of time.

Some hold the view that Joel lived around the middle of the fifth
century before the common era. Others maintain he lived before the
other prophets, which would place his life somewhere in the latter part
of the ninth or even the beginning of the eighth century, inasmuch as
the book does not mention Assyria, which would mean an earlier date,
nor Babylon of the sixth century, a later date. There is no reference to
the Northern Kingdom, Israel, nor to any ruling king. The references to
the wall of Jerusalem (Chapter II, Verses 7 and 9) appear to imply the
period of restoration after the exile when the wall was rebuilt and the
second Temple was in existence. This would bring the Book of Joel after
Nehemiah (c. 445 BJ.C.E.) or the middle of the fifth century.

Comprising four chapters, the book is divided into two parts: the first
tells a vivid story of an extraordinary invasion of swarms of locusts which
threaten agriculture and livestock with destruction and whose repeated
ravages are so intense that even the Temple services cannot be maintained because fruits and vegetables have been annihilated. This is the

JOEL

form taken of God's chastisement of a sinning people. The second part of
the book tells of the people's repentance and God's promise of blessings,
abundance, relief, and hope.

There is evidence that the Prophet Joel actually experienced the
dreadful plague of locusts which he uses as a lesson for his message. In
its visitation, he sees signs of the approaching day of judgment. Winged
desert locusts, resembling grasshoppers, travel in flights of destructive
swarms over great distances. Maintaining military formation, they swoop
down upon crops, cattle, and buildings with savage ferocity and devour-
ing appetites, blotting out the skies and the sun. This plague, not unknown to the peoples of Syria, Palestine, and Egypt, is interpreted as a
scourge of God, in wreaking havoc and terror.

> They leap on the city,
> They run on the wall,
> They climb up into the houses
> They enter windows like thieves.
> Before them the earth quakes,
> The heavens tremble;
> The sun and the moon are blacked out,
> And the stars withdraw their brightness.
>   (Chapter II, Verses 9, 10.)

> The field is wasted,
> The land mourns;
> For the grain is wasted,
> The new wine is dried up,
> The oil languishes.
>   (Chapter I, Verse 10.)

When the plague results in famine, the rituals of the Temple cease for
lack of offerings. Joel summons the priests and ministers to lament the
misfortune visited upon the people. There is no hope, Joel holds, save
in repentance and prayer, so he urges the priests and the people to
penitence that the destruction from the Almighty may be stayed.

> Sanctify a fast,
> Call a solemn assembly,
> Gather the elders
> And all the inhabitants of the land

163

To the House of the Lord your God,
And cry to the Lord. . . .
                    (Chapter I, Verse 14.)

Is not the food cut off
Before our eyes,
Yes, joy and gladness
From the House of our God?
The grains shrivel under their hoes;
The garners have been laid desolate,
The barns have broken down;
For the corn is withered.
                    (Chapter I, Verses 16, 17.)

Joel insists that the repentance be sincere and not merely ceremonial.

Yet even now, says the Lord,
Turn to Me with all your hearts,
With fasting, weeping, lamentations;
Rend your hearts, and not your garments,
And turn to the Lord your God;
For He is gracious and compassionate,
Long-suffering, and abundant in kindness. . . .
                    (Chapter II, Verses 12, 13.)

The second part of the book presents God's promise to rescind the plague and to restore the fruitful seasons. The interval implies that the people have obeyed the prophet's call to repentance and that God has accepted their contrite hearts. Joel now announces the glad tidings of a new era in creation for the land and for its inhabitants. All will change. The horrifying locust swarms will depart and the blessed rains will fall. The land will be productive again. Good will be showered upon the people as reward for their obedience and faith.

Do not fear, O land, be glad and rejoice;
For the Lord has done great things.
Do not be afraid, you beasts of the field;
For the pastures of the wilderness do spring with grass.
The tree bears its fruit,

JOEL

The fig-tree and the vine do yield their strength. . . .
You will eat in plenty and be satisfied,
And will praise the name of the Lord your God. . . .

(Chapter II, Verses 21, 22, 26.)

The prophet continues his message of hope. He describes the future glory of Judah. He declares that spiritual gifts will descend upon the people so that all will be endowed with clearer perception of divine truth.

It will come to pass afterward,
That I will pour out My spirit upon all people;
Your sons and your daughters will prophesy,
Your old men will dream dreams,
Your young men will see visions,
And also upon the servants and upon the handmaids
Will I pour out My spirit.

(Chapter III, Verses 1, 2.)

Israel will be delivered and restored. Judgment will overtake the nations who have oppressed them. Joel predicts a great crisis. In a digression in prose (Chapter IV, Verses 4-8), mention is made of the coming doom of Tyre and Sidon of Phoenicia and of Philistia, when God will restore Judah and Jerusalem after the captivity.

Zion will be blessed:

It will come to pass on that day,
That the mountains will drop sweet wine,
The hills will flow with milk,
All the brooks of Judah will flow with waters;
A fountain will come forth from the House of the Lord,
And will water the valley of Shittim. . . .
But Judah will be inhabited forever
And Jerusalem from generation to generation.

(Chapter 4, Verses 18, 20.)

The book of Joel ends with the benediction, "And the Lord dwells in Zion." Although brief, the book is broad in dimension, drawing its ser-

165

mon from plague, symbolic of punishment, to repentance and hopeful glory in the end of days. Joel, the prophet of repentance, covers many doctrines with emphasis on the value of prayer and fasting, while not discounting the importance of significant rituals. Like the fraternity of prophets, Joel insists that true repentance comes from the heart, that religious acts and deeds must accompany the ceremonial of the service in order to merit validity.

AMOS

AMOS IS THE FIRST OF THE LITERARY PROPHETS WHOSE words, enshrined in the third book of the Twelve Prophets, form the earliest prophecy that has survived. Many of the fundamental doctrines Amos formulated and preached were adopted by succeeding prophets and transmitted down through the ages.

Amos lived and prophesied in the critical, turbulent days of Jeroboam II who reigned as king of Israel from 786 to 745 B.C.E. and in the days of King Uzziah of Judah. He experienced the earthquake which shook the land so severely it remained forever after in the memory of people, and the eclipse of the sun of 763 which he mentions in Chapter VIII, Verse 9: "Says the Lord God . . . I will cause the sun to go down at noon,/ And I will darken the earth in the clear day." Like his younger contemporary Hosea, Amos lived through the decline and fall of Israel in 722 B.C.E.

The prophet describes himself as a herdsman and a dresser of sycamore trees. He lives simply in Tekoa, in the hill country of southern Judah by the Dead Sea, about twelve miles south of Jerusalem. Although he is familiar with the agriculture and commercial life of central Palestine and its cities, he approaches them as an outsider. He lives the life of the semi-nomad who is accustomed to the wide spaces of the southern plains and hills. While he is engaged in his lonely occupation, he feels the stirring of God's spirit within him, calling him to go to Israel, and there to proclaim the coming destruction. He is to announce that punishment will be meted out for injustice and unrighteousness

167

which are rife. Amos responds to the divine call and leaves his rustic homestead to fulfill his mission.

Appearances indicate prosperous times for Israel and Judah. The people believe that God has blessed them with abundance and they expect even greater glory to come to Israel. But Amos, and later Hosea, are able to penetrate beneath appearances and what they see is disturbing and frightening. Since the days of King David, Israel and Judah have been steadily growing out of the ancient nomadic social and economic order into that of an agricultural and commercial state. The transition is attended by social upheavals which had already become evident a century before Amos. Small proprietors prevalent up to the middle of the ninth century have given way to large estates worked by serf labor. Social evils of all kinds and forms, oppression of the needy, injustices, unrighteousness prevail. Worship has become perfunctory and without feeling. Popular religion does not help toward righteousness.

Amos sees on one hand an extravagant luxury and on the other the poverty of the majority of the people from whom all virility has been sapped. The country is disintegrating from within and will soon be demolished by the Assyrians. What Amos has observed incites him to anger. His indignation knows no bounds over the indolence and selfishness of the wealthy, the misery and poverty of the common people. His thundering words have become exemplars for all social reformers. He will not permit himself the ease of witnessing evil and remaining silent.

Amos is the Prophet of Justice. He has no social program to offer. Instead he calls people back to the God of their ancestors and insists that the nation can find safety only in moral and spiritual reform. To his mind the God of Israel is the Lord of creation, of history and of universal morality and God's supreme demand is for justice which alone will save the people from their impending fate.

Religious practices must stem from the heart and be the outgrowth of justice and righteous living. Violation of ethical standards is bound to bring a severe rebuke from God, who demands justice and righteousness. These are the two key words of the ministry of Amos, applicable to all individuals as well as to national life, to all nations, Israel included.

Amos is thoroughly convinced that Israel is God's elect nation among the families of mankind and that this distinction carries with it great responsibilities. The covenant between God and Israel cannot, however, serve as a protective shield. To the contrary, Israel's violations will bring worse punishment precisely because of the covenant. Thus Amos, prophet of stern justice, arrives on the scene to proclaim the unpopular message to an incredulous people who see only good living and prosperity all about them as far as the fortunate few are concerned.

AMOS

* * *

There are three divisions in the Book of Amos. The first two chapters introduce the theme. Like all nations, Israel will be punished, because, like them, the people have violated God's basic ethical and social laws. The second section of four chapters continues to sharpen the theme; the people's complacency is to be shaken. The last three chapters contain a series of visions. Similes, metaphors, symbols describe the coming destruction. There is another call for return to God before it is too late. The last eight sentences end on a hopeful note—a glorious picture of the Golden Age. God and the people are brought together again.

The book opens with fierce impact, a powerful prophecy of the destined punishment. Judgment will be passed upon the various nations, each described by name. Their iniquities will be visited upon them. The prophet then turns to Judah, which will also bear responsibility, and for Israel, Amos reserves his strongest, most stinging and denunciatory language. Israel is no exception and will be given no special privileges. Prior protections will not be repeated. The penalty will prove more severe because of the covenant and because Israel has not controlled the spread of social evils; a betrayal of the trust God has reposed in Israel.

You only have I known of all the families of the earth;
Therefore I will visit upon you all your iniquities.
Will two walk together,
Except they have agreed?
(Chapter III, Verses 2, 3.)

Israel's relationship with God has been a close one, united by mutual understanding. This is no longer true. Israel has strayed and now God and Israel no longer walk together. Amos denounces selfishness, disregard for the needy, and exploitation of the poor:

Here this word, you cows of Bashan,
Who are in the mountain of Samaria,
Who oppress the poor, who crush the needy,
Who say to their lords: Bring, that we may feast! . . .
Therefore, because you trample on the poor,
And take from him exactions of wheat;
You have built houses of hewn stone,
But you will not live in them,

You have planted pleasant vineyards,
But you will not drink of their wine.
For I know how many are your transgressions,
And how mighty are your sins;
You who afflict the just, who take a ransom,
Who turn aside the needy in the gate. . . .
Hear this, O you who would crush the needy,
And destroy the poor of the land,
Saying: When will the new moon be over, so that we may
    sell grain;
And the Sabbath, that we may sell wheat?
Making the ephah small, and the shekel great,
Falsifying the balances of deceit;
That we may buy the poor for silver,
And the needy for a pair of shoes,
And sell the refuse of the corn. . . .
The Lord has sworn by the pride of Jacob:
I will never forget any of their deeds.
(Chapters IV, Verse 1; V, Verses 11, 12; VIII, Verses 4-7.)

These are the sins of people against people; the sins of greed and
vanity. They are therefore sins against God. Prosperity is only apparent;
the great body of people live in poverty and in debt. The laborers in the
town often have to pledge their possessions to buy grain for food and the
farmers have to borrow funds and mortgage their homes and acres. If
the crops fail, they lose their livelihood and are reduced to selling themselves or their children into bondage. The wealthy, however, do enjoy
influence in high places, controlling appointments to public offices so
that in turn officials fear to refuse their wishes, and even judges in
courts are controlled by their appetite for bribes so that it is an evil
time.

Amos points out that God does not seek sacrifices which are requests
for favors. God has laid down rules for ethical daily living under the
Law. Amos knows his own people, that they scrupulously observe the
rituals and therefore mistakenly believe their observances are acceptable
to God. The people are pious in their own way, but their deeds belie
their piety. Amos is impatient also with the exaggerated worship at
Bethel, Dan, Gilgal or Beer-sheba:

I hate, I despise your feasts,
I will take no delight in your solemn assemblies.

Though you offer me burnt offerings, and your meal-
    offerings,
I will not accept them;
Nor will I regard the peace offerings of your fat beasts.
Take away from Me the sound of your songs;
And let Me not hear the melody of your psalteries.
But let justice well up as waters,
And righteousness as a mighty stream.

                          (Chapter V, Verses 21-24.)

In desperation Amos pleads with the people to avoid devastation by establishing true justice:

Seek good, and not evil, that you may live;
So that the Lord, the God of hosts, will be with you, as
    you say.
Hate evil, and love the good,
And establish justice in the gate;
It may yet be that the Lord, the God of hosts,
Will be gracious to the remnant of Joseph.

                        (Chapter V, Verses 14, 15.)

The last section of the book offers a series of five brief but vivid visions. Each tells the story of the future. Amos has the clearness of insight which is natural to one who is in solitary communion with nature, as he is in his calling as a shepherd and the tender of sycamore trees. He experiences the intense realization that he is chosen to deliver the word of God.

The first vision is that of a swarm of locusts who descend during harvesttime to consume the production of long toil. The second vision is of a destructive fire. Both symbolize Israel's forthcoming doom. Amos pleads with God to be merciful:

O Lord, cease, I beseech You;
How shall Jacob stand, for he is small.
The Lord repented concerning this;
"It shall not be," says the Lord God.

                    (Chapter VII, Verse 5.)

The third vision is that of the wall and the engineer's plumbline. A wall, erect and straight when built, now shows signs of imminent collapse. Amos intercedes no longer. He is convinced that God acts justly because the people have been found wanting in justice and righteousness.

At this point, a dramatic personal meeting at Beth-el between Amos and the high priest Amaziah is recorded. The priest is greatly alarmed when he hears the dire predictions of doom by Amos.

Amaziah thereupon sends a messenger to Jeroboam, king of Israel, saying: "Amos has conspired against you . . . the land is not able to bear all his words . . . for he says Jeroboam shall die by the sword, and Israel will surely be led away captive." (Chapter VII, Verses 10, 11.) Amaziah accuses the prophet of treason against the king and his throne. He appears before Amos in his regal, official garments and furiously expels the prophet from Beth-el forever.

O you seer, go away to the land of Judah. Earn your bread and prophesy there, but do not prophesy any more at Beth-el, for it is the king's sanctuary and it is a royal house. (Chapter VII, Verses 12, 13.)

Amos is undismayed by Amaziah's rebuke, responding with pride that he is not a professional prophet. By this he implies that he regards himself as a special envoy who speaks in the name of God:

I was no prophet, nor was I prophet's son; but I was a herdsman, and a dresser of sycamore trees; and the Lord took me away from following the flock, and said to me: Go, prophesy to My people Israel. (Chapter VII, Verses 14, 15.)

Disregarding the expulsion, Amos predicts the downfall of the household of Amaziah along with the others.

The fourth vision of Amos compares Israel to a basket of summer fruit at the end of the season, overripe and needing to be discarded. So, also, will Israel meet its end.

The fifth and last vision portrays God standing beside the altar at Beth-el. It tells, in effect, that not only the people but the house of worship is included in the general destruction. No one will escape. No one will be saved.

The final sentences of the book turn to a more hopeful theme. Redemption will come and a better future; more glorious times are ahead. Amos sees the return of Israel to glory and splendor under the re-established kingdom of David.

On that day I will raise up
The tabernacle of David that has fallen,
And close up its breaches;
I will raise up his ruins,
And I will build it as in the days of old. . . .
I will turn the captivity of My people Israel,
They will rebuild the wasted cities and live in them;
They will plant vineyards, and drink of its wine;
They will also make gardens and eat of their fruit.
I will plant them upon their land,
And they shall never again be uprooted
From their land which I have given them,
Says the Lord your God.

(Chapter IX, Verses 11, 14, 15.)

Thus the Book of Amos closes on the theme that the covenant between God and Israel will yet be restored.

Many of the doctrines propounded by later prophets find their original source in the book of Amos.

To Amos, God is the God of all humanity. God's requirements of righteousness are not limited to any one people; they apply to all people. Israel, though chosen of God, is not privileged in the sense of being absolved from acting justly and righteously. On the contrary, the covenant imposes greater responsibility. It follows, therefore, that Israel's punishment, if it violates the standards, is to be more severe. Moreover, these principles of conduct apply with equal force to every individual.

In observance of the ritual, it must not be supposed, Amos teaches, that mere practice or mere external expression without moral and good behavior is acceptable. Just and righteous actions, ethical and moral living, are required before the ritual can have any meaning.

One of the Bible's most forceful, magnetic characters, the impress of stern Amos on Judaism is indelible. His profound conception of a universal God, his unequivocal love for and defense of the poor and the oppressed, his fearless, dauntless denunciation of any form of injustice and immorality, his demands for proper conduct and living, establish Amos firmly in the higher echelons of religious leaders of history.

OBADIAH

OBADIAH, FOURTH BOOK OF THE TWELVE IS THE SHORTEST IN
the Bible, with only one chapter of twenty-one sentences and a single
theme: at last Edom has received its just deserts!

Nothing is known about the prophet nor is there any direct suggestion
in the book itself which may throw light on when he lived and where he
prophesied. Some ascribe a very early date to the book, as early as the
eighth century B.C.E. Most scholars, however, prefer to place Obadiah
in some time around the destruction of Jerusalem in 586 B.C.E. They
deduce the approximate date from three sentences which vividly depict
ruin and desolation, and from a number of sentences which bear striking
resemblance to the words of Jeremiah.

With graphic wording, coupled with a lively, imaginative mind, Obadiah prophesies the downfall of Edom, the enemy of Israel. His accusations and predictions are all the more stirring and pathetic because
Edom, southern neighbor of Israel, is descended from Esau, the brother
of Jacob. In spite of common descent, enmity exists between the Edomites and Israelites. When Israel was being laid waste, Edom did not act
like a brother. Edom not only refrained from lending a helping hand but
stood by awaiting Israel's decimation, and even joined the assault and
participated in the resulting spoils.

The Edomites occupy the mountainous country south of the Dead
Sea, hence the reference to their rocky dwellings. The aid referred to is
the assistance they gave to the Babylonians against Jerusalem in 586
B.C.E. which was never forgiven. In its early part, Obadiah belongs to

174

Obadiah

the first half of the sixth century B.C.E., the opening paragraph of the Prophet Malachi appearing to refer to the same event.

With strength and fervor, Obadiah begins his brief condemnation of Edom. Edom will fall because of the violence wreaked on brother Jacob.

For the violence done to your brother Jacob shame will
   cover you,
And you will be cut off forever.
On the day when you stood aloof,
On the day when strangers carried away his substance,
And foreigners entered his gates,
And cast lots upon Jerusalem,
Even you were one of them. (Verse 10)

You should not have gazed on the day of your brother,
On the day of his disaster;
Nor should you have rejoiced over the children of Judah
On the day of their destruction;
Nor should you have spoken proudly
On the day of distress.
You should not have entered the gate of My people
On the day of their calamity;
Yes, you should not have gazed on their affliction
On the day of their calamity,
Nor laid hands on their substance
On the day of their calamity.
You should not have stood in the crossway. . . .
As you have done, it shall so be done to you;
Your dealing will return upon your head.
(Verses 12-15.)

For all nations who oppressed and mistreated Israel, the day of reckoning is rapidly approaching. For Israel, however, Obadiah reserves his promise of restoration. He envisions that Israel and Judah will be reunited once more and that ". . . the kingdom will be the Lord's."

Obadiah's is a simple message of hope. He preached to a people whose homes had just been razed. Their low spirits needed encouragement, and Obadiah's words assuaged their sorrow.

Obadiah's prophecy appears on the surface to be one of vengeance and anger. Yet one reads behind the words a story of faith in God, in the Lord's supremacy over all the world, and in the Lord's ultimate justice.

One detects an urgent call to the nations of the world to live peacefully one with the other. We remember Obadiah's pointing finger . . . "you should not have," a profound expression which says in effect, this is not the way nations on earth should live. They ought not to take advantage of one another, but learn to live together and to help each other in times of stress. Else, only destruction and evil can result. Obadiah does not preach vengeance, but against causeless enmity and hatred, and in behalf of faith in God and in God's justice.

JONAH

THE FIFTH BOOK OF THE TWELVE IS DEVOTED TO JONAH, generally identified as the prophet of the same name recorded in II Kings, Chapter XIV, Verse 25: "He restored the border of Israel from the entrance of Hamath to the sea of the Arabah, according to the word of the Lord, the God of Israel, which He spoke by the hand of His servant Jonah, the son of Amittai, the prophet, who was of Gath-hepher." The reference is to Jeroboam II, who reigned in Samaria for forty-one years. This therefore places the life of Jonah in the middle of the eighth century, while the message of his ministry, it is generally held, was not reduced to writing until some time in the fifth century after the destruction of Judah and Jerusalem.

The Book of Jonah contains no prophecy in the accepted sense of the term in the prophetic books. Through the use of symbolism or imaginative story, the message is conveyed. Its primary theme is the universality of God who loves all and rules over all people, forgiving anyone who repents and acknowledges his wrongdoing. Jonah records a noble expression of the universality of God and true religion, bearing on the sublime theme of God as just, kind, merciful, loving all creatures, treating all equally. The book teaches the principle that God is everywhere and no one can escape the Lord's presence.

The story begins with a call from God. Jonah is to go to the wicked city of Nineveh, the capital of Assyria, to proclaim the imminent punishment to be visited upon it and those who live there, because of their

177

great sins. Jonah, the reluctant prophet, tries to evade the mission. He is afraid and refuses to obey. Instead, in an attempt to flee from God's will, he embarks for Tarshish. On the high seas a terrible storm arises, threatening to engulf the ship and take the lives of passengers and mariners. Heavy loads are cast overboard in desperate efforts to lighten the ship's weight, to no avail. The storm rages more fiercely than ever and the lives of all are in danger. Meanwhile Jonah is fast asleep in the ship's hull. When Jonah is found he is roundly reprimanded and asked to pray to his God—"if it so be that God will think of us"—for immediate deliverance.

The mariners believe that someone on board ship is responsible for the violent tempest. They cast lots to discover the guilty one and it falls to Jonah, who admits he is running away from God's behest. They surround Jonah and question him:

"Tell us, we pray you, for whose cause this evil is upon us. What is your occupation? Where do you come from? What is your country? and of what people are you?" And he said to them, "I am a Hebrew; and I fear the Lord, the God of heaven, who made the sea and the dry land." (Chapter I, Verses 8, 9.)

The men now know that Jonah is fleeing from the presence of the Lord and that therefore he is the cause of the storm. Jonah suggests that, inasmuch as he is responsible, he be cast into the raging sea. He is thrown overboard, and soon the sea becomes calm. The storm subsides and the people and the ship are saved. The people greatly fear God, and offer a sacrifice to the Lord and vow further offerings upon their return home.

Chapter II tells of the great fish sent to swallow up Jonah and to imprison him for three days and three nights. As Israel prays for deliverance from the dark depths of exile and is rescued, so Jonah is saved from the whale so that he may continue on his mission to Nineveh. In his despair, Jonah cries out to God a magnificent prayer reminiscent of the Psalms:

I called out of my affliction
To God, and He answered me;
Out of the belly of the netherworld I cried,
And You heard my voice.

178

For You cast me into the depth,
In the heart of the seas,
The flood was all around me;
And Your waves and billows
Passed over me.
Then I said, "I was cast out
From before Your eyes";
Yet I will look again
Toward Your holy temple.
The water encircled me all around,
Even to my very soul;
The deep embraced me;
The weeds were entwined around my head.
I went down to the bottoms of the mountains;
The earth with her bars closed upon me forever;
Yet, You brought up my life from the pit,
O Lord my God.
When my soul fainted within me,
I remembered the Lord;
And my prayer reached You,
In Your holy temple.
Those who regard lying vanities
Forsake their own good.
But I will sacrifice to You
With the voice of thanksgiving;
What I have vowed I will pay.
Salvation is of the Lord.

(Chapter II, Verses 3-10.)

God hears Jonah's prayer and instructs the fish to cast him up on dry land. He has submitted completely to God's will and has learned his lesson of unquestioning obedience. Again, God commands him to go to Nineveh. Jonah proceeds unhesitatingly to the capital of Assyria with God's message.

Yet forty days and Nineveh shall be overthrown. (Chapter III, Verse 4.)

The inhabitants are impressed after listening to the warning uttered by God's prophet. They acknowledge their wrongdoing and repent.

179

Their king dresses himself in sackcloth, proclaims a fast, and calls upon his people to cry mightily to God.

When God sees that the people are sincere, the contemplated punishment is rescinded. The city for the time being is saved. Jonah, however, is grieved because he feels he has failed in his mission and is angered because he had been sent to preach an imminent punishment which has not been fulfilled. He feels that he avoided coming to Nineveh in the first place because the people would gladly repent and make the voyage unnecessary.

I pray you, O Lord, did I not say this when I was still in my own country? Therefore I fled beforehand to Tarshish; for I knew that You were a gracious God and compassionate, long-suffering, and abundant in kindness, and repent of the evil. Therefore, now, O Lord, take, I pray You, my life from me; for it is better for me to die than to live. (Chapter IV, Verse 2.)

God rebukes Jonah and then Jonah goes out from the city. He sets up a little booth and sits under it in the shade to see what will happen in Nineveh. A large, fast-growing plant, a gourd, rises to shelter him from the hot sun and gives Jonah great comfort. The next morning, however, the gourd plant has withered because God has sent a worm to injure it from within. When the sun rises, God prepares a hot east wind, and the sun beats on Jonah's head so that he is faint and begs that he may die. And here by analogy God teaches Jonah a lesson.

You had pity on the gourd for which you did not labor nor make it grow, which came up in the night and perished in the night. Should I not have pity on Nineveh, that great city, in which there are more than six score thousand people who cannot discern between their right hand and their left hand, and also much cattle? (Chapter IV, Verses 10, 11.)

God feels compassion for the people. God is the God of all creatures. God will punish or save, depending on deeds. All may come to God for forgiveness and pardon.

Jonah questions whether the Ninevites are worthy of receiving the lofty messages of God's forgiveness, and he is taught by God that they, too, are worthy to receive God's love and compassion which extends to all. This explains why the entire Book of Jonah has been selected as the prophetic portion which is read in the synagogue at the afternoon service (Minhah) on Yom Kippur, the Day of Atonement.

MICAH

THE SIXTH BOOK OF THE TWELVE IS NAMED FOR MICAH, WHO was born in the earlier part of the eighth century. He is a younger contemporary of Hosea and Isaiah and was active during the reigns of the eighth-century kings Jotham, Ahaz, and Hezekiah of Judah. Unlike Isaiah, who lived in the city of Jerusalem, Micah was a country man. He is called the Morashtite because he is a native of Moresheth-Gath (Chapter 1, Verse 14), meaning a daughter village of Gath in Shephelah, a district in the lowlands of Judah in which his interest is manifest (Chapter I, Verses 10-15).

The days of Micah's active ministry followed the period of Jeroboam II's reign over Israel. It was Jeroboam II who brought political prestige, prosperity, and glory to his country. A sense of security prevailed as a flourishing commerce with foreign countries meant good living, luxury, and a pervading sense of happiness. With the eyes of a prophet, Micah saw a thin veneer of wealth and ease covering a decaying society. There was a constant, concentrated pursuit after material goods, the prime motivation of many, with concomitant social evils rampant. There was little regard for the less fortunate, the poor, the stricken who were exploited and oppressed. The qualities of human love, charity, compassion, sympathy were almost nonexistent, and poverty, misery and suffering were much in evidence. Micah emphasizes the fundamental principles of prophetic religion—justice, mercy, and humility.

More than other prophets, Micah understands the agony of the common people. He himself is a humble villager and has been called the

182

prophet of the poor. He knows poverty from personal experience, and his sympathies are with those suffering from social wrongs. As he lashes out against injustice and oppression, he condemns the rich who have wealth at the expense of the less fortunate. He threatens and promises by a combination of the sternness of Amos, who also originated in the country, and the compassion of Hosea.

Destruction is inevitable, as both Israel and Judah must be punished for their evildoing, and their special relationship with God will not spare them. As a chosen people their obligations are greater and they must be more ethical than other nations. With equal passion, Micah tries to teach and to elevate his people, presenting the essence of God's demands: justice, mercy, and humility.

The fall of Samaria fills neighboring Judah with apprehension. Micah's antipathy to militarism is strong as he prophesies that the evil has come to Judah and reaches to the gate, even to Jerusalem as he declares at Moresheth. His fervor and passionate expressions in favor of the ethical side of religion hold the powerful wealthy to account for social inequalities.

While the approaching humiliation of Israel will indeed be agonizing, Micah sees another future developing, another dawn rising. Gazing into the distance, he sees afar off in the end of days how the kingdom will be re-established when the faithful remnant will be restored to the land under the leadership of the messianic redeemer. Then all the nations of the world will recognize that God rules over all the world. They will acknowledge God's greatness and demands. Peace, justice, and righteousness will be ushered in, and will reign forever more. This twofold prophecy of Micah is similar to the teachings and visions of the other prophets. His particular strength lies in his powerful presentation and his concise formulation.

The seven-chapter book is divided by theme and subject matter into three parts. The first three chapters describe the prophet's vivid vision of the destruction. The next two have a different theme—the future of peace and justice. In the last two chapters, Micah's prophecy rises to sublime and noble emotional heights.

Micah opens with harsh words foretelling God's punishment, how it will happen and what the effect will be. The destined judgment will come to both Israel and Judah. Israel's destruction is imminent and Judah's desolation is sure to follow. Micah selects the capital cities as the symbols of his prophecy. They are both the centers of all the social evils, fountains of irreligiousness and consequent iniquity. Micah's first utter-

ances indicate the majesty and greatness of God coming to judge the
world:

Behold, the Lord coming from His place,
Will come down and tread upon the high places of the earth.
The mountains will melt under Him,
And the valleys will disintegrate
As wax before the fire,
As waters that are poured down a steep place. . . .

(Chapter I, Verses 3, 4.)

As God's prophet, Micah must speak up. He must carry the message
through the length and breadth of the country. Thus far he has spoken
in generalities. Now he becomes more specific. His perspective narrows. He directs his thoughts to certain groups, condemning each for its
share in the social evils extant:

Woe to those who plan iniquity
And work evil upon their beds!
When it is morning, they execute it,
Because they then have the power.
They covet fields, and seize them;
And houses, and take them away;
Thus they oppress a man and his home,
A man and his heritage.

(Chapter II, Verses 1, 2.)

Those who are guilty are stung and embarrassed by his frank words.
They are uncomfortable and try to stop Micah's accusations.

"Do not preach," they admonish him, but the prophet is compelled to
continue. He replies: Has God done this? Is God responsible?

With a change in tone, Micah pauses to mollify by speaking tenderly
and lovingly of the restoration to come in the end of days. He allows his
feelings of affection for his people to become apparent as he projects
into the future:

I will surely assemble all of you; O Jacob,
I will surely gather the remnant of Israel;

MICAH

I will render them all as sheep in a fold;
As a flock in the midst of their pasture. . . .
And the Lord is at their head.
> (Chapter II, Verses 12, 13.)

He cannot, however, linger long in this reverie, in this flight into the dim future. He therefore returns to reality. Resuming his attacks on injustice, turning now to the powerful judges of the land who have denied what is due to the people who come to them for help, he charges that certainly the judges, the authorities, who should dispense justice, should have been in the forefront in dispensing justice and observing God's laws.

Listen, you heads of Jacob,
And rulers of the house of Israel:
Is it not for you to dispense justice?
Who hate the good, and love the evil;
Who rob them of their skin
And their flesh from off their bones. . . .
> (Chapter III, Verses 1, 2.)

Micah now turns his attention to the false prophets. They have contributed to the demoralization of the people by creating an unreal sense of security, by not acting in accordance with moral standards but according to the gifts they receive. His most biting invective Micah reserves for the rulers and prophets who have led their people astray:

Listen, you heads of the house of Jacob,
And rulers of the house of Israel,
Who abhor justice, and pervert all equity
Who build up Zion with blood, and Jerusalem with iniquity.
The leaders judge for reward,
The priests teach for hire,
The prophets divine for money;
Yet lean on the Lord, and say,
Is not the Lord in our midst?
No evil will come upon us.
Therefore will Zion for your sake be plowed as a field,

And Jerusalem will become mounds,
And the mountain of the house as the high places of a forest.
(Chapter III, Verses 9-12.)

Divesting himself of bitterness and grief, Micah reflects on the future. In the second part of the book, he stands transfixed, in prophetic ecstasy, gazing beyond the world. He sees a beautiful vision of the future glory and restoration of Zion. True, Israel will suffer now but will be reborn. The day will come when all nations will recognize God's greatness. They will acknowledge God's universality over all the world. War will be abolished. Peace will reign.

His vision is almost word for word the magnificent portrayal of the end of days found in Isaiah. Micah's radiant words glow with prophetic fire.

It will come to pass in the end of days,
That the mountain of the Lord's house will be established
    on the top of the mountains.
And it will be exalted above the hills;
People will come to it in droves.
Many nations will come and say:
Come and let us go up to the mountain of the Lord,
And to the house of the God of Jacob;
He will teach us His ways,
And we shall walk in His paths;
For out of Zion will go forth the Law (Torah),
And the word of the Lord from Jerusalem.
He shall judge between many peoples,
And shall decide about mighty nations far away;
They shall beat their swords into plowshares,
And their spears into pruning-hooks;
Nation shall not lift up sword against nation,
Nor shall they learn war any more.
But they shall sit every man under his vine and under
    his fig tree;
And none shall make them afraid;
For the Lord of hosts has so asserted.
(Chapter IV, Verses 1-5.)

MICAH

Micah now strikes at the heart of his sublime revelation: the relationship between God and Israel. How is God to be served? What are God's demands? What are people's roles in life and in relation to the Lord? God speaks to Israel, asking: What have I done? Wherein have I failed? What unkept promises did I make? Are My demands excessive? Are they unreasonable? God invites the people to testify. But the people do not respond. By implication they admit the accusations. One can almost feel the sensitive pleading:

Listen, O mountain, to the Lord's controversy,
And you enduring rocks, the foundations of the earth;
For the Lord has a controversy with His people,
He pleads with Israel.
O My people, what have I done to you?
And where have I failed you?
Testify against Me. . . .

(Chapter VI, Verses 2, 3.)

The people are silent. They seek guidance. How is God to be served? How shall they come to God? What shall they do? They seek instruction. Shall they come with burnt offerings and sacrifices? Is this the way to serve God? No, says the prophet, not through sacrifices can one come to God. Not even with thousands of ram offerings can Israel show its gratitude.

And now Micah reaches his greatest heights as he proclaims concisely and precisely the simple and noble demands God makes.

It has been told to you, O man, what is good,
And what the Lord requires of you;
Only to do justly, and to love mercy, and to walk humbly
with your God.

(Chapter VI, Verse 8.)

Thus does Micah condense the individual's duty to God and to other people.

We have learned of coming punishment as we have been assured of a glorious future. We have been told what the demands are that God makes of people. Micah's last chapter moves rapidly to the close of his prophecies. It combines his many-sided feelings. He is deeply grieved as he looks about him on the evils that exist. He bemoans the present and what he sees. He makes a final survey of the present society. He looks for upright people but he is sorely disappointed. As for himself, says the prophet, his undeviating faith and his trust are in God:

> But as for me, I will look to the Lord;
> I will wait for the God of my salvation;
> My God will hear me. (Chapter VII,
> Verse 7.)

With compassion, Micah ends his ministry. He knows his attacks have been scathing. He has not, however, lost his affectionate tenderness for his people. Micah offers a psalm, an appeal to God for mercy and forgiveness. In his heart, he knows that the future will be better. For this he prays with all his soul:

> Who is a God like You, who pardons iniquity,
> And disregards the transgression of the remnant of
> His heritage?
> He does not retain His anger forever.
> Because He delights in mercy.
> He will again have compassion upon us;
> He will subdue our iniquities;
> You will cast all our sins into the depths of the sea.
> You will show faithfulness to Jacob and mercy to Abraham,
> As You have promised our fathers in days of old.
>   (Chapter VII, Verses 18-20.)

Micah's lofty themes, a cry for social justice, for peace, and a world without wars have stirred the hearts of people throughout the ages. His divinely inspired messages have penetrated the fibers of religion and religious ideals. They live today as they have vibrated within people's minds from the times of antiquity to the present day.

NAHUM

NAHUM, MEANING "RICH IN COMFORT," IS THE SEVENTH BOOK of the Twelve. All that is known of the Prophet Nahum is that he is an Elkoshite, but even the locality of the people denoted is uncertain. However, it is known that Nahum's prophecy lies between the time of the capture of Thebes (No-amon) and its destruction in the year 663 B.C.E., and 612 B.C.E., the date of the fall of Nineveh, capital of Assyria, conquered by the Babylonians and the Medes.

The main features of this three-chapter volume of poetry of a high order are: First, Nahum's prophecy contains a singleness of purpose and theme. His attention is to the coming annihilation of Assyria's beautiful capital city of Nineveh because of its maltreatment of many nations, especially Israel. Second, there is no reference to the evils and sins of Judah. Nahum does not denounce his own people as did the other prophets. Nor does he speak of Judah's obligation to God. By implication, Judah is a good and righteous people. Third, Nahum's emphasis is on vengeance and retribution, not emphasized by other prophets.

The literary style of this obscure prophet is unparalleled in prophetic literature. It reaches heights of sublimity in words which are sharp, vigorous, realistic, full of fire. The phrases are terse, compact, yet full and deep, rich in poetic feeling. Nahum's power of description is so realistic that it draws the reader into what is transpiring. The vivid imagery excites the mind and inflames the emotions as the champion of the vanquished speaks as an outraged human being against the conquerors.

189

THE PROPHETS

The first chapter gives an exalted picture of God appearing in judgment as defender of oppressed people. God is long-suffering, patient, and forgiving, yet great in power, and therefore God will not allow the guilty to be cleared without punishment. The enemies of Israel will be destroyed.

The Lord is a jealous and avenging God. . . .
He is long-suffering, and great in power,
And will by no means clear the guilty. . . .
The mountains shake before Him,,
And the hills melt;
The earth is upheaved at His presence,
Yes, the world, and all who live in it.
Who can withstand His indignation?
And who can abide the fierceness of His anger?
His fury pours out like fire,
And the rocks are broken before Him.
(Chapter I, Verses 2, 3, 5-6.)

God will, however, protect and save those who put their trust in the Lord. God is good to those who have implicit faith in the Lord; they need not fear.

The Lord is good,
A stronghold on the day of trouble;
He knows those who take refuge in Him.
(Chapter I, Verse 7.)

To oppressors, tyrants, ruthless leaders, God will withhold protection. An end will be made of those who afflicted Israel when they plundered the people and opposed the God of justice. Once the enemies are destroyed, they will not rise up again.

Nahum has introduced the prophecy of the fall of Assyria. In the second chapter, he proceeds to offer a vivid narration of the actual physical devastation. In his overpowering portrayal, there is a mingling of fantasy and realism. With Nahum we witness the invasion. We watch, breathlessly, the flight of the citizens in the face of the attackers. The heavy city walls are battered until they tumble down. Assyria's splendor and glory crumble into an ignoble heap of ruins. There is rejoicing among the people of Judah who will soon see the complete end of its oppressors. The burden of life will be eased as Judah will be restored to pristine glory.

A challenger has come up against you;
Guard your defenses,
Watch the way, strengthen your loins,
Fortify your power mightily!
For the Lord restores the pride of Jacob,
As well as the pride of Israel;
For the attackers have made them bare
And marred their branches.
The shield of his mighty men is painted red,
The valiant men are dressed in scarlet;
The chariots are fire of steel on the day of his preparation,
And the cypress spears are made to poison.
The chariots rush madly in the streets,
They jostle each other in the fields;
Their appearance is like torches.
They run to and fro like streaks of lightning.

(Chapter II, Verses 2-5.)

Nahum describes the unavailing efforts of the Assyrian leaders to retrench, to re-form their ranks, to set up stronger fortifications, to store up more provisions and water. Yet it is predestined that evil Nineveh be destroyed and nothing can prevent the catastrophe. So complete will be the devastation of the power of Assyria, the nation will never rise again. Nahum compares Assyria to a ferocious lion who secures its victim and shows no mercy.

Where is the den of lions,
Which was the feeding place of the young lions,
Where the lion and the lioness walked,
And the lion's cub, and none made them afraid? . . . .

(Chapter II, Verse 12.)

Nahum now directs his words specifically to the capital city of Nineveh. What are its crimes? Ruthlessness, treachery, deceit, dishonesty. He philosophizes that a people which tyranizes must in the end itself expect tyranny. Assyria and its chief city Nineveh will receive a just recompense for the cruelties to their victims. The third chapter is devoted to a breathtaking description of the razing of the city:

Woe to the bloody city!
It is full of lies and robbery;
The prey does not depart.
Hark! The noise of the whip, and hark! The noise of
    the rattling of wheels;
Prancing horses and bounding chariots;
The horsemen charging,
The flashing sword, and the glittering spear;
There is a mass of slain and a heap of dead;
There is no end of bodies,
They stumble on their corpses. . . .

        (Chapter III, Verses 1-3.)

The invaders will have no difficulty capturing Nineveh. No matter how impregnable it seems, the city will succumb quickly, easily.

All your fortresses will be like fig trees with the first-ripe figs;
If they are shaken, they will fall into the mouths of the eaters.

        (Chapter III, Verse 12.)

With a blaze of irony and sarcasm, the prophet chides the inhabitants. He taunts them to build greater strongholds and fortifications, increase the population, work diligently for defense. Nineveh nevertheless is doomed not to rise again, he insists.

Nahum's prophecy closes on a note of confidence and exultation. There is jubilation when the joyful news of the fall of the oppressor is conveyed to Judah.

Looking beyond the sternness expressed by the prophet, we find in the highest degree his justified moral indignation. The injustice typified by the powerful and wealthy Nineveh moves him to condemnation. He believes this nation of Assyrians, which "has multiplied its merchants more than the stars of heaven," like every other nation, is accountable to a basically moral world, that God's judgment is based on reason, predicated on a basic teaching holding that nations, as people, must live in accordance with God's principles of justice and morality, and that only righteous governments can maintain a nation securely. Nahum's poetic prophecy therefore teaches the principle that not only will evil be punished but right and justice will in the end triumph.

HABAKKUK

NOTHING IS KNOWN ABOUT THE LIFE AND HABITAT OF HABAK-
kuk, whose name is borne by the eighth book of the Twelve Prophets. It
is believed that he lived around the end of the seventh century, since
Nineveh had already fallen and the days were drawing near for the capture of Jerusalem, and the exile of its people to Babylonia.

The noble message Habakkuk delivers in three brief chapters has become part of religious language and thought. The prophet searches for
answers to the age-old question of the meaning of justice which per-
plexes him because he sees righteous people suffer while the wicked
apparently prosper and enjoy the blessings life has to offer.

The first part of the book presents a dialogue with God in which he
queries whether it is justice for foreign countries to plunder his people,
oppress them, succeed in their treachery, enjoy their power, while less
sinful people suffer afflictions. This suffering of good people and the joy
of the wicked have caused the people to lose faith in the Torah. They no
longer regard the law of Moses as a living guide, as God's law, so that
the prophet cries to God against continued violence and injustice:

How long, O Lord, shall I cry out
And You will not hear?
I cry to You of violence
And You will not save.
Why do You show me wrong,

194

And cause me to see misconduct?
Why are spoiling and violence before me?
So that there is strife and contention?
Therefore the Law is not observed,
And justice never goes forth; . . .

(Chapter I, Verses 2-4.)

God answers the challenge by saying that the Chaldeans have already begun to rise up, "a bitter and impetuous nation that marches through the breadth of the earth," whose formidable resources are invincible and who will destroy the wicked. They may prosper now but their success is not enduring. With their swift horses sweeping across the plains, they come as the divine instruments to punish the wicked and annihilate their land.

Their horses are swifter than leopards,
They are fiercer than the wolves of the desert;
Their horsemen spread themselves;
Yes, their horsemen come from afar,
They fly as vultures rushing to devour.

(Chapter I, Verse 8.)

Habakkuk listens to the spoken word but is not satisfied. To the contrary, he is bitterly distressed, for God's words indicate that the people will be completely destroyed. True, they are not all perfect. There are wicked to be found among them. Should they indeed all be wiped out? Will God permit this? Is this justice and does this not exceed God's mandate of sending the Chaldeans to swallow up Israel? They are intended to correct and not to destroy.

Habakkuk confronts God a second time:

Are You not from everlasting?
O Lord my God, my Holy One?
We shall not die.
O Lord, You have ordained them for judgment.
O Mighty One, You have established them for correction.
You who have eyes too pure to see evil,
You cannot look at iniquity,
Why do You permit treachery

And remain quiet when the wicked swallow up
The man who is righteous.

(Chapter I, Verses 12, 13, 17.)

I will stand on my watch,
Place myself on the tower,
And will wait to see what He will say to me
And what I shall answer when I am reproved.

(Chapter II, Verse 1.)

God answers by demanding patience and by declaring that the righteous will live by faithfulness:

The Lord answered me and said:
Write the vision down
And make it plain upon tablets
So that a man may read it quickly.
For the vision is for the appointed time,
It declares of the future and does not lie;
Though it may tarry, wait for it;
Because it will surely come, it will not delay.
Behold, his soul is puffed up, it is not upright in him;
But the righteous shall live by his faith.

(Chapter II, Verses 2-4.)

The last sentence (Verse 4) forms Habakkuk's eternal message. Faithfulness, steadfastness, undeviating devotion to God will ultimately triumph.

The prophet now turns his attention to the conquering hosts. He cites a series of five woes or threats upon Babylonia because it has despoiled Judah.

Woe to him who increases that which is not his. . .
Woe to him who gains evil gains for his house. . .
Woe to him who builds a town with blood. . .
Woe to him who gives his neighbor drink. . .
What profit the graven image. . . . Woe to him who says
to the wood: "Awake." . . .

(Chapter II, Verses, 9, 12, 15, 18, 19.)

HABAKKUK

In metaphor and directly, the woes underscore grasping rapacity, proud self-aggrandizements, cruel exactions, exulting triumph, or senseless idolatry. Habakkuk's final woe attacks idol worshipers. Full of biting sarcasm, it reaches a climax as the graven image is contrasted with the living God in a magnificent passage often used, bespeaking God's greatness and omnipotence.

> The Lord is in His Holy Temple;
> Let all the earth be silent before Him.
> (Chapter II, Verse 20.)

The last chapter, with its expression of thanksgiving, joy, faith, and trust, is one of the remarkable lyrical odes of literature. The prophet now turns to God, without questioning, and entreats God to intercede for the people. As he previously challenged, so does he now humbly pray:

> O Lord, I have heard of Your renown and I am afraid;
> O Lord, revive Your works in the midst of the years,
> In the midst of the years make them known;
> In anger, remember compassion.
> (Chapter III, Verse 2.)

The prophet envisions God approaching with all the Lord's glorious paraphernalia and retinue of war in answer to his prayer. God comes to champion the Chosen People and to overthrow their enemy. The world may be cast into a state of chaos which is designed to bring ultimate salvation to Israel:

> God comes from Teman,
> And the Holy One from Mount Paran.
> His glory covers the heavens,
> And the earth is full of His praise.
> A brightness appears as the light;
> Rays has He at his side;
> And there is His power hidden.
> Before Him goes the pestilence,
> And fiery bolts go forth at His heels.

He stands and surveys the earth,
He beholds and the nations tremble;
The everlasting mountains are dashed to pieces,
The ancient hills bow;
His ways are everlasting. . . .
You come forth for the deliverance of Your people.
For the deliverance of Your anointed.
                    (Chapter III, Verses 3-6, 13.)

Habakkuk has complete confidence in Israel's salvation. Through pain and anguish the people will yet rejoice in God's manifold blessings. Habakkuk reaches the peak of eternal faith.

I will rejoice in the Lord,
I will exult in the God of my salvation.
The Lord God is my strength,
He makes my feet like hinds' feet.
And he makes me to walk on high places.
                    (Chapter III, Verses 18, 19.)

The preaching, begun with skepticism and doubt, with questions, challenges, and demands, is brought to a close on a deep note of unquestioning confidence and absolute dependence on God which is the glory of the religion of the Bible and the important contribution of Habakkuk to the spirit of Judaism. His message inspires hope; it encourages the righteous who have maintained their devotion to God, God's principles, and God's way of Life. They know that they will triumph, for the righteous shall live by their faith.

ZEPHANIAH

ZEPHANIAH, NINTH BOOK OF THE TWELVE, COMPRISES THREE compact chapters. Some scholars trace the lineage of Zephaniah ("whom God had hidden") to his great-great-grandfather Hezekiah, king of Judah. Of a distinguished, noble family, the prophet was well educated and influenced by the seventh-century prophets Habakkuk and Jeremiah, his contemporaries.

A citizen of Jerusalem, he did not hesitate to criticize royalty while sparing the king himself. The teachings of Zephaniah fit the conditions of the seventh century, immediately prior to the reformation instituted by King Josiah in 621 B.C.E. The evils he deplored are similar to those alluded to in II Kings, Chapter XXI, characteristic in Judah until King Josiah was moved to action by the finding of the scroll in the Temple.

After the fall of Nineveh in 612 B.C.E., the Assyrian court removed to Haran, which was also taken in 610 B.C.E. Thus fell Assyria, an empire which had dominated Palestine for two centuries and was a political threat in the west for a thousand years. The Scythians threaten Judah from the north. Zephaniah's prophecy is one of a large group of prophecies against historic enemies including Edom, Philistia, Moab, Ammon.

The gloom of political milieu is relieved by the promise of a territory extending from the Mediterranean to the Syrian desert. After a period of punishment, God's jealousy against Judah is turned to jealousy for the Chosen People, and in this Zephaniah agreed with Zechariah and Haggai in which the remnant are comforted by the return of God to Zion and the dispersed exiles are brought back.

Zephaniah severely denounces evil and injustice, addressing himself to both the leaders and the people because they have strayed from the paths of righteousness. He thunders the message of catastrophe. He says, however, that annihilation will not be complete. A remnant, a faithful group, will survive, and, duly chastened and humbled, will lead others to accept God's sovereignty. Zephaniah also brings comfort and hope, prophesying a new era when the hearts of people will have been changed to the ways of God.

What differentiates Zephaniah from other prophets is his tremendous command of realistic language in his terrifying portion and threat, and not positive moral teaching as the main burden of his preaching. In comparatively few verses, he presents the major doctrines of sin, suffering, retribution, repentance, and salvation. Three words describe the running theme in this slight volume: warning, penance, promise. The significant event of destruction for the wicked is called by the prophet "the day of the Lord." For judgment day, he presents an allegory portraying a great sacrifical feast in which the people inhabiting the earth—all those who adopted foreign customs, clothes, and traditions with strange rites—are themselves the sacrifices. And who are to be the guests? They are the invaders sent by God to punish the evildoers.

This is God's proclamation:

I will consume everything completely
From off the face of the earth,
Says the Lord. . . .
I will cut man off from the face of the earth. . . .
And those who worshiped the host of heaven upon
   the housetops,
And those who worship, who swear to the Lord
And swear by Malcam. . . .
Hold your peace at the presence of the Lord God;
For the day of the Lord is at hand,
For the Lord has prepared a sacrifice,
He has consecrated his guests.
And it shall come to pass on the day of the Lord's
   sacrifice,
That I will punish the princes, the king's children,
And all who are clothed in foreign apparel.
On the same day will I also punish those who leap over
   the threshold,
Who fill their master's house with violence and deceit. . . .

And I will punish the men who rest on their lees,
Who say in their heart:
'The Lord will not do good, nor will He do evil.'
(Chapter I, Verses 2, 3, 5, 7-9, 12.)

Zephaniah then resorts to mellowness in appealing to the people to repent and turn from unrighteous living before it is too late:

Seek the Lord, all you humble of the earth,
Who have fulfilled His ordinance;
Seek righteousness, seek humility. . . .
(Chapter II, Verse 3.)

He assures the small group of the faithful that they will not be forgotten. Salvation shall be theirs. They will, indeed, be compensated with the lands and possessions of the enemy.

It shall be a portion for the remnant of the house of Judah,
On which they will feed;
In the houses of Ashkelon will they lie down in the evening;
For the Lord their God will remember them,
And turn away their captivity.
(Chapter II, Verse 7.)

Like other prophets before him, Zephaniah turns his denunciation upon the foreign countries, the Philistines, the Moabites, Ammonites, the Ethiopians, Assyrians. He condemns them for their contempt, hostility, and intrusion. Nor does he spare his own city, Jerusalem, for whom he reserves his strongest words, which are wrung from his anguished heart.

In the third chapter Jerusalem is arraigned before Zephaniah's wrath:

Woe to her who is sullied and polluted,
To the oppressing city!
She did not listen to the voice,
She did not accept correction;

She did not trust in the Lord,
She did not draw near to her God.
Her princes within her are roaring lions,
Her judges are wolves of the desert;
They do not leave a bone for the morrow.
Her prophets are wanton
And treacherous people;
Her priests have profaned that which is holy,
They have done violence to the law. . . .

(Chapter III, Verses 1-4.)

Zephaniah now reaches the promise for his people after "the day of the Lord." To the faithful remnant, he pictures the glorious Golden Age. He tells them to be patient, to wait and watch. The nations will be gathered together. They will have knowledge of God and will unite in worshiping God. A new race of people will inhabit the earth who will live better with justice. Changed attitudes and changed hearts will bring a noble era of peace.

The remnant of Israel will not do wrong,
Nor speak lies,
Nor will a deceitful tongue be found in their mouth;
For they will feed and lie down,
And none will make them afraid.

(Chapter III, Verses 12-13.)

He summons the people to offer an ode of thanksgiving to God, to be joyous and glad because they will be restored to God's favor with an even greater affection when the exile will be over and forgotten. Zion, Israel, will once again be under God's care and loving protection. The world will give recognition and respect to Zion.

Sing, O daughter of Zion,
Shout, O Israel;
Be glad and rejoice with all your heart,
O daughter of Jerusalem. . . .
The Lord your God is in your midst,
A mighty One who will save;
He will rejoice over you with joy,

ZEPHANIAH

He will be silent in His love,
He will rejoice over you with singing. . . .
At that time I will bring you in,
And at that time I will gather you;
For I will make you to be a name and praised
Among all the peoples of the earth. . . .

(Chapter III, Verses 14, 17, 20.)

Denouncing the unrighteousness of his age, Zephaniah is merciless on those guilty of intrigue, dishonesty, evil and idolatry. He extends a promise of comfort and hope to those who live righteously or repent of their wickedness. He concludes his message with a prophecy of the Golden Age, a glorious world in which all people will worship one God, live harmoniously with each other, and where peace will reign eternal.

HAGGAI

THE BOOK OF HAGGAI, TENTH OF THE SECTIONS DEVOTED TO the Twelve, is also the first of a small segment of three books—Haggai, Zechariah, and Malachi—which form a separate group of successive prophets whose ministry covers a specific post-exilic period in Jewish history. This group treats of events after the destruction of Jerusalem, the end of the kingdom of Judah in 586 B.C.E., and the beginning of the exile to Babylonia.

The prophets who preceded Haggai, Zechariah, and Malachi were active in the time surrounding the fall in 722 B.C.E. of Israel, Northern Kingdom of Palestine, and during the period of Judah's devastation. A few prophets preached after the Babylonian exile began but these three appeared much later. Haggai and Zechariah were chiefly concerned with the rebuilding of the Temple of Jerusalem (Second Temple) in the latter part of the sixth century. The prophet Malachi, whose book closes the writings of the prophets, preached sixty or seventy years thereafter. While little is known about Haggai, it is indicated by his book that he prophesied for a brief four months during the year 520 B.C.E.

When most of the inhabitants of Judah were brought to Babylonia after their lands were confiscated and the Temple was shattered, Palestine became a province of the Babylonian empire, which maintained its world supremacy for half a century, and its decline began as Persia became the rising world power. Cyrus the Great of Persia entered Babylon in 544 B.C.E. and when it was subdued, Palestine became one of the provinces of the newly formed Persian empire. The first emperor, who was given to conciliating his conquered peoples, decreed in the first year of his reign (538 B.C.E.) that the Jewish people who wished to do so might return to Palestine. Many availed themselves of the offer to return to the old homeland, and over forty thousand Jews undertook to return.

Almost immediately after their resettlement, the pioneers began to rebuild the ruined House of God on Zion hill. Amid rejoicing, expressions of thanksgiving and gratitude, they laid the foundations of what was to become Jerusalem's Second Temple. The reconstruction, so enthusiastically undertaken, was not, however, destined to continue. No sooner had they begun when unforeseen forces interfered with the rebuilding plans. There were difficulties with the Samaritans, a group which had settled near Jerusalem who offered to help. Their offer was denied on the grounds that the Temple must be the sole effort of the Jewish people. The Samaritans, in retaliation, conspired to hamper and harry the progress of construction. Their efforts were effective enough to lessen the enthusiastic fervor. Additionally, there were economic considerations. Harvests had been poor so that food supplies were scarce. People had primarily to concentrate on fulfilling their daily needs. The rebuilding of the Temple therefore reached an impasse. This was in 537 B.C.E. The inactivity lasted for about sixteen years.

At this juncture, Haggai appears to resume the building program. The historical background comprises Persia's difficulties with the Egyptian rulers so that, in a maze of intrigue and rivalry between Persia and Egypt, armies are near, around and through Palestine causing the inhabitants to be apprehensive and disturbed. At the same time, Darius I has problems with other rival countries which, one by one, strive to disentangle themselves from the influence of Persia. News of wars and strife is heard throughout the land. Haggai inteprets the tumultuous times as rumblings to precede the coming of the messianic era. He feels that God's sacred Temple must be completely rebuilt to welcome the great and long-awaited Golden Age. Applying religious significance to political events, the prophet believes prevailing adverse conditions are due to the people's apathetic attitude toward building the Temple. The indifference of the populace Haggai interprets as the very reason for the poor harvests and destitute situations. Build the House of God, urges the prophet, and God's manifold blessings will accrue; security and prosperity will be yours.

The people heed the prophetic call and within three weeks begin the reconstruction of the great Temple, laboring zealously for a period of four years to its completion. In the year 516 B.C.E., twenty years after the foundation stones were laid and seventy years after the Babylonian exile began, the Second Temple stands gloriously in Jerusalem, the city of God.

The slight book of two chapters and thirty-eight sentences contains five brief sections of prose permeated with a depth of sincerity and religious conviction. Haggai directs his appeal jointly to Zerubbabel, the governor of Judah appointed by Darius, and to Joshua, the high priest. Zerubbabel is the son of Shealtiel and grandson of King Jehoichin, who was carried off to Babylonia in 585 B.C.E. Joshua is the grandson of the high priest who ministered in the First Temple that same year. Thus the thread of continuity of the monarchy of David and the priesthood has been retained.

In the second year of King Darius, on the first day of the sixth month, Haggai speaks to these two leaders of the people as the book opens, urging them to devote themselves to rebuilding the Holy Temple. The people hesitate, reluctant to resume such a gigantic enterprise. They maintain that the time has not yet come. The prophet first chides them for being preoccupied with building beautiful homes for themselves (those who can afford them) and neglecting the rebuilding of the Temple. He says that the prevalent distress of crop failures is due to God's indignation for delaying the Temple reconstruction. Let them rebuild, he assures them, and God will take pleasure in it and will acknowledge the honor:

Is it a time for you to dwell in your ceilinged houses,
    while this House lies in ruins? . . .
Consider your ways:
You have sown much and brought in little.
You eat, but you do not have enough,
You drink, but you are not filled with drink.
You clothe yourselves, but no one is warm;
And he who earns wages earns wages
For a bag with holes. . . .
Go up to the hills, bring wood, and build the House; I will
    take pleasure in it, and I will be glorified, says the Lord.
                                    (Chapter I, Verses 4-6, 8.)

Restored in spirit by Haggai's encouragement, the people undertake the work without further delay. The second chapter is a further encouragement. The prophet turns to his older contemporaries, who recall the beauty and grandeur of the First Temple of Solomon and find the second structure, beautiful as it is, mean in comparison. (The language suggests that Haggai is old enough to have seen the Temple of Solomon destroyed in 586 B.C.E.) Haggai is concerned about this attitude, for it may well undermine the initiative of the workers. In one of his more eloquent messages, he asserts that the Second Temple will outshine the first. God will soon bestir and inspire all of the nations of the world and the choicest gifts of gold and wealth will pour willingly into the Temple to adorn the Lord's House.

Who is left among you who saw this House in its former glory? How do you see it now? Is not such a one as nothing in your eyes? Yet now be strong, O Zerubbabel, says the Lord; and be strong, O Joshua, son of Jehozadak, the high priest; and be strong, all you people of the land, says the Lord, and work; for I am with you. . . . I will shake all nations, and the choicest things of all nations will come, and I will fill this House with glory. . . . The glory of this House will be greater than that of the former, says the Lord of hosts; and in this place will I give peace. . . . (Chapter II, Verses 3, 4, 7, 9.)

Two addresses are now delivered, the first directed to the priests who are asked ritual questions dealing with purity and impurity. The prophet is not concerned with the literal answer. He draws the moral that it is much easier for the wicked to influence the righteous than vice versa. He goes further and associates his thinking with the experience of building the Temple. He shows that those who oppose the rebuilding can readily influence the proponents of restoration. Some say that the question is related to the matter of the Samaritans being involved in the rebuilding, as they had requested. The content would indicate a decision to permit only Jews to share in the building of the Temple.

The prophet's final address is given on the twenty-fourth day of the month. He looks to the future and speaks encouragingly to Zerubbabel, governor of Judah, assuring him of God's special favor and protection in the impending catastrophe of kingdoms and nations to which the prophet had formerly pointed as preceding the glorification of God's House.

With the prophet Zechariah, Haggai's role is vitally crucial. His earnestness, zeal, and contagious enthusiasm animated the Jewish people who had returned sixteen years earlier from their exile in Babylonia, to undertake the overwhelming enterprise of rebuilding the ruined Temple of Solomon. Haggai's love for the Temple and his conception of its centrality in Jewish life inspires the congregation to sustain the arduous rebuilding in Jerusalem of the House of God. It may be said that Haggai's four months of active ministry directed and changed the course of Jewish history as well as of Judaism itself.

ZECHARIAH

ZECHARIAH, ELEVENTH BOOK OF THE TWELVE, IS ALSO SEC-
ond of the separate group of three: Haggai, Zechariah, Malachi, the
post-exilic prophets active after the destruction of the government of
Judah and the beginning of the Babylonian exile in 586 B.C.E. The other
prophets were active at the time surrounding the fall of the Northern
Kingdom of Israel in 722 B.C.E. and in the period of the downfall of
Judah. A few prophets preached somewhat after the beginning of the
exile. However, Haggai, Zechariah, and Malachi were active toward the
close of the exilic period. Haggai and Zechariah were directly involved
in the building of the Second Temple in 520 to 516 B.C.E. The words of
Malachi were heard sixty or seventy years thereafter.

The prophecies of Zechariah are dated exactly in 520 B.C.E. (Chapter
I, Verses 1 and 7) and in 518 B.C.E. (Chapter VII, Verse 1) and are
found in the first eight chapters of the book which bears his name. The
historical setting was similar to that of Haggai. Almost fifty years had
elapsed since the inhabitants of Judah were carried off into Babylonia
during which time the Jews, counseled by the prophet Jeremiah,
learned to live peacefully in the land of their captors and to become
good citizens. However, the Babylonian nation began to lose its prestige
and power as another nation rose in its place to dominant world power.
When Persia conquered Babylonia in 539 B.C.E., the then province of
Palestine became subject to Persia.

In Babylon, the city of merchants, the fortunes of the exiles greatly
improved and many grew opulent through mercantile pursuits, acquir-

ing influence in court circles. When Nebuchadrezzar was followed upon the throne by his son Evil-merodach, the latter, in his first year of rule, released King Jehoiachin from prison and accorded the Jewish king some royal honors. This is the last event recorded in the Book of Kings. Thus the movement of restoration was under way, but Evil-merodach reigned only two years and the last king of Babylonia, Nabonidus (555-538) was occupied in repelling the attacks of the Medes under Astyages. When the Persians vanquished the Medes, Cyrus became master of Babylon. A cry of jubilation came from the Jews and was even greater when, in the spring of 538, King Cyrus issued a royal declaration from his summer palace at Ecbatana, granting permission for the Jews to return to Jerusalem to rebuild the Temple of God and surrendering to them also their sacred Temple vessels. The book of Ezra records the historic trek of thousands of Jews from Babylonia who became pioneers once more in the promised land of their ancestors.

Zechariah, probably among the returnees from Babylon, a member of the priestly group, and a younger contemporary of Haggai, began his active ministry two months after Haggai. The general portent of his message is similar: to inspire the people to complete the rebuilding of the Temple in Jerusalem.

The Book of Zechariah—much longer and more complex than that of Haggai—contains fourteen chapters, divided into two major parts, the first section: Chapters I to VIII and the second part Chapters IX to XIV. Unlike Haggai, Zechariah uses the strong approach, calling for repentance and denouncing evil. He sees the doom of nations that have oppressed Israel and at the same time envisions the coming of the messianic era. Many of his verses have become part of the daily prayerbook and have been adopted in the synagogue ritual. His most characteristic narration is the vision, in which technique he resembles the prophet Ezekiel. Zechariah experiences eight visions, all following the same pattern. Looking into the heavens whence the vision originates, he inquires of an accompanying angel the interpretation of the vision, which in each instance shows God's intervention on behalf of the Jewish people.

The book begins with a brief, firm call to repentance. The year is 520 B.C.E. The reigning Persian king is Darius. Zechariah speaks to the returnees, urging them to cling to their worship of God, reaffirming their faith. He points out that their ancestors heard the prophets speak but did not heed their warnings. He offers the basis of an understanding between themselves and God. If they change their ways and accept God wholeheartedly, God will shower them with blessings. Zechariah pleads for them to renew their rebuilding of the Temple as a token of their love of God.

ZECHARIAH

*   *   *

Each of the eight night visions of Zechariah bears an individual message. In totality they serve to banish disturbing thoughts and fears, portraying God's manifestation in the world. We see Zechariah's concept of God governing the universe, God's concern for the people and promise to establish Jerusalem as the Holy City of Peace. We learn of the prophet's ideas of sin, ethics, morals, ritual, and religious ceremonial.

The first vision depicts a man with four horses, each of a different color, the leader riding on a flaming red horse. These are God's four messengers sent throughout the world. An angel explains the vision for Zechariah. The nations enjoy security. Only Jerusalem experiences unrest and turmoil, but this will change. Jerusalem, too, will have peace. God will fulfill promises of mercy:

> I will return to Jerusalem with compassion: My House will be built in it, says the Lord of hosts, and a line will be stretched over Jerusalem. Again, proclaim, saying: Thus says the Lord of hosts: My cities will again overflow with prosperity; and the Lord will yet comfort Zion, and will yet choose Jerusalem. (Chapter I, Verses 16, 17.)

The second vision is that of the four horns and the four craftsmen, which, explains the angel, signify the four powers which have overthrown and scattered Judah and Israel and who in turn will be overthrown by the craftsmen.

The third is that of the man with the measuring line. A young man traverses the boundaries of Jerusalem and measures the area, to establish the new ramparts when he is suddenly recalled and told there is no further need for measuring as no new walls are necessary. God himself will be the protector of Jerusalem. God will be the wall about the city.

> Run, speak to this young man and say: Jerusalem will be lived in without walls. . . . For I myself, says the Lord, will be a wall of fire all around her, and I will be the glory in her midst. (Chapter II, Verses 8, 9.)

As part of this vision, Zechariah issues a call to all Jewish people to return from exile to Zion. With the Temple rebuilt, God will dwell there and it will be a time of rejoicing for all:

211

Sing and rejoice, O daughter of Zion; for lo, I come, and I will dwell in your midst, says the Lord. Many nations will join themselves to the Lord on that day, and will become My people and I will dwell in your midst. (Chapter II, Verses 14, 15.)

In the next vision, the prophet imagines Joshua the high priest standing in unclean clothes before the angel of God. At his side Satan accuses him and God rebukes Satan. Joshua's unclean robes are removed and replaced with regal, priestly garments. He is charged with various duties of his position, including proper conduct, observance of the commandments, leadership of the people in the laws of God, and diligence in maintaining the ritual in the Temple. Joshua is thus vindicated and consecrated to the primary position of spiritual leadership.

The fifth vision is the golden candlestick with a constant flow of oil. There is a bowl above the candlestick. Along each side stands an olive tree. These trees feed the bowl through two golden spouts, and the bowl, in turn, feeds into the candlestick through seven individual pipes. Again Zechariah asks his angelic guide for the meaning:

Then he answered me, saying: "This is the word of the Lord to Zerubbabel, saying, Not by might, nor by power, but by My spirit, says the Lord of hosts. (Chapter IV, Verse 6.)

The candlestick represents the spirit of God and the two olive trees are symbolic of Joshua and Zerubbabel, who are jointly to lead the people. As God's spirit is invisible, so will the unseen inspire Zerubbabel to complete the rebuilding of the Temple. Thus the fourth and the fifth visions are directed to the two leaders appointed to rule, one of the priesthood and the other of royalty. Both will be constantly inspired by the divine spirit which flows uninterruptedly.

Vision six follows immediately. Zechariah sees a parchment scroll flying through the air. It is unusually large. There is writing on it. This vision is explained as a curse against evil; and it means that all the wicked will be wiped out. The land will be completely purged.

The seventh vision is that of the woman in the measure. The prophet sees a woman sitting in a measure. A round piece of lead nearby, lifted up, is seen covering the woman. The woman in the measure is then lifted and carried off into Babylon. The vision, Zechariah learns, explains the woman as sin personified: "This is wickedness." Wickedness is carried away and completely removed from Judah, thus purifying and cleansing the land.

The last vision is that of the four chariots. Zechariah sees the chariots coming from between two mountains of brass. The horses are of varied colors, red, black, white, and bay. These are messengers of God. They have presented themselves before God, received instructions, and are now relaying God's messages throughout the world. They travel to different corners of the earth and their duty: to bring punishment upon the powers which threaten Israel. Zechariah learns that the chariot which sped north, that is, to Babylon, has eased God's spirit because already judgment has been imposed upon it.

The prophet is now commanded to make crowns of gold and silver, brought from the people still in Babylon through a delegation. He is to place a crown upon the head of Joshua, the high priest, and also tell him that God's appointed, meaning Zerubbabel, will complete the building of the Temple. A counsel of peace and harmony is to exist between them.

The visions concluded, Zechariah now (two years later) turns to answer a question submitted by a delegation. It is similar to those discussed previously by the prophets. Should fasting on various sad occasions in Jewish history still be observed? The Temple is being rebuilt! Should the custom of mourning be continued? Zechariah's answer is in direct line with the prophets of the past. He speaks for God as he asserts that there is little value in fasting unless it is accompanied by moral improvement. Human love and social justice are primary. Fasting is but a means. Ritual and religious ceremonial are not substitutes for justice, righteousness, and mercy.

Speak to all the people of the land and to the priests, saying: When you fasted and mourned in the fifth (Tisha B'Av, ninth day of the month Av) and in the seventh month (Tzom Gedaliah, Fast of Gedaliah) for these seventy years, did you at all fast for Me? And when you eat and drink, are you not those who eat and those who drink? . . . Thus has the Lord of hosts spoken, saying: Execute true justice and show mercy and compassion every man his brother; do not oppress the widow, nor the orphan, the stranger, nor the poor; let none of you devise evil against his brother in your heart. (Chapter VII, Verses 5, 6, 9, 10.)

Indeed, Zechariah, in the following chapter goes further on this issue of fasts. He gives a more direct answer to the question posed as he foresees the conversion of fasts to feasts because the destruction will, in the future, have been reconstructed:

Thus says the Lord of hosts: The fast of the fourth month (Shiva Asar B'Tammuz, Seventeenth Day of the month of Tammuz) and the fast of the fifth (Tisha B'Av, Ninth Day of the month of Av) and the fast of the seventh (Tzom Gedaliah, Fast of Gedaliah, and the fast of the tenth (Asarah b'Tevet), shall become to the House of Judah events of joy and gladness and cheerful holidays; therefore, love truth and peace. (Chapter VIII, Verse 19.)

It is interesting to observe that the fast days mentioned are still observed today, all pertaining to the destruction of the Temple, the only exception being Tishah B'Av which also commemorates other national calamities. The fast of the fourth month commemorates the breach in the walls of Jerusalem and entrance into the city by the Chaldeans (II Kings, Chapter XXV, Verse 3; Jeremiah, Chapter LII, Verses 6 and following). The fast of the fifth month commemorates the destruction of the Temple. Historically, the Second Temple was also destroyed on the same day and other calamities occurred on this day, such as the fall of Betar to the Romans, the attempt by the Crusaders to conquer Jerusalem on that day in 1099, expulsion of Jews from England in 1275, etc. The fast of the seventh month, third Tishri, commemorates the assassination of Gedaliah, the Jewish governor appointed over the people left in the land by Nebuchadnezzar (II Kings, Chapter XXV, Verse 25). The fast of the tenth month commemorates the Chaldean beginning of the siege of Jerusalem (II Kings, Chapter XXV, Verse 1).

The last chapter of the first section contains ten brief messages, divinely inspired, dealing with the days that are coming. In each Zechariah uses the introductory phase "Thus says the Lord." All maintain the spirit of hope for Jerusalem. It is God's proclamation of love for Zion and God's intent to return to Jerusalem to dwell there.

Thus says the Lord: I will return to Zion and will dwell in the midst of Jerusalem; and Jerusalem will be called the City of Truth; and the mountain of the Lord of hosts the Holy Mountain. (Chapter VIII, Verse 3.)

ZECHARIAH

Zechariah paints a beautiful Jerusalem of the future with Zion at its center, a city in which old and young will rejoice. A new era will dawn with the scattered exiles returning to the Holy City. Fear will be banished. The land will be fertile and productive. In this masterful manner Zechariah encourages his people to persevere in the building of the Temple. He assures them that with its rise a new world will come into being. He gives them a pattern for a renewed way of life.

These are the things that you shall do: Speak every person the truth with his neighbor; execute the judgment of truth and peace in your gates; and let none of you plot evil in your hearts against his neighbor; and do not love false oaths; for all these are things that I hate, says the Lord. (Chapter VIII, Verses 16, 17.)

The prophet speaks of the time when all nations will seek God. They will hear of God's greatness and make their way to God. Zechariah prophesies that many peoples will attach themselves to the Jewish people in their eagerness to join them in the worship of God or to be recognized with them as belonging to the people of God.

We will go with you, for we have heard that God is with you. (Chapter VIII, Verse 23.)

Scholars differ about whether the second part of Zechariah is part of the same author's words and writings. Some say another prophet or perhaps two were involved. Others believe the contents of the next six chapters apply to a much later period, even as late as the Maccabean period, around 175 B.C.E. Others hold that it describes an era before the exile to Babylon. The traditional view, however, is firm that the last chapters continue the theme of the first. Themes are similar, although there may be a difference of emphasis. Zechariah may have preached the first part in the earlier days of his life and the second part in the later years. The words may have been said after the actual building of the Temple. We must remember that a prophet has insight and an ability to capture a scene based on many factors and insights and to foretell what may occur.

Zechariah took note of the world's political situation with its grave threats. Greece, the new power, was on the rise. This meant a threat to his homeland. But he did not allow these factors to destroy his belief that in the end Jerusalem would be the City of Peace, and that all the nations of the world would come to acknowledge God.

Zechariah loses himself in reverie as he stands, his eyes transfixed, gazing into time and space, and depicting the scenes of the glorious messianic age. The whole future, unreal now, but real to the prophet, is recorded. He first speaks of including all of the countries surrounding Israel in the kingdom, mentioning them by name. Then he portrays the messianic age, the coming of the Messiah—from the Hebrew word mashiach, "one who is anointed"—and the many changes which will take place, including the cessation of war, the discarding of war implements, and the homecoming of the exiles.

> Rejoice greatly, O daughter of Zion,
> Shout, O daughter of Jerusalem;
> Behold, your king comes to you,
> He is triumphant and victorious,
> Lowly, riding upon a donkey.
> (Chapter IX, Verse 9.)

Zechariah pleads with the people to prepare for this event. He urges them to discard idolatrous worship. Prosperity and blessings come from God alone, not from idols. The worship of idols has indeed caused all the disasters of Israel. In the end, Israel and Judah will be restored to their regal position:

> I will strengthen the House of Judah,
> And I will save the House of Joseph,
> And I will restore them for I have compassion upon them . . .
> I will also bring them back from the land of Egypt. . . .
> I will strengthen them in the Lord;
> And they will walk up and down in His name,
> Says the Lord.
> (Chapter X, Verses 6, 10, 12.)

What a comforting thought that Jerusalem will be restored! Once again the Holy City will be elevated to its rightful place. Judah will be purged of evil. When the idols will be completely destroyed, the relationship of old between God and the chosen people will be reaffirmed and revitalized:

> They will call on me by My name,
> And I will answer them;
> I will say: You are My people,
> And they will say: The Lord is our God.
> (Chapter XIII, Verse 9.)

Jerusalem is delivered. Zechariah looks beyond the city and the land of Israel. The people are gathered into a narrow area about the City of Peace, the source which will be tapped by the nations of mankind. To it all will direct their minds and hearts. And from it, they will draw understanding of the greatness and universality of God who will be recognized and worshiped by everyone. This thought has been incorporated into the daily synagogue service:

> And the Lord will be King over all the earth;
> On that day will the Lord be One and His name One.
> (Chapter XIV, Verse 9.)

All nations will come to worship God on the Festival of Tabernacles, Sukkoth, also known as the Feast of Booths, when the bounty given by God, in the season of harvest, becomes a universal thanksgiving. The messianic era will be at hand.

With this prophecy Zechariah's words come to an end. Together with Haggai, he aroused, he inspired, he encouraged the people to complete the Second Temple. Zechariah's simple but carefully worded pronouncement, "Not by might, nor by power, but by My spirit, says the Lord of hosts," has become a clarion call for godliness.

Zechariah's divinely inspired message has moved people to strive for the great future when peace and security will be manifest, when One God will be worshiped.

MALACHI

THE BOOK OF MALACHI, THE LAST PROPHET OF ISRAEL, IS likewise the last of the Twelve. His book completes the second part of the Bible known as The Prophets (Nevi'im). Haggai and Zechariah were active during the rebuilding of the Second Temple, whereas Malachi preached about 450 B.C.E. in the middle of the fifth century. He was a contemporary of Ezra the Scribe and Nehemiah the Governor, who were factors of paramount importance in reorganizing the Jewish community.

In previous eras, more than one prophet of major stature was usually active. Malachi, however, stands alone as the prophet of his era. The Second Temple was completed in 516 B.C.E. and its ritual resumed by the priests ministering at the service. Haggai and Zechariah had brought popular confidence to a high point. As years passed, however, there were disappointments. The prosperous times the prophets had promised had not materialized. Religious enthusiasm began to wane. Economic conditions did not improve. Unprecedented poverty existed with harvests unfruitful. The people began to feel bitter discouragement. They expressed their despondency by questioning the truth of the prophetic words. They doubted their own beliefs. They questioned their faith in God. They had built the Temple. Where were God's promised blessings? The skepticism affected not only the people but their leaders as well. The priests—who should have known better—became lax in the performance of their duties. They ignored the strict rules and laws of the sacrifices, closing their eyes to violations.

MALACHI

In this depressed atmosphere, it is not surprising that moral disintegration set in. Standards bent from conformity. Divorce became a common occurrence. Intermarriage with foreigners weakened the loyalty of Israel's faith and corrupted the integrity of the community. Malachi begins his ministry with a despondent, hostile people. The people are not amenable to listening to the word of God. Many begin to lose their faith and only a small group of Jews persist in maintaining their trust in the prophetic utterances and teachings. Malachi has a difficult task. His unshakable conviction that God will triumph, his magnetic personality, and oratorical ability bring him a large measure of success in his ministry. He wins a place in the forefront of the great Hebrew prophets.

No indication is given in the book as to Malachi's identity or origin, nor is any lineage recorded in outside sources. Some hold that no such prophet by the name of Malachi lived, since the meaning of his name is "my messenger." "Behold I send my messenger" (Chapter III, Verse 1) implies that the book may be anonymous. It is unnecessary, however, to question the reality of the prophet. The words written here, the masterful, convincing voice of Malachi, make him a real person and a brilliantly dynamic speaker for God.

Malachi utilizes the technique of dialogue. He makes a statement and follows with a question which may very well be in the minds of his listeners. He deliberately formulates his statement to anticipate the question. Then he elaborates and returns to his first assertion with example, facts, proof. He knows that his message, designed to purge indifference of worship and immorality from conduct, will not be readily acceptable. Yet he perseveres. His purpose is to inspire the people once more with love of God. He himself feels this love and demands of himself that he convey its blessings to others. He tells his listeners that they have failed, not God. Firmly he admonishes them: that they should comply with the laws of the Temple ritual and that their failure to do so has brought about the conditions prevalent.

The age-old question, "Why do the righteous suffer while the wicked prosper?" confronts Malachi as it did the earlier prophets and later on as it puzzles Job. Malachi does not evade it. He says the people's disloyalty to God and their neglect of the service are responsible. God does indeed love them. Has God not made a distinction in preserving their land while the land of neighboring Edom was destroyed? Does this not show God's love for the chosen people? They must be patient. The day of judgment is not far distant when each person will receive just due. The wicked will be punished; the righteous will be rewarded.

Malachi demands not only strict adherence to the laws of the ritual but high ethical standards as well, pleading thereby for the spirit which underlies the observance. The prophet attacks the adulterers, the perjurers, those who oppress the widows and children. His most magnificent rhetorical question is a sublime pronouncement of the fatherhood of God and the brotherhood of man.

Have we not all one father?
Has not one God created us?
Why do we deal treacherously every man against his brother?
(Chapter II, Verse 10.)

The three chapters of the book can be divided into two parts. The first and almost all of the second sets forth God's demands plus a denunciation of those failing to live up to the standards of Judaism. The second part consists of Malachi's forecast of the coming judgment day.

He opens the book by declaring God's love for Israel which has not lessened. He compares their state to their neighbor Edom, whose progenitor is Esau, brother of Jacob:

I have loved you, says the Lord.
Yet you ask, "Wherein have You loved us?"
Was not Esau Jacob's brother?
Says the Lord;
Yet I loved Jacob
But Esau I did not. . . .
(Chapter I, Verses 2 and 3.)

God has not failed the people, but they have neglected God. He turns to the priests and arraigns them figuratively. Has God been recognized as Father? Has God received proper respect and honor? The day will come when the Temple will be the center of inspiration for all the people on earth and therefore Israel ought to render to God and to the Temple in the Holy City respect and honor.

A son honors his father,
And a servant his master;
If then I am a father,
Where is My honor?
And if I am a master,

MALACHI

Where is My respect?
Says the Lord of hosts.
To you, O priests, who despise My name,
And you ask: "Where have we despised Your name?" . . .
This has been your doing . . .
For from the rising of the sun even to its setting
My name is great among the nations,
Says the Lord of hosts. . . .

(Chapter I, Verses 6, 9, 11.)

Malachi pleads that the priests become the inspired messengers of God:

And now this commandment is for you, O you priests. . .
For the priest's lips should keep knowledge,
And they should seek the law at his mouth;
For he is the messenger of the Lord of hosts.

(Chapter II, Verses 1, 7.)

Malachi turns his attention to marriage failure. He rebukes the faithless for their divorces. Divorce is treachery. Intermarriage is treachery.

Have we not all one father?
Has not one God created us?
Why do we deal treacherously every man against his
  brother,
Profaning the covenant of our fathers?
Judah has dealt treacherously,
Abominations have been committed in Israel and in
  Jerusalem;
For Judah has profaned the holiness of the Lord whom
  He loves,
And has married daughters of strange gods. . . .
Yet you say: "Wherefore?"
Because the Lord has been witness
Between you and the wife of your youth,
Against whom you have dealt treacherously,
Though she is your companion,
And the wife of your covenant. . . .

221

For I hate putting away,
Says the Lord, the God of Israel. . . .
>   (Chapter II, Verses 10, 11, 14, 16.)

To people who have lost their faith, God gives assurance that the day of judgment will correct all inequities.

Behold, I will send My messenger,
He will clear the way before Me. . . .
Then will the offerings of Judah and Jerusalem
Be pleasant to the Lord,
As in the days of old,
And as in ancient years.
I will come near to you to judgment;
And I will be a swift witness
Against the sorcerers, and the adulterers,
The false swearers;
And those who oppress the laborer in his wages,
The widow and the fatherless. . . . .
>   (Chapter III, Verses 1, 4, 5.)

Behold, I will send My messenger,
He will clear the way before Me. . . .
Then will the offerings of Judah and Jerusalem
Be pleasant to the Lord,
As in the days of old,
And as in ancient years.
I will come near to you to judgment;
And I will be a swift witness
Against the sorcerers, and the adulterers,
The false swearers;
And those who oppress the laborer in his wages,
The widow and the fatherless. . . . .
>   (Chapter III, Verses 1, 4, 5.)

The names of the righteous will be inscribed in the heavenly book of remembrance. God's time will come when the wicked will be punished and the righteous will triumph. The final words of the prophet are filled

222

with sincere zealousness for God and the chosen people. The prophet earnestly exhorts the people never to forget their Torah which Moses, the greatest of all prophets, bequeathed as their spiritual heritage. He assures them that God will send Elijah, the messenger of good tidings:

Remember the Law of Moses, My servant,
Which I commanded him in Horeb, for all Israel,
Statutes and ordinances.
Behold I will send you
Elijah the prophet before the coming
Of the great and awesome day of the Lord.
He will turn the hearts of the fathers to the children
And the hearts of the children to their fathers. . .
                    (Chapter III, Verses 22-24.)

This is the fitting conclusion of Malachi and of the second part of the Bible as the prophet entwines the work of all of the prophets with the first part, the Torah of Moses, exhorting the people to make it part of their lives. Faith in God and scrupulous compliance with the laws of religious ceremonial and of ethical conduct will assure the coming of a better day.

PART III

THE
WRITINGS

Ketuvim

∽⌒∽⌒∽⌒∽⌒∽⌒∽⌒∽⌒∽⌒∽⌒∽⌒∽⌒∽⌒∽⌒∽⌒∽⌒∽⌒∽⌒∽⌒∽⌒∽

PSALMS

T HE BOOK OF PSALMS OPENS THE KETUVIM, WRITINGS, WHICH constitute the third and last section of the scriptures, following the Torah, Pentateuch, and Nevi'im, Prophets. It is of interest to note that the first letters of these sections form the contraction TeNaKh (kh being a softened version of the letter K) frequently used to denote all three parts of the Bible.

The Writings are a composite of twelve books, each different in style, content, and purpose. Some are narrative (Ruth, Esther, Daniel), some historical (Ezra, Nehemiah, I and II Chronicles), others are prophetic in spirit (Daniel). The Book of Proverbs provides a distillation of wisdom and reflections on conduct, whereas the Book of Ecclesiastes and the Book of Job are masterpieces of religious philosophy. The Song of Songs, devoted to human and exalted love, and Psalms, an anthology of varied themes, containing some of the deepest expressions of the human heart, are classified as religious poetry.

The thread of unity is that the twelve books (thirteen if I and II Chronicles are counted separately) were collected after the period of the Prophets (from Amos, c. 750 to Malachi, c. 400 B.C.E.). The Greek name for this section (from the Septuagint, Greek version of the Bible) is Hagiographa, meaning Sacred or Holy Writings. The term Septuagint applies to the earliest Greek translation of the Bible, receiving its name for the seventy (more exactly, seventy-two) translators sent by the High Priest Eleazar of Jerusalem to Alexandria at the request of Ptolemy II Philadelphus (288 to 247 B.C.E.) known as a ruler of eclectic literary tastes. The Greek version of the Pentateuch of Moses dates from the beginning of the third century and in the second century before the common era—when it had become customary to read not only the Law but the Prophets in public—the bulk of the second section of the Prophets was similarly translated. After the destruction of the Temple in Jerusalem in 70 B.C.E. the authoritative Hebrew text was fixed by the rabbis of Palestine, but a new version (Aquila) of the long familiar Greek Bible was prepared which remained long in usage.

* * *

The Book of Psalms (Sefer Tehillim, or simply, Tehillim, "praise songs") are mainly hymns of praise to God. More than any other biblical volume, Psalms, containing one hundred and fifty chapters, has infiltrated religious ritual into the human reservoir of spiritual expression. Universal in appeal and scope, their breadth of thought and mood are not limited to person or group. The Psalms belong to all people. The simplicity of faith expressed in the Psalms claims a distinct place for this influential book in public worship and private devotions. Their tender, gentle, melodious strains, captivating the very essence of life, stir the heartstrings as they resound heavenward to God. Everyone—whatever a person's station in or attitude to life—can find in their matchless phrases the reflection of personal feelings and emotions. The worshiper can identify with the poet who expresses mutual sentiments in the verses.

When in distress, there are words of another's pain and anxiety. One who suffers feels the similar hurt and anguish of a kindred soul. One who looks hopefully for help and deliverance sees the poet translate one's heartfelt feelings into language. One blessed with plenty, with joy and gratitude, who wants to express thanks to God, finds the thoughts in words. The wrongdoer discovers passages which convey feelings of guilt and shame. One who longs to talk with God finds the right phrases in the Psalms which help to express feelings. A person seeking to understand a people's history, their trials, problems, their covenant with God, their deviations, consequent punishment, and their longing for Zion, will here find a guide for verbal expression.

In a word, therefore, the Psalms are a guide to all people. They reflect the entire range of human feelings: hardship, sorrow, joy, faith, humility, doubt, pain, hurt, sin, despair, thanksgiving; whatever the experience, whatever the mood, these and many more nuances of thought are conveyed in this great human document, because the religion of the psalter is closely related to prophetic teaching. The Psalms include petitions, laments, imprecations, meditations, historical reviews.

The Psalms reflect not only the soul of the individual, they mirror the heart of the nation. They reveal how the Jewish people responded to periods of crisis, how they called for God's help, how they reacted to joyous events, how they thanked God for bounty. How did the people respond when their magnificent Temple was destroyed? How did they feel when the Second Temple was built and dedicated? The Psalms tell us with a depth of feeling about the pain of the destruction of Jerusalem, the joy of the return, and the glory of the Temple's restoration. Reverting to ancient times, the Psalms tells us how King David, the shepherd son of Jesse, expresses his love for his people and for his son Prince Absalom.

The Psalms not only epitomize the human element of Jewish history, they teach the great religious truths of Judaism; of God and the world; God's handiwork; of humanity, God's creation. They teach of Israel, God's chosen; of humanity at large; how people may live the righteous life by following the path of goodness, as well as the byways of evil. Mercy and justice are glorified.

The Psalms are people's guides for everyday living. Little wonder, then, that they comprise the basis of the synagogue service. The daily morning service is composed largely of Psalms, as is also the service of the Sabbath, Festival, and High Holy Day mornings. The Sabbath Eve's inaugural service is taken almost entirely from Psalms. On the Festivals, New Moons, and Hanukkah an additional series referred to a Hallel, Praise, is added. The person who prays, therefore, following the prayer-book, is in a real and literal sense reading and praying the Psalms.

The chapters vary in theme but display a unity of spirit. Unlike both the Torah and Nevi'im, and even other volumes of Ketuvim they show an individual-to-God direction, an upward relationship. The individual speaks to God. It is to God the individual turns—I to You. In the Psalms God permeates the heavens, earth, nature, history, human society, the Temple, and finally narrows to the personal religion in which a person looks directly to God. The Psalms express humanity's humble gratitude for God's providence, abundance, and blessings.

Many of the Psalms, dating back to the days of King David (the tenth century before the common era), were written by him, the poet and sweet singer of Israel. Indeed, according to tradition David is the author of all. "Moses gave Israel the five books of the Torah and correspondingly David gave them the five books of the Psalms." Seventy-three of the one-hundred and fifty Psalms carry the editorial heading "Mizmor l'David" meaning "A Song of David" or "To David." At the end of Psalm LXXII the editor has noted "The prayers of David, son of Jesse, are ended." We do not know when the Book of Psalms was finally formulated nor who codified the book, excluding some and including others from a vast source of material. Some sources hold that the book reached its present form during the third century B.C.E. Others suggest that the editing was performed during the period of the Scribes, following Ezra the Scribe and Nehemiah the governor of Judah, about the middle of the fifth century. Still others maintain that some were written as late as the Maccabean period, early third century before the common era.

There are five divisions of the book of Psalms: Book I, Chapters I to XLI; Book II, Chapters XLII to LXXII; Book III, Chapters LXXIII to LXXXIX; Book IV, Chapters XC to CVI; Book V, Chapters CVII to CL. The division is not, however, based on any single theme applying to each group. The books probably derive from a number of lesser and smaller groups of Psalms, previously compiled and now formed into one larger collection. Even within these five books there are smaller groupings. For example, there are the "Songs of Ascent" (Shirei Hamaalot, Chapters CXX to CXXXIV) which probably describe the singing by the Levites as they ascended the same number of steps within the Temple.

The Psalms are in rhythmical but unrhymed verse, most frequently of a three-beat line. Many were sung in various processionals and religious performances by the Levites during the service. Six distinct instruments are mentioned in Psalm CL: "the blast of the horn," "the harp," "the timbrel," "stringed instruments and the pipe," "cymbals, loud-sounding and clanging." In this final Psalm there is mention of the accompanying dancers. The singing was, like the dancing, by professional choirs with a response from the worshipers of "Amen" and "Hallelujah."

There are the Korahite and Asaph Psalms, composed by members of the Levite families bearing these names. There are the Hallel Psalms. In addition, there are those Psalms attributed to Moses, Solomon, Heman, Ethan, and others. Thus the divisions cannot be considered in terms of theme. Each does end in a similar vein with what is called a doxology, expression of thanks, to God. The end of the first section includes the words:

Blessed be the Lord, the God of Israel, from everlasting to everlasting. Amen, and Amen. (Chapter XLI, Verse 14.)

The first Psalm, "The Two Ways," is a fitting prologue to the entire book. It concisely presents the kind of life the individual designs.

Happy is the man who has not walked in the counsel
  of the wicked,
Nor stood in the way of the sinners,
Nor sat in the seat of the scornful.
But his delight is in the law of the Lord,
And on Whose law he meditates day and night.
He will be like a tree planted by streams of water,
That brings forth its fruit in its season,
And whose leaf does not wither;
In everything he does he will prosper.
Not so the wicked;
They are like chaff which the wind scatters.
Therefore the wicked will not stand in the judgment,
Nor sinners in the congregation of the righteous.
For the Lord considers the way of the righteous;
But the way of the wicked will be destroyed.

(Book I, Psalm I)

A number of Psalms tell of the individual's cry to God for succor. In distress, frightened, powerless in the face of enemies, one seeks relief from God with faith that the Lord will hear and answer, easing one's fears and dispelling one's doubts. The most bitter grief of King David was brought him by his son Absalom who rebelled against his father and sought his life. King David had to flee from the son he deeply loved, and only his faith in God sustained him in those dark hours as a fugitive and then the horror of Absalom's death. The following Psalm whose historical superscription is given as "A Psalm of David When He Fled From Absalom His Son" reflects the poignant vicissitudes of life:

Lord, how many have become my adversaries!
Many there are who rise up against me.
Many there are who say of my soul:
There is no salvation for him in God,
But You, O Lord, are a shield around me;
My glory, and the lifter up of my head.
With my voice I call to the Lord,
And He answers me from His holy mountain.
I lie down and I sleep;
I awake for the Lord sustains me.

I am not afraid of ten thousands of people
Who have set themselves up against me,
Arise, O Lord; save me, O my God;
For You have smitten all my enemies on the cheek. . . .
Salvation belongs to the Lord;
May Yours blessing be on Your people.

(Book I, Psalm III.)

A Psalm praying for healing of illness:

O Lord, rebuke me not with Your anger.
Nor chasten me with Your wrath.
Be gracious to me, O Lord, for I am weak;
Heal me, O Lord, for my bones are afraid.
My soul also is hurt;
And You, O Lord, how long?
Return, O Lord, deliver my soul;
Save me for Your mercy's sake.
For in death there is no remembrance of You;
In the grave who will give You thanks?
I am weary with my groaning;
. . . I wet my couch with my tears.
My eye is dimmed because of vexation;
It ages because of all my adversaries.
Leave me, you workers of iniquity;
For the Lord has heard my weeping.
The Lord has heard my supplication;
The Lord receives my prayer.
All my enemies will be ashamed and afraid;
They will turn back, they will be suddenly ashamed.

(Book I, Psalm VI.)

A Psalm concerning humanity's role within God's creation:

When I look at Your heavens, the work of Your fingers,
The moon and the stars, which You have established;
What is man, that You are mindful of him?
And the son of man, that You think of him?
Yet You have made him but little lower than the angels,

And have crowned him with glory and honor.
You have given him dominion over the works of Your hand;
You have put all things under his feet:
Sheep and oxen, all of them,
The beasts of the field;
The fowl of the air, and the fish of the sea;
And whatever passes through the paths of the seas.
O Lord, our Lord,
How glorious is Your name throughout the world.

(Book I, Psalm VIII.)

The Psalms often speak of good and evil. Who is a godly person? One who walks with sincerity, uprightly, with dignity, with integrity, speaking the truth, doing right, judging all others by their true character rather than by appearances, and honoring those who show reverence for God.

A Psalm of David:
Lord, who shall sojourn in Your tabernacle?
Who shall dwell on Your holy mountain?
He who walks uprightly, and does righteousness,
And speaks truth in his heart;
Who has no slander on his tongue,
Nor does evil to his fellowman,
Nor takes up a reproach against his neighbor;
In whose eyes a vile person is despised,
But he honors those who fear the Lord;
He who swears to his own hurt, and does not change;
He who puts not out his money on interest,
Nor takes a bribe against the innocent,
He who does these things shall never be moved.

(Book I, Psalm XV.)

King David, great warrior, ruler and statesman, who brought power and glory to his people, remembered his early youth when he was a shepherd tending his flocks on the hills. The sheep, whom the shepherd loves, have faith in him and are therefore free from cares. David conceives of God as the Great Shepherd caring for and protecting His flocks. Men who have faith in God are well protected in their daily lives.

233

The Twenty-third Psalm, a precious gem, a pearl, is the supreme expression of God's goodness and man's gratitude:

A Psalm of David:
The Lord is my shepherd; I shall not want.
He makes me to lie down in green pastures,
He leads me beside the still waters.
He restores my soul;
He guides me in straight paths for His name's sake.
Yes, though I walk through the valley of the shadow of death,
I will fear no evil,
For You are with me;
Your rod and Your staff, they comfort me.
You prepare a table before me in the presence of my enemies;
You have anointed my head with oil; my cup runs over.
Surely goodness and mercy will follow me all the days of my life;
And I shall dwell in the house of the Lord forever.

(Book I, Psalm XXIII.)

Here, in its magnificence, is the inspiring Psalm David sang as he walked in the joyous procession in the streets of Jerusalem when the Holy Ark of the Covenant, housing the Torah of Moses, was triumphantly borne to Jerusalem:

The earth is the Lord's and the fulness thereof;
The world, and those who live in it.
For He has founded it on the seas,
And established it upon the floods.
Who will ascend to the mountain of the Lord?
And who will stand in His holy presence?
He who has clean hands and a pure heart;
Who has not taken My name in vain,
And has not sworn deceitfully.
He will receive a blessing from the Lord,
And righteousness from the God of his salvation.
Such is the generation of those who seek Him,
Who seek Your face, even Jacob. Selah.
Lift up your heads, O you gates,
And be you raised up, you everlasting doors;
That the King of glory may come in.

"Who is the King of glory?"
"The Lord strong and mighty,
The Lord mighty in battle."
Lift up your heads, O you gates,
Lift them up, you everlasting doors;
That the King of glory may come in.
"Who then is the King of glory?"
"The Lord of hosts;
He is the King of glory." Selah
(Book I, Psalm XXIV.)

A prayer of thanksgiving for a gracious, beneficent God who has blessed the people with a wonderful harvest:

You who hear prayer,
To You do all men come. . . .
You have remembered the earth, and watered her,
  greatly enriching her,
With the river of God which is full of water;
You prepare for them corn,
Watering her ridges abundantly,
Settling down her furrows,
You make her soft with showers;
You bless her growth.
You crown the year with Your goodness;
And your paths drop abundance.
The pastures of the wilderness do drop
And the hills are girded with joy.
The meadows are clothed with flocks;
The valleys also are covered with corn;
They shout for joy; they sing.
(Book II, Psalm LXV.)

Attributed to Moses and called by his name, the Ninetieth Psalm, one of the most sublime of human documents, concerns God's eternity and the human being's mortality, the brevity of life being all the more reason for people to seek strength, fortitude, and peace in God who is eternal.

A Prayer of Moses, the man of God:
Lord, You have been our dwelling-place throughout all
   generations.
Before the mountains were brought forth,
Or before You formed the earth and the world,
From everlasting to everlasting, You are God.
You turn man to contrition;
And say, "Return, you children of men."
For a thousand years in Your sight
Are but as yesterday when it is past,
And like a watch in the night.
You carry them away as with a flood; they are as a sleep;
In the morning they are like grass which grows up.
In the morning it flourishes and grows up;
In the evening it is cut down and withers. . . .
We bring our years to an end as a tale that is told.
The days of our years are three-score years and ten,
Or even by reason of strength four-score years;
Yet their pride is but travail and vanity;
For it is speedily gone, and we fly away. . . .
So teach us to number our days
That we may secure for ourselves a heart of wisdom. . . .
O satisfy us in the morning with Your mercy;
That we may rejoice and be glad all our days.
Make us glad according to the days in which You have
   afflicted us,
According to the years in which we have seen evil.
Let Your work appear to Your servants,
And Your glory on their children.
Let the graciousness of the Lord our God be upon us;
Establish also upon us the work of our hands,
The work of our hands establish it.

                         (Book IV, Psalm XC.)

One of the most quoted psalms is that of the humble person turning
trustfully to God as his rock, fortress and refuge.

O You who dwell in the covert of the Most High,
And abide in the shadow of the Almighty,
I will say of the Lord, who is my refuge and my fortress,

My God, in whom I trust,
That He will deliver you from the snare of the fowler,
And from the threatening pestilence.
He will cover you with His pinions,
And under His wings will you take refuge;
His truth is a shield and a buckler.
You will not be afraid of the terror by night,
Nor of the arrow that flies by day;
Of the pestilence that walks in darkness,
Nor of the destruction that stalks at noonday.
A thousand may fall at your side,
And ten thousand at your right hand;
It shall not come near you. . . .
There will no evil befall you,
Nor will any plague come near your home. . . .
He will call upon Me, and I will answer him;
I will be with him in time of trouble;
I will rescue him, and bring him to honor.
With long life will I satisfy him,
And make him to behold My salvation.

(Book IV, Psalm XCI.)

The Sabbath eve synagogue service includes seven Psalms: Book IV, XCII, XCIII, XCV-XCIX. The psalmist calls upon all to come and worship God. The poet looks to nature and bids her join in offering prayer to God. How good it is to give thanks to God. It is for all of us, the poet proclaims, to rejoice and to be glad and to serve God in the beauty of holiness.

We give excerpts from these Psalms, beginning with XCII which is titled The Sabbath Hymn:

It is good to give thanks to the Lord,
And to sing praises to Your name, O Most High;
To declare Your lovingkindness in the morning,
And Your faithfulness at night. . . .
How great are Your works, O Lord!
Your thoughts are very deep.
An ignorant man does not know,
Nor does a fool understand this. . . .

(Book IV, Psalm XCII.)

O come, let us sing to the Lord;
Let us shout for joy to the Rock of our salvation.
Let us come before His presence with thanksgiving,
Let us shout for joy to Him with psalms. . . .

(Book IV, Psalm XCV.)

O sing to the Lord a new song;
Sing to the Lord, all the earth.
Sing to the Lord, bless His name;
Proclaim His salvation from day to day.
Declare His glory among the nations,
His marvelous works among all the peoples. . . .
Honor and majesty are before Him;
Strength and beauty are in His sanctuary. . . .
O worship the Lord in the beauty of holiness;
Tremble before Him, all the earth. . . .

(Book IV, Psalm XCVI.)

The heavens declared His righteousness,
And all the peoples saw His glory. . . .
Light is sown for the righteous,
And gladness for the upright in heart.
Be glad in the Lord, you righteous ones,
And give thanks to His holy name.

(Book IV, Psalm XCVII.)

Shout to the Lord, all the earth;
Break forth and sing for joy, sing praises. . . .
Let the sea roar, and the fullness thereof;
The world, and those who dwell in it;
Let the floods clap their hands;
Let the mountains sing for joy together;
Before the Lord, for He comes to judge the earth;
He will judge the world with righteousness.
And the peoples with equity.

(Book IV, Psalm XCVIII.)

Six Psalms, called Hallel, meaning praise, (CXIII to CXVIII) form a series reserved for the synagogue service celebrating the three Pilgrim Festivals: Pesach, Shavuoth and Sukkoth, and also on Rosh Hodesh, the New Moon day, Hanukkah and—since 1948—on Yom HaAtzmaut, Israel Independence Day, which occurs on the fifth day of the month

of Iyar, usually in the month of May.
From the Hallel, some excerpts:

Hallelujah!
Praise, you servants of the Lord,
Praise the name of the Lord.
Blessed be the name of the Lord
From this time forth and forever.
From the rising of the sun to its setting,
The Lord's name is to be praised. . . .

(Book V, Psalm CXIII.)

When Israel went out of Egypt,
The house of Jacob from a people of strange language;
Judah became His sanctuary,
Israel His dominion.
The sea saw it and fled;
The Jordan turned backward.
The mountains skipped like rams,
The hills like lambs. . .

(Book V, Psalm CXIV.)

Not for our sake, O Lord, not for our sake,
But for Your name's sake grant glory,
For Your mercy, and for Your truth.
Why should the heathen question:
"Where is their God now?"
But our God is in the heavens;
Whatever pleased Him, He has done.
Their idols are but silver and gold,
The work of men's hands.
They have mouths, but they cannot speak;
Eyes have they, but they cannot see;
They have ears, but they cannot hear;
Noses have they, but they cannot smell;
They have hands, but they cannot handle;
Feet have they, but they cannot walk;
Nor do they speak with their throats. . . .
The Lord who has been mindful of us, will bless—
He will bless the house of Israel;
He will bless the house of Aaron.
He will bless those who revere the Lord,

Both small and great.
The Lord increase you more and more,
You and your children.
Blessed may you be by the Lord,
Who made heaven and earth.
The heavens are the heavens of the Lord;
But the earth has He given to the children of man.
(Book V, Excerpts from Psalm CXV.)

I shall walk before the Lord
In the lands of the living. . . .
I will lift up the cup of salvation,
And call upon the name of the Lord.
(Book V, Psalm CXVI, Verses 9, 13.)

Praise the Lord, all you nations;
Laud Him, all you peoples!
For His mercy is great toward us;
And the truth of the Lord endures forever.
Hallelujah.
(Book V, Psalm CXVII.)

Psalm CXVII with only two verses is the shortest in the entire collection of the Psalter, whereas Psalm CXIX with its one hundred and seventy-six verses is the longest. There are twenty-two stanzes, each comprising eight verses, each group beginning with a letter of the Hebrew alphabet, the twenty-two letters being equally represented: Aleph, Bet, Gimel, Dalet, He, Vav, Zayin, Khet, Tet, Yod, Kaf, Lamed, Mem, Nun, Samekh, Ayin, Pe, Tzadi, Kof, Resh, Shin, Tav. The longest Psalm is reserved for a magnificent tribute to the Torah as a way of life.

Happy are they who are upright,
Who walk in the law of the Lord.
Happy are they who keep His testimonies,
Who seek Him with their whole hearts. . . .
Blessed are You, O Lord;
Teach me Your statutes. . . .
Deal bountifully with Your servant, that I may live,
And I will observe Your word. . . .
Give me understanding that I may keep Your law

And observe it with my whole heart. . . .
I will never forget Your precepts. . . .
Oh, how I love Your law!
It is my meditation all day long. . . .
Your word is a lamp to my feet,
And a light to my path. . . .

(Book V, Psalm CXIX.)

Some have called the group of Psalms known as Ascents (CXX to CXXIV) "a Psalter within the Psalter." Each of fifteen successive Psalms begins with the introductory phrase Shir Hamaaloth, "A Song of Ascents." Some scholars hold that the Psalms correspond to the fifteen steps on which the ministering Levites walked in the Temple, pausing on each to sing a Psalm. Others believe they were chanted when the Israelites came to Jerusalem and the Temple on the Pilgrimage Holidays. Since Jerusalem was situated on an altitude above other parts of the country, the approach to the Holy City was by ascent. The first of this group has been called the perfect Psalm since it contains a perfect expression of trust in God who will help, guide and support, will never slumber and will ever watch and guard.

A Song of Ascents.
I will lift up my eyes to the mountains;
Whence will my help come?
My help comes from the Lord,
Who made heaven and earth.
He will not let your foot to be moved;
He who guards you will not slumber.
He who guards Israel neither slumbers nor sleeps.
The Lord is your guardian;
The Lord is your shelter on your right hand.
The sun will not smite you by day,
Nor the moon by night.
The Lord will guard you from all evil;
He will guard your soul.
The Lord will guard you as you come and go,
From this time forth and forevermore.

(Book V, Psalm CXXI.)

Another psalm of joy expresses the triumph of Zion restored after the exile:

A Song of Ascents.
When the Lord brought back the exiles to Zion,
We were like those who dream.
Our mouths were filled with laughter,
And our tongues with singing;
Then it was said among the nations:
"The Lord has done great things for them."
The Lord has done great things for us and we rejoiced.
Turn our captivity, O Lord,
As streams in the dry land.
Those who sow in tears
Will reap in joy.
Though he bears the measure of seed,
Who goes on his way weeping,
He will come home with joy, bearing his sheaves.

(Book V, Psalm CXVI.)

Another tender Psalm expresses the love for Zion by one who has witnessed the destruction of Jerusalem and vows never to forget the Holy City:

By the rivers of Babylon,
There we sat down, and we wept,
When we remembered Zion.
On the willows in its midst
We hung up our harps.
For there those who led us captive asked of us words of song,
And our tormentors asked of us mirth;
"Sing us one of the songs of Zion."
How shall we sing the Lord's song
In a foreign land?
If I forget you, O Jerusalem,
Let my right hand forget her cunning,
Let my tongue cleave to the roof of my mouth,
If I remember you not;
If I set not Jerusalem
Above my chiefest joy. . . .

(Book V, Psalm CXXXVII.)

PSALMS

One of the most noble hymns of praise is the one-hundred and forty-fifth Psalm CXLV, which holds an important place in Jewish liturgy. Introduced by two verses from other Psalms (Psalms LXXXIV, Verse 5, and CXLIV, Verse 15) and known as "Ashray," it is included as a central part in the morning service, and is part of the afternoon ritual. The verses are:

"Happy are they who dwell in your house,
They are forever praising You."
(Psalm LXXXIV, Verse 5.)

Happy is the people of prosperity,
Yes, happy is the people whose
God is the Lord.
(Psalm CXLIV, Verse 15.)

A Psalm of Praise of David.
I will extol You, my God, O King,
And I will bless Your name forever and ever.
Every day will I bless You;
And I will praise Your name forever and ever.
Great is the Lord, and highly to be praised;
His greatness is unsearchable.
One generation shall laud Your works to another,
And shall declare Your mighty acts.
On the glorious splendor of Your majesty
And on Your wondrous works, will I meditate.
Men will speak of the might of Your tremendous acts;
And I will tell of Your greatness.
They will spread the fame of Your great goodness,
And will sing of Your righteousness.
The Lord is gracious, and full of compassion;
Long forbearing and abundant in kindness.
The Lord is good to all;
His tender mercies are over all His works.
All Your works will praise You, O Lord;
And Your faithful ones will bless You.
They shall speak of the glory of Your kingdom,
And talk of Your might;
To let men know His mighty acts,

And the glorious majesty of His kingdom.
Your kingdom is an everlasting kingdom,
Your dominion endures throughout all generations.
The Lord upholds all who fall
And raises up all who are bowed down.
The eyes of all look hopefully to You!
And You give them their food in due season.
You open Your hand,
And satisfy every living thing with favor.
The Lord is righteous in all His ways,
And gracious in all His works.
The Lord is near to all who call upon Him,
To all who call on Him in truth.
He will fulfill the desire of those who revere Him,
He will also hear their cry and save them.
The Lord preserves all those who love Him,
But all the wicked will He destroy.
My mouth shall speak the praise of the Lord;
Let all men bless His holy name forever and ever.

(Book V, Psalm CXLV.)

Another verse (Psalm CXV, Verse 18); "We will bless the Lord from this time forth and forevermore," concludes the recitation of this Psalm in the ritual.

The Book of Psalms, which began with the individual's choice of good or evil, rises to the heights of ecstasy. The poet now extols God in a paean of praise; voices are joined with musical instruments and dancers whirl in a glory of harmonious movements as the psalmist bids everyone and everything that breathes to praise the Creator of the universe and all that is in it.

Hallelujah.
Praise God in His sanctuary;
Praise Him in the firmament of His power.
Praise Him for His mighty acts;
Praise Him according to His abundant greatness.
Praise Him with the sound of the horn;
Praise Him with the psaltery and harp.
Praise Him with the timbrel and dance;

Praise Him with stringed instruments and the flute.
Praise Him with the loud-sounding cymbals;
Praise Him with the clanging cymbals.
Let everything that has breath praise the Lord.
Hallelujah!

(Book V, Psalm CL.)

PROVERBS

THE BOOK OF PROVERBS, SECOND IN THE THIRD DIVISION OF
the Bible—the Sacred Writings—has for centuries been a source of popular quotations. In Hebrew, it is called Mishlei, from the word "ma-
shal," meaning proverb, example, likeness, compare. Other names
which have been given to this book are: Sefer ha-Hokhmah, Book of
Wisdom, and Sefer Derishat ha-Hokhmah, Book of the Search for
Wisdom. It is in the literary form of poetry with parallelism of the
verses its most prominent characteristic.

Proverbs is also one of three volumes which comprise a group known
as the Wisdom Literature of the Bible, the others being Job and Ecclesiastes. The authors of this literature were the wise men or sages, less
known by name and deed, who lived side by side with the priests and
prophets of Israel. The wise men, to whom the young people were attracted because of the practicality of their message, taught the meaning
of a good life to their listeners and followers. They formulated the teachings of the Torah of Moses into concrete terms applicable to daily living.
Of these wise men, King Solomon was considered the chief exponent.
Instead of praying to God for wealth and power, he prayed for a wise
and understanding heart, which was granted him. Indeed, tradition ascribes authorship not only of Proverbs but also the Song of Songs and
Ecclesiastes to Solomon. A rabbinic teaching says that Solomon wrote
Song of Songs in his youth, Proverbs in middle age, and Ecclesiastes
toward the end of his life.

PROVERBS

Solomon composed hundreds of proverbs and sayings which form the kernel of this book to which many wise men contributed. It is recorded in I Kings, Chapter IV, Verse 32, that Solomon spoke three thousand proverbs. Some authorities hold that the Book of Proverbs was compiled from sayings in the pre-exilic era, that is, the period just before the destruction of the Temple of Jerusalem in 586 B.C.E. Indications are that the book was in its present form approximately 400 B.C.E., the period of the Sopherim, Scribes, who followed Ezra the Scribe. All agree, however, that the proverbs had their origin in the age of Solomon.

In general, the Book of Proverbs is disconnected in form yet has a marked degree of unity pervading the whole, as a book of guiding principles for daily living. It confirms its own statement of purpose (Chapter I, Verses 1-6) that it is intended to teach wisdom to people, especially to the young and inexperienced as well as to those having some knowledge of wisdom. It offers simple and direct counsel. Its underlying theme is what constitutes a good, honest, decent life.

In pearls of wisdom, we are told what to do and what not to do; how to pursue happiness, whose company to seek, whose to shun, how to prepare for life, what happens when we shrink from responsibilities; what to do for our neighbors and what not to do . . . all in succinct, dignified style. The do's are not demanding nor are the don'ts reprimanding. They are merely suggestive.

The book of Proverbs deals primarily with wisdom in its comprehensive meaning, which includes all that is desirable in character, all that is undesirable in folly. Its foundation stone being religion, wisdom fundamentally consists in a right relation of the individual to God . . . "The fear of God is the beginning of wisdom." (Chapter IX, Verse 10). All that pertains to humanity is included within the scope of wisdom so that the book teaches all phases of a person's life. Wisdom therefore is presented in its practical form as related to the tenets of religious teaching rather than a philosophical discourse. It is a limitless reservoir of practical advice, not limited in scope, nor is it a message especially to the Jewish people.

Little appears about ritual, the priesthood, or the messianic era. It is Jewish in the sense that its sources are Jewish. Its messages are not necessarily religious unless we hold that religion encompasses all of life. True it is that the book is founded on belief in God, which is the basis of the entire presentation. Brevity, pithiness, energy are all implied in the very nature of a proverb with its simile, metaphor, or paradox. Proverbs are the teachers who speak to rich and poor, to thrifty and indolent, to the righteous and the wicked, to the proud and the humble. These teachers speak humanly, affectionately, warmly, addressing the listener as "my son."

What do these teachers talk about? Justice, mercy, honesty in business dealings, happy home life, chastity in private life, charity to those in need, ethical standards, love and respect for mother and father, discipline of children, parental love, marital fidelity. They talk about pausing in the race of life to reconsider actions and ways of life, urging one to be wise by seeking wisdom and understanding. By gaining wisdom, a person places himself on the pathway to happiness.

The Book of Proverbs is a book of life. Usually the poetry is in couplets, in the style of parallelism, characterized by a certain number of rhythmic beats. The synonymous proverbs are those in which the second of the two lines repeats somewhat differently the message of the first line:

> How much better is it to get wisdom than gold!
> To get understanding is preferred to silver.
> (Proverbs XVI, Verse 16.)

In an antithetic proverb, the second line has an opposite meaning to the first line:

> The tongue of the wise uses knowledge properly,
> But the mouth of fools pours out foolishness.
> (Chapter XV, Verse 2.)

In the synthetic proverb, the second line continues the same thought as the first line:

> The words of a man's mouth are as deep waters;
> A flowing brook, a fountain of wisdom.
> (Chapter XVIII, Verse 4.)

Some of the proverbs have three and four lines.

The thirty-one chapters of Proverbs contain nine hundred and fifteen proverbs, which are divided into seven sections.

Section I, Chapters I to IX, is the introduction to the main body of proverbs. This may be called the wisdom section because the proverbs extol and glorify wisdom:

The proverbs of Solomon, son of David, King of Israel.

To know wisdom and instruction,
To perceive words of understanding;
To accept instruction in wise dealing,
Justice, and right, and equity;
To give prudence to the simple,
And knowledge and discretion to youth;
The wise man may hear and increase his learning,
And the man of understanding may reach wise counsels;
To understand a proverb and the interpretation;
The words of the wise and their riddles.
The fear of the Lord is the beginning of knowledge;
Only fools despise wisdom and discipline.
(Proverbs, Chapter I, Verses 1-7.)

The above last two verses of Proverbs constitute the motto of the entire book, for true knowledge must begin with a recognition of God.

The individual has the power of choice. One can select the way which leads to joy or the road to death and ruin. Indeed wise is the one who, inspired by reverence for God, pursues the first course. The fool turns away and walks the deceptive path to destruction.

Wisdom is personified as a wonderful woman, a personal friend, a knowing counselor:

She is more precious than jewels,
And nothing you desire can compare with her.
Long life is in her right hand;
In her left hand are riches and honor.
Her ways are ways of pleasantness.
And all her paths are peace.
She is a tree of life to those who lay hold of her,
And those who hold her fast are happy.
(Proverbs, Chapter III, Verses 15-18.)

Wisdom, who was a partner with God in the creation of the world, urges people to follow her. Significantly the Proverbs begin with the home, parents and children, for the basis of wisdom is understanding in the home.

Section II, Chapters X to XXII, Verse 16, forms the main section of the book, titled The Proverbs of Solomon. For the most part the proverbs, in antithetic couplets, reflect social, political, and economic conditions. All told there are three-hundred and seventy-five proverbs. By coincidence (or design) the Hebrew name of Solomon, SHeLoMoH, has a Hebrew numerical value of the identical amount.

Section III, Chapter XXII, Verse 17, to Chapter XXIV contains lengthened couplets constituting warnings to those who deviate.

Section IV, Chapters XXV to XXIX, is similar to Section II and begins with the phrase "These are also the proverbs of Solomon." Many are secular in nature. The last two chapters, however, have ethical and religious overtones. This section serves to emphasize that the ethical teaching of the book is on a high plane. The sages agreed with the prophets that ritual, ceremonial, and external acts, although important for self-discipline, are valueless without an inner reality which enhances conduct itself with sincerity and high morality.

Section V is comprised of one chapter (XXX) attributed to Agur, son of Jakeh.

Section VI is still briefer, with nine verses making up Chapter XXXI, attributed to King Lemuel, who relates the moral guidance received from his mother.

Section VII is comprised of Chapter XXXI, Verses 10 to 31. Here is the famous passage extolling the Jewish woman. It is read in traditionally Jewish homes on Friday evening before the Sabbath meal. The Jewish wife and mother is praised as a paragon of love, devotion and piety. She is industrious, diligent, and concerned for the welfare of her family. She counsels and advises. She encourages and inspires her husband.

A good wife, who can find?
For she is far more precious than rubies.
The heart of her husband trusts in her,
And he has no lack of gain.
She does him good and not evil,
All the days of her life. . . .
She seeks wool and flax,
And works willingly with her hands.
She is like the merchant-ships,

She brings her food from afar.
She rises while it is yet night,
Gives food to her household,
And a portion to her maidens.
She considers a field and buys it,
With the fruit of her hands she plants a vineyard.
She girds her loins with strength,
And makes her arms strong.
She perceives that her merchandise is good.
Her lamp does not go out at night.
She puts her hand to the distaff,
And her hands hold the spindle.
She stretches out her hand to the poor,
She reaches out her hands to the needy.
She is not afraid of the snow for her household;
For all her household are clothed in scarlet.
She makes coverings for herself;
Her clothing is of fine linen and purple.
Her husband is known in the gates,
When he sits among the elders of the land.
She makes linen garments and sells them;
And delivers girdles to the merchant.
Strength and dignity are her clothing,
And she laughs at the time to come.
She opens her mouth with wisdom,
And the teaching of kindness is on her tongue.
She looks well to the ways of her household
And does not eat the bread of idleness.
Her children rise up and call her blessed;
Her husband also and he praises her:
'Many daughters have done valiantly,
But you surpass them all.'
Grace is deceitful and beauty is vain.
But a woman who reveres the Lord, she is to be
praised.
Give her of the fruit of her hands;
And let her works praise her in the gates.

(Chapter XXXI, Verses 10-31.)

The above pearl in praise of woman is an acrostic, each verse beginning with a succeeding letter of the Hebrew alphabet. Other proverbs pay tribute to the Jewish woman:

A virtuous woman is a crown to her husband.
(Chapter XII, Verse 4.)

Whoever finds a wife finds a great good
And obtains favor of the Lord.
(Chapter XVIII, Verse 22.)

Houses and riches are the inheritance of the fathers;
But a prudent wife is from the Lord.
(Chapter XIX, Verse 14.)

SELECTED PROVERBS

ANGER
An angry man stirs up strife,
And a wrathful man causes many transgressions. (XXIX, Verse 22.)

ANIMALS CAN TEACH
There are four things which are small on earth,
But they are exceedingly wise;
The ants are a people not strong,
Yet they provide their food in the summer;
The rock-badgers are but a feeble folk,
Yet they make their homes in the crags;
The locusts have no king,
Yet they all go forth in bands;
The spider you can take in your hands,
Yet she is in the palaces of kings. (XXX, Verses 24-28.)

KINDNESS TO ANIMALS
A righteous man has regard for the life of his beast;
But the feelings of the wicked are cruel. (XII, Verse 10.)

WHAT TO AVOID
There are six things which the Lord abhors,
Seven which are an abomination to Him;
Haughty eyes, a lying tongue,
And hands that shed innocent blood;

A heart that devises wicked plans,
Feet that are swift in running to evil;
A false witness who breathes lies,
And one who sows discord among brothers. (VI, Verses 16-19.)

WHAT BELONGS TO OTHERS
Drink waters from your own cisterns,
And running waters from your own well. (V, Verse 15.)

DISCIPLINE OF CHILDREN
He who spares the rod hates his son;
But he who loves him punishes him at times. (XIII, Verse 24.)

Discipline your son for there is hope;
But do not set your heart on his destruction. (XIX, Verse 18.)

Train a child in the way he should go,
And when he is old, he will not depart from it. (XXII, Verse 6.)

Do not withhold correction from the child;
For though you beat him with a rod, he will not die. (XXIII, Verse 13.)

CHILDREN AND PARENTS
My son, keep your father's commandment,
And do not forsake your mother's teaching. (VI, Verse 20.)

A wise son makes a glad father:
But a foolish son is the grief of his mother. (X, Verse 1.)

Listen to your father who begot you,
And do not despise your mother when she is old. (XXIII, Verse 22.)

Let your father and your mother be glad,
And let her who bore you rejoice. (XXIII, Verse 25.)

CHARITY
He who has a bountiful eye will be blessed;
For he shares his bread with the poor. (XXII, Verse 9.)

He who is gracious to the poor lends to the Lord,
And He will repay him for his good deed. (XIX, Verse 17.)

Whoever closes his ear to the cry of the poor,
He also will cry and will not be answered. (XXI, Verse 13.)

He who gives to the poor shall not want,
But he who hides his eyes will have many a curse. (XXVIII,
Verse 27).

CHASTISEMENT
Better to open rebuke
Than love which is hidden.
Faithful are the wounds of a friend;
But the kisses of an enemy are deceitful. (XXVII, Verses 5, 6.)

COUNSEL
Where there is no counsel, plans are frustrated;
But where there are many counselors, they are established. (XV,
Verse 22.)

Listen to counsel and accept instruction,
That you may gain wisdom in the future. (XIX, Verse 20.)

My son, do not despise the chastening of the Lord,
Do not spurn His correction.
For the Lord corrects him whom He loves,
As a father the son in whom he delights. (III, Verse 11.)

DECEIT
Deceit is in the heart of those who devise evil;
But to the counselors of peace is joy. (XII, Verse 20.)

EXCESSIVENESS
Be not among wine drinkers
Nor among gluttonous eaters of meat,
For the drunkard and the glutton will come to poverty;
And drowsiness will clothe one with rags. (XXIII, Verses 20, 21.)

FAITH
Trust in the Lord with all your heart,
And do not depend on your own understanding.
In all your ways acknowledge Him,
And He will direct your paths. (III, Verses 5, 6.)

PROVERBS

In the reverence of the Lord one has strong confidence,
And his children will have a place of refuge.
The fear of the Lord is a fountain of life,
To avoid the snares of death. (XIV, Verses 26, 27.)

Commit your works to the Lord,
Then will your plans be established. (XVI, Verse 3.)

EQUALITY

The rich and the poor meet together;
The Lord is the maker of them all. (XXII, Verse 2.)

FEAR

Be not afraid of sudden terror,
Neither of the destruction of the wicked when it comes;
For the Lord will be your confidence,
And will keep your foot from being caught. (III, Verses 25 and 26.)

FRIENDS

He who overlooks a transgression seeks love;
But he who harps on a matter alienates a friend. (XVII, Verse 9.)

FAIR-WEATHER FRIENDS

Wealth brings many friends;
But a poor man is separated from his friend. (XIX, Verse 4.)

Many will seek the favor of a generous man;
And everyone is a friend to one who gives gifts. (XIX, Verse 6.)

CHOOSE FRIENDS WISELY

Make no friendship with a man given to anger,
And do not go with a wrathful man;
Lest you learn his ways,
And get a snare to your soul. (XXII, Verse 24.)

FRIENDSHIP

A friend loves at all times,
And a brother is born for adversity. (XVII, Verse 17.)

Most men will proclaim each his own goodness;
But a faithful man who can find? (XX, Verse 6.)

There are friends that one has even to his own hurt;
And there is a friend who stays closer than a brother. (XVIII,
Verse 24.)

FLATTERY
One who flatters his neighbor,
Spreads a net for his steps. (XXIX, Verse 5.)

GENEROSITY
The beneficent soul will be enriched,
And he who satisfies abundantly will himself be satisfied. (XI,
Verse 25.)

GLOATING
Do not rejoice when your enemy falls,
And let not your heart be glad when he stumbles. (XXIV, Verse 17.)

GOSSIP
The words of a whisperer are like dainty morsels,
They go down into the innermost parts of the body. (XVIII,
Verse 8.)

He who goes about gossiping reveals secrets;
Therefore do not associate with one who opens wide his lips. (XX,
Verse 19.)

Where there is no wood, the fire goes out;
And where there is no whisperer, contention ceases. (XXVI,
Verse 20.)

He who is of a greedy spirit stirs up strife;
But he who puts his trust in the Lord will be abundantly gratified.
(XXVIII, Verse 25.)

THE HEART
A merry heart makes a cheerful countenance;
But by sorrow of heart the spirit is broken. (XV, Verse 13.)

All the days of the poor are evil;
But he who has a merry heart has a continual feast. (XV, Verse 15.)

A merry heart is a good medicine,
But a depressed spirit dries the bones. (XVII, Verse 22.)

PROVERBS

HOME
Better is a dry morsel with peacefulness
Than a house full of feasting with strife in it. (XVII, Verse 1.)

By wisdom is a home built,
And by understanding it is established;
By knowledge are the rooms filled
With all precious and pleasant riches. (XXIV, Verses 3 and 4.)

HONESTY
Better is the poor man who walks with integrity
Than one who is perverse in his lips and is also a fool. (XIX,
Verse 1.)

A just balance and scales are the Lord's;
All the weights of the bag are His work. (XVI, Verse 11.)

HUMILITY
When pride comes, then comes shame;
But with the humble is wisdom. (XI, Verse 2.)

It is better to be of a lowly spirit with the humble
Than to divide the spoil with the proud. (XVI, Verse 19.)

Before destruction a man's heart is haughty,
But before honor there is humanity. (XVIII, Verse 12.)

JEALOUSY
Wrath is cruel and anger is overwhelming,
But who is able to stand before jealousy? (XXVII, Verse 4.)

KINDNESS
Let not kindness and truth forsake you;
Bind them about your neck,
Write them on the tablets of your heart. (III, Verse 3.)

LOVE AND HATRED
Hatred stirs up strife;
But love covers all offenses. (X, Verse 12.)

Better is a dinner of herbs where love is,
Than a fattened ox and hatred with it. (XV, Verse 17.)

LONELINESS

The heart knows its own bitterness;
And with its joy no stranger can share. (XIV, Verse 10.)

LYING

He who has a crooked heart will find no good.
And he who has a perverse tongue will come to harm. (XVII,
Verse 20.)

A GOOD NAME

A good name is to be chosen rather than great riches,
And loving favor rather than silver and gold. (XXII, Verse 1.)

YOUR NEIGHBOR

Do not withhold good from one to whom it is due,
When it is in the power of your hand to do it.
Do not say to your neighbor, "Go, and come again,
And tomorrow I will give," when you have it to give.
Do not devise evil against your neighbor,
Seeing that he lives trustingly beside you. (III, Verses 27, 28, 29.)

He who hates his neighbor sins,
But he who is gracious to the humble is happy. (XIV, Verse 21.)

Do not rob the weak because he is weak,
Nor crush the poor in the gate;
For the Lord will plead their cause,
And despoil of life those who despoil them. (XXII, Verses 22, 23.)

Your own friend and your father's friend, do not forsake;
Nor go to your brother's home in the day of your calamity;
Better is a neighbor who is near than a brother who is far away.
  (XXVII, Verse 10.)

PATIENCE

He who is slow to anger has great understanding;
But he who is hasty of spirit exalts folly. (XIV, Verse 29.)

A hot-tempered man stirs up discord,
But he who is slow to anger quiets strife. (XV, Verse 18.)

He who is slow to anger is better than the mighty;

And he who masters his spirit, than he who takes a city. (XVI, Verse 32.)

The thoughts of the diligent lead only to abundance;
But everyone who is hasty, hastens only to want. (XXI, Verse 5.)

PREPARE FOR LIFE
Go to the ant, you sluggard;
Consider her ways and be wise;
For without a chief,
Officer or ruler,
She prepares her bread during the summer
And gathers her sustenance in the harvest time.
How long will you sleep, O sluggard?
When will you arise from your sleep?
"Yet a little sleep, a little slumber,
A little folding of the hands to rest"—
And your poverty shall come upon you as a runner,
And your want as an armed man. (VI, Verses 6 to 11.)

A son who gathers in summer is wise,
But a son who sleeps in harvest time causes shame. (X, Verse 5.)

PRIDE
Pride goes before destruction
And a haughty spirit before a fall. (XVI, Verse 18.)

SELF-PRAISE
Do not boast of tomorrow,
For you do not know what a day may bring.
Let another praise you and not your own mouth;
A stranger and not your own lips. (XXVII, Verses 1, 2.)

NO ONE IS PERFECT
Who can say, "I have made my heart clean,
I am pure from my sin"? (XX, Verse 9.)

QUARREL
The beginning of strife is like letting out water,
Therefore abandon contention before the quarrel breaks out. (XVII, Verse 14.)

It is an honor for a man to keep aloof from strife;
But every fool will be quarreling. (XX, Verse 3.)

THE RIGHTEOUS
The memory of the righteous will be for a blessing,
But the name of the wicked will disintegrate. (X, Verse 7.)

SYMPATHY
Care in the heart of a man bows it down;
But a kind word gladdens it. (XII, Verse 25.)

As in water face mirrors face,
So the heart of man to man. (XXVII, Verse 19.)

THANKSGIVING
Honor the Lord with your substance
And with the first fruits of your produce;
And then your barns will be filled with plenty,
And your vats will overflow with new wine. (III, Verses 9 and 10.)

THE POWER OF THE TONGUE
Where there are many words, there is no lack of transgression;
But he who restrains his lips is wise. (X, Verse 19.)

The mouth of the righteous is a fountain of life;
But the mouth of the wicked conceals violence. (X, Verse 11.)

A man will be satisfied with good from the fruit of his words,
And the works of a man's hands will be returned to him. (XII, Verse 14.)

He who breathes truth speaks righteousness,
But a false witness utters deceit.
There is he who speaks like the piercings of a sword,
But the tongue of the wise brings healing.
The lips of truth will endure forever,
But a lying tongue is but for a moment. (XII, Verses 17 to 19.)

He who guards his mouth preserves his life;
But he who opens wide his lips will come to ruin. (XIII, Verse 3.)

A soothing tongue is a tree of life;
But perverseness in it is a wound to the spirit. (XV, Verse 4.)

Proverbs

A soft answer turns away wrath,
But a harsh word stirs up anger. (XV, Verse 1.)

A man has joy in the utterances of his mouth;
And a word in due season, how good it is. (XV, Verse 23.)

TRUTH
Buy the truth and do not sell it;
Buy also wisdom and instruction and understanding. (XXIII,
Verse 23.)

VENGEANCE
Do not say, "I will do so to him as he has done to me;
I will pay him back for what he has done. (XXIV, Verse 29.)

YOUTH AND OLD AGE
The glory of young men is their strength
And the beauty of old men is the hoary head. (XX, Verse 29.)

JOB

JOB APPEARS AS THE THIRD BOOK OF THE KETUVIM OR SACRED Writings and together with the Book of Proverbs and Ecclesiastes constitutes that portion of the Bible known as the Wisdom Literature.

Probably more praise and reverence have been heaped on this book than on any other in the holy scriptures. The greatest work of Hebrew literature that has come down to us, it has been called a noble book, a book for all people, inasmuch as it concerns the eternal problem of personal destiny and God's ways with the individual here on this earth.

There is no evidence, however, that the memorable book is historical, although a man named Job is mentioned with Noah and Daniel in the Book of Ezekiel, Chapter XIV, Verses 14 and 20, which appears to indicate a historic character who experienced unusual suffering. Most scholars concede that the Book of Job was written about the beginning of the fifth century, about 400 B.C.E. While the Talmud attempts to set dates for this book ranging from the period of the Judges to the time of Ahasuerus, it also allows that Job never was, and never existed but as a typical figure or parable designed to impress the viewpoint of a religious person in great distress in regard to Providence.

In this magnificent drama, a man called Job is caught in the web of a struggle with his own soul and conscience and with his God. From the depths of his despair, he challenges God. Eventually as he rises to an understanding of God's justice and greatness, he reaffirms his faith in the Creator of humanity and of the universe. The Book of Job is a human document, a poignant spiritual experience with every human feeling being expressed. The literary genius of its author strikes a balance of mind and heart, of reason and emotion, in the creation of a believable character fully involved with both.

One of the perennial questions which has tantalized the thoughtful and oppressed the hearts of people for centuries is that of suffering by the innocent. And one of the most beautiful treatments of this problem is the Book of Job, a masterpiece of art and reflection. Job's heart is laid bare, revealing his honesty and integrity. He is at a loss to understand wherein he has failed. The story of Job is familiar enough: a prosperous and very devout Israelite, he is rich in the goods of this world, his happy circumstances credited to his devotion to God, for prosperity is the God-given reward of the just man. Suddenly Job's fortunes turn. He loses his possessions, his loved ones, his health, and his peace of mind and soul. Since suffering is the result of sin, his friends believe he must have offended God in some way. As the drama unfolds the answers are revealed.

The forty-two chapters of this book are divided into three general parts—prologue, dialogue, epilogue. The prologue comprises six scenes. The main portion of the drama in dialogue constitutes a series of addresses by Job, by his three friends and an observer. The friends speak three times each (with one exception). Job speaks a number of times. The epilogue which concludes the biblical drama relates to the prologue and enfolds the whole.

THE PROLOGUE (Chapters I and II)

The narrator speaks with rapidity in a prose which may be delineated as a suddenness of style, as action follows action. Scene One reveals Job, an inhabitant of the land of Uz, as a fine, upstanding, honest person, God-fearing, righteous, of high repute. He and his wife and their seven sons and three daughters are blessed with plenty, his prosperity including a vast estate of seven thousand sheep, three thousand camels, five hundred yoke of oxen, five hundred donkeys, numerous caretakers and servants to minister to him and to his household. Unquestionably, Job is the wealthiest man in the land of Uz. The family is merry of heart and practice the happy custom of feasting together. Each of Job's sons customarily takes his turn as host at a feast to which he invites his parents, brothers and sisters. Following each such celebration, Job rises early in the morning to offer sacrifices to God on behalf of his sons, thinking to himself, "Perhaps my sons have sinned and blasphemed God in their hearts." (The specific sacrifice is a burnt-offering—olah, plural oloth—as distinguished from other kinds, in expiation for evil thoughts and sins.)

Scene Two takes place in heaven. The sons of God come before the Lord who is seated on the heavenly throne. Among them is Satan, who is the Accuser, or Adversary. When God asks Satan whence he comes, he replies: "From going to and fro in the earth and from walking up and down in it." (Chapter II, Verse 2.) God now asks: "Have you seen my servant Job? Ah! There is a man. There is no one like him in all the earth, wholehearted, upright, God-fearing, shunning evil." Satan retorts: "Does Job fear God for nothing? Have you not Yourself made a hedge about him and about his house? You have blessed the work of his hands. His possessions have increased enormously. Why should he not be God-fearing? Just take away his possessions and You will soon see how quickly he will forget the blessings." Deciding to put Job to the test God replies to Satan: "He is in your power. Only Job himself do not touch." Satan thereupon leaves the presence of God and sets out on his mission.

Scene Three takes place on earth where Satan is already at work, testing Job by visiting calamities upon him in quick succession and with astounding suddenness. Job has not recovered from the shock of one when the second calamity befalls and then the third.

On a day when his sons and his daughters are dining and drinking wine in the house of the eldest brother, a messenger arrives and tells Job that as the oxen were plowing and the donkeys feeding beside them, the Sabeans raided and stole them away. The intruders killed all of the servants except the messenger who escaped to report the misfortune to their master. Job is stunned by the news. While the first messenger is still speaking, another man arrives to inform Job that lightning struck and burned to death the sheep and the attending servants and that only he has escaped to inform him. While he speaks still another messenger arrives to report that the Chaldeans, in three bands, attacked, took away the camels and slew all the servants except himself, who miraculously escaped to tell of the disaster. Immediately thereafter, another messenger appears before the stricken Job with the horrifying information that while his children were feasting a great wind which swept in from across the wilderness with stupendous, destructive force demolished the fine house of his eldest son and that all the young people therein were instantly killed; only he, the messenger, has survived the catastrophe of nature.

In this manner, by a series of swift tragedies, Job finds his wealth impaired, he himself childless, and his home life shattered. While his whole life pattern crumbles, he remains unshaken in his faith and begins stoically the mourning practices, expressing his faith in words which have become immortal:

Naked came I out of my mother's womb,
And naked will I return there;
The Lord gave and the Lord has taken away;
Blessed be the name of the Lord.

(Chapter I, Verse 21.)

Scene Four takes place in heaven. Once more we see Satan before the throne of God who asks him if he has seen Job and if Job has retained his faith and held firm. Satan responds: "Indeed he has maintained his faith. This is because You have not touched his body. Just You touch him himself and You will see how he will capitulate, lose his faith, and curse You." God now tells Satan to do what he will to subject Job to further tests. Only one limitation is imposed—Job's life is to be spared. Leaving the Lord's presence, Satan returns again to earth.

Scene Five takes place on earth. The once healthy, strong-limbed and proud landholder, husband and father is now stricken with a horrible affliction of boils from his feet to his head, bringing him intense pain. Added to his physical suffering Job endures the harsh words of his wife, who angrily taunts him: "Do you still maintain your faith even now? Curse God and die!" Job reprimands her. "You speak like an impious woman. Shall we receive good from God and not accept the evil?" (Chapter II, Verse 10.)

Scene Six reveals Job and his wife sitting dejectedly in mourning. Meanwhile, three friends of Job who have heard of the tragedies which have befallen him, decide to visit him to offer words of comfort. They come together and, seeing Job from a distance in his misery, they do not recognize him. They are shocked to see how he has changed. Incredulous, they show their grief for their friend by rending their garments in the usual custom of mourning. Unable to speak, they sit down sympathetically with Job and his wife. As nobody can speak of the unspeakable, they sit together for seven long days and nights in stony silence. Thus ends the prologue.

THE DRAMA (Or Dialogue, Chapters III to XLII, Verse 6)

The main part of the Book of Job now begins. Job will speak. Each of the three friends will speak three times in cycles. Each will try to comfort Job. We will see him confused and bewildered, hear his outcries of honest hostility, anger, cynicism. Some of the friends will be outspoken, callous, others tender, understanding. Job will deny that he has committed evil. Gradually he will advance from answers to piercing questions. He will ultimately see God's magnificence and reaffirm his faith in God, although he will not understand everything and never will.

The first act contains Job's discourse, a monologue. For seven days and nights they have sat without uttering a word. The friends look at Job and see a stricken man, bitter, hurt, bewildered by his fate. He cannot understand why these calamities have been visited on him. Wherein has he sinned? Has he not always been faithful? Has he not always had faith in God's justice? Slowly, a tiny sliver of doubt begins to edge around his mind. The doubt intensifies, striking at his mind and making his temples throb. It pounds at his heart and unleashes his tongue. In an outburst which startles the friends, Job's anguish gushes forth and he curses the day on which he was born:

May that day on which I was born perish,
And the night in which it was said
"A male-child is being born!"
Let that day be darkness;
Let not God above seek it,
Nor light shine upon it. . . .
Why did I not die in the womb?
Why did I not perish at birth?
Why did the knees receive me?
Or why the breasts that I should suck?
For I should have lain down and died;
I should have slept; then I would have been at rest—
With kings and counselors of the earth,
Who built monuments for themselves;
Or with princes who had gold,
Who filled their houses with silver. . . .
Why is light given to him who is in misery
And life to the bitter in soul,
Who long for death, but it does not come;
And dig for it more than for hidden treasures. . . .
For the thing which I feared has happened
And that which I dreaded has befallen me.
I was not at ease, nor was I quiet,
I had no rest, but trouble came.
(Chapter III, Verses 3, 4, 11-14, 20, 21, 25, 26.)

JOB

Job's rhetorical questions surprise his three friends, Eliphaz the Temanite, Bildad the Shuhite, and Zophar the Naamathite. They have come to console and they must try. Eliphaz approaches Job, reminding him of consolation in suffering he has given to people. Eliphaz speaks gently:

If one ventures a word to you, will you be offended?
Yet who can refrain from speaking?
You have taught many,
And you have strengthened weak hands.
Your words have supported those who were falling,
And you have strengthened feeble knees.
But now it has come to you and you are weary;
It touches you and you are frightened.
Is not your fear of God your confidence,
And the integrity of your ways your hope?
Remember, who ever perished because he was innocent,
Or where were the upright cut off?
As I have seen, those who plow iniquity,
And sow trouble, reap the same. . . .
For affliction does not come from the dust,
Nor does trouble spring from the ground. . . .
Happy is the man whom God corrects,
Therefore, despise not the chastening of the Almighty.
For He wounds and He binds up.
He smites and His hands make whole. . . .
Hear this and know that it is for your good.
(Chapter IV, Verses 2-8; Chapter V, Verses 6, 17, 18, 27.)

Job is not comforted, as he believes vehemently in his own innocence. Instead his anguish and pain deepen.

What is my strength, that I should wait?
And what is my end, that I should be patient?
Is my strength the strength of stones?
Or is my flesh made of brass?
Is it that I have no help within me,
And that wisdom is driven away from me? . . .
My brothers have dealt deceitfully as a brook. . . .
They were disappointed because they had hoped;

They came here and were ashamed.
For now you have become His,
You see my tragedy and you are afraid. . . .
Teach me, and I will be silent,
Make me understand where I have erred. . . .
I will not restrain my mouth,
I will speak out of anguish of my spirit,
I will complain out of the bitterness of my soul. . . .
If I have sinned, what do I do to You, O You watcher of men?
Why have you set me as a mark for You,
So that I have become a burden to myself?

(Chapter VI, Verses 11-13, 15, 20, 21, 24;
Chapter VII, Verses 11, 20.)

In the second act, his friend Bildad, visibly shaken by Job's outburst, steps forward and asks Job to cease his self-praise and to put an end to his claims of innocence. God is a God of justice and therefore it must be Job who has committed wrong. Bildad clings to the teaching that Job or his children must have sinned, for such severe punishment implies guilt. He, too, urges Job to admit his wrongdoing and to pray and God will surely answer. Bildad says:

How long will you say these things,
And the words of your mouth be like a mighty wind?
Does God pervert judgment?
Or does the Almighty pervert justice?
If your children have sinned against Him,
He delivered them into the power of their transgression.
If you would earnestly seek God,
And supplicate to the Almighty God;
If you were pure and upright,
Surely He would arise for you,
And make the habitation of your righteousness prosperous.
And though your beginning was small,
Your latter days will be greatly increased. . . .
God will not cast away an innocent man.
Nor will He uphold the evildoers.

(Chapter VIII, Verses 2-7, 20.)

JOB

Job vociferously denies he has done wrong, and in a crescendo of feeling he suddenly quite boldly challenges God and God's justice and decides that God has abandoned him to the wicked. Close to self-pity, Job pleads dejectedly: "Let me alone," and withdraws from his friends who have not helped him.

Truly, I know that this is so,
But how can man be just with God?
If one should wish to contend with Him,
He could not answer Him once in a thousand times.
He is wise in heart and mighty in strength;
Who has hardened himself against Him and prospered? . . . .
I am innocent—I regard not myself,
I hate my life.
It is all one—therefore I say:
He destroys the innocent and the wicked. . . .
Let Him take away His rod from me,
And let not His terror frighten me;
Then I would speak and not fear Him,
For I am not so with myself. . . .
I will say to God: Do not condemn me;
Let me know why You contend with me.
Is it good for You to oppress,
That You should despise the work of Your hands,
And favor the counsel of the wicked? . . . .
Are not my days few? Cease then,
Let me alone,
That I may find a little comfort. . . .

> (Chapter IX, Verses 2-4, 21, 22, 34, 35;
> Chapter X, Verses 2-4, 20.)

The two friends who have come to help have only angered and discouraged Job. In the third act, his friend Zophar, who has closely watched Job's reactions, now speaks. He is blunt, sharp, even harsh, and will not let Job have the last word. He says, in effect: You are wicked and evil and must have done wrong and you ought to be grateful that God has not punished you more severely. Be honest with yourself! Turn to God! Have faith in God. That faith will give you security, peace, and hope.

Should not a multitude of words be answered?
And should a man full of talk be considered right?
Your boastings have made men hold their peace,
And you have mocked, but none have made you ashamed.
You have said: "My doctrine is pure,
And I am clean in Your eyes."
O that God would speak
And open His lips to you;
That He would reveal to you the secrets of wisdom,
That sound wisdom is manifold!
Know then that God exacts of you less than your iniquity
    deserves. . . .
If you set your heart properly,
And stretch out your hands toward Him—
If iniquity is in your hand, put it away,
And do not let unrighteousness exist in your tents—
Surely then will you lift up your face without blemish;
Indeed, you will be steadfast and will not fear,
For you will forget your misery;
You will remember it as waters that have passed away;
And your life will be brighter than the noonday;
And the darkness will be like the morning,
And you will be secure, because there is hope;
You will look around and will take your rest in safety.
And you will lie down, and none will make you afraid.
(Chapter XI, Verses 2-6, 13-19.)

At a loss, Job turns from the friends he cannot understand to God. He frankly tells his friends that his reasoning powers are equal to theirs and he will now turn to the Almighty, for his faith is unswerving.

My eye has seen all this,
My ear has heard and understood it.
What you know, I also know;
I am not inferior to you.
Nonetheless, I want to speak with the Almighty,
And I want to reason with God. . . .
Though He slay me, yet I will trust in Him;
But I will defend my ways before Him. . . .
Only do not do two things against me,

Then I will not hide myself from You:
Withdraw Your hand far from me,
And let not Your terror make me afraid.
Then call, and I will answer,
Or let me speak, and You reply to me.
How many are my iniquities and my sins?
Let me know my transgression and my sin.
Why do you hide Your face,
And consider me Your enemy?

(Chapter XIII, Verses 1-3, 15, 20-24.)

In his pleading and confrontation Job turns to the question of life after death, as he sinks to the depths of despair.

Man born of a woman
Is of few days, and full of trouble.
He comes forth like a flower, and withers;
He flees also as a shadow, and does not continue. . . .
Look away from him, so that he may rest,
Till he will accomplish, as a hireling, his day.
For there is hope of a tree,
If it is cut down, it will sprout again,
And its tender branch will not cease.
Though its root in the earth becomes old,
And its stock dies in the ground;
Yet through the scent of water it will bud,
And bring forth boughs like a plant.
But man dies, and wastes away,
Indeed, man perishes, and where is he? . . . .
O that You would hide me in the grave,
That You would keep me secret, until Your wrath
    passes,
That You would appoint me a set time, and
    remember me!—

(Chapter XIV, Verses 1, 2, 6-10, 13-14.)

Thus ends the first cycle of addresses by Job's friends. Job has not been comforted nor impressed with their arguments. The more he resists, the more determinedly they cling to their inherent beliefs; and by the same token the more they persist, the more resistant Job becomes and the more certain of his innocence. The friends continue their efforts in two further cycles in the spiritual drama.

Eliphaz, no longer subtle nor gentle, imputes sins of varied proportions to Job. Zophar also determinedly states that Job should realize that the wicked must eventually fall. Job protests that the evil do prosper everywhere. While rejecting his friends' arguments, Job does not close his own mind. Herein is the greatness of his character. When his friends complete the third cycle, Job is ready with words of grandeur and beauty which reveal his insight into awareness of God's presence. He begins to understand, to acquire wisdom concerning the laws and principles by which the world moves and God's centrality in it. Only God has full knowledge of the universe; for people who cannot attain the wisdom of God, the fear of God is wisdom.

Wisdom! where shall it be found?
And where is the place of understanding?
Man does not know its price,
Nor is it found in the land of the living.
The deep says, "It is not in me";
And the sea says, "It is not with me."
It cannot be gotten for gold,
Nor can silver be weighed for its price. . . .
Where then, does wisdom come from?
And where is the place of understanding?
Seeing that it is hidden from the eyes of all the living,
And kept away from the birds of the air. . . .
God understands its way,
And knows its place.
He looks to the ends of the earth,
And sees under the whole heaven; . . . .
And to man He says:
"The fear of the Lord, that is wisdom,
And to depart from evil, that is understanding."
(Chapter XXVIII, Verses 12-15, 20, 21, 23, 24, 28.)

Job relives his life and revels in his past glories. He surveys the past and the present and despairs of his low estate. Once again he protests his innocence.

He now regards his present state:

But now they make sport of me,
They who are younger than I. . . .
They hate me, they run far away from me,
And do not hesitate to spit at me. . . .
I cry to You and You do not answer me,
I stand up and You look at me.
You have turned cruel to me,
With the might of Your hand, You persecute me. . . .
(Chapter XXX, Verses 1, 10, 20, 21.)

With all the fervor of his soul, he protests his innocence:

Does He not see my ways,
And count all my steps?
If I have walked with falsehood. . .
If my heart has been enticed by a woman. . .
If I despised the cause of my servants. . .
If I have withheld what the poor needed. . .
If I have seen a wanderer in want of clothing. . .
If I have lifted up my hand against the fatherless. . .
If I have rejoiced because my wealth was great. . .
If I beheld the sun when it shined. . .
If I rejoiced at the destruction of one who hated me. . .
O that I had one to hear me!
Here is my signature, let the Almighty answer me—
O that I had the indictment written by my adversary. . . .
(Chapter XXXI, Verses 4, 9, 13, 16, 19, 21, 25, 26, 29, 35.)

"The words of Job are ended." (Chapter XXXI, Verse 40) Job's brilliant summary, with its set of principles as a guide for life, comes to a close. He rests his case.

A young bystander named Elihu, who has been watching the enactment of the entire drama, offers his views. Unlike Job's other friends, Elihu is haughty, addressing Job in intimate terms. He asserts he is amazed at the weak arguments of the friends. He apologizes for his youth and says that wisdom need not be limited to older people, nor does it necessarily come with age. God speaks to people in many ways. God works in mysterious ways.

It is incomprehensible that the Ruler of the world is unjust. God is infinitely great, wise, and just. Elihu calls on Job to desist from his complaints and his desire to confront God and instead to acknowledge God with reverence and humility.

The interruption is ended. Job has confronted God, continuing his cry of why? God now presents the answer, teaching Job the Lord's greatness and majesty. Job learns of the immensity of the universe, how small humanity is in comparison, and how impossible it is for people to understand everything. One's intellect is limited and one must therefore accept the principle that there is a divine purpose which is omniscient. It is no longer a question of innocence or guilt. Job's innocence and spiritual integrity are indeed irrefutable. When Job is humbled by the perception of God's immeasurable greatness, his perspective is thereby enlarged. He has struggled for an explanation of God's ways with humanity. Now he accepts God without needing to know the reason. He is assured by the revelation and is satisfied, "For I know that my redeemer lives." (Chapter XIX, Verse 25.) His problem is not solved as he has expected but is seen rather from a higher vantage point: God and he are one. He no longer questions God's moral integrity.

The Book of Job therefore tells us that problems may not be explained by logic, intellectual arguments, or divine feats but by simple faith and trust in a gracious God whose personal friendship and concern are of greater value than the comforters or counselors who think they must defend God.

God speaks to Job out of the whirlwind, revealing the vast panorama of creation to convince Job that complete wisdom is only in God.

Then the Lord answered Job out of the whirlwind:
Who is it who darkens counsel
By words without knowledge?
Gird up your loins like a man,
And I will ask of you and you answer me.
Where were you when I laid the foundations of the earth?
Tell me, if you have the understanding.
Who determined its measurements?
Or who stretched the line upon it?
On what were the foundations set?
Or who laid its cornerstone?
When the morning stars sang together,
And all the sons of God shouted for joy?
Or who shut in the sea with doors,
When it burst forth from the womb. . . .

JOB

Have you entered into the springs of the sea,
Or have you walked in the recesses of the deep?
Have the gates of death been revealed to you?
Or have you seen the gates of the shadow of death?
Have you comprehended the expanse of the earth?
Declare if you know all this. . . .
Have you entered the treasuries of the snow,
Or have you seen the treasuries of the hail. . . .
How is the light distributed,
Or the east wind scattered upon the earth? . . . .
Does the rain have a father?
Or who has begotten the drops of dew. . . .
Do you know the laws of the heavens?
Can you establish their rule on the earth. . . .
Can you send lightning that they may go,
And say to you, "Here we are"?
Who has put wisdom in the inward parts?
Or who has given understanding to the mind. . .
Do you know the time when the wild goats
of the rock give birth? . . . .
Have you given the horse his strength? . . . .
Does the hawk soar by your wisdom? . . . .
Does the vulture mount at your command,
And make her nest on high?
(Chapter XXXVIII, Verses 1-8, 16-18, 22, 24, 28, 33, 35, 36;
XXXIX, Verses 1, 19, 26, 27.)

Job answers the voice of God with great humility:

I am of small account; what shall I answer You?
I lay my hand on my mouth.
Once I have spoken, but I will not answer again,
Indeed, twice, but I will continue no more.
(Chapter XL, Verses 3, 4.)

Job's perspective has changed. He has previously understood God only through past teachings. His comprehension dictated that there was no place for the suffering of the righteous. Now, he has understood God's splendor in all its dazzling glory. God is good and righteous. Job, too, though he may suffer, is also righteous. Job's answer is submissive, humble, penitent.

I know that You can do everything,
And that no purpose can be withheld from You.
Who is he who hides counsel without knowledge?
Therefore have I said what I did not understand,
Things too wonderful for me, which I did not know.
Listen, I pray You, and I will speak;
I will ask of You and declare to me.
I had heard of You by hearsay,
But now my eye sees You,
Therefore, I despise myself and repent
Because I am dust and ashes
(Chapter XLII, Verses 2-6.)

Job admits his human limitations. He no longer needs to know why he has suffered. God knows. That is enough for him. He is comforted and is finally at peace with himself because it is God's will. Job rises above his fate.

THE EPILOGUE (Chapter XLII, Verses 7-17.)

The drama is over. God is known to Job. The "still small voice" has reconciled Job with his suffering and with God. God rebukes the friends of Job for not better understanding the problem of suffering which is not the result of sin or wrongdoing. Job intercedes on behalf of his friends and they are forgiven. Job is restored to position and wealth. He ends his days after a long and full life.

And the Lord changed the fortune of Job and gave him twice as much as he had before . . . and blessed the latter life of Job more than his beginning. He had fourteen thousand sheep, six thousand camels, a thousand yoke of oxen and a thousand donkeys. He had also seven sons and three daughters . . . and in all the land there were no women found so fair as the daughters of Job. . . . After this Job lived a hundred and forty years and saw his sons and his sons' sons, even four generations. So Job died, being old and full of days.
(Chapter XLII, Verses 10-17.)

SONG OF SONGS

IN HEBREW, THE TITLE OF THIS BOOK, THE FOURTH VOLUME in the Sacred Writings, is Shir HaShirim. It is the first of the Five Scrolls (Hamesh Megilloth) comprising the Song of Songs (or Canticles), Ruth, Lamentations, Ecclesiastes, and Esther, all of which are publicly read or chanted in the liturgy of the synagogue. The Song of Songs, with its emphasis on the beauty of springtime, is read on Passover.

Tradition ascribes its authorship to King Solomon, the Book of Kings (I Kings, Chapter V, Verse 12) recording that Solomon composed a thousand and five songs. Of these his choice or best song is included in this volume of the Ketuvim, written (according to Jewish lore) in his youth. The same tradition holds that Solomon composed Proverbs in his middle age and Lamentations in his declining years, based on the Midrash or Jewish homiletic treatises on the Bible which date from the fourth century. Different schools of thought, however, vary in opinions regarding these portions of the scriptures.

The name of God is not mentioned in the Song of Songs at all, and its inclusion in the Biblical canon was a matter of heated dispute. It would hardly have found acceptance for inclusion in the canon but for the theory of its Solomonic authorship and its religious significance. The latter was asserted by the famed scholar Rabbi Akiba ben Joseph (d. 132 A.C.E.), first of the compilers of the oral tradition which eventually became the Talmud, who said: "All the Ketuvim are holy, but the Song of Songs is the holiest Holy of Holies," and he forbade its recitation or singing in the contemporary wine-houses. Publicly read in the Syn-

277

agogue on Passover, it is also read by some in the home after the joyful Seder meal, and it is read every Friday before the Sabbath eve service. In the traditional prayerbook the Song of Songs is placed immediately before the Sabbath service and it is of interest to note that it is the only book of the Bible included in the daily prayerbook.

The story of the Song of Songs is of a passionate love told in a series of love lyrics of great beauty, warm and exciting. Some find eighteen love songs in the book of eight chapters, others twenty-three separate poems. There are monologues, dialogues, expressions of love by a shepherd, a young and beautiful maiden and a king. Whispered endearments are repeated until the climax of the drama is reached in the telling declaration:

Many waters cannot quench love,
Nor can the floods drown it.
(Chapter VIII, Verse 7.)

In the verses of this superb book are portrayed the impatient lover whose heart longs for the loved one and the beloved who in turn yearns for the lover. They seek and find each other. In striking imagery and graceful language, love unfolds in the beauty of refreshing springtime, young buds puncturing dry, dormant bark and soft breezes gently touch flushed, inviting cheeks. The union of love, the sacredness and dignity of the passionate life stimulus, is presented as the central element of human life, enshrined forever in this immortal literary masterpiece.

Why was this amatory poem included in the scriptures? Through its genius the Song of Songs captures the reverence of love, holiness being the key to the mystery of its inclusion. There is an ecstasy in love which elevates this unforgettable literature to holiness.

This epic poem has been accepted throughout the ages as an allegory of the relationship between God and Israel. The lover is God and the beloved is Israel. God seeks love from Israel and Israel from God. The language of the poem feelingly describes the spiritual marriage solemnized on Mount Sinai eternally sealing the divine union of God with the Chosen People. Prophets often spoke of God and Israel in terms of bridegroom and bride. The idea of bridegroom and bride is also found in a Sabbath ritual. The Sabbath is viewed as a bride and Israel as a bridegroom; the love relationship is extolled each week by the reading of the Song of Songs on Friday eve before the Sabbath service.

SONG OF SONGS

* * *

On the other hand, the Song of Songs has been viewed by some as a collection of old wedding songs chanted at a marriage festival when by custom the bridegroom and bride became king and queen for seven days, during which time love songs were sung in their praise and honor. Every bride's beauty was compared to Abishag, the Shulamite, "the fairest of the fair" in all the land, and every bridegroom was compared to King Solomon, most resplendent of the monarchs of antiquity.

Some read into the book a narrative of King Solomon, a beautiful maiden, her shepherd lover. The daughters of Jerusalem encourage her to accept the king's offer of marriage. A young girl from Shulem (or Shunem), afterward called Shulamith, tends sheep at the behest of her mother and brothers, who are not pleased about her affection for the shepherd and devise ways to sever the tie. She is sent to the vineyards where she is seen by Solomon's entourage moving along the road en route from winter to summer home. She accepts the invitation of the charioteers to accompany them awhile and is persuaded to perform her lovely dance. Then she is ready to return home. But the servants bring her by force to the king's palace where Solomon, having fallen in love with her, offers her his love and by implication his kingdom. She cannot turn her heart to the monarch because it already belongs to her shepherd lover, even though the ladies of the court, the daughters of Jerusalem, plead the king's love. Shulamith is impervious. Love triumphs and holds fast.

She dreams of her love and imagines he comes and takes her away with him. Awakening, she goes forth to pursue him and is deterred by the watchman. Finally the king ceases to importune the maiden and sends her home, where she is joined by her lover and they are welcomed by the friends who encourage her to relate the tale of her wanderings and her stay at court. She reveals the temptations of wealth and position and assures her listeners of her abiding love for her betrothed. Turning to her handsome lover, she sings these exquisite words:

Set me as a seal upon your heart,
As a seal on your arm;
For love is as strong as death,
Jealousy is cruel as the grave;
Its flashes are flashes of fire,
A most vehement flame.
                    (Chapter VIII, Verse 6.)

THE WRITINGS

In the greatest of all love stories, the poem carries the strongest of human emotions to its highest pitch of excitement, speaking in the gentle language of love, lyrically, liltingly, and almost dancingly. With a language of its very own, fully fifty words appear to have been created for it which do not appear elsewhere in the scriptures. Here is related in poetry the very force of life, given biblical sanction and understanding, which has drawn human beings together for the creation of families, peoples, and nations. This, indeed, is the sacred fire with its aura of the divine reflecting God's richest blessings, for true love is godly, teaches the Song of Songs.

Let him kiss me with the kisses of his mouth,
For your love is sweeter than wine.
Your perfumes have a goodly fragrance;
Your name is as perfume poured out,
Therefore do the maidens love you.
Take me with you, and we will run;
The king has brought me into his chambers;
We will be glad and rejoice in you,
We will extol your love more than wine!
Sincerely do they love you. . . .
Tell me, you whom my soul loves,
Where you feed, where you make your flock rest at noon;
Why should I be like one who covers up,
Beside the flocks of your companions?
                                    (Chapter I, Verses 2-4, 7.)

The maiden compares her love to Spring, with its renewal of life in the rebirth of nature when the earth stirs and brings forth its verdure. This Spring song is therefore read on the Passover in the synagogue.

Hark! my beloved! behold, he comes
Leaping over the mountains, bounding over the hills.
My beloved is like a gazelle or a young deer.
Here he stands behind our wall,
He looks in through the windows,
He peers through the lattice.
My beloved speaks and calls to me,
"Rise up, my beloved, my fair one, and come away.
For lo, the winter is past,

The rain is over and gone;
The flowers appear on the earth;
The time of singing has come,
And the voice of the turtle-dove is heard in our land;
The fig-tree sprouts its green figs.
And the vines are in blossom, giving forth their
fragrance.
Rise up, my beloved, my fair one, and come
away. . . .

(Chapter II, Verses 8-13.)

How shall I describe his charms to you? What is his mien?

My beloved is white and ruddy,
Distinguished among ten thousand.
His head is of the finest gold;
His locks are curled,
And black as a raven.
His eyes are like doves,
Beside springs of water,
Bathed in milk,
And fitly set.
His cheeks are like a bed of balsam-flower,
As banks of sweet herbs;
His lips are like lilies,
Distilling flowing myrrh,
His arms are like rods of gold
Set with jewels;
His body is like polished ivory
Overlaid with sapphires.
His legs are like pillars of marble,
Set on bases of fine gold;
His form is like Lebanon,
Excellent as the cedars.
His speech is most sweet;
He is altogether desirable.
This is my beloved and this is my lover,
O daughter of Jerusalem.

(Chapter V, Verses 10-16.)

Then the lover describes the woman he adores with a tenderness which has become immortal:

You are beautiful, my love; you are beautiful!
Your eyes are like doves behind your veil;
Your hair is like a flock of goats,
That trail down from Mount Gilead.
Your teeth are like a flock of shorn ewes, all shaped alike,
When they have come from the washing;
Where they all are paired,
And not one of them is missing.
Your lips are like a thread of scarlet,
And your mouth is lovely,
Your temples, behind your veil,
Are like a slice of pomegranate.
Your neck is like the tower of David,
Built for trophies,
On which hang a thousand shields,
All armor of mighty men,
Your two breasts are like two fawns,
Twins of a gazelle,
Pasturing among the lilies. . . .
You have ravished my heart with a glance of your eyes,
With one bead of your necklace.
How sweet is your love, my sister, my bride!
How much better than wine is your love!
(Chapter IV, Verses 1-5, 9, 10.)

From the Song of Songs have come quoted phrases and verses, titles of books and plays, for here in one human document is superb recognition in the abiding and sublime power of love as the primary emotion of life.

RUTH

THE SCROLL OF RUTH, THE FIFTH BOOK OF THE SACRED WRIT-
ings, is one of the Five Scrolls, Hamesh Megilloth, which includes the
Song of Songs, Ruth, Lamentations, Ecclesiastes, and Esther. Like the
others which are read publicly, Ruth is read in the synagogue on Shavuoth, the harvest festival commemorating the receiving of the Torah by
Moses on Mount Sinai. In the Septuagint, Greek translation of the Bible, the Book of Ruth follows the Book of Judges.

Jewish tradition assigns authorship to Samuel, although varying views
credit the date of its composition from the time of King David, tenth
century, to periods as late as that of Ezra and Nehemiah, middle of the
fifth century B.C.E. It is believed that the great interest in the ancestry
of King David is among the primary purposes for the inclusion of this
delightful epic in the Biblical canon. The old history books name no
ancestor of David beyond his father Jesse of Bethlehem. In this book it
is told that the son born to Ruth, Naomi's daughter-in-law, and her
second husband Boaz, is named Obed, who became the father of Jesse,
father of King David. (Chapter IV, Verses 17-22.)

The Book of Ruth is thus connected also with Bethlehem, the birth-
place of David, and there is some connection between Ruth and Moab
found in I Samuel (Chapter XXII, Verse 3) which indicates knowledge of
some relationship between Moab and David, since David brought his
parents to Mizpah, to the King of Moab, for refuge during the time of
his flight from King Saul when he was maintaining his stronghold at the
cave of Adullam with his followers. It is interesting to note that inter-

marriage with the Moabites, who were descendants of Lot, nephew of Abraham, was regarded with aversion at certain periods, as indicated in Deuteronomy, because they had deviated from the religious faith of Israel and also because they stood in the way of the Israelites when they came out of Egypt.

Yet, Ruth, a Moabitess, is presented with great sympathy and therefore according to some scholars, may have been offered in this light to counteract the drastic reforms of Ezra and Nehemiah which were not everywhere acceptable since it meant the breaking up of marriages and families.

Family love and kindness repaid is the theme of this gentle, tranquil story which enshrines the love of one human being for another. It is set in a blessed, ideal world in which people care about each other. The historical setting is the time of the Judges, about 1100 B.C.E., a time of changing headships, turmoil, and warfare. It tells of landowners and working people who earn their livelihood and thank God for their blessings, of men and women who live the simple, country life. We see the owners of estates who are modest, even if affluent, and take a personal interest in the work side by side with their tenants. We see farmers, farm hands, tillers of the soil, husbands and wives together in the fields, finding serenity and peace. For whatever reasons this story was written, everyone accepts its simple beauty, its magnanimous spirit, its wonderful manifestation of humanity.

One is reminded of the love which pervades the Song of Songs. Here in place of the passionate, romantic, unbridled love of extreme youth, we have the love of a devoted, mature woman who has tasted life; she is understanding, intelligent and perceptive, her love manifested in family loyalty, sincerity. One senses that Ruth is beautiful. The enduring beauty of the spirit shines in her eyes and the warmth of her smiles as she walks in an aura that exceeds even physical loveliness. Through the ages she has remained a symbol of womanliness—a charming, gentle, kind, respectful, discerning, and interesting personality who possesses the secret of true friendship revealed in her modest, even-tempered ways.

Naomi, too, is an understanding woman. The mother of Ruth's first husband, Naomi is concerned for her children, equally for her daughters-in-law as for her sons. In her maternal, devoted nature, she has a deep interest, real and honest, in the welfare of her sons' wives. Furthermore, the love Naomi bears her husband and her two sons survives even their deaths, in that the tie which originally united them into a family is not severed by the grave. Naomi and Ruth depend all the more on each other for comfort, succor, and sustenance in a bond of trust and affection.

Go, return each of you to her mother's house. May the Lord deal kindly with you as you have dealt with the dead and me. The Lord grant that you may find rest, each of you, in the house of her husband. (Chapter I, Verses 8, 9.)

While Naomi feels her aloneness she realizes she can no longer help her daughters-in-law. "What else can I do for you?" she asks plaintively. "I have no more sons to take you in marriage. You have been kind to me and you have helped me in the time of my need and despair. Now your time has come to return to begin your lives anew. God will bless you for your kindness and loyalty to me." Without waiting for their response, Naomi kisses each young daughter-in-law good-bye. They weep as they embrace Naomi, yet both refuse to leave her alone and abandoned.

The four chapters begin simply, proceed smoothly, and draw to a close with the same quiet dignity. The story opens in the small town of Bethlehem and concludes there. In the time of the Judges (which era began in the twelfth century B.C.E.) there was a man there by the name of Elimelech, a wealthy landowner, generally admired and respected. Now it happened that the land was not fruitful no matter how hard the people worked; the earth would not respond and the famine came. In despair, Elimelech took his wife, Naomi, and their two sons, Mahlon and Chilion, from Bethlehem to Moab where he sought to provide for his family and to re-establish himself. Unfortunately, before long Elimelech died. Naomi is now a widow with two sons in a strange land. In due time, both of the sons are married to Moabite women, Ruth and Orphah. For ten years all is well until both of Naomi's sons, Mahlon and Chilion, die. Bereft of her own husband and mourning the loss of her two sons, Naomi now has to comfort her two grieving daughters-in-law, Ruth and Orphah.

When Naomi hears that times have greatly improved in Bethlehem, she decides to return to her old home, believing that life will be easier there near her own family. The story reaches an interesting impasse when the widowed Ruth and Orphah together decide to go with their mother-in-law. They accompany her until they reach a crossroad when Naomi, reflecting on the strange situation, pauses in the journey and urges her daughters-in-law not to go any farther with her but to return promptly to their own homeland. "No! We will go back with you to your people." (Chapter I, Verse 10.)

Naomi now insists. She pleads with the young women: "Return, go back to your own home. I cannot help you any longer! What else can I do for you?"

"For it grieves me deeply for your sakes, for the hand of the Lord has gone forth against me." (Chapter I, Verse 13.)

Orphah, the widow of Naomi's son Chilion, is finally persuaded. Obediently she kisses her mother-in-law and departs. Ruth, the widow of Mahlon, is equally persistent. She understands Naomi's hurt and loneliness and decides not to abandon her. Naomi tries again. Orphah has returned, she says. Follow her example. But Ruth is adamant in her refusal. In deeply stirring and sincere words which reach the highest pinnacle of filial loyalty, Ruth passionately pleads with the mother of her dead husband.

Entreat me not to leave you and to return from following you; for where you go I will go, and where you lodge I will lodge; your people will be my people and your God my God; where you die I will die and there will I be buried. (Chapter I, Verses 16 and 17.)

Overwhelmed by Ruth's expressed devotion, Naomi finally relents, and together the two women proceed to Naomi's home in Bethlehem. News of their return spreads quickly and people speak to Naomi, the widow of Elimelech, remembering the youthful Naomi as she appeared in the days before she left with her husband. The sight of her now, her face lined with sorrow, shocks them into remarking, "Is this Naomi?" They have, of course, forgotten how much has happened over the years. When Naomi hears how changed they have found her, she feels even older, more alone and more bitter. Tearfully she says:

Do not call me Naomi (sweet, pleasant) but Marah (bitter),
for the Almighty has dealt bitterly with me. I went away full
and the Lord has brought me back empty. (Chapter I, Verses
20, 21.)

The welcome has not been warm but disturbing. Nevertheless, Naomi
feels a sense of security now that she is in her own homeland. All the
more poignant is the devotion borne Naomi by Ruth, who loves the
older woman for herself and cares not that time and grief have ravaged
Naomi's youthful physical beauty. Naomi and her daughter-in-law Ruth
have returned at the beginning of the barley harvest. Naomi is too
proud to ask for help but she sends Ruth to glean the ears of the corn in
the field of Boaz, a kinsman of Naomi, being the nephew of Elimelech,
described as "a mighty man of valor." Ruth does not seek special consideration because of relationship. Like the other workers of the poor, she,
too, gleans what is left when the reapers bring in the harvest. According
to Jewish law, a landowner may not pick up gleanings once his reapers
have passed a row, because what is left is designated for the needy.

While Ruth is gleaning with the other people in the fields, the landowner Boaz comes to greet his workers with the friendly words, "The
Lord be with you." They respond with appreciation, "The Lord bless
you." Boaz surveys the work, and upon noticing the newcomer Ruth, he
inquires, "Who is she?" His servants tell Boaz she is Ruth, a Moabite
woman who has just returned with her mother-in-law Naomi. Hearing
this and realizing she is related to him by marriage through Naomi,
Boaz calls to Ruth to come near him, as he wishes to befriend her.
Thereupon he tells Ruth not to glean anywhere else but to feel free to
come to all of the harvest lands which he owns. Ruth humbly expresses
her gratitude, asking why he is so generous and he replies:

All that you have done for your mother-in-law since the
death of your husband has been fully told to me, and how
you left your father and mother and came to a people you did
not know before. May God repay you for what you have done
and a full reward be given you from the Lord, the God of
Israel, under whose wings you have come to take refuge.
(Chapter II, Verses 11, 12.)

Boaz thereupon invites Ruth to sit with the others at mealtime and he tells his servants and workers to be most considerate to her. At the end of the day, Ruth returns home and joyfully tells Naomi of her good fortune. With the sharpness of her own sorrow dulled by time, Naomi thanks God.

Blessed be the Lord, whose kindness has not forsaken the living or the dead. (Chapter II, Verse 20.)

Naomi tells Ruth that Boaz is a relative through marriage and, according to Jewish law, he has certain privileges and duties which include the first rights to redeem or buy the property of a dead relative before it is offered publicly and to assume the obligation to perpetuate the name of his deceased next of kin. This he can do by marrying the wife of the departed. Although this may not be the strict meaning of the law which imposed the duty of a brother of the departed, it appears to have been common custom and is at least within the spirit of the law.

A sense of renewed security comes to both Naomi and Ruth as they gather enough grain for themselves throughout the harvest season. When the harvest is completely gathered, Naomi, devotedly interested in Ruth's happiness and future, delicately suggests to Ruth that she seek betrothal with Boaz. Lovingly, deftly, careful not to hurt or embarrass her, Naomi outlines her plans to Ruth, who obediently follows Naomi's motherly advice.

The young woman goes to the place where Boaz is overseeing the winnowing of the barley and where he is to spend the night. Surprised by Ruth's presence, Boaz asks why she has come. Without circumlocution, Ruth quietly explains her situation and asks him to take her in marriage. Sensitive to Ruth's reputation, Boaz agrees to take whatever steps are necessary, reminding her there is another relative, Elimelech's brother, who must have first matrimonial rights to redeem Elimelech's properties, a Jewish law he will not violate. He will await developments.

The next morning, Boaz goes to the gate of the city where courts of justice hold their session. There he sees Elimelech's brother. He assembles ten elders, and in their presence Boaz informs Elimelech's brother of his ancestral rights under the law. The brother agrees to buy the land. Boaz then advises him of his obligation to perpetuate the name of the deceased. The brother declines to assume this obligation. As next of kin, Boaz, in the presence of the elders of the city, exercises his right of redemption by buying all of the property of Elimelech and his sons

Chilion and Mahlon, and with tenderness of expression takes Ruth to be his wife. The elders bless him and their marriage.

We are witnesses. May the Lord make the woman who is coming into your house like Rachel and Leah, who together built up the house of Israel. May you prosper in Ephrath and be renowned in Bethlehem; and may your house be like the house of Perez, whom Tamar bore to Judah, because of the children that the Lord will give you by this young woman. (Chapter IV, Verses 11, 12.)

The union of Ruth and Boaz is blessed with a son called Obed. Naomi finds much comfort in her new "grandson." The women tell her that the child will be to her a "restorer of life and a nourisher of her old age," for the daugher-in-law who loves her is better to Naomi than seven sons. "And Naomi took the child and laid it in her bosom and became nurse unto him." (Chapter IV, Verse 16.) The women of the city are so taken with the love Naomi showers on the little boy that they exclaim "There is a son born to Naomi!" Naomi, indeed, regards her grandson as her own. His name, Obed, meaning "to serve," expresses the hope that he will serve God and humanity.

The genealogy given in the closing verses traces the ancestry of David to Perez, father of Hezron, who was the father of Ram; Ram was the father of Amminadab; and Amminadab was the father of Nahshon; and Nahshon became the father of Salmon, who was the father of Boaz, the husband of Ruth, their son being Obed, who became the father of Jesse, the father of King David.

Gratitude is part of the theme of the Book of Ruth. In goodness, God guides people, not forsaking them. Naomi and Ruth find comfort again in a new life. The Creator who gave the Torah on Mount Sinai, the event celebrated by Shavuoth, the Feast of the Giving of the Torah, reveals kindness and blessings in the story of Ruth who was irresistibly drawn to the religion of Israel and whose happiness is reborn in the season of the harvests, Shavuoth, also known as "Hag HaBikkurim," the festival of the first fruits.

LAMENTATIONS

THE BOOK OF LAMENTATIONS, SIXTH IN THE SACRED WRITINGS, is the third of the Five Scrolls, comprising Song of Songs, Ruth, Lamentations, Ecclesiastes, and Esther. Read publicly in the synagogue, Lamentations is chanted on Tishah B'Av, the ninth day of the eleventh month in the Jewish calendar (July-August) and known as the national day of Jewish mourning because the day commemorates the destruction of both Temples and other catastrophes which befell the Jewish people. Like the Book of Esther, Lamentations has a special melody which reflects its own solemn, somber theme.

In the Septuagint, Greek translation of the Bible, it was placed after Jeremiah. In Hebrew it is called Ekhah, the exclamatory particle meaning "how!" taken from the first word of the book, but in the course of time it was called Lamentations. (The practice of adopting the first important word as a title is followed also with the first five books of the Bible.) In rabbinic literature, Lamentations is referred to as Kinoth, meaning elegies or dirges. The booklet used on Tishah B'Av for the reading is so known, a book of sorrows, a sad volume.

Lamentations is a collection of five dirges, poetical elegies applied to the fall and desolation of Jerusalem in 586 B.C.E. composed during the period when the walls of the Holy City lay in ruins.

A striking feature of the book is the acrostic structure which because Lamentations was utilized liturgically, may have added to the ease of memorizing the lines. In the Book of Lamentations it first becomes apparent that Hebrew poetry has meter, and the first four elegies came to

290

be known as Kinah, limping or elegiac meter well suited to the elegy and dirge.

Tradition says that the poet of Lamentations is the prophet Jeremiah. The tragic destruction of Jerusalem is presented as God's punishment, thus teaching lessons of the past of the children of Israel and keeping alive the nation's faith in the face of overwhelming disaster. There is deep sorrow in the poems but shining through them is a radiant hope for the future. God prophesied that the Holy Temple, the City of Jerusalem, would meet with misfortune because the people had turned away from God's laws. Judah would crumble under the devastating strength of the armies of the Babylonian King Nebuchadnezzar, and thousands would be deported to Babylonia for the long exile.

The five sorrowful songs (or chapters) follow a clear pattern. The first, second, and fourth are true elegies or poetic laments appearing in alphabetic acrostic, twenty-two verses for the twenty-two letters of the Hebrew alphabet and each opening with the word Ekhah, "How!"

The third chapter's alphabetic acrostic is tripled, and thus has sixty-six verses, each Hebrew letter beginning three successive verses. Chapter V, while not following the acrostic pattern, consists of twenty-two verses, relating it, in this sense, to the Hebrew alphabet.

In Hebrew literature, a city is referred to in the feminine gender and therefore Jerusalem is regarded as a woman bereft and grieving, her children slain, or humbled and humiliated, her feet surrounded with rubble of the destroyed city. Through the cries of despair runs a thread of hopefulness. The poet cries out for faith in God's mercy which never fails. God may punish, but God also pardons. He prays that God will heed a dejected people and return them to their pristine glory.

How does the city sit all alone,
That was once full of people!
How has she become like a widow!
She who was great among the nations,
How has she become a tributary!
And princess among the peoples.
She weeps bitterly at night,
Her tears are on her cheeks;
She has no one to comfort her
Among all her lovers;
All her friends have dealt treacherously with her,
They have become her enemies.
Judah has gone into exile because of affliction,
And because of hard servitude;

She dwells among the nations,
She finds no rest;
All her pursuers have overtaken her
Within her distress. . . .
Arise, cry out in the night,
At the beginning of the watches;
Pour out your heart like water,
Before the presence of the Lord;
Lift up your hands toward Him
For the lives of your young children
Who faint for hunger
At the corner of every street.
"See, O Lord, and consider
To whom You have done this . . ."

(Chapter I, Verses 1-3;
Chapter II, Verses 19, 20.)

Jerusalem herself speaks as a woman:

For these things do I weep;
My eye flows over with tears,
Because a comforter is far away from me,
One who could refresh my soul.
My children are desolate
For the enemy has prevailed. . . .
O Lord, I am in distress,
My inwards burn;
My heart is stirred within me,
For I have been rebellious.
In the street, the sword bereaves,
At home it is like death. . . .
For my sighs are many,
And my heart is faint. . . .

(Chapter I, Verses 16, 20, 22.)

The poet extols God and God's mercy.

Surely the Lord's mercies are not consumed,
Surely His compassions do not fail.
They are new every morning;

Great is Your faithfulness.
"The Lord is my portion,"
"Therefore I will hope in Him."
The Lord is good to those who wait for Him,
To those who seek Him.
It is good that a man should quietly wait
For the salvation of the Lord. . . .
For the Lord will not cast off forever.
Though He causes grief, He will have compassion
In keeping with His many mercies.
For He does not afflict willingly,
Nor grieve the children of men. . . .
Let us search and try our ways
And return to the Lord.
Let us lift up our hearts with our hands,
To God in the heavens. . . .

(Chapter III, Verses 22-26, 31-33, 40-41.)

The book of sorrows ends on a note of hope for the future and faith in God's restoration of Israel to grace:

The crown has fallen from our head;
Woe to us! for we have sinned.
For this our hearts are faint,
For these things our eyes have grown dim;
For the mountain of Zion which lies desolate,
Foxes walk on it.
You, O Lord, reign forever,
Your throne endures from generation to generation.
Why do You forget us,
And forsake us for so long a time?
Turn us to Yourself, O Lord, and we shall return.
Renew our days as of old. . . .

(Chapter V, Verses 16-21.)

ECCLESIASTES

ECCLESIASTES, THE SEVENTH BOOK OF THE SACRED WRITings, and the fourth of the Five Scrolls (Hamesh Megilloth), consisting of Song of Songs, Ruth, Lamentations, Ecclesiastes, and Esther, is read publicly in the synagogue on Sukkoth, the Festival of Tabernacles, celebrating the bringing in of the harvest. The rather incongruous association of the realistic Book of Ecclesiastes with the joyous festival is probably due to the desire to emphasize that true enjoyment is to be found in the more simple things in life—the results of people's yearly work terminating in the bountiful harvest, the satisfaction in gathering in the grain, a basket of summer fruit, loading the oxcarts with clusters of grapes.

The English name, Ecclesiastes, derives from the Greek translation of ecclesia meaning assembly. The word Koheleth comes from the Hebrew word kahal, meaning congregation, assembly or community, and for this reason, he, Koheleth, a teacher of Jerusalem, having spoken or taught before an assembly or congregation, has been called the Preacher or the Teacher. Tradition says that Solomon was the author of this volume, as he is reputed to have composed the Song of Songs and Proverbs. The book begins with the statement that Koheleth is the son of David (i.e., Solomon) and king of Jerusalem. Many scholars place the time of its writings from the fifth century B.C.E. to the first century of the common era. Most biblical authorities agree that the time of compilation is somewhere between the third and fourth century B.C.E.

ECCLESIASTES

The narrator, Koheleth, called the sad, gentle preacher, is perplexing to us. What does the Preacher desire most in life? For what is he striving? And why is he so given to fatalism? Is he truly a biting, cynical, skeptical doubter? Why, indeed, was the book included in the sacred biblical canon among the prophets who called for justice, mercy, and righteousness? It was included by the sages because in its keen perception of humanity's transitory existence it is one of the most vivid, fascinating, charming, and exciting books of the scriptures, ever fresh, ever modern, vital, effervescent. Koheleth disturbs the complacent tranquility of the religious mind as he evokes philosophical questions which pierce the heart of the matter. What, he asks, is there to life? What is its real meaning? None can deny the world's injustice, its evil, its greed, human vanities. When one ponders on the brevity of life, it is only natural to wonder why one should strive so hard. What is there to gain? Where are we heading?

The brooding preacher sows the seeds of doubt, knowing full well that in the end of his discourse he will bring his listeners back to God after a spiritual journey through the mires of disbelief, poverty, injustice, the pitfalls of youth, the bitterness of old age seen through the eyes of cynicism and fatalism. Nevertheless this wise guide will give the traveler sagacious counsel and finally return the traveler to a sense of security in religious faith. Meanwhile long-treasured views will have been dislodged in considering the basic truths of one's life and its endeavors. What is achievement? For whom? How long will the achiever be remembered? What is the purpose of life? To study? To procreate? To serve God? To work? To love? Whoever and wherever you are, whatever your station in life—wealthy, poor, wicked, righteous—everyone's end is the same. Is it not frightening? For what then are the strivings when human life is finite. Everything is a delusion. Koheleth calls it a "chasing after the wind." All is transitory. "Vanities of vanities, all is vanity."

All life is a profound mystery, an enigma impossible to fathom. The brilliant, restless mind searches the hidden recesses of thought and meditations, now along one path, now along another, wandering and wondering. Koheleth encourages the mind to formulate ideas and expects his listeners to join him in the groping quest. He asks for honesty, disdaining façade, pretense and sham. He fosters a freedom of the mind, no matter where it may lead. This freedom results in searching, evaluating, balancing, and tempering. There are contradictions and inconsistencies that are a part of life which never hews to a straight and narrow line in its flowing course.

The surface contradictions in the book of Koheleth almost excluded it from the biblical canon, but the tradition of its Solomonic authorship persuaded the selecting rabbinical editors in its favor. Fundamentally its philosophical "end of the matter" teaches that an individual's whole duty is to revere God and to keep the commandments. It is true that Koheleth incited wholesome doubts in religious faith, but he countered this by always maintaining a firm faith in God. He does not ask for unequivocal acceptance of his thoughts which would only contradict his entire purpose of stimulating others to think for themselves. As a mediator, he speaks throughout the book in the first person except where he offers maxims and proverbs. Apparent in his philosophy there is the persuasive power of his deceptively plain simplicity.

In sum, Koheleth awakens the mind from its lethargy as he preaches his basic theme of making the best of life by the pursuit of happiness, actually enjoying life and the good things it offers. To Koheleth, God is ever present. His philosophy teaches that all enjoyment comes from God—it is God's gift. Complete denial of pleasure is not, therefore, the theme of Ecclesiastes. One is encouraged instead to enjoy life's fleeting blessings, with the capacity and strength to do so having its source in God who rules over humanity and nature.

Like the Book of Proverbs, the Book of Ecclesiastes has twelve chapters, suggests ways of achieving success, offers gems of wisdom for the good life, and sound advice to young and old. The main theme is projected in the first third of the book. The prologue introduces Koheleth, the author, and forthwith asserts the monotony of life, in the ways of the world and nature. Here is a teacher who differs from other prophets. He does not with passionate oratory summon the people to repentance. He simply states without preliminaries that life is certainly hopelessly monotonous and futile.

After the prologue, Koheleth speaks from his own experience, revealing how he has looked everywhere for personal happiness in wealth and varied pleasures, but has found in them only emptiness, futility, and vanity. Nothing worthwhile is enduring. People should therefore eat, drink, and make their souls merry. These pleasures are not forbidden by God and it is foolish not to take advantage in moderation of these God-given blessings.

In Koheleth's belief, everything is predestined. Immutable circumstances control fate. He considers various worldly matters, justice, reward and punishment, labor of people and beasts. He delivers a masterful address contrasting youth and old age and encourages people of all ages to enjoy life to the fullest extent of their powers.

In the epilogue an editor speaks of Koheleth, telling how the Preacher taught by using many proverbs, his premise to revere God and to keep the commandments being the whole duty of the individual.

ECCLESIASTES

From Koheleth we learn to have faith, to be patient, to be discreet, to thank God for the gift of life and to enjoy it as best we can.

Koheleth theorizes that nothing is worthwhile. The present is like the past, the past is like the present; nothing is new, it is all the same, tiring and wearisome.

Vanity of vanities, says Koheleth,
Vanity of vanities, all is vanity.
What benefit does a man have of all the work,
In which he works under the sun?
One generation goes and another comes,
But the earth endures forever.
The sun rises and the sun goes down,
And hastens to its place of rising.
The wind blows toward the south,
And turns around to the north,
It whirls around continually,
And the wind returns to its own circuit.
All the streams run into the sea,
Yet the sea is not full.
To the place where the rivers flow,
There they flow again.
All things are full of weariness.
Man cannot say it,
The eye is not satisfied with seeing,
Nor the ear filled with hearing.
What has been is what will be,
What has been done is what will be done,
And there is nothing new under the sun.
Is there a thing of which it is said, "See, this is new."
It has already been in previous ages. There is no recollection of former things, nor will there be any remembrance of things that are to come with those who will come afterward.

(Chapter I, Verses 1-12.)

Koheleth changes his style from poetry to prose, as he attests to his personal experiences, his achievements, his garnering of wealth, his love of women. All is vanity.

I devoted myself to seeking and searching out wisdom concerning all things that are done under the heaven . . . I have seen all the works done under the sun, and behold all is vanity and a striving after wind . . . I devoted myself to knowing wisdom and to knowing madness and folly . . . I perceived that this also was striving after wind. . . (Chapter I, Verses 13, 14, 17.)

I said to myself, "Come now, I will make a test of mirth and enjoy pleasure, and behold this also was vanity." I said of laughter, "It is made," and of mirth, "What does it accomplish?" I sought to pamper my body with wine and my heart to guide me with wisdom, and to lay hold of folly till I might see what was best for people to do under the heaven the few days of their lives. I made me great works, I built houses, I planted vineyards, I made gardens and parks, and I planted trees in them of all kinds of fruits. I made pools of water, to water the forest of growing trees. I acquired male and female servants and had servants born in my house; also I had great possession of herds and flocks, above all that were before me in Jerusalem. I gathered for myself silver and gold. . . . So I was great. . . . And whatever my eyes desired, I did not keep from them. I did not keep my heart from any joy, for my heart rejoiced of all my labor . . . Then I looked on all works that my hands had wrought . . . and behold all was vanity and a striving after wind, and there was no benefit under the sun. I hated all my labor in which I worked under the sun, knowing that I must leave it to the one who will come after me. And who knows whether he will be a wise man or a fool? Yet he will rule over all the works in which I toiled and showed myself to be wise under the sun. This also is vanity. . . . (Chapter II, selected verses.)

There is nothing better for a man to do than to eat and drink and enjoy the pleasure of his labor. This also, I saw, is from the hand of God. (Chapter II, Verse 24.)

The whole range of human experience is captured in Koheleth's masterpiece on the virtues of timeliness.

For everything there is a season, and a time for every purpose under the heaven.

A time to be born, and a time to die;
A time to plant, and a time to uproot;
A time to kill, and a time to heal;
A time to destroy and a time to build up;
A time to weep and a time to laugh;
A time to mourn and a time to dance;
A time to scatter stones and a time to gather them together;
A time to embrace and a time to refrain from embracing;
A time to seek and a time to surrender;
A time to keep and a time to cast away;
A time to tear and a time to sew;
A time to be silent and a time to speak;
A time to love and a time to hate;
A time for war and a time for peace.

What benefit does he have who works? I have seen the task which God has given to people to be exercised with it. He has made everything beautiful in its time; also He has set eternity in their hearts, yet so that man cannot find out the work that God has done from the beginning to the end. I know that there is nothing better for them than to be happy and to derive pleasure as long as they live. Also, that every man should eat and drink and take pleasure in all his labor, is the gift of God. I know that whatever God does, endures forever; nothing can be added to it, nor can anything be taken from it; and God has made it so, that men should revere Him. . . . (Chapter III, Verses 1 to 14.)

Koheleth considers the oppressed and bewails their fate. They have no comforter, no one to speak in their behalf. His pessimism deepens. He begins to feel that death is better than life because the dead at least do not experience pain and suffering. He sees competition in labor instead of cooperation, with little peace of mind coming from the rivalry. He considers the loneliness of the person who accumulates a fortune and hoards it. He considers the value of companionship. How much better it is to share some of one's treasures with another. With his slightly amused regard of human foibles, Koheleth is the perfect philosopher of the secular. Human life is at its best with a periphery of divine grace practically expressed in good manners one person to another, giving substance to security and well-being.

While pessimism and doubt tug and gnaw at the heart and mind, and while it may appear that faith is struck a crushing blow, it is indeed faith which, in the end, triumphs. So teaches Koheleth.

MAXIMS FROM KOHELETH

PEACE OF MIND
Better is a handful with quietness
than both hands full with travail and vexation of spirit. (Chapter IV, Verse 6.)

COMPANIONSHIP
Two are better than one, because they have a good reward for their labor. For if they fall, one will lift up his fellow, but woe to him who is alone when he falls and has not another to lift him up. (Chapter IV, Verses 9-10.)

WATCH YOUR STEP
Guard your foot when you go to the house of God, and be ready to listen. . . . (Chapter IV, Verse 17.)

MAKE YOUR PRAYERS BRIEF
Do not be rash with your mouth nor let your heart be quick to utter a word before God, for God is in heaven and you are on earth. Therefore, let your words be brief. (Chapter V, Verse 1.)

IF YOU VOW, PAY YOUR PLEDGE
When you make a vow to God, do not delay paying it, for He has no pleasure in fools. Pay that which you vow. It is better that you should not vow than vow and not pay. (Chapter V, Verses 3, 4.)

THE MORE YOU HAVE, THE MORE YOU WANT
He who loves money will not be satisfied with money, and he who loves wealth will not attain it . . . (From Ibid, Verse 9.)

WORK IS GOOD AND HEALTHY
Sweet is the sleep of a toiler, whether he eat little or much. But the satiety of the rich does not let him sleep. (From Ibid, Verse 11.)

SEIZE THE DAY
Better is the seeing of the eyes than the wandering of the desire . . . (From Chapter VI, Verse 9.)

ECCLESIASTES

WHAT'S IN A NAME
A good name is better than precious oil. (From Chapter VII, Verse 1.)

THINK SERIOUSLY OF LIFE
It is better to go to a house of mourning,
Than to go to a house of feasting;
For this is the end of all men,
And the living may learn a lesson.
(From Ibid, Verse 2.)

ACCEPT CONSTRUCTIVE CRITICISM
It is better to hear the rebuke of the wise,
Than for one to hear the praise of fools.
(From Ibid, Verse 5.)

HOW ANGER DESTROYS!
Be not quick to anger,
For anger rests in the bosom of fools.
(From Ibid, Verse 9.)

THE GOOD OLD DAYS
Do not say: How is it that the earlier days were better than these?
For it is not from wisdom that you ask this! (Chapter V, Verse 10.)

DO NOT WORRY TOO MUCH
Consider the work of God, for who can make straight that which He has made crooked? In the day of prosperity, be joyful, and in the day of adversity, consider that God has made one as well as the other, so that man should find nothing after he is gone. (Chapter VII, Verses 13, 14.)

DO NOT BE EXCESSIVE
Be not overly righteous; nor make yourself overwise; why should you destroy yourself? Be not wicked overmuch, nor be foolish. . . . (Chapter VII, Verses 16, 17.)

THE STRENGTH OF WISDOM
Wisdom gives strength to the wise man more than ten rulers of the city. (Chapter VII, Verse 19.)
Whoever keeps the commandments will experience no trouble, and a wise man's heart discerns time and judgment. (Chapter VIII, Verse 5.)

The words of the wise spoken quietly
Are more acceptable than the cry of a ruler among fools.
(Chapter IX, Verse 17.)

WE ARE ALL HUMAN
There is not a righteous man on earth who does good and never
sins. (Chapter VII, Verse 20.)

IT IS LATER THAN YOU THINK
Go your way, eat your bread with enjoyment,
And drink your wine with a merry heart;
For God has already approved your action.
Let your garments always be white,
And let your head lack no oil.
Enjoy life with the woman whom you love all the days of your life,
which He has given you under the sun, because that is your por-
tion in life and in your work at which you labor under the sun.
What you are able to do, that do with all your might for there is no
action, nor thought, nor knowledge, nor wisdom, in the grave to-
ward which you are going. (Chapter IX, Verses 7-10.)

FALLING INTO YOUR OWN TRAP
He who digs a pit shall fall into it,
And whoever breaks down a fence shall be bitten by a serpent.
(Chapter X, Verse 8.)

REAP THE HARVEST OF KINDNESS
Cast your bread upon the waters,
For you will find it after many days. (Chapter XI, Verse 1.)

SHARE WHAT YOU HAVE
Give a portion to seven and even to eight,
For you do not know what calamity will happen on earth. (Chapter
XI, Verse 2.)

DO NOT WHILE AWAY THE TIME
He who watches the wind will not sow,
And he who gapes at the clouds will not reap. (Chapter XI,
Verse 4.)

IN SPITE OF UNCERTAINTY, LIVE, WORK, ENJOY
As you do not know what is the way of the wind,
Nor how bones grow in the womb of a pregnant woman;

Even so do you not know the work of God
Who does all things.
In the morning sow your seed,
And in the evening do not be idle;
For you do not know which shall prosper, this or that,
Or whether they both alike be successful.
The light is sweet,
And it is a pleasant thing for the eyes to see the sun.
For if a man live many years,
Let him rejoice in them all,
And let him remember the days of darkness,
For they will be many.
All that comes is vanity. (Chapter XI, Verses 5-8.)

YOU ARE ONLY YOUNG ONCE
Rejoice, young man, in your youth;
And let your heart cheer in your youthful days,
And walk in the ways of your heart,
And in the desires of your eyes;
But know, that for all these things,
God will bring you into account.
Remove sadness from your heart.
And put away evil from your body,
For your childhood and youth are vanity.
Remember then your Creator in your youthful days,
Before evil days (old age) come,
And the years draw near when you will say:
"I have no pleasure in them." (Chapter XI, Verse 9; Chapter XII,
Verse 1.)

THE END OF THE MATTER
The end of the matter, everything having been heard:
Revere God and keep His commandments,
For this is every man's whole duty. (Chapter XII, Verse 13.)

With these words, the last sentence of the Book of Ecclesiastes,
Koheleth sums up all of his life and humanity's role in God's world.

ESTHER

THE BOOK OF ESTHER, THE EIGHTH BOOK OF THE SACRED
Writings, Ketuvim, is also the fifth of the Five Scrolls (Song of Songs,
Ruth, Lamentations, Ecclesiastes, Esther). The Book of Esther, which is
read publicly in the synagogue on the festival of Purim, is also chanted
to the tune of a special cantillation or melody which reflects musically
both the deep pathos and the triumphant joy of the holiday, based on
this book.

The inspiring story of the Jewish heroine Esther is read from a parchment scroll on which the narrative has been inscribed by hand in Torah
scroll style. It is similar to the Torah scroll in that the parchment is
rolled. The Torah scroll, however, has two wooden handles, called etz
hayyim (the tree of life), for the rolling of the parchment. The scroll of
Esther, on the other hand, has either one or no wooden handles. Without a handle, it has the true appearance of a scroll or letter and vividly
symbolizes the important letter of communication which is the central
feature described in the story. While the Five Scrolls of the Sacred
Writings are known as Megilloth, the Hebrew word for scrolls, the mere
use of the word Megillah (the scroll) always implies the Scroll of Esther.

It is believed that the account based on historical incident was written
about the fifth century B.C.E. The Ahasuerus of the book is equated by
some to Xerxes, who ruled Persia between 485 and 465 B.C.E. Others
say that the events took place during the rule of Artaxerxes II, King of
Persia between 404 and 361 B.C.E. The author was undoubtedly a Per-

304

sian Jew of high literary artistry, intimately acquainted with the Persian royal court and its intrigues, with particular sensitivity to the ways of human beings, their strivings, moods, and responses. The writing is indicative of an abiding faith in God, in the eternal principles that right will triumph, and the indestructibility of the Children of Israel.

The word God is omitted from the story, although it is made clear that God's providence guides the people, recognized in Mordecai's assertion to Esther, "If you do nothing to help, relief and deliverance will come from another source." The reason given for excluding God's name was that the Megillah would be read during the time of hilarious, excessively joyous celebration. The religious implications are of an intense nationalism and there are overtones of the faith in God which is glorified in the saving of the Jews from destruction at the hands of Haman. Mordecai and Esther are indeed God's instruments in the Persian era of Israel's history.

The story of Esther is probably the most popular and cherished of the books of the Bible. At the end of the first century of the common era, it was still disputed among the rabbis whether it should be included in the canon. With its depth of feeling, the drama has stirred the imagination of a whole people from time immemorial, imparting strength and courage to the Jewish people, renewing their faith in the heritage of their forefathers.

After the Babylonians took Jerusalem, in 586 B.C.E., the exiled leaders, nobles, priests, and a large part of Judah settled in Babylonia, becoming loyal citizens as counseled by the prophet Jeremiah. When the Persians in turn conquered Babylonia, the Jews gave allegiance to the Persian king. The period of peace for them ended when a tyrant came who hated the Jews. This was Haman, the Agagite, in the reign of King Ahasuerus, who plotted their destruction but was foiled by the courage of a beautiful Jewish girl who interceded with the king and saved her people. Haman is the symbol of other dictators and autocrats who have sought to eradicate the Jew for no reason other than his faith.

Esther (Hadassah, meaning myrtle) has been reared in Persia by her cousin Mordecai, a man devoted to his people and a hero of his faith, for whom the king's favorite Haman nurses a bitter hatred. This villain plans the annihilation of all the Jews in the empire, but his evil plot is ruined by Esther, who acts on the instructions of Mordecai. Haman is maneuvered into a position in which he himself is hanged on the very gallows he has had prepared for Mordecai.

The story unfolds against the elegant background of the Persian king, ruler over one hundred and twenty-seven provinces, in the royal court, his private chambers, the queen's quarters, and rooms of the hand-maidens attached to the court. In one scene, the home of Haman is the setting for two brief conversations.

In the third year of his reign, Ahasuerus receives all of his princes, favorites, advisers, and court attendants, the commanders of the armies of Persia and Media, nobles, governors of the provinces. For one hundred and eighty days he shows them the wealth of his great kingdom. Upon their completion, he holds a magnificent banquet in the enclosed garden of the royal palace at Shushan (Susa). Meanwhile the lovely queen Vashti gives a feast for the women of the royal palace and women guests.

When the week for merrymaking draws to a close, the exuberant king bids his comely wife Vashti to grace the feast with her royal crown to accent her loveliness. Vashti refuses the royal request, for the feast has reached climactic proportions of celebration. Surprised, embarrassed, the affronted king turns to his counselors for advice. A serious breach has been committed. What shall he do? The shocking disobedience of the queen is unprecedented.

The counselors recommend that to avoid possible repercussions in the kingdom whereby wives may be influenced to act as audaciously as the queen, Vashti must serve as an object lesson, and as punishment she should be removed from her throne. The king agrees. Letters are dispatched throughout the land stating that "every man should bear rule in his own home" to assert his mastership and lordship over his household.

When Vashti is deposed and time assuages King Ahasuerus' anger, his counselors advise him to seek very fair young maidens of the land, who would assemble in the palace and there prepare themselves to be presented one by one to the king. The one who pleases him will become queen in place of Vashti.

The ancestors of Mordecai were among those who suffered in the Babylonian exile (which began in 586 B.C.E.). Mordecai is a descendant of those who fled with the king of Judah from Jerusalem and is therefore entitled to certain honors and status.

Now there was a certain Jew in Shushan the capital, whose name was Mordecai, the son of Jair, the son of Shimei, the son of Kish, a Benjaminite, who had been carried away from Jerusalem among the captives carried away with Jaconiah, King of Judah, whom Nebuchadnezzar, King of Babylon, had carried away (Chapter II, Verses 5-7.)

He has reared his cousin Esther since she was left an orphan in early childhood and she has, indeed, been like a daughter to him and he a father to her. Since the girl has great beauty, Mordecai, urged on by a sense of destiny, sends her to the royal court as a contestant for the queenhood. She is not to reveal her faith, for Mordecai is aware that a Jewess would not be permitted to participate. Esther's graciousness impresses those in charge of the women's quarters. Mordecai anxiously hovers about the palace grounds and makes daily inquiries about his young relative's welfare.

One by one, the maidens visit the monarch until Esther's turn comes. Her manner, her beauty and charm captivate the king and she wins his love. He places the crown on her beautiful tresses and proclaims her his queen.

Meanwhile her kinsman Mordecai sits at the gates and overhears two of the king's servants, who guard the entrance of the palace, plot to assassinate the king. He reports this to Esther, who, in turn, tells the king. She mentions it in Mordecai's name. The traitors are quickly arrested and summarily executed; the event is duly recorded in the official chronicles of the day.

We learn that Haman becomes grand vizier or premier of the land and the people bow down respectfully before him. However, Mordecai is conspicuous for his refusal to prostrate himself before the official. The king's servants ask Mordecai why he fails to pay the respect due to Haman as the king's deputy. Mordecai replies that he cannot pay such homage because he is a Jew. When Haman hears of this, he is incensed.

"This is treason!" he storms, and in a rage he determines to destroy all the Jews of the kingdom, including Mordecai's family. He plans the massacre and even casts lots to select the day. The Hebrew word for lot is pur, plural, purim, (Feast of Lots). The thirteenth day of the Hebrew month of Adar (February-March) a month before Passover, is chosen and Haman now informs the King:

There is a certain people scattered and dispersed among the peoples in all the provinces. Their laws are different from any other people's. They do not observe the king's laws. It is not to the king's advantage to keep them. Therefore, if it please the king, let it be decreed that they be destroyed, and I will pay ten thousand talents of silver into the king's treasury. (Chapter III, Verses 8-9).

While the king assents to the dastardly proposal, he spurns the silver. He gives Haman his royal ring with which to seal the proclamations of the throne. Haman now issues the dreadful order signed by the king. Copies of the document are dispatched throughout the vast Persian empire and the people learn of the imminent doom of many Jews who have lived in peace among them.

The king and Haman sat down to drink, but the city of Shushan was perplexed. (Chapter III, Verse 15.)

Haman's vile act, even though bearing the seal of royal approval, will not be submissively accepted by the populace. When Mordecai hears of the evil decree, he dons garments of mourning and terror spreads among the hapless Jewish people throughout the land. There is fasting, weeping, wailing by people in sackcloth and ashes.

Esther sends fresh garments to Mordecai, who, in his grief, refuses to don them. Whereupon she then sends her trusted steward Hatakh to ascertain all he can from Mordecai. Mordecai reveals what has transpired. He sends the message to Esther, urges her to go to the king, make known her Jewish origin, and to intercede on behalf of her people. The queen responds to the message, saying that the king has not called her into his presence, and one may not, under penalty of death, come to the king's chambers without being summoned.

Disappointed and angered, Mordecai sends back a stern rebuke to Esther.

Do not think that you will escape in the king's house more than all the other Jews. For if you keep your peace at this time, relief and deliverance will come from another place, but you and your father's house will perish. And who knows whether you were not sent to the kingdom for such a time as this? (Chapter IV, Verses 13, 14.)

Mordecai has told Esther that her selection as queen has been providential, that she has a vital obligation to her people. The queen is convinced, and responds with alacrity, instructing Mordecai to call on every Jew to fast for three days. She and her maidens will also fast. Then after the lapse of three days, she will approach the king whether or not she is summoned. "And if I perish, I perish."

ESTHER

Esther plans how to present her appeal at the most opportune moment. On the third day, the queen, arrayed in her royal regalia, presents herself in the inner court of the king's palace. Not daring to enter, she waits to be ushered in, for the king must extend his golden sceptre to indicate his recognition of her. When the king sees his lovely wife, he unhesitatingly reaches out his sceptre, inviting her to enter.

What do you wish, Queen Esther? What is your request? Ask, even to half the kingdom, it will be given to you. (Chapter V, Verse 3.)

Esther graciously extends an invitation to the king and to Haman to attend a dinner in her quarters. The king sends word of his acceptance to Haman. When both monarch and vizier attend the banquet, the royal husband inquires as to what thoughts are troubling his queen. However, Esther hesitates to reveal her true purpose, feeling the time is still not propitious. She therefore, invites her guests to return the following day for another great dinner, promising that she will then confide in the king. Her guests agree to come.

The happy and radiant Haman does not conceal his intense joy. Is not high honor being paid him even by the lovely Queen Esther? His felicity is dampened, however, when he observes Mordecai as he leaves the palace. Mordecai makes no move to recognize Haman who, with hatred burning in his soul, returns home to boast of his great achievements, recounting his wealth, his high position in the government, and his wide public recognition. He admits, however, that the very sight of the Jew Mordecai has marred his success. When his wife callously suggests Mordecai's removal, Haman comes to the dreadful decision to have his enemy hanged. Thereupon he orders a gallows to be erected, fifty cubits high. Although he must first seek the king's permission for the execution, he is quite certain it will be granted. Still riding his crest of glory and honor, Haman has now sealed Mordecai's fate. Now, when the king, being disturbed, cannot sleep, he decides to listen to some readings until he is tranquil. He calls a servant to read to him from the book of daily chronicles, the official records in which there is recounted the episode of how Mordecai foiled the plan of the guards who had plotted to assassinate the king. His curiosity suddenly aroused, Ahasuerus inquires what has been done to express royal gratitude to Mordecai. What honor and what dignity have been accorded to this man in acknowledgment of so deep a debt to the savior of the king?

Meanwhile, Haman, with the idea fixed in his mind that Mordecai

309

must be removed, hastens in the middle of the night to the king to secure permission for executing Mordecai, certain that authority will be granted. Coincidentally, Haman arrives and awaits the pleasure of the king in the outer chamber. When the monarch learns that Haman has been waiting for some time, he summons him into his presence and without preliminaries poses to Haman the question he has been pondering in regard to the form his gratitude to Mordecai should take.

"What shall be done to the man whom the king desires to honor?" asks the king.

Haman instantly comprehends that the person the king has in mind is himself, and he already relishes the rewards to be bestowed upon him. He therefore responds that the man should be attired in regal apparel, seated on a royal horse, and escorted by one of the king's noble princes through the thoroughfares of Shushan, proclaiming he is the man whom the king delights to honor. The king listens attentively and thoughtfully to Haman's suggestion. Great is the consternation and bewilderment of Haman when he hears the king order him to do exactly as suggested not in honor of himself, Haman, high official of the realm, but for his bitter enemy Mordecai the Jew. The king seems to emphasize the "Jew!" Humiliated and crestfallen, Haman returns to his home. The contrast of the vizier's exhilaration of the previous day with the deep gloom caused by the unexpected event of the tables being turned against him is overwhelming. Haman carries out the order of the king.

The climax of the book is reached as Haman's advisers and his wife soberly express the truth of the matter.

If Mordecai, before whom you have begun to fall, is of the seed of the Jews, you will not prevail against him, but will surely fall before him. (Chapter VI; 13.)

They realize that there is a force operating which is not in favor of Haman. Haman's career is in swift decline. As Haman listens to the prophecy of his own doom, he is summoned by invitation to the second banquet proffered by Queen Esther. Once more the king inquires of his queen what thoughts depress her. Without hesitation this time, Esther respectfully pleads for her own life as a Jewess and for the lives of her people who have been destined to be destroyed by the terms of the edict fostered by their enemy Haman. The king demands to know who this culprit is who dares such a measure as slaughter of a people.

Who is he and where is he who dares presume in his heart to
do so? (Chapter VII, Verse 5.)

Esther rises from her banquet chair and fearlessly points her finger
directly at the vizier of Persia, while she denounces him as "an adversary and an enemy, this wicked Haman."

Horrified by the dramatic turn of events, Haman cringes in fear. The
king, who is also shaken, abruptly leaves the banqueting hall, convulsed
with rage. Haman remains seated in the presence of the queen, knowing full well he is facing complete defeat. He pleads for his life, for some
understanding of his situation, nurtured by unbridled ambition and lust
for glory and power, but Esther seems not to hear him. Now the king,
who has regained his composure, returns, but is silent. With a simple
gesture from the monarch, the condemned Haman is summarily removed from the royal presence. When the king is informed by a palace
guard that Haman had indeed erected a gallows for the execution of
Mordecai, he promptly orders that Haman be hanged from the very
same gallows prepared for Mordecai, and thus the villain falls into his
own trap.

Justice truly triumphs as the king designates that the properties and
possessions of wealthy Haman be placed at the disposal of Queen Esther. Haman is replaced by Mordecai as premier. It is remembered that
the evil decree to destroy the Jews issued by Haman and sealed by the
king's signet ring has become an irrevocable law. Esther therefore presents the problem to the king, who instructs her to write letters of instruction to the Jews that they defend themselves by striking back when
the fatal thirteenth day of Adar, appointed by the decree, arrives. So it
is done. Riders are sent again, the third time in the narrative, to apprise
the people of the land of the new ruling.

The balance of the account is commentary. Mordecai is attired in
royal garments, the sight of him in his elegance eliciting great joy and
happiness among the people.

And Mordecai went out from the presence of the king in
royal robes of blue and white, with a great golden crown and
a mantle of fine linen and purple. The city of Shushan
shouted and rejoiced. The Jews had light, gladness, joy and
honor. In every province and in every city where the king's
commandment and his decree came, there was gladness and

joy among the Jews, a day of feasting and a holiday. (Chapter
VIII, Verses 15, 16.)

When the thirteenth day of Adar arrives, the Jews retaliate, comply-
ing with the king's decree. An additional day of rejoicing is established
for the capital city of Shushan and the two become permanent days of
feasting, merrymaking and sending of gifts to each another.

The greatness of Ahasuerus and of Mordecai are restated. Mordecai
especially is praised. He is promoted to the position of premier and is
commended for "seeking the welfare of his people and speaking peace
for all his people."

DANIEL

The book of daniel ("god is my judge"), ninth of the
Sacred Writings—written partly in Hebrew and partly in Aramaic—falls
into two distinct parts: Chapters I to VI record the personal experiences
of Daniel and of his three friends during a fifty-year period from the
days of Babylonian King Nebuchadnezzar, who in 586 B.C.E. destroyed
Judah and carried the Jewish people into captivity in Babylonia, until
the reign of Persian King Cyrus, conqueror of Babylon (541 B.C.E.).
Cyrus permitted the Jews to return to their ancient homeland in 538
B.C.E., to rebuild the Holy Temple and to repopulate the city of Jerusalem. The second part of the Book of Daniel, Chapters VII to XII,
relates four visions which have symbolic significance.

The Septuagint or Greek translation places this book among the
Prophets. Jewish tradition has included it in the Sacred Writings, together with the Books of Ezra and Nehemiah, which follow immediately. Historically, perhaps, the book should have been assigned to a
place following the Books of Kings. Traditional sources ascribe the editing to the Men of the Great Assembly (Keneset Hagedolah) or the so-
called Men of the Great Synagogue, the group of religious leaders
organized by Ezra which continued into the common era as the San-
hedrin, a body of seventy-one notables and sages, with the high priest,
as a rule, the presiding officer. Dates of writing of the Book of Daniel
range from the sixth to the middle of the second century B.C.E., the
latter period coinciding with the time of the Maccabean revolt, the
event celebrated by Hanukkah, the Feast of Lights. Some believe that

313

the visions in Daniel are veiled allusions to the experiences of the Jewish people during the reign of the Syrian king Antiochus Epiphanes (175—164 B.C.E.).

What were the circumstances which gave birth to the memorable and historically significant holiday of Hanukkah? During the Hellenization of Palestine, while Rome throttled Macedonia, Egypt renewed its claims upon Palestine. The high priest Jason was replaced by Menelaus, brother of Simon, Temple treasurer. Menelaus offered a higher tribute to King Antiochus, and when he returned from an Egyptian expedition, Menelaus in 169 B.C.E. conducted him into the Holy of Holies and permitted the complete spoliation of the Holy Temple. When King Antiochus suffered disappointment in Egypt he allowed a vengeful advance upon Jerusalem on a Sabbath when the unresisting inhabitants suffered the soldiers to burn the city and take women and children into captivity. The walls of the city were razed and the gates burned. This depredation was followed by a royal edict horrifying to the Jewish people.

The edict was ostensibly designed to unite all peoples; it suspended the practice of the Jewish religion upon pain of death, and ordered general acceptance of the Greek religion. Thereupon the Temple of Jerusalem became the sanctuary of Olympian Zeus. On the fifteenth day of Kislev (168 B.C.E.) a great statue of the god was set upon the altar in the Temple and on the twenty-fifth day of the month heathen sacrifices were offered, followed by riotous revels. Persecution of the Jews was rampant.

The author of the Book Daniel, according to this view, interpreted these events as the final onslaught on God's people and the Holy City where four world empires held sway since Nebuchadnezzar's conquest of Judah: Babylonian, Median, Persian and Greek. Against the heathen powers the Angel Michael warred to deliver the Jewish people.

The deliverer came in the person of Judah the Maccabee (The Hammer) one of the five sons of the priest Mattathias, the Hasmonean of Modin, near Jerusalem. Judah organized a rebellion, and his forces routed the Syrians marching on Jerusalem. The Jewish uprising was in a measure part of a general revolt of the East against the West. Judah and his men occupied the Temple hill, found the sanctuary desolate, the altar profaned, the gates burned, the chambers of the priests destroyed. They took down the heathen altar and built a new altar. New holy vessels were fashioned, and on the twenty-fifth day of Kislev, exactly three years after its desecration, the Holy Temple of Jerusalem was solemnly rededicated. The lamps of the golden candlesticks were lighted and for eight days the Feast of Dedication (Hanukkah) was observed.

The visions of the Book of Daniel speak of God's sovereignty over the world; they are vivid portrayals of God's salvation of the faithful and those who recognize God's power. The Book of Daniel (last to be included in the collective writings of the Bible) is one of tremendous courage and hope at a time of the Jewish struggle for survival. It is a stirring document of faith which records the lives of those loyal Jews who under threat of death refused to profane the laws of the Torah, endeavoring to practice the religion of Judaism with stamina, fearlessness, fortitude, and divinely inspired courage.

The first six chapters tell of the personal experiences of Daniel and his companions in relation to various kings. Each narrative is related through the medium of symbol and allegory. The opening chapter of the book reveals Daniel and his friends in the court of King Nebuchadnezzar, who brought the Jews into their captivity in Babylonia in 586 B.C.E. The monarch instructs his chief officer Ashpenaz to select a choice number of young Israelites of royal and noble families to be trained for entry into the service of the court. Those chosen are Daniel, Hananiah, Mishael and Azariah, who are given the Babylonian names of (Daniel) Belteshazzar; (Hananiah) Shadrach, (Mishael) Meshach, and (Azariah) Abed-nego. These young men are to be instructed in the Babylonian language and culture for three years before entering the service of the king.

The friends are to receive wine and food from the royal tables as a mark of high favor. Daniel and his friends, however, determine that they would not wish to violate Jewish dietary laws by partaking of the king's food. Daniel therefore approaches the king's steward and finds favor in his eyes so that the official is willing to comply with Daniel's request that he and his companions partake of their customary food. The steward expresses concern lest the youths be underfed and thus show a marked physical difference when they are brought before the king. They may appear undernourished and fatigued compared to the others in training who have partaken of the prescribed court food. Daniel persuades the officer to let the Hebrew youths try their own diet for ten days. Daniel and his group sustain themselves on vegetables. When the period is over, they appear even more healthy and heavier than the other young men who ate the king's food.

God has imbued the four young Israelites with wisdom and understanding, with the skill to interpret dreams and visions even beyond the scope of all the wise men and magicians in the kingdom of Babylonia. Impressed with their brilliance, keen understanding and erudition, they become palace favorites, and the king advances them to high positions in his realm.

In Chapter II, Daniel is given his first opportunity to interpret dreams. Nebuchadnezzar has experienced a frightful dream that troubles him so much he cannot sleep. He summons his wise men and magicians, who inquire what his dream portrayed. The king tells them he will not reveal the content of the dream to them but they must, under penalty of death, not only interpret it but present the content of the dream. After consultation, they implore the king to describe at least the dream itself, otherwise only the gods can comply with the unreasonable request. Nebuchadnezzar is infuriated and insists they are trying to maneuver for their own protection. The wise men assure the king that his demand based on his premise of withholding facts is impossible to fulfill:

There is not a man on earth who can declare the king's matter. No great and powrful king has ever asked such a thing of any magician or enchanter. (Chapter II, Verse 10.)

Nebuchadnezzar summarily orders all the wise men to be executed. The horrified wise men seek out Daniel for his advice since the decree affects him and his companions, who are likewise numbered as wise men. Daniel asks Arioch, the captain of the king's guard, why the decree is so harsh, and learns from him about the dream of the king. Daniel goes to his king and begs for time to interpret the royal dream. Then Daniel returns home and asks his companions to join him in praying to God to reveal the secret of the dream so that they may not all die. His prayer is answered in a vision of the night and Daniel offers a beautiful prayer of thanks:

Blessed be the name of God
Forever and ever.
For wisdom and might are His;
He changes times and seasons;
He removes kings and enthrones them;
He gives wisdom to the wise,
And knowledge to those who have understanding;
He reveals the deep and secret things;
He knows what is in the darkness,
And the light dwells with Him.
I thank You and praise You,
O God of my fathers,
Who has given me wisdom and strength,
And has now made known to me what we asked of You,

DANIEL

For You have made known to us the king's matter.
(Chapter II, Verses 20-23.)

Daniel asks Arioch, the king's captain, to take him immediately to the king. Presented to the monarch, Daniel tells him that he is ready to describe the dream and to interpret it. Like Joseph of Egypt, Daniel says there is a God in heaven who interprets dreams and who has revealed what it portends.

The vision, explains Daniel, is a mighty image of unsurpassed brightness, frightening in its appearance. The head is of fine gold, the breast and arms of silver, the body and thighs of brass, the legs of iron, the feet part iron and part clay. You saw, Daniel continues to explain, that a stone was cut out by unseen hands which struck and destroyed the image, breaking it into hundreds of fragments, the minute pieces being scattered everywhere. But the stone that demolished the image was transformed into a huge mountain which filled the earth.

"This is the dream, and we now will tell the king its interpretation," says Daniel with authority.

"You, O King," states Daniel, "to whom God has given power and strength, glory and dominion, are the head of fine gold. After you, another kingdom, inferior to yours, will arise, and then a third. The fourth kingdom will be as strong as iron. It will break and destroy all before it. Like the mixed substance of clay and iron of the legs and feet, that kingdom will be a divided one, but there will be some strength in it characterized by the iron. The rulers shall marry one another but they shall not adhere to each other even as clay and iron do not. During the reigns of these kings, the God of heaven shall set up a kingdom which shall never be destroyed; nor shall the kingdom be left to another people; but it shall break in pieces and destroy all these kingdoms, and it shall endure forever." (Chapter II, Verse 44.)

God will set up an indestructible messianic kingdom. This is indicated by the stone cut out of the mountain but not with the hands of men, and it crushed in pieces the iron, the brass, the clay, the silver, and the gold. This is the messianic kingdom; it will remain forever.

Nebuchadnezzar, deeply impressed by the majesty of the vision, acclaims God as the greatest ruler in the world:

Truly, your God is the God of gods and Lord of kings, and a revealer of secrets, for you have been able to reveal this secret. (Chapter II, Verse 47.)

317

The king gives Daniel many costly gifts and makes him ruler over the whole province of Babylon and chief prefect over all the wise men. Daniel requests that the king appoint his three friends, Shadrach, Meshach and Abed-nego, over the affairs of the province of Babylon.

In Chapter III there is shown how a powerful heathen ruler is brought to the recognition and acknowledgment of God as ruler of humanity. This chapter contains the long, familiar narrative of the fiery furnace and how faith in and loyalty to God provided salvation and protection. It is related that Nebuchadnezzar orders a colossal golden image to be fashioned about ninety feet high and nine feet wide and placed in the plain of Dura. He commands all of his officials, governors, judges, treasurers to attend the dedication and demands that all must worship this graven image whenever the sound of the horn or other designated musical instrument is heard. The Babylonian officials worship the image, but Daniel and his companions do not comply, by arranging to avoid participation in the pagan ceremonies. The jealous wise men of the kingdom take the opportunity to bring Daniel into disgrace by accusing the Jewish rulers, of whom Daniel is one, of refusing to worship as the king has commanded all citizens. Nebuchadnezzar, who is angered when he learns of the recalcitrant Jewish officials, learns upon questioning them that the accusation brought is correct and he offers the men the opportunity to vindicate themselves. They firmly refuse, asserting their willingness to suffer even martyrdom rather than violate the religion of Judaism which recognizes only the one invisible God.

O King, we have no need to answer you in this matter. If our God whom we serve is able to deliver us, He will deliver us from the burning fiery furnace and from your hand. But if not, know, O King, that we will not serve your gods, nor worship the golden image you have set up. (Chapter III, Verse 16-18.)

Enraged by their audacity, Nebuchadnezzar orders the furnace to be heated seven times hotter than usual, and the three companions, Shadrach, Meshach, and Abed-nego, to be bound securely and cast into the furnace, which is so fiercely hot that the men who cast in the friends are themselves ignited and burned to death. The king, who stands nearby witnessing the scene, suddenly is astonished and greatly alarmed. He cannot believe what he sees.

Did we not cast three bound men into the midst of the fire?
(Chapter III, Verse 24.)

When the courtiers answer in the affirmative, the king looks again and reports:

I see four men, unbound, walking in the midst of the fire;
they are not hurt. And the fourth looks like a son of the gods.
(Chapter III, Verse 25.)

The king calls to the three men to leave the furnace. "Shadrach, Meshach and Abed-nego, servants of the Most High, come out and come here."

The three men emerge, unsinged, unhurt. The king, who clearly recognizes that here is the very hand of God, bursts into a triumphant song:

Blessed be the God of Shadrach, Meshach and Abed-nego, who has sent His angel, and delivered His trusting servants, who have changed the king's command, and have offered their bodies rather than serve and worship any god except their own God. Therefore, I issue a decree that any people, nation, or group that speaks against the God of Shadrach, Meshach and Abed-nego, shall be punished and their houses reduced to rubble; for there is no other God who is able to save in this way. (Chapter III, Verses 28, 29.)

The king then promotes the men to higher positions in the province of Babylonia.

Chapter IV, a personal testimony by Nebuchadnezzar, emphasizes the theme of God's supremacy. The king speaks throughout in the first person, telling of his dream in which men are subject to the will of God. In the dream, he is greatly frightened when he sees a gigantic tree in the midst of the earth which grows until it reaches tremendous proportions even into the heavens. A beautiful tree, it is visible at a great distance. Laden with fruit, the leaves are full, and animals lie in its shade. Birds find a haven of refuge in its rich foliage and heavy branches. Suddenly, narrates the king, he sees an angel descend from heaven and order the tree to be cut, its leaves shaken, its fruits scattered. The animals and birds are chased away until nothing is left of the huge tree except its stump.

When the king summons his wise men, they cannot interpret his dream. Daniel gives the explanation without fear, although he knows how threatening is its signficance. The king is the tree, strong and powerful, but he will be cut down and driven among men. He will lose his mind, and for seven years live like an animal until he recognizes that God rules all life; then he will be restored. Daniel urges his monarch to do good, to be kind and merciful to the poor. Events occurred according to Daniel's interpretation. Twelve months after the dream, as Nebuchadnezzar walks about the royal grounds, enjoying the expanse of his realm, boasting of his greatness, the dream is fulfilled. The king loses his reason and wanders about, living like an animal. When the period of seven years is over, the king at last recognizes God's greatness and is restored to his original position of glory.

Chapter V is concerned with a later period in the reign of Belshazzar, son of Nebuchadnezzar. This is the traditional view, for historically no son by the name of Belshazzar sat on the throne of Babylon. Belshazzar, son of Nabonidus, last king of Babylon, here supposed to be son of Nebuchadnezzar, is depicted as hosting a magnificent feast for a thousand of his lords. Upon tasting the excellent wine, Belshazzar deems it worthy of special service. He therefore commands that there be brought out the golden and silver sacred vessels which his father Nebuchadnezzar had taken from the Holy Temple in Jerusalem. The guests drink the wine from them and praise the gods of gold, of silver, of brass, of iron, of wood, and of stone. In the same hour, there appears a man's handwriting upon the plaster of the wall of the king's palace at the very height of the enjoyment and hilarity of the feast. The king sees the palm of the writing hand. Four words are inscribed: "Mene, Mene, Tekel, Upsharsin." The fearful king summons the enchanters, astrologers, and the magicians to interpret for him the handwriting on the wall, but they are unable to do so. Learning what has happened, the queen enters the banquet house and suggests that there is a man in the kingdom in whom there is the spirit of surpassing wisdom, Daniel, whom the king's father, Nebuchadnezzar, made master of his magicians and astrologers. She suggests that the man be called to interpret the writing on the wall.

When Daniel is brought into the royal presence, the king offers him great wealth and many gifts if he is able to read and explain the mysterious writing. Daniel bids them keep the gifts and offers to explain the significance of the words without reward. Daniel speaks of the glory of

DANIEL

the reign of Nebuchadnezzar, the king's father, who suffered a period of madness and exclusion from other people until he had come to recognize that God rules the kingdom of people. Nebuchadnezzar understood the power of God, says Daniel, who is aware of this royal history, but his son Belshazzar does not. On the contrary, Belshazzar has defiled and affronted God by using the holy vessels plundered from the Temple in Jerusalem and by praising other gods of metal, wood, and stone and not God to whom he owes his very being. Therefore, explains Daniel, the writing inscribed on the king's palace wall forecast the future:

"Mene, Mene, Tekel, Upharsin" is translated: You are weighed in the balance and found wanting.

This is the interpretation:
Mene (counting), God has numbered your kingdom and brought it to an end.
Tekel (weighed), you are weighed in the balances and found wanting.
Peres (divided), your kingdom is divided and given over to the Medes and Persians. (Chapter V, Verses 26, 27.)

The king clothes Daniel in royal purple, a chain of gold is placed around his neck, and a proclamation made that he is to rule as one of the three in the kingdom. The prophecy of doom comes true when the Babylonian king is assassinated that very night.

In Chapter VI, when Darius of Media becomes king, he places a hundred and twenty satraps to govern throughout the kingdom and over them are three rulers. Of these, Daniel distinguishes himself because of the spirit of God within him. He causes a great deal of envy among the king's officials, who seek his removal from power by disgracing him in the eyes of the king. They decide to attack Daniel's integrity through his faith in God:

We shall not find any ground for complaint against this Daniel unless we find it in connection with the law of his God. (Chapter VI, Verse 6.)

They recommend that the king issue a law to the effect that for thirty days the people of the kingdom worship the monarch of the realm. Whoever fails to do so shall be cast into the den of lions to be devoured.

The king, unaware of the true intent of the plotters, agrees. The plotters begin their careful observation of Daniel when the new law becomes effective. He goes home to pray, as is his daily custom. The plotters follow him and find him praying to God. They quickly bring him to the king. They insist that the king comply with his irrevocable law, and the king now realizes that the intent of the plotters is to destroy his brilliant official. In spite of his own compassion for his favored ruler, he has no alternative under the law but to consign him to the lion's den.

Your God whom you serve continually, He will deliver you. (Chapter VI, Verse 17.)

A stone is placed at the mouth of the cave and the king's signet ring is impressed on it. The distressed and disconcerted king returns to his palace and spends a restless night fasting in behalf of his servant Daniel. Early in the morning, he hastens to the den and calls out:

O Daniel, servant of the living God, is your God, whom you serve continually, able to deliver you from the lions?

And Daniel replies from within the cave:

O King, live for ever! My God has sent His angel, and has shut the lions' mouths. They have not hurt me. For I was found to be innocent before Him and also before you, O King, I have done no wrong.

The king orders Daniel released.

. . .And no manner of hurt was found upon him because he had trusted in his God.

Thereupon King Darius issues a proclamation, calling on all of his subjects, the people and nations of the earth, that they revere the God of Daniel:

For He is the living God,
And steadfast forever.
His kingdom that which will not be destroyed,
His dominion will endure even to the end;
He delivers and rescues,
And He performs signs and wonders
In heaven and on earth;
Who has delivered Daniel from the power of the lions.
(Chapter VI, Verses 27-29.)

So Daniel prospered in the reign of Darius and in the reign of Cyrus the Persian.

The second section of the Book of Daniel contains a series of four visions related in the first person by Daniel. The visions are incredibly fantastic, employing symbolism of beasts and monsters to foretell the future, the rise and fall of kings and kingdoms until the messianic era, the messianic kingdom which will last to the end of time. Daniel views the righteous remnant of Israel struggling through the epochs and emerging the victor and successor to all temporal power.

Chapter VII presents the first vision. Four animals emerge from the sea, comparable to an eagle-winged lion, a bear, a leopard, and a beast with ten horns and a little horn. The beast is put to death and the kingdom is offered to one "like the son of man" who comes from the clouds of heaven. Daniel reveals the significance of the vision: the four animals represent the four empires, Babylonia, Media, Persia, and Greece; the ten horns symbolize the Seleucids, and the little horn is Antiochus IV known also as Antiochus Epiphanes (175 to 164 B.CE.) who persecuted the Jews for three years or "a year, two years and a half year." The rule of the universe shall thereupon pass to "the people of the saints of the Most High" or the righteous remnant of Israel.

Chapter VIII shows the vision of the two-horned ram which attacks westward and southward, with no rivals until a unicorned goat smites him. The horn of the goat is broken and gives place to four horns, out of one of which arises "a little horn." It grows exceedingly powerful and prevents the celebration of the sacrificial worship for two thousand, three hundred evenings and mornings (1,150 days, or about three and one half years). The archangel Gabriel interprets the dream to Daniel: The two-horned ram represents the empire of the Medes and of the Persians. The goat symbolizes the empire of Alexander the Great, and the five horns his successors.

Chapter IX indicates that Daniel meditates on the predictions of the Prophet Jeremiah (Chapter XXV, Verse 11; Chapter XXIX, Verse 10) and receives from the archangel Gabriel an exegesis in poetic form of the Jeremiah prophecy. The number "seventy" refers not to years but to "weeks of years," thus meaning 490 years. During the first half of the last week (171 to 168 B.C.E.) the enemy will cause the worship of the Lord to cease and the "abomination and desolation" will stand in the very sanctuary until, at the end of history, it is overthrown. This appears to be the reference to the colossal image of Olympian Zeus placed in the Holy Temple of Jerusalem in the desecration by Antiochus Epiphanes in 168 B.C.E.

The final vision indicates that the last Persian king is vanquished by a powerful ruler of Greece (Alexander) whose empire is divided into four kingdoms. The southern kingdom of the Egyptian Ptolomies is engaged in a bitter struggle with the northern kingdom, Seleucids, Syria, until King Antiochus Epiphanes of the north causes the sacrificial offerings to cease and then is slain in the war with the southern king. The archangel Michael will appear, those whose names are written in the book will be saved, the dead will arise from their graves, and the reign of righteousness will be ushered in.

Those who are wise will shine as the brightness
   of the firmament;
And those who turn the many to righteousness,
   as the stars forever and ever.
                                        (Chapter XII, Verse 3.)

The fantastic visions presented and interpreted, Daniel gazes out upon the land and the people. He prays to God for the restoration of the Holy Temple. He brings to mind the words of Jeremiah, prophet of the destruction in 586 B.C.E. who saw Judah destroyed and Jerusalem reduced to rubble. He recalls the tears of the weeping prophet and that Jeremiah declared that the exile would endure for seventy years. The Archangel Gabriel is sent to reassure Daniel of the future restoration of the Temple. Daniel's other visions assure him that in the messianic era the righteous will triumph. Blessings and blessedness will replace evil, and God will reign supreme.

EZRA

THE BOOK OF EZRA, TENTH OF THE KETUVIM, CONTINUES THE narrative with which the Book of Daniel ends in the reign of King Cyrus of Persia (546 to 530 B.C.E.). It is followed by the Book of Nehemiah, originally joined with the Book of Ezra. The oldest Hebrew codices treat Ezra-Nehemiah as a single book calling the combination of the two books by the name of Ezra. In the Septuagint or Greek translation the books are still united.

Ezra, a priest of the Persian period, lived in Babylonia, and tradition ascribes to him the writing of the books of Ezra, Nehemiah, and Chronicles (down to his own name and completed by Nehemiah). Some scholars believe the books were written later by someone known simply as the Chronicler. Ezra is one of the dynamic personalities of Jewish history whose impact on the course of Judaism is enduring. He stands mighty among the greatest figures of Judaism.

In response to Ezra's personal petition to the king, he is granted royal permission to go to Palestine to re-establish the laws of God. His commission involves the propagation of the law and the organization of the courts to enforce it. Ezra's stern, drastic measures bring about the resuscitation of Judaism from the low ebb of its assimiliation with foreign peoples and their religions. Fervently he summons the Jewish people to renew their covenant with God, inspires them to reaccept the Torah and to vow to keep the laws and the statutes of the founders of Judaism.

When he wins the respect and cooperation of the Jewish nobles, the leaders of the Temple and the important people who support him in his reforms, Ezra authorizes the "Men of the Great Assembly" or Great Synagogue, which as a body establishes many of the Jewish institutions which, by force of continuity, are still in existence today. He inaugurates a number of traditions which are adopted for all time. His universally accepted enactments become the very warp and woof of Judaism.

Ezra, called "scribe of the words of the commandments of the Lord and of the Lord's statutes to Israel" (Chapter VII, Verse 11), is regarded as first of the group of soferim (plural for the Hebrew word sofayr, scribe) who followed the prophets as sages and leaders of Israel. It is Ezra who makes the Torah the constitution of the Jewish commonwealth which is established upon the return of the exiles from Babylonia.

The Book of Ezra, a valid, historical source, is written in both Hebrew and Aramaic. The Jews spoke Aramaic, which at this time was more extensively used as a vernacular than Hebrew. Ezra incorporates specific dates and records into his book.

Ezra's vigorous narrative relates to the Jewish people during two periods of their history. The first (Chapters I to VII) in which he is not present deals with the return of the Jewish people from the Babylonian exile to Jerusalem in 538 B.C.E to the rebuilding of the Second Temple in 520 to 516 B.C.E., during which time the prophets Haggai and Zechariah are active in their ministries. The records of the second period (Chapters VII to X) tell of the significant two years, 458 to 457 B.C.E., from personal experiences and are substantially autobiographical. They offer Ezra's own reaction to current events.

The historical portion opens with the proclamation of the Persian king Cyrus, who has recently conquered Babylon, whose state policy is to offer as much autonomy as possible to conquered peoples in his empire. A year after ascending the throne in 546 B.C.E. Cyrus announces the granting of permission to the exiled Jews to return to their home land. He orders his treasurer to return to the Jews the five thousand silver and gold Temple vessels which Nebuchadnezzar, King of Babylon, had taken as plunder from Jerusalem at the time of its destruction and had placed in the house of his own gods. To those Jews not desiring to go to Palestine, Cyrus issues a call that they plan to assist the pioneering Jews with material goods and to contribute to the undertaking.

A proclamation throughout the realm is recorded in exact, official protocol and in simple Hebrew:

Thus declares Cyrus, king of Persia: All the kingdoms of the earth has the Lord, God of heaven, given me. He has charged me to build Him a house in Jerusalem, which is in Judah. Whoever is among you of His people—may God be with him—let him go up to Jerusalem, which is in Judah, and build the house of the Lord, the God of Israel—He is the God who is in Jerusalem. And whoever is left, in any place he lives, let the men of his place help him with silver and gold, with goods and beasts, besides the free-will offering for the house of God in Jerusalem. (Chapter I, Verses 2-4.)

Response to the edict is made by 42,360 people, not counting 7,337 slaves. The homecomers return to the Holy Land under the leadership of Zerubbabel, the son of Shealtiel, and nephew of Sheshbazzar, son of King Jehoiachin of Judah who was the captive of the Babylonians. Zerubbabel is appointed governor of the new community. Plans for the rebuilding of the Holy Temple commence and a spirit of gladness pervades the city.

The ceremony of laying the foundations of the Temple structure is accompanied with triumphal expressions of praise and gratitude:

They sang one to another, praising and giving thanks to the Lord: for He is good; for His mercy endures forever toward Israel. (Chapter III, Verse 11.)

The happiness of the people was not complete, for there were mixed feelings among them. The older people, who had known the grandeur and splendor of the First Temple, were crestfallen when they saw the much smaller foundations being laid for the Second Temple. In their hearts they wept, for they could not erase the memory of the beauty of the First Temple from their minds and the difference in architectural magnificence depressed them. The young people, on the other hand, whose vision was not hindered by recollection of the glory of the First Temple, were deeply impressed by the potentially beautiful edifice rising before them.

But many of the priests, Levites and heads of fathers' houses, the old men who had seen the first house, wept loudly when they saw this house standing before their eyes; and many shouted aloud for joy; so that the people could not distinguish between the sound of the joyful shout from the sound of the people's weeping. (Chapter III, Verses 12, 13.)

The wonder of return to the homeland is dimmed by external sources as the building of the Temple incurs strained relationships. Difficulties arise almost immediately and the usual obstacles of enterprise which are destined to last for a number of years. In the neighboring country of Samaria, people known as Samaritans had settled from other places and had been brought from Babylonia and elsewhere by the King of Assyria. (II Kings, Chapter XVII, Verse 24 and following). They had adopted the worship of the one God and wished to participate in the Temple being constructed for God's worship. They therefore approached Zerubbabel and the other leaders with the offer to join the Jews in the building of the Temple:

Let us build with you; for we seek your God, as you do. And we have offered to Him since the days of Esarhaddon, King of Assyria, who brought us here. (Chapter IV, Verse 2.)

Zerubbabel and the other leaders decline the offer of assistance by the Samaritans because they desire to preserve and to maintain their distinctive religion in its purity and are themselves charged with the duty of the Temple's rebuilding.

You have nothing to do with us in building a house to our God. But we ourselves together will build to the Lord, the God of Israel, as King Cyrus, the king of Persia, has commanded us. (Verse 3.)

Thus scorned, the Samaritans retaliate by devising a baffling series of hindrances by which they seek in every way to undermine the efforts of the Temple rebuilders and to frustrate their plans. They go to the extreme of writing a communique to King Artaxerxes accusing the Jews of building a potentially rebellious and evil city, adding obliquely that if he searches the official record, he will find this allegation to be true. They are bold enough to maintain that if the reconstruction of the Temple be allowed, the Jews will refuse to pay expected tribute and thus preclude any revenue the king might normally anticipate. The threat to the exchequer arouses the interest of the king who replies to the leaders of the Samaritans acknowledging the letter of complaint. In effect, the response of the king is his command to halt the rebuilding. Everything is at a standstill. The Samaritans have succeeded—at least temporariliy.

Some years later the prophets Haggai and Zechariah begin to reinspire the people with the urgent necessity of continuing to rebuild the Temple. The Jews respond enthusiastically and resume the sacred, holy effort, not without intervention, however, for Tattenai, the nearby governor, demands to know by whose authority they are now rebuilding: "Who gave you the decree to build this house and to finish this structure?" (Chapter V, Verse 3.)

The Jewish leaders reply that King Cyrus had granted permission. They prevailed upon him to allow the work to proceed while he writes for verification to the present King Darius. The long epistle to the Persian court is duly recorded. It concludes with a request for direction in the matter. Darius responds tht he has had the official records searched and has found it to be true, that Cyrus, his predecessor, had, indeed, authorized and encouraged the return of the Jewish people to Jerusalem. The letter from Darius continues that he has ordered Tattenai to permit and furthermore to assist in the Temple rebuilding, forbidding any kind of interference. He further instructs that financial aid be given from the king's coffers if needed. With this encouragement, the rebuilding proceeds with renewed vigor. Before long, the Holy Temple is rebuilt and ready for the services of the ritual. A grandiose dedication ceremony, replete with appropriate expressions of joy and accompaniment of feasting, officially brings the Second Temple into being. The year is 516 B.C.E.

The construction of the Second Temple inaugurates a lengthy period of Jewish history which becomes known as the Second Jewish Commonwealth.

The first part of the Book of Ezra is concluded.

Ezra himself appears in the second part of the book, introduced by a detailed geneaology, tracing his lineage back to Aaron, the High Priest, brother of Moses and Miriam. Ezra is presented as a "ready scribe in the law of Moses."

It is of interest to note that a period of sixty years, from the time of the completion of the Second Temple until Ezra's arrival on the scene, is omitted and knowledge of what transpired during these six decades remains obscure. The book then records that King Artaxerxes of Persia granted Ezra the priest official permission to proceed to Jerusalem, set up a court system of judges and magistrates and to teach the people about their God and religion.

For Ezra had set his heart to seek the law of the Lord and do it, and to teach Israel statutes and ordinances. (Chapter VII, Verse 10.)

Ezra acknowledges the authorization in a lengthy document. The king not only allows Ezra and his followers to go but promises assistance from the king's tributaries. He forbids any harm to the group during their travels to the Holy Land. The document thus imparts to Ezra much authority in Jerusalem. Ezra expresses his profound gratitude to the monarch:

Blessed be the Lord, the God of our fathers, who has put such a thing as this into the king's heart, to beautify the house of the Lord in Jerusalem; and who has extended mercy to me before the king and his counselors, and before the king's great princes. I was strengthened, for the hand of the Lord my God was upon me, and I gathered together leading men of Israel to go up with me. (Chapter VII, Verses 27, 28.)

After Ezra's personal prayer, the book details the names of the leaders who join him on the journey. En route, Ezra assembles his party at the river Ahavah and finds that there are no Levites in the group, who are essential because they are the ministers in the Temple. The Levites are summoned and become part of the massive caravan to Jerusalem. Ezra is greatly concerned about the burdens of travel on the road, and the threat of an ambush by marauders. He hesitates, however, to ask for further help from the already gracious king. After he proclaims a fast and prays fervently for God's protection, his confidence is restored. The travelers proceed to Jerusalem happily without incident.

Upon Ezra's arrival, he is shocked and grieved when he learns of the prevalence of mixed marriage, especially among the priestly and Levitical classes, which portends the deterioration of the Jewish people. It is unbelievable to him that even the leaders of the people, the exemplars, should have so strayed from the Torah by taking foreign wives and giving their sons to foreign daughters. His grief moves Ezra to express himself forcefully and he mourns and prays to God for guidance. Israel has sinned, and has made itself impure by intermarriage and the adoption of foreign ways. What is to be done? The answer is in stern reformation. One of the leaders approaches Ezra and inspires him to take firm and fearless action. There is no alternative for the salvation of Judaism:

Arise, for the matter belongs to you, and we are with you. Be of good courage and do it. (Chapter X, Verse 4.)

Encouraged, Ezra summons an assembly of all the people. Three days are allowed for them to gather. It is a national meeting. When all are present, Ezra rises and courageously, and determinedly, fully aware of his drastic measures, calls upon the people to surrender their foreign wives and to confess their wrongdoing. Stirred by his impassioned pleading and power of persuasion, the people respond affirmatively.

Then all the congregation answered and said with a loud voice "As you have said, so it is for us to do." (Chapter X, Verse 2.)

A court of princes, a commission, is set up to proceed in orderly fashion in the reformation of Ezra.

The last section of the Book of Ezra enumerates the one hundred and thirteen men who have taken foreign wives and who are affected by the decision agreed upon by the people. The book ends on this note of achievement. Further events in the life of Ezra are recorded in the Book of Nehemiah which follows.

NEHEMIAH

THE BOOK OF NEHEMIAH, ELEVENTH OF THE SACRED WRIT-
ings, contains genealogical listings and other valuable historical facts and
events. It covers the period of the middle of the fifth century, described
in Ezra, and was by Jewish tradition joined into one volume called Ezra.

The Jews had returned to Jerusalem in Judah in 538 B.C.E. under the
decree of Cyrus the Great and had completed the building of the Second Holy Temple which was dedicated formally in 516 B.C.E. Six historically obscure decades pass before the time of Ezra who received
permission from the king of Persia, Artaxerxes I, in 458 B.C.E. to go to
Jerusalem and there initiate a legal system of judges and magistrates,
and to teach the people about God and their religion.

Ezra founded the institution known as the Men of the Great Assembly
who interpreted the Torah and inaugurated customs and traditions
which are still part of today's synagogue ritual. He was the first of the
Scribes (Soferim in Hebrew) who followed the prophets as sages and
teachers of Israel.

The thirteen chapters of Nehemiah may be divided into two almost
equal halves. The first seven are Nehemiah's personal reminiscences,
his request for permission to go to Jerusalem, his arrival, his efforts to
rebuild the city walls, and the successes in instituting reforms. The second part covers primarily the dramatic, almost traumatic experience of
Ezra's reading of the Torah of Moses to the people assembled in the
presence of their leaders and their acceptance and renewal of the covenant with God.

NEHEMIAH

Nehemiah ("the Lord has comforted") settles in Shushan (Susa), capital of Elam, the winter residence of the Persian kings. He becomes the royal cupbearer, one of the oldest and highest court positions in ancient Babylonia which remains an honor among the Persians, much desired by the Persian nobles and usually awarded to persons of distinguished lineage. He becomes governor (pechah) or commissioner by appointment of the Persian monarch. In this capacity, out of a deep love of God and his people, Nehemiah courageously sets about to rebuild the walls around Jerusalem, restoring their beauty and utility. His devotion to the cause of his people's reconstruction captivated their imagination.

The Book of Nehemiah tells the story of a brilliant, dedicated administrator, a masterful organizer, who projects goals for his people and then strives to achieve them. Through his own writings, his own words, we are given the opportunity to observe the life of a zealous man of God in action. We see his confrontation of military tactics, his conquest of social and economic difficulties and solution of religious problems.

The book opens as Nehemiah, as an official in the court of Artaxerxes, learns of the deplorable situation of his people in Jerusalem. Hanani and other Jews visit at Shushan and Nehemiah is informed of the misery of the Jewish people, scorned by their neighbors and defenseless because the walls of Jerusalem have been broken down and the gates burned. This causes him great sadness of spirit, evident on his countenance. The king, who observes his depression, inquires about the cause, and the cupbearer reveals his concern for the place of his ancestors' sepulchres, requesting permission to go to Jerusalem to assist his people. His petition is granted. The king appoints Nehemiah governor of Judah with the rights and privileges of that office. He is accompanied by captains of the army and given official documents of identification.

When he has been in Jerusalem three days, keeping his identity secret, he rises in the middle of the night as the city sleeps to acquaint himself personally with the needs of the community, inspecting the entire area. When the extent of the task is known, he declares his position to the people. Before Nehemiah's journey to Jerusalem he had obtained a letter from the king to Asaph, the keeper of the king's park (royal forests) to obtain timber for fashioning beams for the city gates and for the walls of the city. (Chapter II, Verse 8.) After his survey, the governor calls upon the people to begin rebuilding the walls. They respond without hesitation.

The process of reconstruction suffers the usual hindrances from both external and internal forces. Neighboring officials and rulers ridicule their efforts and conspire to stop the work. Nehemiah inspires the people with courage to continue.

Do not be not afraid of them. Remember the Lord, who is great and revered, and fight for your brethren, your sons, your daughters, your wives, and your homes. (Chapter IV, Verse 8.)

Nehemiah, a practical administrator, provides protection to the workers by designating half the people to work and the other half to stand guard. The workers have spears in one hand and tools in the other.

When our enemies heard that it was known to us, and that God had frustrated their counsel, we all returned to the wall, each to his work. From that day on, half of my servants worked on construction, and half held the spears, shields, bows, and coats of armor. And the leaders stood behind all the house of Judah. Those who built on the wall, and those who bore burdens, everyone with one in his hand and with the other held a weapon. And I said to the nobles and to the rulers and to the rest of the people: "The work is great and we are separated on the wall, one far from another; wherever you hear the sound of the horn, come to us, our God will fight for us. (Chapter IV, Verses 9—14.)

His most vigorous opponent is the Horonite Sanballat (Chapter II, Verse 10) governor of the province of Samaria just north of Judah and Tobiah, the Ammonite, governor of Ammon, region of Transjordan just east of Judah. His enemies try to lure Nehemiah into a trap, but he understands their intrigues. They threaten to accuse him in a written report to the king that he is plotting rebellion and that his true ambition is to declare himself king of Judah. Nehemiah refutes the accusation but his enemies persist and prevail upon some of the Jews to betray and entrap their leader. Nehemiah resists the attempts.

When the people complain that they are being taken advantage of because of their poverty, Nehemiah becomes highly incensed and summons the offenders, demanding that they desist from their unjust doings. He assembles the elders and firmly announces:

> What you are doing is not good. Should you not walk in the
> fear of our God because of the reproach of the heathen, our
> enemies?" (Chapter V, Verse 9)

Moved by Nehemiah's appeal, the wrongdoers agree to reform.
Nehemiah forges ahead and the walls around Jerusalem are completed
in fifty-two days, the people having worked "from the rising of the
morning until the stars appeared." (Chapter IV, Verse 15.) The walls are
rebuilt, strengthened and the gates set. The dedication ceremony includes the people walking in procession around the walls. Nehemiah's
leave is extended until the thirty-second year of Artaxerxes I, 433 B.C.E
(Chapter V, Verse 14.)

He returns to his duties in Shushan and then secures another leave to
proceed to Jerusalem as matters there require his firm hand. He has his
opponent Tobiah dispossessed from the rooms he is using in the Temple, works toward repopulating Jerusalem, restores the Sabbath observance, reinstitutes popular contributions for the support of the Temple
and organizes its administration, and takes steps to redeem those Jews
who have been sold into slavery to pagan masters.

Beginning with Chapter VIII, the book devotes itself to recounting
the achievements of Ezra, telling how the people gather around him and
ask that he teach them the laws of Moses. They want to acquaint themselves with the Torah from which neglect has estranged them. The
scriptures relate how Ezra dramatically reads the Torah in the presence
of groups of men, women, and children, how they stand and listen over-
awed by the power and majesty of the words of God. They rejoice as
they hear how the giving of the Torah to Moses on Sinai in the wilderness is vividly recalled. They express their feelings deeply:

> Ezra the Scribe stood on a wooden pulpit. . . . He opened
> the book in the presence of all the people. When he opened
> it, all the people stood up. Ezra blessed the Lord, the great
> God. And all the people answered, "Amen, Amen," lifting
> up their hands; and they bowed their heads, and worshiped
> the Lord . . . So they read in the book, in the Law of God,
> distinctly, and gave the sense, and caused the people to un-
> derstand the reading. Nehemiah, the governor, and Ezra,

the priest and scribe, and the Levites who taught the people, said, "This day is holy to the Lord your God; do not mourn nor weep." (Chapter VIII, Verses 4-7, 9.)

The book now presents a long, beautiful, penitential psalm which may be termed a mosaic of scriptural allusions, in regard to God's role in history, God's greatness and power, God's selection of the Jews as party to the sacred covenant, God's guidance through the paths of time, recounting Israel's deviation and return. The climax of the poem is reached in a solemn pledge to reform, to renew the covenant with God, and to vow loyalty to the Torah. The Torah now becomes the possession of each and every follower of Judaism. The Levites, the leaders, the priests, led by Nehemiah, sign the document containing a number of reforms which they promise to undertake. The reforms deal with the avoidance of intermarriage, observance of the Sabbath, responsibility to the Temple, holiday celebrations, and other rituals.

Because of all this we make a firm covenant and write it; and our princes, our Levites, and our priests set their seal to it. . . . The rest of the people, the priests, the Levites, the porters, the singers, the Temple servants, and all who have separated themselves from the people of the land to the law of God, their wives, their sons, their daughters, all who have knowledge and understanding, vowed to walk in God's law, which was given by Moses, the servant of God, and to observe and do all the commandments of the Lord our God, and the Lord's ordinances and statutes." (Chapter X, Verses 1, 29, 30.)

The covenant renewed, signed and sealed, the walls of Jerusalem are exuberantly, ceremoniously, and reverently dedicated. Amidst joy and thanksgiving, singing and music, the Jewish people restore the ancient glory of Israel, the Holy Temple, and the rebuilt walls of Jerusalem.

Ezra the Scribe, and Nehemiah the Administrator, have emerged as the greatest of inspired leaders in the crucial years of the history of Judaism.

I CHRONICLES

THE BOOK OF CHRONICLES, THE TWELFTH OF THE HOLY
Writings, divided into two books, concludes the scriptures. The general
meaning of Chronicles is "events of the times," called in Hebrew, Divray Hayamim, which translates literally as "words of the days."

I Chronicles is composed of twenty-nine chapters; II Chronicles has
thirty-six chapters. While tradition ascribes the writing of Chronicles to
Ezra the Scribe, some maintain that the lengthy volume, much of it
repetitious of the Books of I and II Kings, was the work of a writer
known simply as the Chronicler. Most authorities agree that it was compiled between the middle of the fourth and the middle of the third
century B.C.E. (350 to 250 B.C.E.)

Recording the days and times of the monarchies of the Jews and concluding with their destruction, Chronicles, while chronologically following the Books of Kings, was placed after the entire history because, in a
real sense, it condenses and compresses the sweep of Jewish life from
the creation of the world to the proclamation of the Persian King Cyrus,
who sanctioned the return of the Jews in the year 538 B.C.E. to their
homeland from Babylonian captivity. The chronicler covers the history
of the Jewish people, its growth, development, rise, glory, and decline.
The books end on a note of hope, the re-entry into the Holy City of
Jerusalem.

The volume is much deeper in both content and purpose than meets
the eye. The first nine chapters are devoted to genealogies from Adam
to King Saul, and of Levitical families. There follows a narrative of

events in Judah and Jerusalem from the reign of David to the end of his kingdom, and of Judah. While genealogies may be arid reading chapter after chapter, the painstaking recording of lineage of families has a significant purpose. The chronicler writes with feeling about the Temple, its varied services, the ministers who led the worship, and all its detailed rituals and observances. He writes with love and adoration. His historical coverage and perspective is religiously rooted and history is interwoven with religious faith and trust.

The chronicler teaches implicit devotion to God. It is God who truly rules over the whole world. It is God whose providence guides the destinies of people and nations. History is not a matter of chance or accident. There is divine purpose in it. Those who are righteous and follow the principles of God will be rewarded and blessed, whereas punishment will be meted out to the wicked. Success and failure derive from God. The whole encircling of the massive historical period of Jewish history and life stems from this religious premise. The chronicler has carefully sifted historical events to suit his purpose. He has emphasized and de-emphasized. He has excluded accounts in other books and added other events. There is no reference to the kingdom of Israel except as it affects the Southern Kingdom of Judah.

The narrative moves from epoch to epoch, from period to period, from age to age. Presented is a meticulous listing of ancestors. Then there is a pause, an historical incident, with a parallel elsewhere. Lineage is recorded from Adam to Noah, from Noah to Abraham, from Abraham through his sons, from Jacob through his sons, pausing to comment on some of the sons of Jacob who have descendants holding important positions. Enumerated are the ancestors of the Levites, who are selected to be the ministers of God in the Holy Temple. The fathers and patriarchs of the kings, the house of David are carefully recounted. The chronicler dwells on the house of Saul, first king, records his genealogy, rise, death and burial.

Recounted are many interesting details in the life of David, his coronation, successes, greatness, reverence of God, his desire to bring the Ark of the Covenant to Jerusalem, which became known as the City of David, and to build a Temple for God as the Lord's dwelling place. David's charge to Solomon, the enumeration of the duties and responsibilities of kingship, the classifications of the priests and Levites in the Holy Temple to be built, his devout, impressive prayer and thanksgiving to God for blessings to the people are recorded. I Chronicles closes with the death of King David when he is full of years and honors.

David, the son of Jesse reigned over all Israel. The time that he reigned over Israel was forty years: seven years he reigned in Hebron, and thirty years and three years he reigned in Jerusalem. He died in a good old age, full of days, riches and honor; and Solomon his son reigned in his stead. (Chapter XXIX, Verses 26-28.)

II CHRONICLES

II CHRONICLES OPENS WITH THE DECLARATION THAT GOD IS with King Solomon and tells how he sought God's blessing. Solomon's life, vision, request for wisdom, and God's beneficence is recounted in the first nine chapters as is the construction of the magnificent Holy Temple, Solomon's diplomatic relationships with foreign rulers and the visit of the fabulous Queen of Sheba.

Solomon the son of David was strengthened in his kingdom, and God was with him and magnified him extensively. Solomon spoke to all Israel, to the captains of thousands and of hundreds, and to the judges, and to every prince in all Israel, the heads of the fathers' houses. Together with the entire congregation, he went to the high place at Gibeon; for there was the tent of meeting of God, which Moses the servant of the Lord had made in the wilderness. . . . (Chapter I, Verses 1-3.)

Solomon presents offerings to the Lord. It was during that night that God appeared to Solomon and said: "Ask what I shall give you," and Solomon asks for wisdom and knowledge to judge God's people which God grants in addition to unsurpassable wealth and honors.

Solomon prays that whatever droughts, famines or pestilences are visited upon the people, if they will stretch forth their hands toward the house of God, He will hear and forgive and "render to every man according to all his ways, whose heart you know—for You, even You alone know the hearts of the children of men—that they may revere You, to walk in Your ways all the days they live in the land which You gave to our fathers." (Chapter VI, Verses 30, 31.)

When the Holy Temple was dedicated, King Solomon, together with all of Israel, held a feast for seven days and all Israel with him, a very great congregation. God revealed to Solomon that the magnificent Temple will be destroyed if God was forsaken by the people.

The balance of the book through to the thirty-sixth chapter summarizes the reigns of the monarchs of Judah and some of the kings of Israel as they relate to Judah, the events of the monarchy, the strife, rivalry, evil, deviation from the path of God which ultimately lead to the path of the destruction of the kingdom of Judah, its capital city of Jerusalem and its Holy Temple.

Solomon's son Rehoboam, who succeeds him to the throne at forty-one years of age, forsakes the laws of God and of Israel. In the five years of Rehoboam's reign, the king of Egypt, Shishak, comes with his armed chariots, conquers the fortified cities of Judah and takes away the treasures of the Temple and of the palace. Then Rehoboam humbles himself before the Lord and reigns for seventeen years in Jerusalem. The chronicler repeats the reigns of the many kings down to Jehoiachin who was eight years old when he began to reign. Jehoiachin reigned three months and ten days in Jerusalem when the Holy City was captured, the Temple sacked, the House of God and palaces burned, the walls of Jerusalem broken down and the people brought into captivity in Babylon where they lived until God stirred up the spirit of Cyrus, King of Persia, who would fulfill the prophecy of Jeremiah.

The narrative reaches a triumphal note when the king of Persia issues his historic edict in behalf of the Jews, which permits their return to Judah in order to rebuild their Temple.

So declares Cyrus king of Persia: "All the kingdoms of the earth has the Lord, the God of heaven, given me; and He has charged me to build Him a house in Jerusalem, which is in Judah. Whosoever there is among you of all His people—the Lord his God be with him—let him go up." (Chapter XXXVI, Verse 23.)

THE WRITINGS

This well known passage, emphasizing the importance of the return from the exile and the rebuilding of Solomon's Temple, serves as the concluding statement of the Holy Scriptures. It ends the thirty-nine books in its three divisions, the Pentateuch, the Prophets, and the Sacred Writings, which began with the sublimely majestic passage of Genesis, Chapter I, Verse 1: "In the beginning God created the heaven and the earth."

THE BIBLE
AND THE
DEVELOPMENT OF
JEWISH LIFE

THE TORAH, MEANING PENTATEUCH, IS THE CONSTANT source of Judaism. It is not, however, the only source.

In its larger sense, Torah is both the *Written Law* and the *Oral Law* interpreted in the Talmud, transmitted orally in the earlier centuries of this era, first reduced to writing in 249 C.E., and finally codified in 499 C.E. Interpretations of the Written Torah by rabbis and scholars thereby established an expanded basis for Jewish living, observance, and celebration. Jewish life is rooted in both Torahs—becoming one unity. When we speak of Torah today, we refer to the enlarged, all-encompassing source of Judaism.

Both Torahs are authoritative, and considered divine in the traditional theological concept. Torah is the process of threading forward age by age, period by period, from the beginnings of the Written Torah. The *Ethics of the Fathers* records the process succinctly: Moses received the Torah on Sinai and handed it down to Joshua; Joshua to the Elders; the Elders to the prophets; and the prophets to the Leaders of the Great Synagogue. In every religious era, such as the Bible period, the Talmud period, the Scribes period, the Gaonic period, the Early Expositors period, the Later Expositors period, and today's Scholar Period, challenging issues arose and life changed.

Through the interpretive process adjustments were made within the context of the religious regulations without having to violate the laws of both Torahs. Interestingly, the framework and rules of this interpretive process developed by the rabbis in the earlier Talmudic period, on how to interpret the Written Bible and bring it forward dynamically, are included in every morning's traditional synagogue service. They are taken from the literature called *Sifra*; the preamble states: "Rabbi Ishmael says the Torah may be interpreted or expounded in accordance with the following thirteen logical principles." The principles are then enumerated. When new problems arise they are confronted within an interpretive program, through which decisions are reached.

When we declare, "The Torah says or Jewish Law says" we mean that in an ongoing, ever-continuing process we move in both directions of time. This process is called Halacha, literally meaning "walking," but connoting Jewish Law in its Jewish legalistic structural sense. This ought not imply that legalistics are the only ongoing processes establishing positions in Judaism. Interpretation broadly incorporates every aspect of life. Judaism stresses both idea and activity, thought and practice, concept and execution, faith and performance. Faith or belief alone is not sufficient to express Jewish life: deeds are required to live a Jewish way of life.

Judaism is a dynamic, living faith, and the legal process, Halacha, has drawn its sustenance and source from the Bible. Indeed, every celebration, observance, custom, and practice is based on the Bible, directly or through the Talmud. Time thus brings the Bible forward into life. Here are a few examples:

a) The Bible speaks of the Covenant—the Brith. It is an event and an injunction. It describes the experience of God and Abraham in establishing the Covenant. The circumcision of Isaac is the external sign of that Covenant. It is the Testament between God and Abraham and, through Abraham, the Jewish people. The Talmud amplifies and explains not only the event, its theology, its religiosity, but also the obligations, regulations, and practices which revolve around the tradition of circumcision. Discussions and codes continue the process. The simple declaration in the Bible that it is a prime duty of every Jewish father to circumcise or to have his son circumcised on the eighth day of birth in order to be brought into the Covenant of Abraham, finds details about the father, child, the time, manner, role of the circumciser or Mohel, the godparents and other practices discussed and explained in various codes through history.

b) The issue of abortion is rooted in the Bible. The book of Exodus describes the account of a woman who had a miscarriage as a result of being pushed. The lost fetus is not considered a "person" in the sense that murder or a life-for-life punishment is imposed. That is the bare statement of the Bible. The Talmud, committed to interpretation, takes the account up for comment and explanation. Is the fetus a separate life or is it an appendage of the mother? Is it a person or not? What happens

344

in the event of danger to the life of the mother? Does physical danger to the mother also mean mental threats to the mother's life? Nuances are discussed, debated, and argued. Decisions are proclaimed which become the Halacha, the Law. Laws which were declared in one period, 500 A.C.E., for example, served as the bases of discussions in 800 A.C.E, 1200 A.C.E., and 1800 A.C.E., and are still discussed today.

c) Attitude toward the dead is another example. In Jewish law one must be buried within twenty-four hours of death. The basis is the biblical account of a criminal who is executed publicly. He must not be allowed to hang overnight. It is a disgrace to God's creature to allow the body to remain exposed. This approach of respect for the dead has become the basis of Jewish funerals. From this passage, the rabbis began to interpret when, how, and what kind of funerals to observe, flowers, caskets, when to delay the funeral, eulogies, burial of suicides in Jewish cemeteries, etc.

d) Another excellent example is the observance of the Sabbath. The Bible makes only limited references, saying simply "there shall be no work on the Sabbath." But what is work, how do we know what one should abstain from doing? The Bible does not say. A complete tractate of the Talmud is devoted to the Sabbath, discussing the many issues, rules, and regulations of Sabbath observance. The interpretative process reveals dynamism as the subjects are expounded, evaluated, and decided.

Every Jewish holiday is proclaimed in the Bible but it is left to the interpreters of the Talmud and later rabbinic discussants and scholars to make the injunctions come alive. The Day of Atonement, Yom Kippur, is a good example. The Bible simply says this is a fast day. But how, when, under what circumstances—all the details of a full-day's service were developed during scholarly discussions throughout time and became the structured guides of the day's experience.

Concepts and ideals which are attainable or aspiring goals are drawn from the Bible. When one speaks about God and people we draw ideas from accounts in Genesis. Justice is exemplified in Abraham's challenge to God in the Sodom and Gomorrah episode. Liberty is sharpened in the Biblical passage, "Proclaim liberty throughout the land unto all the inhabitants thereof." Freedom, its quest and striving, finds its source in the Passover/Exodus trauma. Thanksgiving and its harvest experience is deduced from the description of the holiday of Sukkoth, Feast of Booths. All of these ideals have biblical foundations. At various ceremonials, Psalms are read. The famed twenty-third Psalm is offered at funerals and unveilings. It is also read in Sephardic ritual, before the chanting of Kiddush, the blessing over wine and sanctification of the Sabbath.

In addition, portions of the Bible and Talmud are part of the daily worship service. Psalms, for example, form the basic pattern of prayers, especially in the morning service. Additional psalms are read on Sabbaths and holiday. A number of passages from Proverbs are included in the early morning service primarily for the instruction of children.

The declaration of Israel's Affirmation of Faith, the Shema ("Hear, O Israel, the Lord our God, the Lord is One"), is the nucleus of each morning and evening service—daily proclamations of identity with the Bible.

The Priestly Benediction offered in synagogues on Sabbaths and Festivals is a reminder of the Bible as the source of God's blessings. The Exodus is recalled in every morning and evening service and is mentioned prominently on Sabbaths and holidays. The Haggadah, the booklet used at the Passover Seder ceremony, is developed from biblical statements.

The daily use of the Tallit, the prayer shawl, is based on the Biblical injunction in Numbers 15.37-41 which deals with "fringes" which are the essence of the prayer shawl purpose.

When one dons Tephilin, or phylacteries, to worship in daily morning service, three passages from the Prophet Hosea (Chapter II, 21) are declared as the straps are wound around the fingers to form the Hebrew word Shaddai, Almighty.

The life of the Bible is expressed in other ways. Each year the entire Pentateuch is read. The readings are divided into 54 portions, one for each Sabbath. On some Sabbaths two portions are read so that the entire Torah can be covered annually. When the Torah Scroll is taken from the ark and returned to it, passages from the Bible are chanted. Congregants summoned to the Bema recite blessings. And with the reading of each portion, the rabbi propounds not only the historic and human accounts of the Bible but also the laws and guides of life. In addition, a section from the Prophets is assigned for each Sabbath. And on Festivals, selections dealing with the holidays are read. Thus, the Torah becomes the core around which every Sabbath and holiday service revolves.

The Five Scrolls, known as Hamaysh Megilloth, are read publicly in the synagogue: (1) The Song of Songs is read on the Sabbath during the Intermediate Days of Passover (Shabbath Hol Hamoed). (2) Ecclesiastes is read during the Sabbath of the Intermediate Days of Sukkoth, the Feast of Booths or Tabernacles, or on Shemini Atzereth, the Eighth Day of the festival. (3) The book of Ruth is read on Shavuoth, Feast of

Weeks. (4) The Book of Lamentations is read on Tish'ah Be-Ab (Ninth of Ab), the Jewish fast day of mourning which commemorates the destruction of the two Holy Temples and other catastrophes. (5) The Book of Esther is read on Purim, the Feast of Lots.

The entire Book of Jonah is chanted on Yom Kippur, the Day of Atonement, during the afternoon service.

On Rosh Hashanah, the New Year, the biblical readings are not about the ideas of the New Year, self-introspection, communion with God, or prayer for the coming year. Rather, they tell the story of Abraham and Isaac, the testing of Abraham through the planned sacrifice of Isaac, and the expulsion of Hagar. The account of the sacrifice of Isaac is recalled through the sounding of the Shofar, the ram's horn.

The Sabbath preceding this Passover is called the Great Sabbath, on which afternoon it is the tradition for the rabbi, basing his lecture on the Exodus account, to present the various laws and customs applying to the proper celebration of the holiday.

To better explain what the Bible is, I quote from this commentary by the former chief rabbi of England, Joseph Hertz:

The stories of Genesis, and especially the story of Joseph, have at all times called forth the admiration of mankind. Dealing with the profoundest thoughts in terms of everyday life, yet a child is thrilled by the story; and at the same time the greatest thinkers are continually finding in it fresh depths of unexpected meaning (Ryle). Like summer and the starry skies, like joy and childhood, these stories touch and enthrall the human soul with their sublime simplicity, high seriousness and marvellous beauty. And they are absolutely irreplaceable in the moral and religious training of children. The fact that, after having been repeated for three thousand years and longer, these stories still possess an eternal freshness to children of all races and climes, proves that there is in them something of imperishable worth. There is no other literature in the world which offers that something. This is recognized even in educational circles that are far removed not only from the traditional attitude towards the Bible, but even from the religious outlook. The uniqueness of these stories consists in the fact that there is in them a sense of overruling Divine Providence realizing its purpose through the complex interaction of human motive. They are saturated with the moral spirit. Duty, guilt and its punishment, the conflict of conscience with inclination, the triumph of moral and spiritual forces amidst the vicissitudes of human affairs—are the leading themes. And what is pre-eminently true of Genesis applies to the whole of Bible history. Not by means of abstract formulae does it bring God and duty to the soul of man, but by means of lives of human beings who feel and fail, who stumble and sin as we do; yet who, in their darkest groping, remain conscious of the one true way—and rise again. Witness the conduct of the brothers of Joseph when they had fully grasped the enormity of their crime. "By the study of what other book," asked the agnostic T.H. Huxley, "could children be so much humanized and made to feel that each figure in the vast procession of history fills, like themselves, but a momentary space in the interval between the eternities; and earns the blessings or the curses of all time according to its effort to do good and hate evil?"

What is true of the stories and the accounts of the Bible is also true of Jewish life and guides of life. For example, on Yom Kippur, the holiest day of the year, it is surprising and fascinating that the traditional Torah readings do not include the great ideas of self-evaluation and thought, but rather the laws of incest from the Book of Leviticus. The rabbis pointed out that the essential unit of Jewish life is the family. The family must be clean and pure. The rabbi who wishes to speak of morality on the Day of Atonement, or of issues that have been exacerbated in today's society, may well use the Bible as that day's text, and refer to Talmudic thinkers, analysts, and scholars who have discussed the subjects in other periods.

Thus, the Bible, beyond its simple narration or reading, becomes a living source of study. Every present-day concern in life, e.g., homosexuality, incest, marital relations, drugs, and indeed the question of smoking (within the context of one negatively affecting one's own health, which is against biblical law), is rooted in the Bible.

It is exciting to note that in the daily morning service, immediately after the thirteen hermeneutical principles of logic for the interpretation of the Torah are read, a special doxology, captioned Kaddish, is read. Many have heard about Kaddish. It is generally understood to refer to the prayer which mourners recite three times daily in a synagogue when they have lost parents or other close relatives. The original Kaddish, however, applied not to mourners but was recited for scholars. The text is the same for both except for an additional paragraph in the scholarly Kaddish which reads: "And to Israel, and to our scholars, and to their disciples, and pupils, and to all who engage in the study of the Torah, here and everywhere, may there be abundant peace, grace, loving kindness, mercy, long life, and salvation from their Father in Heaven, and let us say, Amen."

Judaism is a dynamic, living religion in its largest, all-life-encompassing sense.